The Modern Architectural Landscape

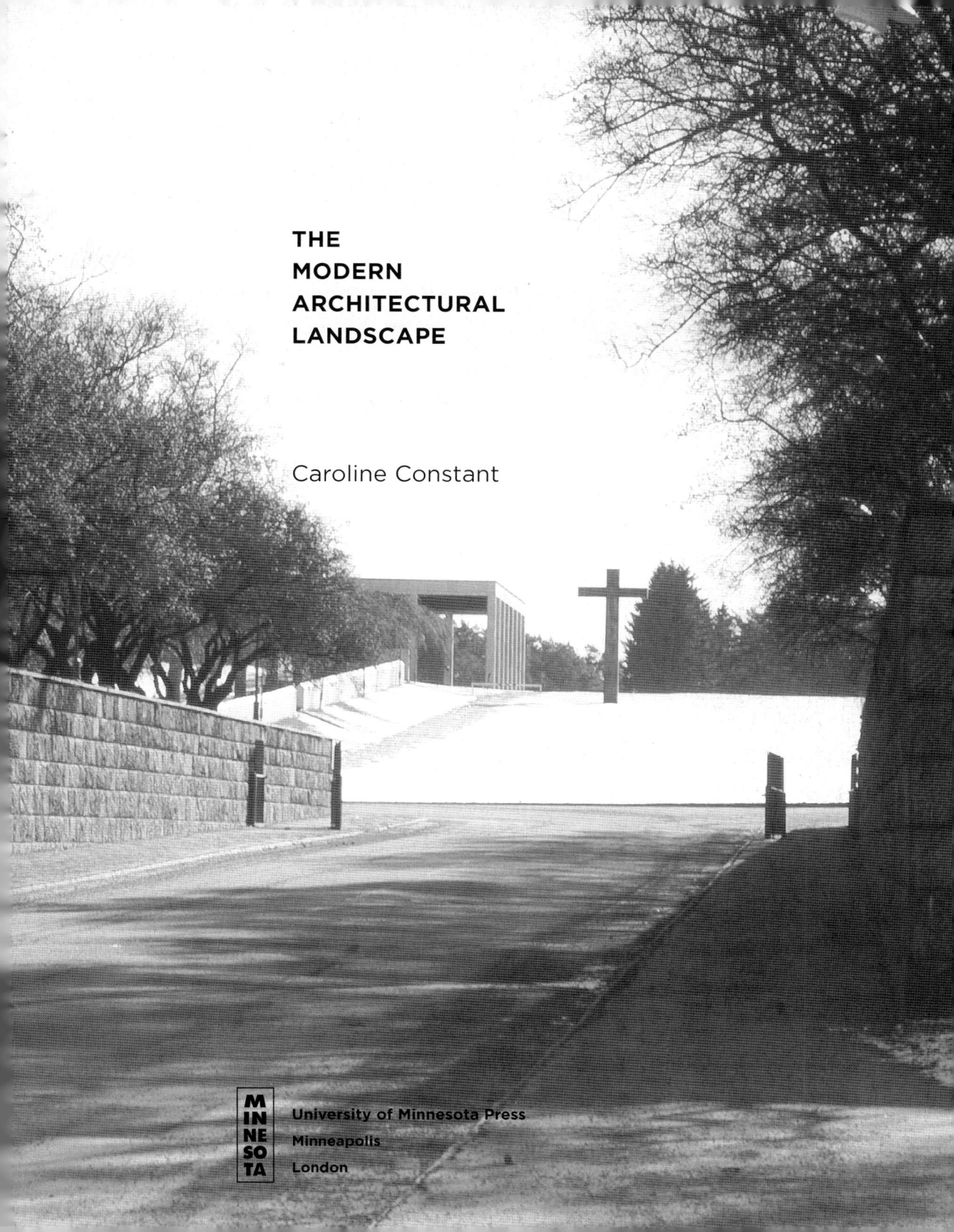

THE MODERN ARCHITECTURAL LANDSCAPE

Caroline Constant

University of Minnesota Press
Minneapolis
London

This book is supported by a grant from the Graham Foundation for Advanced Studies in the Fine Arts.

The University of Minnesota Press gratefully acknowledges financial assistance provided for the publication of this book by the David R. Coffin Publication Grant of the Foundation for Landscape Studies, the Office of the Vice President for Research publication subvention program, and by Taubman College of Architecture and Urban Planning, the University of Michigan.

The University of Minnesota Press gratefully recognizes the work of Edward Dimendberg, editorial consultant, on this project.

Every effort was made to obtain permission to reproduce material in this book. If any proper acknowledgment has not been included, we encourage copyright holders to notify the publisher.

Unless otherwise credited, contemporary photographs were taken by the author.

For information on previously published material in this book, see page 289.

Title page photograph: View to open entry landscape of the Woodland Cemetery, Stockholm, by Erik Gunnar Asplund and Sigurd Lewerentz, 1915–40.

Copyright 2012 by Caroline Constant

All rights reserved. No part of this publication may be reproduced, stored in a retrieval system, or transmitted, in any form or by any means, electronic, mechanical, photocopying, recording, or otherwise, without the prior written permission of the publisher.

Published by the University of Minnesota Press
111 Third Avenue South, Suite 290
Minneapolis, MN 55401-2520
http://www.upress.umn.edu

Library of Congress Cataloging-in-Publication Data

Constant, Caroline.
   The modern architectural landscape / Caroline Constant.
   Includes bibliographical references and index.
   ISBN 978-0-8166-7307-0 (hardback)
   ISBN 978-0-8166-7635-4 (paperback)
 1. Architecture—Environmental aspects. 2. Architecture, Modern—20th century.
3. Landscape architecture—History—20th century. I. Title.
   NA2542.35.C64 2012
   712′.50904—dc23
                                       2012001203

Printed in the United States of America on acid-free paper

The University of Minnesota is an equal-opportunity educator and employer.

19 18 17 16 15 14 13 12   10 9 8 7 6 5 4 3 2 1

CONTENTS

	Preface	vii
	Acknowledgments	xiii
	Introduction: Toward a New Architectural Landscape	1
ONE	Social Idealism and Urban Landscape
Sunnyside Gardens vs. Römerstadt	25
TWO	The Barcelona Pavilion as Landscape Garden
Modernity and the Picturesque	45
THREE	The Urban Landscapes of Erik Gunnar Asplund
Architecture between "Nature" and the City	61
FOUR	Toward a Spiritual Landscape
The Woodland Cemetery and Swedish Burial Reform	77
FIVE	A Landscape "Fit for a Democracy"
Jože Plečnik at Prague Castle	93
SIX	Collaborative Fruits
Garrett Eckbo's Communal Landscapes	115
SEVEN	From the Virgilian Dream to Chandigarh
Le Corbusier and the Modern Landscape	149

EIGHT	Hilberseimer and Caldwell	169
	Intersecting Ideologies in Lafayette Park	
NINE	The Once and Future Park	191
	From Central Park to OMA's Parc de la Villette	
	Afterword	225
	Notes	227
	Publication History	289
	Index	291

PREFACE

> Gardening, conceived as the art within whose range fall all the problems of man's aesthetic relations to the natural environment, is today through its relation to modern architecture an even more important aspect of civilization than in the Baroque and Romantic age, when gardens, superficially considered, attracted a far greater share of aesthetic attention.
>
> —Henry-Russell Hitchcock Jr. (1937)

Because landscape architecture was emerging as a distinct profes-sional and academic discipline during the early part of the twentieth century, it is often assumed that architects were uninvolved in shaping new attitudes toward the field. This study challenges that assumption by examining landscapes designed by architects, either individually or in collaboration with other architects, planners, or landscape architects. Approaching landscape as an essential component of modern architecture's constructive endowment of material with social value, this reexamination focuses on the precise material forms and ideological underpinnings of landscapes conceived of by architects, understanding them as salient to the formulation of both modern architecture and the modern landscape. One ambition of this book is to challenge received understandings of the modern architectural project by foregrounding its social and cultural foundations in landscape. A further objective is to probe the nature of the architecture–landscape continuum in contemporary Western design practices. Only when architects and landscape architects understand the scope and complexity of their individual areas of expertise, as well as their potential points of convergence and conformity, will the two forms of discourse succeed in formulating significant contributions to contemporary culture.

This series of essays examines diverse approaches to landscape design in the work of certain architects practicing in Europe and the United States between 1915 and the mid-1980s. Case studies involve landscapes in the public realm, rather than the private garden, which was a primary focus of much Western landscape theory and practice during the early decades of the century. These public landscapes do more than accommodate the functional needs of the evolving mass society in parks, playgrounds, places of assembly, allotment gardens, child-care facilities, and so on. They give formal expression to the Modern Movement's underlying social and political ideologies, engaging the symbolic potential of the modern landscape—particularly in its ability to engage new, more democratic forms of social organization.

This collection, organized roughly chronologically, focuses on the cultural significance of particular landscapes designed by architects—understanding them as diverse ways of interpreting the world and our place within it. Case studies engage tensions between two aspects of landscape that arise from the term's etymological origins: those embodying customary social practices *(Landschaft)* and the more abstract landscapes of visual spatial relationships *(Landskap)*.[1] They mediate between the traditional conception of space as a palpable entity and the modern conception of space as a continuum without prior accents of meaning, between the physical space of materiality and the mental space of cognition and representation. Thus they challenge distinctions between the cultivated landscape ("second nature") and the symbolically ordered landscape ("third nature") far more than in preceding eras, when the art of garden design was primarily an elitist enterprise.[2]

This series of essays reflects no single line of development, but rather comprises a mosaic of issues and approaches. Certain examples are well known to architects, landscape architects, and historians, while others lie outside the mainstream of conventional histories of modern architecture and/or landscape, yet in all cases the architectural aspects of the projects have been more closely scrutinized than have their qualities as landscapes. This collection reflects an effort to invert that emphasis, focusing primarily on the landscape dimension of each example and its broader cultural relevance. The stylistic terms of these case studies are therefore less significant to this account than their ability to engage a spirit of place relative to underlying cultural values or political ideologies, which constitutes a significant aspect of their broader contribution to the history of architecture and landscape design.

Certain of these essays probe the language of these modern architectural landscapes and their symbolic potential, while others examine their capacity to sustain a cultural, social, or political critique. Jože Plečnik's interventions in the landscape of Prague Castle, while lying outside the formal terms associated with Modern Movement architecture, nevertheless challenge contemporary issues of figuration versus abstraction as means of reinvigorating cultural memory under a new democratic system of government in Czechoslovakia. In more conventionally "modern" stylistic terms, Mies van der Rohe's pavilion representing the democratic Weimar Republic at the Barcelona International Exposition of 1929 and Le Corbusier's capital complex at Chandigarh in newly independent India engage historic landscape precedents strategically; in Barcelona, Mies invoked aspects of picturesque landscape principles in terms of their relevance to contemporary architectural discourse, while in Chandigarh Le Corbusier drew upon the symbolic dimension of traditional Mughal gardens, seeking to impart regional as well as "universal" significance to his design. In his park for the Stockholm Public Library, Erik Gunnar Asplund utilized means by which contemporary landscape expression could reinforce a sense of regional identity, an ideology subsequently associated with the Stockholm school of park design. Stockholm's Woodland Cemetery, envisioned by Asplund and Sigurd Lewerentz as part of an ongoing critique of contemporary approaches to death, fulfills the avant-garde aspiration to reintegrate art and life consistent with Social Democratic political aims while incorporating references to historic Swedish landscapes—ideas that Lewerentz pursued to radically different formal ends on the open site of his Malmö Eastern Cemetery.

Several essays involve landscapes influenced by examples realized under divergent political systems. A comparative analysis of two housing projects derived from Ebenezer Howard's garden city principles—Sunnyside Gardens (Queens, New York) and Römerstadt (Frankfurt)—reveals the challenges involved in applying ideas that originated in a Social Democratic society to conditions of American capitalism. Similarly indebted to the Social Democratic principles of the Weimar Republic, Detroit's Lafayette Park is a highly successful urban renewal project, yet its communal landscape paradoxically isolates that housing complex from its surrounding urban fabric, raising troubling issues concerning its ideological underpinnings.

One essay falls outside this general rubric to examine the work of landscape architect Garrett Eckbo, a lifelong advocate of collaboration with architects on equal terms. In a series of housing projects carried out as a member of an interdisciplinary team, Eckbo developed an approach to landscape design that operated in counterpoint to prevailing planning trends that equated social organization with formal organization. Moreover, the cooperative housing proposals that Eckbo carried out with architect Gregory Ain raise issues of collaboration among equals, a line of inquiry of increasing relevance to contemporary practice. Whereas Eckbo considered architecture and landscape architecture to be equivalent undertakings, his work points to significant differences between the disciplines and the need for collaborators to understand and respect the merits, limitations, and potential correspondences in their respective areas of expertise if they are to play an effective role in transforming the physical environment.

The book closes with an analysis of a more recent example, Rem Koolhaas/OMA's proposal for Parc de la Villette in Paris, a project emanating from an international design competition that has prompted significant disciplinary reevaluations among landscape architects and architects; although these have emanated primarily from the proposal's open-ended character and avoidance of a formal solution, the greater significance of this design tactic lies in its associated social and political implications. By establishing an infrastructural framework whereby the park's formal and programmatic genesis would remain subject to ongoing negotiation among potential users, Koolhaas not only denied the authorship traditionally associated with efforts of the architect/landscape architect but also re-animated the concept of *Landschaft*—that is, landscape as an embodiment of customary social practices and direct human experience—not by working the land, as in the case of Römerstadt, but through public participation in the site's development and use through unspecified processes of social and political negotiation. With his Parc de la Villette, Koolhaas embraced the notion of the public sphere as a site of contention among diverse interest groups, affirming the potential for public agency with respect to social space in a plural democracy.

These essays were written over a period of twenty-five years. Although marked by the critical and historical circumstances under which they were written, they engage issues of ongoing speculation. Although each essay can be read independently, together they form a single project. Probing the interdisciplinary ramifications of landscape as a medium, they combine ideas about architecture, landscape architecture, and urban design with theories of social and/or public space.

As part of a larger history that remains to be written, this collection of essays responds only indirectly and fragmentarily to Hitchcock's challenge concerning the broader cultural significance of contemporary garden art as the expression of humankind's relationship to the natural environment. Hitchcock assumed that the answer lay in part in the relationship of "gardening" to modern architecture. These essays take their cue from that assumption but refrain from value judgments concerning the hierarchy of the disciplines.

ACKNOWLEDGMENTS

Many individuals contributed directly and indirectly to this project: the late William Sheldon, professor of architecture at Princeton University, who opened my eyes to the cultural significance of the modern landscape; former colleagues Elizabeth Meyer (now at the University of Virginia) and Mirka Beneš (now at the University of Texas at Austin), who helped forge interdisciplinary interests among students at the Graduate School of Design (GSD), Harvard University; students who participated in my landscape seminar at the GSD, particularly Julie Bargmann, Anita Berrizbeitia, Farshid Moussavi, Charles Rose, Mary Anne Thompson, and Wynne Yelland, with whom the conversation continues; former University of Michigan colleagues Karen M'Closkey (now at the University of Pennsylvania) and Peter Osler (now at Illinois Institute of Technology); fellow travelers Dorothée Imbert and Marc Treib. Mary Daniels at the GSD's Frances Loeb Library and Rebecca Price of the University of Michigan library deserve special mention for their ongoing assistance and support of my research over the years. For memorable conversations about the Woodland Cemetery and Barcelona Pavilion, I am indebted to the late Robin Evans, whose spirit lives on for those who learned so much from him.

I am grateful to Ed Dimendberg, who brought my work to the attention of the University of Minnesota Press, and to Julia Czerniak and an anonymous reader, who provided invaluable feedback on an earlier version of this manuscript, as did several of the Press's board members. Their suggestions contributed significantly to the book's ultimate form. Those who critiqued individual essays are credited in the notes to the relevant chapters. At the University of Minnesota Press, Pieter Martin offered invaluable editorial support, and Kristian Tvedten's scrupulous attention to detail and persistence in obtaining illustration permissions were essential to bringing this project to fruition. Laura Westlund's efforts in overseeing the book's production made my work all the easier, while Judy Selhorst's editing skills contributed in valuable ways to its final outcome. Finally, I am greatly indebted to Rachel Moeller at the Press and to Neil West at BN Typographics West for their invaluable contributions to the layout.

Several institutions contributed support for this work, which began in earnest with a research grant from the Graham Foundation for Advanced Studies in the Fine Arts in 1989. My research in Sweden was sponsored by a Fulbright Fellowship, with additional funding from the Peter and Birgitta Celsing Foundation, the Swedish Building Research Council, and the American–Scandinavian Foundation. Most recently, a Helmut F. Stern Fellowship at the University of Michigan Institute for the Humanities provided me a year in which to complete the manuscript, and I am grateful to my colleagues there and to institute director Daniel Herwitz for crucial feedback and support.

INTRODUCTION

TOWARD A NEW ARCHITECTURAL LANDSCAPE

If we understand landscape as the medium through which the social, political, and physical structures that endow the ground with cultural value are brought into relationship with the immense scale of natural phenomena, then landscape is the means by which the structure of the ground is made intelligible. As W. J. T. Mitchell argues, landscape is simultaneously "a medium of exchange, a site of visual appropriation, [and] a focus for the formation of identity."[1] It is an active medium that engages ongoing processes, evoking not only a means to artistic, economic, social, and political ends but also the reciprocal "manner in which landscapes act on and shape *us,* as if agents in their own right."[2] Thus, as J. B. Jackson reminds us, the word *landscape* implies more than an aesthetic vehicle or a product of human manufacture; it is a cultural phenomenon with communal resonance: "In our modern sense of the word it means that which underscores not only our identity and presence, but also our history."[3]

The emergence of the discipline of landscape architecture in the United States and much of Europe during the late nineteenth and early twentieth centuries reflects a trend toward increasing professional specialization that was an outgrowth of the Industrial Revolution. In common with other modern professions, landscape architecture engages social and political as well as technical issues and relationships. The designed landscape is not only a significant means by which human societies transform their world, reflecting the organization of society around technical forms of production, it also encompasses a medium of power, functioning in turn as an agent of social organization. The designed landscape is never neutral; it involves structures of experience that, even when they seem profoundly individualized, are in fact profoundly social.

Paradoxically, it is to this period that cultural historians trace the decline of landscape as a significant aspect of Western culture. According to geographer Denis Cosgrove, during the late nineteenth century "landscape as a way of seeing, a symbolic construction [i.e., *Landskap*], largely replaced landscape as a direct human experience and expression of collective social order within a specific geographical and environmental context [i.e., *Landschaft*]."[4] Basing his claim on the economic shift from feudalism to capitalism, Cosgrove assumes that the relationship between humankind and land lost its relevance with the achievement of capitalist modes of production. As a result of this detachment, he reasons:

> Landscape today is preeminently the domain either of scientific study and land planning, or of personal and private pleasure. It no longer carries the burden of social or moral significance attached to it during the time of its most active cultural evolution.[5]

Historian John Barrell broadens Cosgrove's contention with his assertion that, toward the end of the eighteenth century, the liberal arts gave up their service to the general public good and fragmented into instances of personal expression.[6] In 1999, landscape architect and theorist James Corner reinforced such assumptions of a historic decline in titling a collection of essays that he edited *Recovering Landscape* to mark the recent resurgence of interest in the discipline.[7] These theorists overlook the changing social circumstances under which landscape—liberated from the social and spatial confines of the elitist private garden—became a significant agent of the reintegration of art and life sought by architects of the European avant-garde during the early twentieth century.[8] Such reintegration involves the practical as well as the spiritual and symbolic dimensions of landscape, not in order to recover traditional precapitalist modes of engagement with the land but to achieve a comparable sense of place in the interest of furthering avant-garde social objectives. This ideological shift—from the relatively restricted and private domain of the garden to the more open and public realm of landscape—is reflected in a corresponding shift in terminology from *garden design,* which Henry-Russell Hitchcock Jr. and Joseph Hudnut continued to use during the 1930s, to *landscape architect,* which Frederick Law Olmsted invoked to describe his work as early as 1862.[9]

In 1914 Harvard president emeritus Charles W. Eliot made a claim for the resurgence of the discipline on social grounds: "The profession of landscape architecture is going to be—indeed, it already is—the most direct professional contributor to the improvement of the human environment in the twentieth century."[10] Eliot's argument—that access to the benefits of the natural environment would improve the mental and moral health of society as a whole—is indebted to Olmsted's premise that among the social benefits of public parks is "the prospect of coming together, all classes largely represented with a common purpose . . . all helping to the greater happiness of each."[11] During the first half of the twentieth century, numerous architectural and landscape theorists and practitioners reiterated this idea of social betterment to be achieved through governmental provision for public landscapes. For example, German architect and planner Martin Wagner speculated that providing parklands as urban amenities would have an associated economic benefit by contributing to the personal happiness, and thus the social health, of the citizenry, an idea reiterated by French landscape architect Achille Duchêne.[12]

Although the premise that social ills could be alleviated by improvements to the physical environment was a commonplace among architects of the European avant-garde, landscape architects were often slow to undertake initiatives in this direction during the early twentieth century, instead focusing much of their attention on the private garden, as Christopher Tunnard lamented in 1942. Tunnard asserted the need for the discipline to pursue the aesthetic and social imperatives of the architectural avant-garde: "*Modern landscape design is inseparable from the spirit, technique, and development of modern architecture.*"[13] Thus it was inevitable that a certain professional rivalry would emerge as landscape architects struggled to define the terms of their discipline's particular boundaries, working procedures, and areas of expertise in relation to those of architecture.

While architecture and landscape architecture share tensions between the artistic and scientific or technological aspects of their respective enterprises, they engage the world around us by different means and at vastly different scales of concern.[14] Like architecture, landscape is a spatial milieu imbued with cultural significance; unlike architecture, it is an inherently unstable medium, grounded in the volatility of natural processes. Corner theorizes his discipline as one that entails the reciprocity between nature (i.e., "stewardship of the land") and culture (i.e., the sphere of aesthetics and art).[15] It involves cultural interpretations of humankind's place

INTRODUCTION   3

in the world in relation to both natural and urban realms. Thus, while both architecture and landscape architecture operate through physical and symbolic mediation, engaging the broader cultural significance of a locale as well as its forms, there are significant differences in the disciplines' respective scales of operation, as well as their areas of expertise.

There is often a further difference in their operational procedures. Whereas an architect might respond primarily to the topographic features of a site, elaborating on or transforming its existing order to recalibrate its significance or impart new meaning to it, a landscape architect generally works from a deeper understanding of a particular locale, including its environmental qualities—its ecology, hydrology, geology, and horticulture—as well as its morphology, thus drawing upon its subsurface and atmospheric attributes as well as its more overt visible features.[16] Landscape architecture accordingly engages broader concerns not only symbolically but also physically, in terms of its territorial domain and environmental impact.

While acknowledging the disciplines' areas of mutual concern, Elizabeth Kassler, curator of architecture and design at the Museum of Modern Art in New York, elaborated in a museum publication of 1964 upon the negative consequences of collapsing distinctions between them:

> Over-insistence on landscape art as planning and building and space creation can have unfortunate consequences, aggravated in this day of "personality cult" architecture. It promotes irrelevant geometry, and easily turns formality into formalism. It encourages the designer to assert himself where he might wisely be quiet and fosters, among those of lesser talent, a busy kind of showmanship that is distasteful in buildings and repellent when applied to the vast impersonal truths of nature. Worst of all, it discourages the designer from approaching his natural materials with the deep perception that can come only from profound understanding together with a certain degree of humility. Because of the extraordinary character of these special materials, landscape art has a possibility that lies beyond architecture. It can offer an experience of architecture. It can also offer, with or without the assistance of architecture, an experience of universal nature.

Accordingly, as Kassler argued, one should bring broader interpretive means to the theoretical discussion of landscape, independent of its relationship to architecture:

> We demand a close relationship between indoors and outdoors, but wish the landscape to be itself, not an architectural appendage. If a landscape is to be or become itself, it must be understood through every interpretive instrument. It must be understood through the ancient intuitions of sight and smell, touch and hearing, and through that sense by which we feel a place, not as a static fact, but as a phenomenon joining past to future, time to eternity; through the shiny new tools of science; and through the bird's eye view of flight—flying has changed the way we see and feel.[17]

Like Corner, Kassler understood the discipline of landscape architecture in its broadest sense, as conjoining experiential, scientific, symbolic, and spiritual modes of being in the world.

Almost twenty years later, the relationship between landscape architecture and architecture was the topic of a series of essays in the American periodical *Landscape Architecture*, where Garrett Eckbo bemoaned the "professional, academic, and legal boundaries" between the disciplines in an essay provocatively titled "Is Landscape *Architecture*?"

> In spite of the moderating impact of the modern movement, we are still conditioned by formal vs. informal, architecture vs. nature—conflicts which make true landscape architecture impossible. To be true, landscape architecture must do what its name implies—it must integrate landscape and architecture. True landscape architecture produces systems of relations in which neither "landscape" nor "architecture" loses its integrity, disappears, or becomes mere decoration for the other.

Stressing that the disciplinary boundaries should remain fluid, Eckbo concluded: "All of this, of course, is subject to definition, and these vary with the source. Ironically, none will be final or definitive, nor should they be."[18]

Focusing on societal concerns rather than disciplinary disputes, Eckbo's contemporary James C. Rose endorsed "forgetting the mean, little, professional boundaries which we have inherited from the stagnant era, and developing continuity in our environment expressive of Twentieth Century communal needs."[19] Such a spirit of social ethos and interdisciplinary cooperation epitomizes the values Dean Joseph Hudnut imparted to design education at Harvard University in 1936, when he merged the faculties of architecture, landscape architecture, and city planning in the

Graduate School of Design, where Eckbo and Rose received their professional training.

As landscape architects at the forefront of their profession, Eckbo and Rose repeatedly sought to reach an architectural audience through essays published in the country's leading architectural journals: *Pencil Points, Architectural Record, Architectural Forum,* and *California Arts and Architecture*.[20] Although these dealt primarily with a theme pertinent to architects and landscape architects alike—the small-scale residential garden—in 1939 and 1940 the editors of *Architectural Record* solicited a series of essays on the recreational aspects of landscape from Eckbo and Rose, together with their Harvard classmate Daniel Kiley. There the trio addressed programmatic means for stimulating public use of landscapes in urban, rural, and "primeval" settings—a particularly salient issue during the preceding decade owing to the economic impact of the worldwide depression.[21]

European attempts to promote mutual understanding among professionals of both disciplines include L'Association Internationale des Architectes de Jardins Modernistes (the International Association of Modernist Garden Architects, or AIAJM), founded in 1938 by landscape architects Jean Canneel-Claes and Christopher Tunnard, from Belgium and England, respectively. Modeled on the Congrès Internationaux d'Architecture Moderne, or CIAM (founded ten years earlier), the AIAJM sought to explore interdisciplinary issues, considering garden design a discipline with social responsibilities, intimately related to architecture and urbanism; accordingly, the group solicited membership from architects, urban designers, sculptors, painters, and writers, as well as landscape architects.[22] During this period Tunnard was a regular contributor to the *Architectural Review* (London), and Canneel-Claes wrote articles for several Belgian architecture periodicals.[23] Prompted by the First International Congress of Garden Architects, held at the Paris International Exposition of 1937, the French periodical *L'Architecture d'aujourd'hui* published a special issue on the architecture of gardens that included essays by architect Albert Laprade and landscape architects André Vera and Jean-Charles Moreux.[24] A related group effort was the *New Architecture* exhibition organized the following year by the MARS (Modern Architectural Research) Group at Burlington Galleries, London, which included a section on "architecture in the landscape" espousing the conceptual unity of the two milieus.[25] That same year Tunnard and *Architectural Review* editor J. M. Richards—both members of the MARS Group—advocated cooperation between architects and landscape architects in a television program broadcast on the BBC.[26]

During the interwar period the Weimar government had institutionalized such interdisciplinary collaboration in its efforts to address the recreational and housing needs of the urban populace in Germany, and French landscape architects were often involved in postwar reconstruction efforts undertaken by architects and planners. Individuals from both disciplines also worked to promote mutual respect and understanding; for example, Danish landscape architect Gudmund Nyeland Brandt held a chair in landscape gardening at the School of Architecture of the Academy of Fine Arts from 1924 to 1940 and forged close professional relationships with architects in order to augment the impact of landscape issues on the building process, while Carl Theodor Sørensen, his successor at the Academy of Fine Arts, collaborated with numerous architects associated with the Modern Movement.

Despite such broad efforts to bridge the disciplinary divide, certain landscape architects continue to perpetuate the myth, promulgated by Hitchcock and Philip Johnson in the exhibition *Modern Architecture,* held at New York's Museum of Modern Art in 1932, of the untouched landscape as the most appropriate background for modern architecture. Brandt had attributed such romanticism to ideological differences between the disciplines:

> The modernists . . . take insufficient interest in gardens. In itself, that is understandable, for an architecture movement that strives for mechanization and material renewal cannot, in these areas, exercise any influence on the garden, which must provide a counterweight to industrialization.[27]

In a more formal vein, American landscape architect Fletcher Steele asserted rather simplistically, "The architect is primarily interested in the objects which he is designing; the landscape architect with the relation of things and the composition of spaces between them."[28] Drawing on this formal dichotomy, Garrett Eckbo subsequently applauded Richard Neutra's *On Building: Mystery and Realities of the Site* (1951) as an antidote to this "tendency of many architects (even the most 'modern') to view the building as the *objet d'art* for which the site is merely a subservient setting."[29] More recently, Gregg Bleam has cited Eero Saarinen's statement that "the total environment is more important than the single building" to contend, "This position was not generally held by many architects practicing during the 1940s and '50s, who typically used plants only as a foil for their buildings rather than as structural elements to connect interior and exterior space."[30] In a related vein, Martha Schwartz argues, "Architecture's myopic and self-serving attitude toward the landscape, as the passive, untouched setting for heroic objects, has been disastrous visually and ecologically."[31] Although such claims could undoubtedly be substantiated through reference to specific examples, they demonstrate a limited understanding of the history of modern architecture and its landscape dimension. More important, they exemplify ongoing concerns about the respective territories of the disciplines.

The relationship between architecture and landscape architecture is neither monolithic nor static, but capable of elaboration and change by means of iterative processes of negotiation. Just as modern architecture and the modern landscape evolved in different ways and at different rates in particular regions, so the two disciplines diverged considerably in their general trajectories and focus. During the nineteenth century, when European and American architecture was characterized by historic eclecticism, aesthetic principles associated with the picturesque landscape tradition were being adapted to diverse geographical situations throughout the Western world, taking on new forms and meanings. In contrast, Western landscapes of the twentieth century are remarkably varied, both ideologically and formally, owing to the particular geographical and cultural contexts in which they are situated as well as to landscape architecture's broad array of disciplinary undertakings, which range from landscape management and ecological studies to the design of specific parks, gardens, and urban spaces. Unlike in architecture, there was no pretense to an "international style" in landscape design; the rejection of historic styles associated with modern architecture was not a primary issue for landscape architects, whose early theorizing often centered on debates about the appropriateness of geometric versus "natural" forms with respect to the private garden. What ultimately diverted landscape architects from this absorption with historically based forms was a new focus on the practical and aesthetic aspects of designing landscapes for the emerging mass society, an ethical concern they shared with the architectural avant-garde.

Landscape Architecture and the Social Ideology of the Architectural Avant-Garde

Public landscapes of the early twentieth century differed in several respects from those of the nineteenth—particularly in their scale of concern, intended audience, and theoretical underpinnings—which increasingly differentiated the professional domain of landscape architecture from that of architecture. Landscape architects were initially slow to confront the shift in scale that occurred in the estates of the landed gentry in England when, according to Horace Walpole, William Kent "leapt the fence and saw that all nature was a garden."[32] Instead, many early twentieth-century landscape practitioners, theorists, and educators focused their initial attention on the private garden, the most obvious point of contention between the disciplines, leading French landscape architect André Vera to contend: "doesn't urbanism make it clear . . . that France should no longer have only small gardens, but become itself a garden?"[33]

Such capitulation to a significant component of bourgeois culture afforded landscape designers opportunities for formal experimentation, prompting Joseph Hudnut to trace the breakdown of the disciplinary boundaries of architecture and landscape architecture to the spatial interrelationship of interior and exterior, which Modern Movement architects frequently posited as a spatial objective.[34] The era's changing social and political climate ultimately led practitioners of both disciplines to shift the scope and content of their concerns as they began to address the housing and recreational needs of the burgeoning urban populace. In advocating increased green spaces as an antidote to the social malaise stemming from urban overcrowding, theorists of the architectural avant-garde initially posited a romantic detachment of architecture from landscape, conceived in naturalistic terms. James Rose pointedly refuted such a simplistic approach to landscape design:

> Isn't it a little inconsistent, and perhaps unfair, to expect a Twentieth Century individual to step out of a stream-lined automobile, and then flounder through a Rousseauian wilderness until he reaches a "machine for living"? We cannot confine living, which is a process, to little segregated compartments that end at the edge of the nearest terrace where we are again asked to adjust ourselves to what, in it highest form, becomes an Eighteenth Century landscape painting.[35]

Indeed, the challenge of formulating appropriate design strategies for such public spaces was primarily left to landscape architects. Pursuing certain of Olmsted's nineteenth-century initiatives, many undertook the design of parkways and other forms of urban and rural infrastructure, in addition to playgrounds and recreational facilities, thus engaging regional planning and ecological issues, which further differentiated the scope of their undertakings from that of architects.

In contrast to the expanded range of work undertaken by landscape architects, the discipline's theoretical output was more focused than that of architecture. In the architectural manifesto—the unequivocal statement of principles that was the preferred form of written exposition for the architectural avant-garde—the form of the built environment is interpreted anew. The premise of a tabula rasa implied an undifferentiated, communal ground plane, which Modern Movement theorists associated with CIAM imbued with quantitative, rather than qualitative, properties. Zoned to accommodate disparate urban functions, the ground plane of the urban metropolis was conceived of as a locus of pedestrian and vehicular movement and residential, work, or leisure activity, yet there was no associated theoretical foundation for elaboration of its collective social and environmental essence. Thus, although architectural theorists' sweeping attempts to reconceptualize the terms for the built environment had strong implications for landscape, it was primarily landscape architects who took up the challenge of addressing those implications in both theoretical and practical terms.

Unlike the utopian qualities associated with such Modern Movement architectural theory, Elizabeth Meyer argues: "Landscape theory is specific, not general. . . . landscape architectural theory is situational—it is explicitly historical, contingent, pragmatic, and ad hoc. It is not about idealist absolutist universals. It finds meaning, form and structure in the site as given."[36] Garrett Eckbo underscored this situational essence of landscape discourse: "Every site is different, every region is different, every climate is different; hence every problem in the organization of space on the land must be solved individually."[37] As a result, landscape theory is often aligned with regional or nationalistic interests and concerns. For example, Leberecht Migge directed his landscape manifesto "Das grüne Manifest" ("The Green Manifesto"), published in 1918 in *Die Tat*—a journal dedicated to political and cultural reform—to a Germanic solution to the problems of urban civilization.[38] Evoking the spirit of *Landschaft,* Migge advocated a return to the soil in allotment gardens and productive urban parklands as spiritual and practical means to address the alienation he associated with modern urban life. In pursuit of his aim of economic self-sufficiency for the German worker, Migge published a second manifesto, *Die wachsende Siedlung* (The growing settlement, 1932), using a biological metaphor to espouse owner-built housing that could be produced incrementally, over time, according to the occupant's particular spatial needs and financial means.

Similarly nationalistic in tone is the "Manifesto for the Revival of French art," which landscape architect André Vera published in the urban planning periodical *Urbanisme* during the early Vichy period. Seeking interdisciplinary means for the various arts to overcome the physical, economic, and moral devastation wreaked by the war, Vera directed his exhortations about the contemporary landscape to architects and urban designers rather than to professionals directly concerned with garden design. Espousing the values of aesthetic beauty and comfort that French decorators consistently prized over the more objective principles associated with the German avant-garde, Vera advocated an imaginative approach to landscape design: "In the provinces and the countryside, Architects, apply yourself to not spoiling the site with your building. The most reliable means, it would seem, is to respond to necessity, not with pretension but with ingenuity." To enhance national pride he urged architects: "Revive the art of gardens. Embellish our return to the land."[39] Architects could accomplish these objectives, he advised, by prioritizing urban spaces over the buildings bounding them, respecting local and regional scenic effects, and making use of indigenous plant species.

Although landscape theorists of the early twentieth century generally eschewed the international ambitions of certain leaders of the architectural avant-garde, Jean Canneel-Claes's landscape manifesto of 1928 provides an exception to this principle. Decidedly idealist and absolutist in tone, it asserts the aims of the AIAJM using concepts based on CIAM precepts and Modern Movement aesthetic principles. In it "garden architecture" is "indissolubly linked to problems of dwelling and urbanism," with design based on functional principles, structural simplicity, and concise formal means of expression based in geometry (especially asymmetry); moreover, the manifesto reasserts the value of the individual artistic genius in establishing a new style suited to the age. Canneel-Claes's declaration and the writings of AIAJM cofounder Tunnard, intended to further the discipline's theoretical discourse and enhance its visibility among architects and related professionals, constitute the most prominent efforts of international theorizing by Western landscape architects during this period. Despite Canneel-Claes's assertion of "a strong similarity of thought and of technical and aesthetic inquiry" among AIAJM members and his affirmation of the importance of responding to the particular qualities of a landscape, the organization was short-lived, perhaps because such broad-based arguments detached from political and social realities ultimately had little currency among the European landscape professionals who made up its primary audience.[40]

Although landscape lacked the material and technical bases for innovation associated with much theorizing about modern architecture, the medium of landscape was particularly suited to addressing the social issues surrounding the reintegration of art and daily life sought by the European avant-garde. Indeed, the changing social, economic, and political circumstances that Modern Movement architects confronted during the early twentieth century had inherent implications for landscape—to the extent that it often became a primary embodiment of their broader aims. This engagement involved novel spatial conceptions that were symbolic as well as programmatic, yet there was a corresponding shift in patronage from individual, private clients to bureaucratic groups or governmental organizations that often prioritized practicality and convenience over artistry, as Fletcher Steele cautioned in 1941.[41] To mitigate the effects of this conflict, Achille Duchêne vehemently proclaimed: "*The style of today will only tolerate luxury in response to a purpose.* The latest standard is to maximize the effect of each expenditure, while seeking to promote the illusion that it surpasses reality."[42] By fulfilling a combination of functional and aesthetic criteria, public landscapes of the era were expected not only to accommodate the leisure needs of the emerging mass society but also to elevate aesthetic sensibilities and foster a sense of solidarity among the populace.

The motivations underlying modern landscape design in Europe during this period differed considerably from those in the United States, where the potential for landscape to engage issues of social reform was relatively muted. In Sweden, the Netherlands, and Weimar Germany, for example, architecture and landscape design were deemed significant agents in furthering the Social Democratic objective of fostering the collectivity of social existence by dismantling social barriers and promoting economic equality.[43] Rapid industrialization during the late nineteenth century prompted large population shifts in these countries, as workers migrated from the rural countryside to urban centers in search of jobs. In response, Swedish cities such as Stockholm purchased large tracts of land in the urban periphery to ensure municipal control of urban expansion and improve access to good-quality housing, thereby stemming the sweeping tide of emigration. Despite the severe economic hardships of the era, architects, landscape architects, and planners were actively engaged in governmental initiatives to realize the dream of a Swedish *folkhem* (people's home)—a rational model for transforming Swedish society to achieve economic and social parity. Four decades of Social Democratic hegemony during the first half of the twentieth century, uninterrupted by political upheaval or direct involvement in war, facilitated the widespread development of public parks and landscapes, new towns and housing projects, all directed toward improving the daily life of the Swedish populace and thereby instilling a sense of national pride.

In the Netherlands the creation of public parks was a long-standing tradition, although such efforts were sporadic until the late nineteenth century, when such amenities were systematically conceived as part of a broader pattern of urban expansion. Large tracts of moors and heaths were brought under cultivation, depleting much of the country's native fauna, while the early twentieth-century reclamation of the Zuiderzee led to construction of new open landscapes on an unprecedented scale. Under the influence of J. T. P. Bijhouwer, chairman of the country's Society of Garden and Landscape Architects, parks such as the Amsterdam Bospark (1929–37) were developed to address the recreational needs of the urban populace in a distinctly Dutch manner. The layout of Bospark makes reference to contemporary Dutch art forms as well as to the site's existing polders while restoring its native plant materials, thus satisfying both aesthetic and scientific (functional and technical) criteria.[44]

Nationalistic tendencies also characterized the German *Volkspark* (people's park) movement, which proliferated during the early decades of the century to promote active engagement of the populace with its natural roots. This involved landscape architects in the creation of unprogrammed urban woodlands and open fields, as well as sports amenities and leisure facilities, while making use of indigenous plant materials.[45] Allotment gardens, instituted to provide a measure of self-sufficiency under conditions of economic hardship, reinstated direct engagement with the land, or *Landschaft*—the foundation upon which landscape practices originated. As a result of such governmental initiatives, the first decades of the century witnessed unprecedented expansion of green spaces, replete with recreational facilities and agricultural plots, in the industrialized urban centers of Germany. German landscape theorists generally eschewed aesthetic criteria in favor of scientific rationalization of landscape design—in both a technical and a sociological sense.[46] Although this rational focus prompted harsh criticism from their European counterparts, who favored a more balanced artistic approach to landscape design and planning, the landscapes that resulted from such rationalization during the Weimar period were not lacking in aesthetic value—a quality Leberecht Migge characteristically attributed to plant growth rather than to design intentions.[47]

American and British landscape architects were slow to take up the broader social and cultural issues that engaged their avant-garde European counterparts. In the United States, designers initially conceived of public parks as relatively unscripted spaces for individual contemplation and social interaction, an idea that derived from Olmsted. Government efforts to address the active recreational needs of the urban populace during the early decades of the twentieth century led to increased programmatic specificity in the design of American parks and recreation grounds, resulting in conflicts between the utilitarian and aesthetic aims of park administrators and designers. War efforts prompted further instances of functional programming directed to social ends: the patriotic "war gardens" and "victory gardens" promoted during and immediately following World War I, or the facilities for migrant and defense workers created by the Farm Security Administration in the late 1930s and early 1940s.[48] By the 1930s, however, as the presence of public parks and recreational facilities became an accepted norm in American cities, the overt reform motivation underlying such park designs diminished considerably, while issues of social betterment continued to figure prominently in the public landscapes of northern Europe, often without a corresponding sacrifice in artistry.

Two separate initiatives of 1937, the First International Congress of Garden Architects, convened at the Parisian International Exhibition *Art et technique,* and the exhibition *Contemporary Landscape Architecture and Its Sources,* held at the San Francisco Museum of Art, reflect these ideological differences between the approaches of European and American practitioners and theorists. In his report on the First International Congress of Garden Architects, chairman Achille Duchêne analyzed the contemporary art of garden design in terms of economic, social, and political realities. Acknowledging the death of the elitist private garden and proclaiming its rebirth in a more powerful form as *"the Art of Gardens envisaged from a social point of view,"* he stressed the recreational, educational, and productive aspects of landscape. Duchêne also ascribed moral virtue to landscape design, citing its power to enrich the working classes both materially and spiritually, "to accustom them to beauty, develop their contemplative and critical abilities, and produce an effect of serenity and order."[49] In addressing the utilitarian aspects of contemporary garden design, he elaborated on diverse programmatic means to enrich the imagination of the broader populace by accentuating the particular character of each site and using simplicity of means to achieve the maximum effect.

While seeking to accommodate the practical and spiritual exigencies of the emerging mass society, Duchêne also commended the role of parks in developing individualism, a quality French designers consistently prized over the collective values of Weimar culture.[50]

In contrast to the French emphasis on the aesthetic potential of utilitarian landscapes, German landscape theorists of the Weimar period focused on their productive and recreational aspects, principles they extended equally to the private garden. Stressing the collective social import of garden architecture, Migge argued that the basis for the garden of the future should not be "aesthetic abilities and learned disciplinary formulae, but rather knowledge of people's economy, in social and technical conditions, [which is] the basis upon which gardens come into existence."[51] Working in collaboration with a wide array of progressive German architects, he directed his primary energies to fostering economic self-sufficiency through the creation of allotment gardens, a prominent feature of *Siedlungen* (housing settlements) of the Weimar period. In his voluminous writings, Migge sought to reverse the theoretical dominance of architecture over landscape, firmly rejecting the proposition that "our activity in the Siedlung is basically concerned with problems of housing." Instead he maintained, "the production of the soil is an organic part of the process of formation of the Siedlung," and "the rational planning of green belts constitutes a central point of the new type of settlement."[52] Consistent with this concept of landscape as providing essential nourishment for the new architecture, Migge prioritized the productive garden, which he considered a technical solution to a technical problem, in contrast to the romantic approach to the park as a refuge from the mechanized world—a role that Duchêne's report continued to sanction.

Like their architectural contemporaries, many American landscape architects of this period were preoccupied with the aesthetic impact of form, a position that differed markedly from the social concerns of European landscape designers. Theoretical discussions in the United States focused on stylistic issues, especially the relative merits of formal versus informal modes of design, essentially derived from differences between the geometric basis of the French and Italian garden traditions and the irregularity associated with the English landscape garden. In the San Francisco exhibition catalog, Fletcher Steele advocated blending formal and informal styles, ignoring the cultural roots of such design approaches in favor of purely aesthetic ends:

> These two styles are mere surface decoration, each in accord with profound instincts in human character. Composition in landscape design may be achieved by either method or by a combination of both. At bottom, the true aim of landscape architecture is one: by use of style, color and form, to create beauty in space composition.[53]

Landscape architect Peter Walker rationalizes this emphasis on aesthetic values in terms of contemporary American culture, in which "there was no perceived widespread need—no technological revolution in the landscape industry, no revolution in political or social terms—to direct the immediate prewar and postwar work in landscape design." Rather, he argues, "what brought modernism to landscape design in the United States was not revolution but evolution: the gradual, profound changes in American middle-class life."[54] Although Walker overlooks the significant impact of the Great Depression, which led to New Deal policies fostering widespread development of infrastructure, recreational, and housing facilities to address the needs of the broader populace, American public landscapes of the 1930s and beyond generally lacked the explicit social agenda and associated degree of programmatic specificity found in the Siedlung landscapes of Weimar Germany or Amsterdam's Bospark, for example; in addition to recreational facilities, American examples generally included an abundance of open areas intended for social engagement and/or individual contemplation as well as active recreation.[55]

European landscape theorists were not exempt from elaborating upon formal design criteria. French landscape designer Jean-Charles Moreux sought to assert the contemporary cultural relevance of disparate historical forms: "In reality there are only two forms of garden, the formal garden, which is the point of contact between house and nature, for it is a product of them both; and the landscape garden, which is an imitation of nature."[56] In the 1910s German landscape architect Walter Engelhardt had similarly sought to mediate between dwelling and landscape through the architectonic garden's synthesis of geometric "cultural" forms and irregular "natural" forms.[57] To bridge these diverse aesthetic categories, Jules Buyssens, a founder of the Belgian Association of Garden Architects (1930), advocated a "new picturesque," which combined the formal attributes of the French landscape tradition with the irregularity of the English landscape garden; moreover, he associated the possibility of choice inherent to this formal combination with "democratic" values.[58] To overcome the limitations of such distinctions between geometric and "natural" approaches to landscape, certain theorists exhorted designers to concern themselves with broader environmental issues. Tunnard argued: "*The right style for the twentieth century is no style at all, but a new conception of planning the human environment,*" while Kassler exhorted members of both disciplines to remember Alexander Pope's advice to "consult the genius of the place in all."[59] In her terms, this would involve an ecologically sound approach, "planned to respect both the nature of man and the nature of nature."[60]

Genius Loci and the Architectural Avant-Garde

Architects have long embraced the principle of genius loci, but in terms of material logic and form, rather than social ideology or human ecology. For example, seeking a material foundational logic for architectural design, Eugène-Emmanuel Viollet-le-Duc, professor of architecture at the Ecole des Beaux-Arts in Paris, drew upon the notion of genius loci in the opening chapters of his *Histoire de l'habitation humaine* (1875), each of which begins with an evocative description of a particular site that provides the conceptual as well as the material foundation for the associated building form. This reasoning has its origins in eighteenth-century efforts to rethink the logic of architectural form by invoking its primitive roots. Architectural theorist Marc-Antoine Laugier likened the city to a forest and the town planner to a gardener, cutting and pruning, taming and cultivating: "One must look at a town as a forest. The streets of the one are the roads of the other; both must be cut through in the same way. . . . Let us carry out this idea and use the design of our parks as plan for our towns."[61] During the mid-nineteenth century Gottfried Semper extended Viollet's material argument to engage the social origins of architecture. Rejecting the primitive hut as the theoretical basis for architectural form, he postulated four primary elements—hearth (or altar, the social and spiritual foundation of architecture), mound, framework, and enclosure—inextricably linking building and ground in a manner capable of infinite elaboration according to particular social and cultural parameters.[62]

Architects have recently sought to reinstate such foundational logic in more general terms. For example, Vittorio Gregotti traces the origin of architecture to humankind's taking charge of the ground, rather than the primitive hut:

> Before transforming a support into a column, a roof into a tympanum, before placing stone on stone, man placed a stone on the ground to recognize a site in the midst of an unknown universe, in order to take account of it and modify it. As with every act of assessment, this one required radical moves and apparent simplicity.[63]

Gio Ponti endorses a related truism with his assertion of the "landscape genesis of architecture," wherein he argues: "The architect . . . must compose landscapes even within his walls. Be it natural or urban, the architect is always constructing a landscape."[64] Yet such assertions of conceptual unity of architecture and landscape belie the limited nature of architectural concerns in relation to those of landscape architects; lacking any theoretical basis for elaboration of the designed landscape, they overlook disciplinary distinctions that have increasing relevance for contemporary practice.

Although the principle of genius loci seemingly contradicted the internationalist ambitions of certain proponents of the new architecture, such as Hitchcock and Johnson, Walter Gropius, or Sigfried Giedion, Modern Movement architects were inclined to embrace the concept, although in vastly different ways and to varied extents. Prominent among these is Frank Lloyd Wright, who gleaned inspiration from the midwestern prairie in his early work and the southwestern prairie in his later work. Drawing upon Viollet's materialist rationale to engage the physical qualities of the locale, Wright argued that one should build "with" rather than "upon" the land, elaborating: "The good ground should greatly determine the fundamental shape, even the style, of every occupation in building, road, or institution in the new city." Hence his assertion to have virtually eliminated distinctions between architecture and landscape: "To see where the ground leaves off and the building begins would require careful attention."[65] Such coalescence of architecture and landscape also characterizes Wright's thinking at the regional scale, manifested in the "organic" logic of his utopian proposal for Broadacre City: "Here architecture is landscape and landscape takes on the character of architecture by way of the simple process of cultivation."[66] Despite his claim of working with the ground, however, Wright tended to aestheticize each site in architectural terms. Imposing his interpretation of the idealized structure of nature upon the specifics of a site led him to create constructions that substitute for landscape—the inverse of Migge's metaphoric concept of the "growing settlement."[67]

Like Wright, Alvar Aalto also sought resonance between architecture and landscape, whether urban, suburban, or rural, constructed or natural. In contrast to the material concordance of architecture and locale to which Wright aspired, Aalto's propensity to ground construction in the Finnish landscape, at once cultural and mythic, involved using elements and materials that retain clear distinctions among them. In 1925 he articulated a fundamental principle of his architecture:

> We Finns . . . are very prone to "forest dreaming," for which we have had ample opportunity up to now. Sometimes, however, we feel that we do not have enough pure nature at our disposal, and then we try to plant the beauty of the wilds at our very doors. In fact we should apply the opposite principle, starting with the environment we live in, and adding our buildings to it, to the improvement of the original landscape.

The function of public buildings, he elaborated, is "to accentuate the landscape."[68] In opposition to the romantic flight from civilization that Wright endorsed, Aalto prioritized acts of human intervention, seeking a symbiotic synthesis of civilization and nature. He deemed such "a simultaneous solution of opposites" the most important prerequisite for human achievement to attain the level of culture.[69] In an imaginary dialogue with Sigfried Giedion, Aalto affirmed the human focus of his work: "True architecture exists only where man stands at the center."[70]

Even Giedion, a prominent spokesman for international tendencies in modern architecture and an advocate of Le Corbusier's radical urban pronouncements, ultimately came to endorse an aspect of genius loci. In *Space, Time, and Architecture* (1941), Giedion drew upon the mediating capacities of landscape to theorize that the parkway, a contemporary form of roadway that is intimately bound to its specific locale, could provide the basis for new conceptions of urban form. In contrast to the engineered roadways of Europe, "laid out for military purposes," he asserted, "the parkway humanizes the highway by carefully following and utilizing the terrain, rising and falling with the contours of the earth, merging completely into the landscape."[71] Particularly notable is Giedion's professed interest in working from the existing topography, rather than from the notion of a conceptual tabula rasa, to generate new forms of urbanism. Arguing for the potential for the parkway to transform the city, rather than to end at the city, he subsequently elaborated:

> The city must adopt the new scale which is identical with that of its bridges and parkways. Only then will the civic center stand amidst greenery. Until then it will stand as a reminder that the structure of the city must be transformed, not in the interest of single individuals but for the sake of the community as a whole.[72]

Although the organic logic that Giedion used in imagining the parkway as a paradigmatic generator of urban form appears to depart from his enthusiastic endorsement of Le Corbusier's urban theories, it recalls the latter's Obus A proposal for Algiers (1931), where an elevated roadway follows the contours of the hilly terrain, determining the form of the housing beneath it.

Indeed, the notion of genius loci was crucial even to an iconoclast such as Le Corbusier. Unlike his approach to architecture and urbanism, which evolved as his radical a priori theoretical assumptions were tested through his built work, Le Corbusier's approach to landscape evolved a posteriori from practice. Thus, despite the militant tone of his utopian urban pronouncements, Le Corbusier carefully calibrated his building designs to the specifics of their locales. With his capital complex for Chandigarh (1952–59), he extended this concern to an explicit engagement with the symbolism of the Mughal paradise garden in an attempt to conflate the traditional Indian concept of the sacred with a modern metaphysic.

The search for a "timeless" mode of expression led other Modern Movement architects to seek a related spirit of mythic archaism by recourse to contemporary forms. In the outskirts of Mexico City, Luis Barragán drew upon the evocative physical qualities of existing lava fields to craft elements of a suburban subdivision—called El Pedregal (the stony place, 1945–53)—out of territory previously deemed uninhabitable. His garden walls, paths, pools, and fountains of natural stone and brightly colored stucco mediate between the dramatic natural features of the region (which he augmented by adding trees with distinctive profiles) and the abstract forms of his architecture; these garden elements echo or contrast colors found in the existing vegetation while establishing an architectonic basis for the buildings. They also frame distinctive views beyond the domain of the subdivision, thus bringing the broader landscape within the purview of El Pedregal's discrete garden volumes. In keeping with the speculative nature of the project and its exclusive clientele, Barragán intended such spaces primarily for private contemplation rather than public interaction. In prioritizing their aesthetic value over their social potential,

Barragán evoked the spiritual serenity of the monastic *hortus conclusus*.[73] His architectonic elements are discrete fragments, seeds to a potential mode of construction, a vision that has been virtually obliterated by subsequent construction within the subdivision. Unlike Jože Plečnik's incremental interventions in the landscape of Prague Castle, Barragán's fragmentary insertions at El Pedregal contributed only momentarily to a broader narrative about place—one that can only be imagined, thanks to their profuse photographic documentation.

On a more moderate scale, Richard Neutra evoked the genius loci to reinforce the physical and psychological health concerns that motivated the interrelationship of modern architecture and landscape in his work. Espousing a "generous opening to health agents and a biologically minded appreciation of the soil in which all life is rooted," he stressed the need to develop the mythopoetic value of landscape by exploiting "the mysteries and realities of the site." Emphasizing distinctions between the abstraction of modern architecture and the specific qualities that could be gleaned from the natural features of a locale, he argued:

> My experience, everything within me, is against an abstract approach to land and nature, and for *the profound assets rooted in each site* and buried in it like a treasurable wonder. The ancients thought those vital assets spirits. By listening intently, you can hear them miraculously breathe in their slumber. You may subtly awaken them to startling values of design truly assured of duration, growth and never-ending life.[74]

Thus, unlike Wright, Neutra deliberately used materials that contrasted those found in the region, stressing the artificiality of his constructions and their ability to operate in dialogue with the landscape's natural features.[75] As Neutra implies, the genius loci is more than a physical concept; it involves a quasi-mystical environmental sensibility that is cultural as well as spiritual.

While acknowledging that "the *genius loci* is open to contestation, both theoretically (as to its meaning) and concretely (as to how to understand a particular place)," geographer David Harvey credits the concept with the power to "tie together time past with time future while acknowledging the importance of memory, the experience of environment, and the capacity for dwelling in the land."[76] Yet the principle of genius loci is clearly insufficient to generate a significant architectural and/or landscape response in itself, as Sidney Robinson cautions: "Rooted location . . . is not . . . the only guarantee of reliable landscape relationships."[77] Complications arise when the site offers little to the poetic imagination or poses particular environmental challenges, as Marc Treib wryly argues: "So much of landscape architecture in the past has been created to *overcome* what the genius of the place offered—for example, by bringing water to the desert or by constructing conditioned enclosures to grow oranges in cold climates—that it's obvious that the genius's ambiguous advice can be taken rather freely."[78] In such examples, it may be necessary to both transcend *and* engage the site's constraints. Indeed, it is essential to transform the exigencies of any situation to address the complex relationship between humankind and the natural world in an evocative and meaningful way.[79]

In certain examples analyzed in this book, built on industrialized parcels or urban renewal sites—Sunnyside Gardens in Queens, New York, or Lafayette Park in Detroit—there was little on the sites or their immediate environs from which to draw inspiration, apart from the existing urban infrastructure. This absence of distinguishing features enabled the respective teams of designers to impose new kinds of order on such sites, in keeping with their utopian social aspirations. Yet such manifestations of idealized order often constitute significant gestures to the broader urban or "natural" milieus in which they are embedded. For example, the designers of Sunnyside Gardens were required to adhere to the existing urban grid—a restriction they turned to their advantage—while the layout of Römerstadt derives in large measure from the undulating contours of its site, part of a land reclamation project in Frankfurt's Nidda River valley. Of the examples scrutinized here, only Lafayette Park maintains an order independent of the site's urban or natural features, an approach that has been imitated formally, although not in substance, in more recent housing developments in the vicinity. The resulting islands of inhabitation are separated by streetscapes virtually devoid of human activity, thus operating to the detriment of the broader urban milieu. The intervening landscape isolates and privatizes such housing projects, rather than uniting them as urban planner Ludwig Hilberseimer intended.

In the best of these projects, the architectural concept derives in significant ways from that for the landscape, despite any difference in authorship that this might entail. Each design is conceived of as part of a larger whole, with interventions consisting of both building elements and landscape elements. Neither architecture nor landscape dominates, but each serves as the complement of the other. Such affinities ultimately derive not from the overarching notion of *Gesamptkunstwerk* but from a purposeful dialogue among a range of related discourses, for, as Julia Czerniak argues, "landscape is too important, ubiquitous, and complex to leave to a single discipline."[80] Significant examples in the public domain, although unfortunately all too rare, are nonetheless important precursors to current notions of interdisciplinarity, engaging inherently different modes of thought or types of knowledge to expand upon the potential that exists within each discipline.[81]

Over the past thirty years, humanist geographers have argued that the issue of constructing a place in the world necessarily involves the complexities of human social and cultural interaction.[82] To address such broad concerns, architects need to be aware, as landscape architects undoubtedly are, of the mediating aspects of their discipline, its potential for establishing relations among a diverse range of issues and scales of undertaking. Only when architects and landscape architects understand the scope and complexity of their individual areas of expertise, as well as their points of convergence and intersection, will the two discourses succeed in formulating significant contributions to contemporary culture. As Homi Bhabha argues: "It is in the emergence of the interstices—the overlap and displacement of zones of difference—that the intersubjective and collective experiences of . . . cultural value are negotiated."[83] To accomplish this objective, as André Vera and Elizabeth Kassler have noted, requires a certain humility. The eighteenth-century English architectural theorist Robert Morris said it best when he advised that the "first care [of the architect] is justly appropriating the Design to the Situation . . . so blending Art and Nature together."[84]

Art historian John Beardsley brings this thought up to date in a message directed to practitioners and theorists of both disciplines:

> I wish to say something about landscape architecture, for design inextricable from the history of the site, from its spatial, material, and phenomenal conditions, and from natural and social ecology, as contrasted with the design merely of buildings—to regard design as part and parcel of nature, as well as of society.[85]

Concluding that "landscape architecture will soon become the most consequential of the design arts," Beardsley echoes a sentiment expressed more explicitly a century earlier by landscape architect Charles Eliot: "Landscape Architecture is an art of design, and in a very real sense covers agriculture, forestry, gardening, engineering, and even architecture (as ordinarily defined) itself."[86] The challenge for architects practicing today is not to reject the hierarchy articulated by Eliot and Beardsley, but to embrace the spirit of such provocations.

ONE

SOCIAL IDEALISM
AND URBAN LANDSCAPE
Sunnyside Gardens vs. Römerstadt

In their 1932 analysis of the "international style" of modern architec-ture, Henry-Russell Hitchcock Jr. and Philip Johnson reinforced historic distinctions between architecture and landscape design, arguing that the natural conditions of the site constitute a pristine entity best left untouched by architects: "Choice of site, and the arrangement of buildings upon the site: these are the prime problems of the international style in relation to natural surroundings." Invoking the myth of the "natural" landscape as the ideal setting for modern buildings, they elaborated: "As far as possible the original beauties of the site should be preserved. Mere open spaces are not enough for repose; something of the ease and grace of untouched nature is needed as well."[1]

Hitchcock reiterated this argument in the catalog for an exhibition, *Contemporary Landscape Architecture and Its Sources,* held at the San Francisco Museum of Art in 1937:

> One single principle is ultimately sufficient to cover all the various current manifestations of intelligent and aesthetically effective human control over the natural environment: that is, the preservation of all possible values previously in existence in the landscape setting with the addition of only the simplest and most practical provision for specific human needs. The essence of sound modern gardening is neither design nor planting, but choice of site.[2]

In this interpretation, the modern landscape is the antithesis of modern architecture; it is a relatively mute phenomenon, its role limited to addressing minimal functional requirements.

According to Hitchcock, the two professions had been in a struggle for dominance since the eighteenth century, when landscape design became the primary embodiment of romantic values. Thus romanticism tended "to reduce architecture to a position of subservience to gardening, to literature, and to painting"—an effect that had been overcome, he noted, by a recent focus on construction.[3] Celebrating the modern reemergence of architecture as a primary cultural endeavor, Hitchcock championed the capitalist values inherent to American individualism, in which the "natural" landscape was valued as a soothing backdrop for the new architecture. He thus denied not only the symbolic potential of the modern landscape, its role in concretizing the place of humankind in the modern world, but also its ability to contribute to a broader architectural vision.

Modern Architecture—International Exhibition, held at New York's Museum of Modern Art in 1932 and organized by Hitchcock and Johnson, included a housing project that challenged these assumptions in significant ways. The curators' aesthetic biases are well known; hoping to end the eclecticism that characterized American architecture of the early twentieth century, Hitchcock and Johnson sought to promote a new aesthetic, "Modern Architecture," or "the international style," as they subsequently termed it.[4] This stylistic unity, comprising abstract white buildings with simple volumes and broad expanses of glass, was the topic of their coeval book *The International Style: Architecture since 1922,* intended to promote a modern aesthetic among contemporary architects, builders, and potential clients. Yet one complex included in the exhibition's Modern Housing section—Sunnyside Gardens in Queens, New York (1924–28), by architects Clarence Stein and Henry Wright and landscape architect Marjorie Sewell Cautley—both departed from the stylistic predilections that motivated Hitchcock and Johnson's choice of works on display and challenged their attitude toward landscape.[5]

What set this moderate-income housing project apart formally from existing urban tenement housing or contemporary suburban developments was not its architecture—redbrick townhouses and low-rise apartment buildings with facades incorporating subtle decorative embellishments—but its site strategy and landscaping. Although the designers subdivided the typical urban blocks according to conventional lot lines (thus acceding to stipulations of mortgage lenders), they instituted forty-year restrictive (left) Aerial view of Sunnyside Gardens in Queens, New York (1924–28), by Clarence Stein, Henry Wright, and Marjory Sewell Cautley, on the cover of promotional brochure *Sunnyside: A Step toward Better Housing*, 1927. Courtesy Frances Loeb Library, Harvard University.

(right) Inner garden court with pergola at Sunnyside Gardens. From Terence Riley, *The International Style: Exhibit 15 and the Museum of Modern Art*, 1992.

covenants and easements to provide for communal landscapes at the centers of the blocks and a network of pedestrian paths weaving through them.[6] Stein and Wright devised a range of housing types and varied their external appearance, creating a syncopated rhythm in the tree-lined streetscape, which Cautley augmented by means of variegated planting in the front yards and inner blocks. At Sunnyside Gardens, landscape dominates over architecture. Indeed, landscape plays a crucial role in the development's success as an urban living environment, a success that derives as much from its radical, anticapitalist assumptions about landownership and control as from its traditional appearance.

In keeping with their stylistic aims, Hitchcock and Johnson incorporated no photographs of Sunnyside Gardens in their exhibition catalog, *Modern Architecture—International Exhibition,* and associated book.[7] Other than Stein and Wright's development plan of 1929 for Radburn, New Jersey (a project in which Cautley also participated), the publications' images of housing complexes are limited to European examples that adhere to Hitchcock and Johnson's stylistic predilections: J. J. P. Oud's Kiefhoek in Rotterdam (1928–30) and two German *Siedlungen*: Ernst May's Römerstadt in Frankfurt (1927–29) and Otto Haesler's Rothenberg in Kassel (1930–32). In the final chapter of their coeval book, devoted to "*Siedlung*," Hitchcock and Johnson alluded to the reason for this omission in an implicit criticism of Sunnyside Gardens' architecture:

SOCIAL IDEALISM AND URBAN LANDSCAPE 27

> Despite the development of group planning along modern lines in America the style of the individual houses in our "garden suburbs" remains traditional. Even where modern construction has been introduced, the sponsors have been loath to provide modern design. Hence our *Siedlungen* are sometimes excellent illustrations of sociological theory, but they are seldom examples of sound modern building and never works of architectural distinction.[8]

Their association of modern architecture with the expression of modern construction techniques limited Hitchcock and Johnson's ability to recognize the contribution of Sunnyside Gardens to contemporary architectural and landscape discourse, which arose from the designers' ambitions to create an amenable communal living environment for moderate-income residents in close proximity to both workplace and natural environs.

Hitchcock and Johnson rejected not only the stylistic aspects of Sunnyside Gardens but also its ideological underpinnings—its grounding in communal social values espoused in the German *Siedlungen,* especially those such as Römerstadt, carried out in Frankfurt between 1925 and 1930 under May's administrative leadership. Arguing that European *Siedlungen* are built "for some proletarian superman of the future," they endorsed an architecture grounded in American individualism:

> Satisfying the particular client is one particular function of architecture that the European functionalists usually avoid. For them such work is without sociological significance. The *Siedlung* implies preparation not for a given family but for a typical family. This statistical monster, the typical family, has no personal existence and cannot defend itself against the sociological theories of the architects.

Stressing quotidian needs rather than utopian social aspirations, Hitchcock and Johnson concluded: "There should be a balance between evolving ideal houses for scientific living and providing comfortable houses for ordinary living."[9]

Lewis Mumford, the well-known urban historian and social critic who served as guest curator for the exhibition's Modern Housing section, provided an assessment of the contemporary situation that differed in several crucial respects from that of Hitchcock and Johnson. While deriding the false romanticism of the American suburban cottage—and thus seemingly supporting Hitchcock and Johnson's aesthetic biases—Mumford cautioned against architectural evaluations based solely on appearances. In the exhibition catalog, he cited Sunnyside Gardens and other

American examples realized by nonprofit development groups, alongside the housing developments around Frankfurt, as examples of progressive urban development. Ideological, rather than stylistic, concerns prompted Mumford's association of Sunnyside Gardens with European examples in which, he argued, "one witnesses the growing integration of modern architecture . . . with the land itself, with human beings and their needs."[10] In Mumford's analysis, the modern integration of architecture and landscape merged practical realities with utopian aspirations in a manner that was replete with symbolic overtones.

Mumford directed his primary criticism to the social assumptions of the American suburban myth, rather than to the stylistic aspects of suburban housing. His notion of human needs incorporated more than access to open space and greenery; it involved communitarian aspirations that were not generally associated with contemporary American cultural values but had inherent implications for landscape—not only its design but also its conditions of use. Mumford advocated a decidedly reformist approach: "a new domestic environment," conceived in terms of the community as a whole, rather than the individual homeowner.[11] What stands in the way of this idea, he surmised, is "belief in abstract individual rights and opportunities which have no reality or efficacy"—a quality he termed "the myth of individual initiative."[12] Arguing that "we have confused good housing with the very limited and abstract matter of ownership," Mumford espoused European examples in which "the unit is no longer the individual house, but the community."[13] He associated modern architecture in general and modern housing in particular with communal values: "Modern housing turns its back upon the romantic individual nourished in the illusion of isolation; accepting the house as part of the community, modern architecture concerns itself with the comprehensive and integrated design of the whole."[14] At Sunnyside Gardens, such communal objectives derive from Stein and Wright's radical planning methods rather than from radical architectural design.

The *Modern Architecture* exhibition and its associated catalog and book were unabashedly promotional: intended to endorse European avant-garde architectural currents among an American audience, especially members of the entrenched architectural profession, its builders and clients. Although Stein, Wright, and Cautley conceived of Sunnyside Gardens as a model for urban reform, it was not the stylistic reform that Hitchcock and Johnson championed. Instead, the Sunnyside designers sought to adapt European housing principles, such as those found in the German *Siedlungen,* to American social, economic, and cultural realities. As Stein

Aerial view of Siedlung Römerstadt, Frankfurt, by Ernst May et al. (1927–29), with Nidda River in foreground, followed in turn by allotment gardens, townhouses with private gardens, and apartment slabs with communal gardens. Photograph by Stadtplanungsamt Frankfurt, 1929. Courtesy Historisches Museum Frankfurt (photograph: Horst Ziegenfusz).

later argued, "Sunnyside was an experiment in community building far more than in housing."[15]

There are strong parallels between Sunnyside and Römerstadt. Both are planned communities, conceived by architects and planners working in collaboration with landscape architects.[16] Their stylistic qualities are less significant historically than their overall planning strategies and attitudes toward open space. Both were influenced by the ideas of British urban planner and garden cities advocate Raymond Unwin, who sought radical means to achieve new patterns of civic life, prioritizing communal life and welfare over individual needs and interests.[17] Their designers addressed the social issues associated with their architecture in four distinct but interrelated ways: technically, through the reorganization of methods of building production; programmatically, through the provision of improved housing conditions; economically, through novel combinations of public and private funding in Frankfurt and the introduction of cooperative methods of ownership in Sunnyside; and formally, through spatial organizations that give expression to the collectivity of social existence. Both were built by limited-dividend building organizations seeking to counter speculative building practices—in the case of Römerstadt with substantial public involvement. Each was situated on the urban fringe: Römerstadt on former swampland that constituted part of a broader program of land reclamation along Frankfurt's Nidda River valley and Sunnyside on a disused railroad yard in Queens, New York. Both developments are essentially satellite communities; lacking means of economic self-sufficiency, their inhabitants rely on existing public transport systems to reach workplaces, shopping, and cultural amenities in the broader urban milieu. Both are primarily residential developments, with similar net density and emphasis on single-family dwellings as the primary housing type.[18] Their designers achieved aesthetic and formal variety through various combinations of unit types, dominated by townhouses adjoining small private gardens. Economic self-sufficiency for the residents was an objective of each, although this was only partially successful—through rental units included in selected townhouses in both developments, as well as allotment gardens in Frankfurt.[19] Owing to planning efficiencies, moreover, buildings constituted only 30 percent of ground coverage, leaving landscape as the dominant means by which the planners' broader communal aspirations were satisfied.

Whereas Römerstadt was one of several projects realized between 1925 and 1930 by May and his team of architects and landscape architects to effectively rehouse 11 percent of Frankfurt's urban population, Sunnyside was an isolated example, with little impact on American housing practices. In large measure, this is because Römerstadt was the product of a specific social, cultural, and political milieu, while Sunnyside Gardens reflected an attempt to overcome certain limitations of its time and place. Particular aspects of Sunnyside also contributed to this discrepancy: the limited power entrusted to its architects and planners, the unassertive character of its buildings, the relative lack of publicity given to the development, and, to a lesser extent, Stein's own modest assessment of the project. Finally, the minimal reception given to Sunnyside ultimately reflects a bias against addressing the modern landscape on the part of architectural historians and critics, exemplified by the writings of Hitchcock and Johnson.

Sunnyside Gardens grew out of an attempt to respond to certain limitations of the capitalist system: to improve the quality and availability of moderate-income housing by restricting the profit motive and facilitating cooperative methods of home and apartment ownership. The project came about thanks to the altruistic aims of developer Alexander Bing, who established the City Housing Corporation in 1924 as a limited dividend corporation to "build better homes and communities."[20] Responding to the relative inability of private enterprise to address the chronic lack of moderately priced housing, the corporation and its designers viewed Sunnyside as "a laboratory in which to work out better house and block plans and better means of construction and financing."[21] More important, it operated as a testing ground for the corporation's ultimate aim: to develop a garden city in the United States. The corporation's motivations—"to improve living conditions, reduce rents and influence the future planning of cities"[22]—not only extended from pragmatic to utopian but also included an explicit political dimension:

> It was the purpose of the City Housing Corporation to create a setting in which a democratic community might grow. This requires space and place to get together easily and agreeably. It means doing things for each other, or together, cooperating in caring for children; adult education; athletic meets; discussion of community affairs, whether those be of a court or block or take place in the interior park under a pergola, or the whole community of home owners, their tenants and the tenants or cooperative owners of the apartments.[23]

Determining the particular attributes of this "democratic" landscape with any precision, however, would remain an elusive goal at Sunnyside.

The political, economic, and social milieu in Weimar Germany differed dramatically from that in the United States, facilitating a more explicit correspondence between social aims and landscape as well as urban form. The German government not only guaranteed its citizens housing suited to their means, but it was also empowered to appropriate land for development purposes—and, beginning in 1918, housing was deemed a "public utility."[24] A 15 percent rent tax imposed in 1924 provided local municipalities with funding for new housing developments. As a center of Social Democratic values, Frankfurt was a locus of working-class movements for housing reform. Under the coalition of Socialist, Democratic, and Center parties headed by Mayor Ludwig Landmann (from 1924), City Architect Ernst May developed a unique model of social planning for the city in which he was able to coordinate closely all offices dealing with planning, construction, and financing. His sweeping bureaucratic powers included compulsory land purchase in the name of the public good.[25]

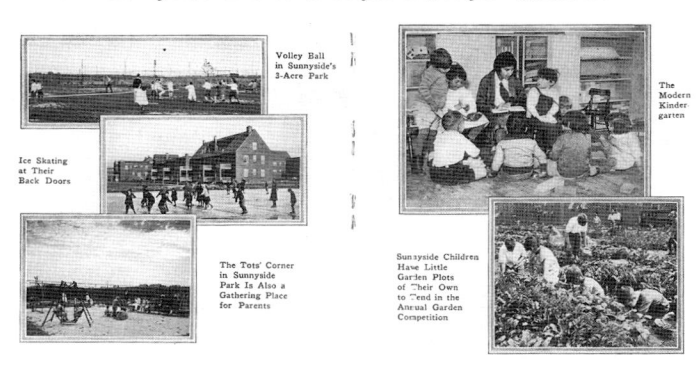

Procedures used by May and the City Housing Corporation to disseminate information about their respective housing projects differed radically in both intended audience and scope. May's efforts to engineer social change through architecture, to instill a new *Wohnkultur* (dwelling culture) in Frankfurt, led him to edit a periodical, *Das neue Frankfurt: Monatschrift für die Probleme moderner Gestaltung* (The new Frankfurt: Monthly publication for problems of modern design, 1926–31), that informed the urban populace and design professionals alike about innovative aspects of the lifestyle available in the housing settlements created under his direction.[26] Essays focused on cultural amenities—cinema and radio, theatrical productions, educational opportunities, and sports—as well as architectural features directed toward improving the conditions of daily life in these new settlements. A segment titled "Frankfurt Register" cataloged large-scale equipment (the Frankfurt kitchen, Frankfurt bath, and Frankfurt bed) as well as smaller household items (chairs, lighting fixtures, cooking utensils, and so on), indicating the extent to which May's program rationalized all aspects of the domestic environment. Despite the prominent role of landscape in the Frankfurt *Siedlungen*, however, it was not a salient theme in the periodical's essays or its imagery. Instead, *Das neue Frankfurt* was replete with "objective" photographs of the equipment and facilities available in support of the new dwelling culture, all directed to fulfilling communal needs rather than individual desires.[27] May's success in addressing the city's dire housing shortage in a contemporary idiom prompted the members of the Congrès Internationaux d'Architecture Moderne (CIAM) to hold their initial meeting of 1929, devoted to the minimal dwelling, in

(left) Cover of *Das neue Frankfurt* 1 (October/November 1926), contrasting Ernst May's approach to housing with conventional urban organization.

(right) Two-page spread promoting Sunnyside as "a wonderful place for children," from *Sunnyside: A Step toward Better Housing*. Courtesy Frances Loeb Library, Harvard University.

SOCIAL IDEALISM AND URBAN LANDSCAPE 33

Frankfurt, bringing his work to the attention of an international array of architects, planners, and historians associated with the Modern Movement.[28] In contrast, the City Housing Corporation directed its modest occasional pamphlets primarily to prospective investors and secondarily to potential occupants, but not to design professionals. The graphic presentation was more conventional in layout and appearance, relying primarily on scenic exterior photographs, which supported the idea of the communal landscape as Sunnyside's primary attribute. In both cases, however, the texts instructed potential occupants about the novel lifestyles afforded by the two developments.

The social grounds for the projects also differed. Unlike the relatively uniform cultural values that characterized the Frankfurt urban populace, who were receptive to social reform and expected the government to provide for basic living needs, the residents of Sunnyside were a socially and economically heterogeneous group. Römerstadt's physical isolation from the city contributed to a pioneering spirit among its early settlers, enhancing the residents' social solidarity. In Frankfurt, moreover, the government owned the land, and thus control over its communal aspects, whereas in the United States private ownership was the norm. Thus, rather than aspiring to engineer social change, Sunnyside's designers attempted to devise formal vehicles capable of fostering social exchange.

The architects' respective approaches to site planning reflect these differing cultural values. At Sunnyside, Stein and Wright were required to maintain the existing urban grid, a restriction they turned to their advantage, whereas in Frankfurt, May devised new kinds of street patterns, providing a hierarchical network of roadways to create superblocks in which the impact of roads is minimized and the communal landscape dominates. Whereas Römerstadt's idiosyncratic superblock pattern accentuates its isolation from the city core, the repetitive block pattern at Sunnyside grounds that settlement in its urban context. May's design team adapted block layout and building types to the contours of the irregular site and created unit plans that reflect solar orientation—as opposed to the varied formal response to the grid at Sunnyside, where the site lacked topographic variety.[29] Römerstadt's superblock layout and accompanying landscape thus distinguish the complex from its broader context, whereas at Sunnyside this distinction is accomplished principally through landscaping alone.

Like the urban parks of America's City Beautiful movement, the Sunnyside landscape reflects the association of social improvement with aesthetic improvement, but the designers rejected the movement's elitist, neoclassical models in favor of the regional vernacular. Cautley used landscape elements to enhance the hierarchy of open space: poplars and London plane trees line the streets, while privet hedges line the walkways; private gardens are bounded by low walls or hedges; finally, irregular clumps of deciduous trees and flowering shrubs differentiate the common gardens, many of which originally contained pergolas to provide shady locales where neighbors might gather. Her planting layout established a range of spaces for various types and degrees of social interaction by differentiating among public, semipublic, and private outdoor zones and establishing their relative separation and/or connectedness.[30] Cautley's concern for the subtle effects of her planting scheme on the day-to-day lives of the inhabitants is evident in her essay "Landscaping in the Housing Project" (1935), where she advocated a layered planting scheme to provide opportunities for supervising children at play from within each dwelling while preserving the privacy of the domestic interior from without.[31]

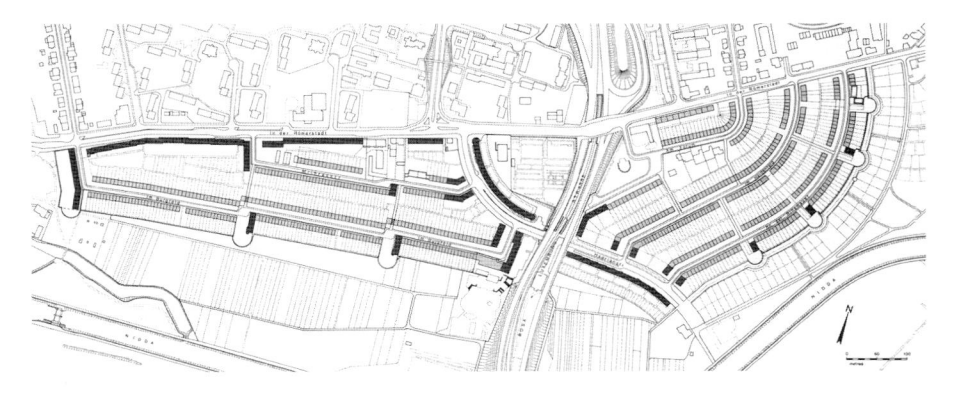

Whereas Stein, Wright, and Cautley sought to instill a sense of community through site beautification and provision of communal open space in Sunnyside Gardens, the Römerstadt landscape was more overtly utilitarian—and politically motivated. It included a sheepfold near the river and laundry drying yards distributed amid the housing blocks, along with allotment gardens for apartment dwellers and private vegetable gardens for the townhouses.[32] To ensure maximum efficiency and productivity there were typological norms for planting these garden plots and courses offered to educate the inhabitants in suitable planting methods. Laboring on the grounds did more than contribute to the residents' self-sustaining potential, however; it also instilled pride in their surroundings—akin to ownership—through active engagement with the land.

(left) Site plan reconstruction of Siedlung Römerstadt (drawn by Christopher Procter). Peter G. Rowe, *Modernity and Housing,* figure 99, page 136; copyright 1993 Massachusetts Institute of Technology; reprinted by permission of The MIT Press.

(right) Site plan of Sunnyside Gardens, 1928. Clarence S. Stein, *Toward New Towns for America,* 1957.

SOCIAL IDEALISM AND URBAN LANDSCAPE   35

Throughout the parkland along the reclaimed Nidda River valley, landscape architects Max Bromme and Leberecht Migge rejected the aesthetic basis of nineteenth-century European park design; instead they laced sports facilities interspersed with nature preserves, an outdoor theater, and gardens dedicated to scientific experiments to facilitate the development of healthy bodies and minds. As Migge argued: "Our settler is no cow farmer, but a fully cultured person of his time. Settlement is improvement."[33] This rationalization of the Nidda valley landscape extended beyond individual self-improvement; by directing mass leisure toward gardening, sports, and education, the Frankfurt government sought to instill moral values among the city's residents and to foster their engagement in emerging forms of mass culture.[34]

The layouts of Römerstadt and Sunnyside also reflect different approaches to the automobile. The private automobile was a minor factor in the planning of Römerstadt, whereas the designers of Sunnyside assumed its prevalence. Providing remote garages enabled them to establish the communal character of the inner blocks while fostering use of that pedestrian environment as well as existing public transport systems. Owing to increases in reliance on private transport in the interim, however, curbside parking has become the norm in both developments; cars now fill the streets of both settlements, as Sunnyside's remote garages have been demolished.

Whereas the Römerstadt landscape strategy was established from the outset, piecemeal development at Sunnyside enabled the designers to institute formal changes over the course of time in response to issues concerning the quality of life in a cooperative setting.[35] The history of this landscape reflects the changing social values and conflicting aims of its occupants. In the central portion of each block, for example, Stein, Wright, and Cautley responded to issues of privacy for the dwelling units in relation to communal amenities and gathering spaces. In the first block to be developed, a single central expanse originally included provision for active recreation—children's playground, wading pool, and tennis court—which proved too intrusive for residents of the adjoining townhouses. In response, the designers shifted such functions to a peripheral location and created smaller, more intimate gardens in the midblock zones, "intended for restful gatherings or for quiet play."[36] The central portions of the residential blocks thus became more contemplative in character, a quality lacking in the immediate vicinity of the Römerstadt housing units.

Sunnyside Gardens inner court *(left)* and U-shaped entry court. Photographs by Gottscho-Schleisner, New York, 1949. Clarence S. Stein, *Toward New Towns for America,* 1957.

With these physical modifications, social and communal organization at Sunnyside also underwent a transformation. Initially it existed at the scale of the residential block, with associations of home owners and renters established to maintain the central gardens and sponsor social events. This changed when the City Housing Corporation made space available for the broader community, which happened in two distinct ways. In 1926, at the request of neighborhood mothers, the corporation provided space in a cooperative apartment building for a kindergarten and play school. Sunnyside Park, established that same year on a far corner of the site, addressed two fundamental needs overlooked in the architects' original conception: while providing for active recreation in proximity to, but not directly adjacent to, the residential units, it included an existing building capable of accommodating social and communal activities at the scale of the community as a whole.[37] The presence of the park and its associated meeting place led to further changes in the community's social organization. A voluntary association of home owners and renters, the Sunnyside Community Association, arose to organize communal undertakings and safeguard the public welfare, while the earlier block associations continued to address concerns at the more immediate local scale. The Community Association fostered recreational activities and holiday celebrations as well as theatrical events (in a log cabin theater erected on the site), a gardening club, children's gardens, a circulating library, and a cooperative for purchasing garden and household equipment.

Efforts by the City Housing Corporation to encourage communitarian values had unforeseen consequences during the Great Depression, when rampant unemployment among residents led them to organize rent and mortgage strikes, which ultimately bankrupted the corporation. The worldwide depression also affected Römerstadt, although owing to government ownership of the land, many attributes of its original landscape are extant.[38] This has meant that Römerstadt residents have been at the mercy of the prevailing political system. For example, in 1933 the National Socialists dissolved the tenants' association, which had been formed to protect the rights of the original settlers and advocate for rent controls. For a few years following World War II, moreover, American military families occupied the settlement. After the Americans vacated, however, 75 percent of the original occupants returned, bringing a renewed solidarity to the community.

The flexible nature of Sunnyside Gardens, its ability to adapt to changing social needs, led Mumford (a longtime resident) to advocate this approach over the rigidity of German housing schemes.[39] Yet legal subdivision of the blocks along conventional plot lines has made the issue of control over the central commons, intermediate pathways, and curbside plots an ongoing source of conflict between those residents who sanction communitarian ideals and those who prioritize individual property rights. Challenges to the restrictive covenants began almost immediately. The corporation established a board of trustees to settle disputes, and a lawsuit of 1932 ended in a court decision supporting the restrictions, which reinforced the board's authority.[40] These problems were exacerbated, however, when the original covenants ended, beginning in 1965. Young newcomers unsympathetic to Sunnyside's social goals began fencing off portions of the central commons that had reverted to private ownership to use as private play areas for their children; some paved over and fenced in front yards to create private parking areas, and others installed locked gates barring entry to pedestrian passages. These territorial changes led to conflicts between the newcomers and members of the older generation, who sought to maintain the communal character of the inner blocks. A series of preservation efforts instituted since the 1970s has been only partially successful, owing to a lack of means to enforce restrictions.[41] Furthermore, methods to fund maintenance of the remaining common areas no longer exist, and many trees and shrubs in the complex are in need of pruning or replacement. Only the single-family row houses grouped around U-shaped entry courts, constructed during the latter stages of Sunnyside's development to provide a transition to extant housing in the neighborhood, have retained their original form. Here permanent easements were established at the outset, since entry to the housing units via the central common space (with private gardens facing narrow alleys to the rear) made strict subdivision along property lines infeasible.

Stein ultimately rejected Sunnyside planning principles, citing a variety of issues: his propensity for urban dispersal; his aspiration to alter the urban grid system to isolate pedestrian from vehicular traffic while providing direct access between housing and communal open space; the need for regional planning powers, such as those espoused by landscape architect Frederick Law Olmsted.[42] Stein's antiurban stance biased his subsequent assessment of Sunnyside Gardens. Echoing Le Corbusier's mandate for "*soleil, espace, verdure*" (sunlight, space, greenery) in his utopian Radiant City proposal of 1933, Stein argued: "*Nature* will dominate, and all cities will be green cities, with parks in the heart of each block and encircling belts of agriculture, natural playgrounds and wilderness. Man's desire for a good life and his love of nature will determine the form of the town."[43] Despite his debt to the Swiss theoretician, Stein opposed the lack of human values in Le Corbusier's urban thinking. He viewed the existing city as an antiquated relic, in need of replacement with suburban models such as Radburn and Baldwin Hills Village (1941), in which pedestrian and vehicular movement are isolated from one another—an idea modeled on Olmsted's layout for New York's Central Park that Raymond Unwin had also advocated.[44] Although Stein's subsequent housing projects, also designed in collaboration with Wright and Cautley, came closer to his ambition to create a garden city in the United States, their lower density made them ineffective as models for addressing the need for affordable housing in an urban context.[45] Sunnyside Gardens reflects a more radical means to house the urban working classes.

In support of his garden city proclivities, Stein opposed "the rigid framework of New York's gridiron," which prevented him from removing streets at Sunnyside to create superblocks in the manner of Römerstadt.[46] He elaborated:

> The gridiron pattern of small blocks and narrow deep lots is a convenience for trade in land—not good living. The conventional city plan cuts neighborhoods into small islands separated by dangerous flows of traffic. It loses the identity of neighborhoods in the pattern without limits or end. It has no focal center or boundary.[47]

Although fears about the threats posed by automobile traffic were then somewhat commonplace, this logic ignores the positive role of the street in contributing to neighborhood identity. Just as May's typological approach allowed him to invest his housing projects with individual character, so the grid allowed Stein and Wright an opportunity to create a distinct neighborhood in conformity with the urban fabric. Landscape not only contributes to this difference but also provides a sense of place at multiple scales, ranging from the relatively idiosyncratic qualities of Sunnyside's private gardens and inner blocks to the broader sense of neighborhood that the tree-lined streetscape affords in weaving the blocks together. The universal quality of the grid is thus mitigated by its ability to absorb local adjustments of a more individual character.

Despite his aspiration for broader design authority, Stein did not aspire to the extensive regulatory powers that May assumed in Frankfurt; instead he proposed a new kind of planning: "to build a substantial setting for neighborhood and family life, rather than to control and regulate."[48] Acknowledging this quality of Stein's practice, the American Institute of Architects awarded Stein its Gold Medal in 1956, stating that his "vision embraced the wider aim of designing for mankind's environment rather than for mere shelter—for a way of life rather than for walls and a roof."[49] In his acceptance speech, Stein elaborated on the expanded role he envisioned for the architect in relation to that of the city planner:

> The architect must deal with the whole environment in which his building is set, of which it forms a part. In short he must become a *community architect*. . . . City planning deals with two-dimensional diagramming, with a city's framework for circulation, and its subdivision into blocks and lots. Its specifications are negative regulations and generalized limitations, such as zoning. They are not positive, specific, constructive requirements, as those for a particular building. Thus the detailed form and mass of a city is not designed, but is merely limited. . . . The architect's work is a dynamic activity that forms part of the realistic production of a structure or group of structures.

In this model, architects would have considerably broader powers than those with which Stein and his team were entrusted in Queens, yet the model also varies dramatically from the process May established in Frankfurt. Stein characterized such efforts, motivated by communal concerns, as "dynamic, not static."[50]

Stein's communal approach echoes that of Raymond Unwin, who saw architecture as "the outward expression of an orderly community of people." Addressing issues associated with designing for a democratic society in his *Town Planning in Practice* (1909), Unwin argued:

Hitherto the growth of democracy, which has destroyed the old feudal structure of society, has left the individual in the helpless isolation of his freedom. But there is a growing new sense of the rights and duties of the community as distinct from those of the individual. It is coming to be more and more widely realized that a new order and relationship in society are required to take the place of the old, that the mere setting free of the individual is only the commencement of the work of reconstruction, and not the end. The town planning movement and the powers conferred by legislation on municipalities are strong evidence of the growth of this spirit of association. To no one can this growth appeal more strongly than to the architect, who must realize that his efforts to improve the design of individual buildings will be of comparatively little value until opportunity is again afforded of bringing them into true relationship with the other, and of giving in each case proper weight and consideration to the total effect. In the planning of our towns in future there will be opportunity for the common life and welfare to be considered first.[51]

While the social ideology underlying Sunnyside Gardens has strong affinities with European reformist attitudes, the historic roots of American communitarian thought lie in the early towns of New England, organized around the town common, as Henry Wright noted in an essay of 1933: "The essential elements of modern community planning were already there: the 'common'—land held by the community around which the village was grouped; rational open spaces; exposure and protection for every house; an orderly arrangement with due regard for human amenities."[52] Landscape architect Fletcher Steele echoed this sentiment with regard to American society in general: "The American way of life has always been communal, since early days when neighbors got together for a barn-raising and to serve each other in a dozen homely ways."[53] Like its historic antecedents, Sunnyside Gardens is a locus of communitarian values that also provides a respite from the vicissitudes of contemporary urban life. Praising its ability to address the American propensity for individuality without sacrificing communal values or resorting to stylistic clichés, Lewis Mumford maintained:

> By eliminating false questions of "style," the architects of Sunnyside have built with genuine style; by achieving variety through the use of different units and in the relations of landscape and garden design to the simple plans of the houses themselves, they have given an individuality

to each block and court, far more positive than the extraneous individuality of style.[54]

Mumford was not the only critic to reject style as the basis for assigning value to such a housing project. Italian architect and Marxist theorist Manfredo Tafuri also singled out Stein and Wright, along with Ernst May, for their significant contributions to architectural practice. It was the social and economic implications of the work of these architects and planners that attracted Tafuri's attention, their attempt to redistribute the capitalist division of labor by rejecting speculative building practices in favor of providing low-cost housing conveniently located in proximity to both workplace and natural environs—a "current [that] interprets architecture as an altogether insignificant phenomenon."[55] In a related vein, Mumford also commended Römerstadt's "monumental treatment of the landscape and city" in his postwar assessment of the *Modern Architecture* exhibition, in which he derided the international style as "a new canon of modernity, . . . a new kind of academicism."[56] He elaborated: "[Römerstadt] remains one of the high points of architectural expression of our time, not by the excellence of its individual buildings, but by the ordered relationship of the whole."[57] In such practices, architecture and landscape are not antithetical phenomena, but mutually reinforcing enterprises.

The landscape of Sunnyside Gardens is an embodiment of cultural aspirations, not merely an aesthetic, an expression of meaningful relations among individuals that is adaptable to social change. While it reflects the social and political difficulties surrounding the use of open land in a contemporary urban setting, Sunnyside Gardens remains a prime example of communal space planning in American cities. It has increasing relevance for a society in which funding mechanisms are no longer averse to communal ownership, in which condominium and cooperative apartments, where the landscape is communally held and maintained, provide compelling and popular alternatives to the private ownership of land.

Like Hitchcock and Johnson, Henry Wright endorsed a minimal functional approach to the modern landscape: to "preserve, as far as possible, the natural landscape, except for providing sites for educational, recreational and community buildings."[58] Yet the landscape of Sunnyside Gardens is a more complex phenomenon. Engaging the repetitive urban grid as a site of potential variation, Cautley differentiated between the garden as an extension of the house and the commons as an extension of the street; she addressed issues of the individual versus the social, the private versus the public, not as distinct polarities, but as extremes to be mediated through landscape design. In its messy vitality, the extant Sunnyside Gardens landscape is neither an elitist enterprise nor a soothing backdrop; it is neither purely functional nor purely aesthetic. Instead, it is an active agent in facilitating the neighborhood's messy "democratic" qualities. If Sunnyside Gardens exemplifies the cultural prominence of landscape during the early twentieth century, then landscape architecture is no longer operating in competition with architecture, but complementary to it—as an essential component for addressing Modern Movement social aspirations.

TWO

THE BARCELONA PAVILION AS LANDSCAPE GARDEN
Modernity and the Picturesque

> A work of architecture must not stand as a finished and self-sufficient object. True and pure imagination, having once entered the stream of the idea that it expresses, has to expand forever beyond this work, and it must venture out, leading ultimately to the infinite. It must be regarded as the point at which one can make an orderly entry into the unbreakable chain of the universe.
>
> —Karl Friedrich Schinkel

To propose that Ludwig Mies van der Rohe conceived of his German Pavilion at the Barcelona International Exposition of 1929 as a landscape may challenge conventional interpretations of his architecture, although these have undergone considerable reevaluation since 1983–86, when the pavilion was being reconstructed on its original site.[1] To assert his debt to the picturesque in this work is a more subversive claim. After all, the picturesque is associated with emotive appeal, formal eclecticism, and artifice, whereas Mies identified his aims with reason, the rejection of formal issues and realism.[2] Mies's debt to the picturesque is not as precedent; rather, it provides a means to transcend the difficulty of his work. Positing the Barcelona Pavilion within the picturesque landscape tradition thus elicits speculation about both the building's significance and the repressed role of the picturesque in modernism.

There is only minor evidence in Mies's writings to support this claim, and it concerns a later project. Describing his Museum for a Small City (1943), he argued: "The barrier between the work of art and the living community is erased by a garden approach for the display."[3] Similarly, creators of eighteenth-century English landscape gardens sought to dissolve the visual distinction between garden and landscape. For Horace Walpole, the ha-ha was "the capital stroke, the leading stop to all that has followed." He credited William Kent with the genius to discern its significance: "He leaped the fence, and saw that all nature was a garden."[4] In the Barcelona Pavilion Mies elaborated upon that earlier leap. Yet his challenge lay not in the visual extension of space, as numerous interpretations of his pavilion have claimed, but rather in the conceptual boundaries of architecture.

Any interpretation of the Barcelona Pavilion as landscape must transcend Mies's tendency, like that of Karl Friedrich Schinkel (who inspired his early work), to challenge *formal* distinctions between architecture and landscape. As Mies argued, "Form is not the aim of our work, but only the result."[5] Indeed, the pavilion's tectonic means are unquestionably architectural. With no programmatic constraints other than to represent the democratic Weimar Republic, the commission to design the German Pavilion in Barcelona afforded Mies the freedom to pursue the expressive possibilities of the discipline. During the 1920s he had begun to abandon the formal logic of the classical idiom, with its mimesis of man and nature, in favor of specifically architectural means. Many of Mies's contemporaries resorted to imagery from other sources, such as engineering, an expedient that bases its claim to validity on that discipline's objective nature. For Mies, however, artistic objectivity derived from the assertion of differences rather than metaphorical similarities. The meaning of the Barcelona Pavilion is not conveyed through a priori formal logic or the representation of some external reality, but is given to sensual and temporal experience.[6] While immersed in the experience of Mies's pavilion, the spectator is simultaneously distanced from it. Such contradictions were nascent in the picturesque.

The picturesque is an elusive concept.[7] Certain discrepancies arise from the term's etymological origins in painting. Alexander Pope first used it, in annotations to his translations of Homer, to refer to a theme appropriate to a history painting—one that represents a significant human action based on verbal narrative, represented iconographically. Pope conceived of his garden at Twickenham in analogous terms; it was a locus of human action, its meaning conveyed to the knowledgeable viewer moving from object to object.[8] By the late eighteenth century, however, the term *picturesque,* as a result of its association with the genre of landscape painting, was more commonly used to refer to the aesthetic qualities of irregularity, roughness, and complexity—and thus to the type of English landscape garden devised to imitate nature. In its appeal to the visual faculty, the picturesque landscape garden depended for its meaning on the interpretive powers of the individual imagination as well as the iconography of its sculptural and architectural elements.

The assertion of aesthetic distance was a primary accomplishment of the picturesque—an effect simulated by the Claude glass, a darkened, concave mirror that could reduce a natural scene to fit into the palm of a hand. While it renders nature an object of manipulation, the picturesque garden is perceived not as a thing in itself but as a series of relationships that are gradually revealed to the moving spectator. For Mies, as for the picturesque landscape designer, the lack of resolution inherent in such contradictions was the starting point for the ongoing process of interpretation.

The term *pavilion* was first associated with garden structures for temporary shelter in the late seventeenth century; such buildings provided the architectural leitmotif of the English landscape garden, which emerged during the following century as a vehicle of the new sensibility. Likewise, the Barcelona Pavilion lacked a specific program; rather, it provided a momentary pause in an itinerary through the exposition's grounds. Rejecting overt historical references, however, Mies undermined the object status of his structure. The pavilion has no facades in the traditional sense. The need for boundaries between inside and outside, functionally necessary in most buildings, does not pertain. Thus the doors, positioned for security rather than to delimit threshold, were removed during the exposition's opening hours to enhance the spatial continuity. As a result, the Barcelona Pavilion is a labyrinth, a "montage of contradictory,

(left) Composite plan and perspective views of Chiswick House, London, and its garden pavilions, designed by Horace Walpole and William Kent and engraved by J. Rocque, c. 1736. J. Badeslade and J. Rocque, *Vitruvius Brittanicus or the British Architect,* volume IV, 1739.

(right) Mies van der Rohe's German Pavilion at the Barcelona International Exposition, 1929. *Cahiers d'Art* 4, nos. 8/9 (1929).

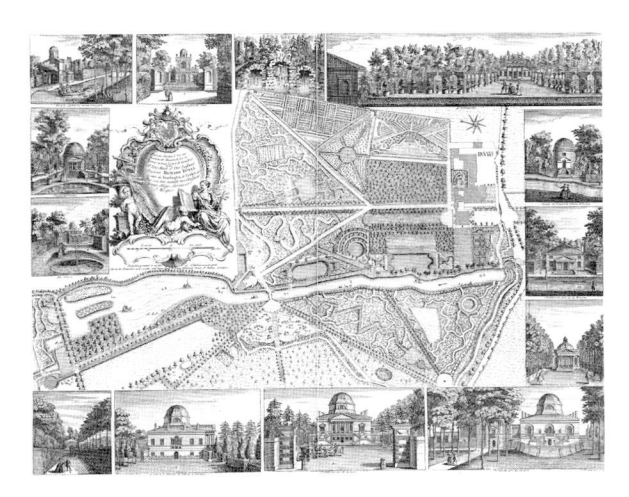

perceptual facts."⁹ Its meaning is generated through the experience of a circuit that suggests parallels with those of the English landscape garden.

Mies's early plan studies indicate his explicit use of picturesque devices. He initially distributed three pedestals for statues throughout the pavilion, each positioned to provide a focal point at the end of a major viewing axis. The sequence is analogous to the picturesque garden's pictorial circuit—a series of points at which views are contrived to arrest the progress of the observer. Moreover, these moments of stasis punctuate the experience of the pavilion and accentuate discontinuities between sculpture and architecture, reflecting those between architecture and landscape in the earliest English landscape gardens.

Ultimately Mies reduced the number of statues to one, that in the inner court, thereby augmenting the continuity of the sequence. There is only one relative point of stasis, and it focuses not on the statue but on a wall of onyx dorée, which Mies from the early conceptual stages of the project endowed with iconic value. By eliminating these sculptural focal points, he rejected pictorial means and overcame a tendency common to the early picturesque garden, that of focusing attention on architectural objects rather than on the intervening landscape. This momentary pause relies not on the contrast between architecture and sculpture but on more subtle distinctions between elements conceived of as part of an architectural system and an isolated architectural element, elevated, like the single column in the Temple of Apollo at Bassae, to the level of the sacred.[10]

Mies's rejection of pictorial means goes beyond that of perspective. Despite certain formal similarities between his plan for a Brick Country House (1924) and Theo van Doesburg's painting *Rhythms of a Russian Dance* (1919), Mies denied that there were any de Stijl influences in his work.[11] The differences are fundamental. In their efforts to avoid a static perspectival vantage point, de Stijl artists and architects sought a more

(left) Mies's early plan study for the Barcelona Pavilion, indicating bases for three sculptures. Collection of the Ludwig Mies van der Rohe Archive, Museum of Modern Art, New York.

(right) Plan of the Barcelona Pavilion as built, 1928. Wolf Tegethoff, *Mies van der Rohe: Die Villen und Landshausprojekte,* 1981.

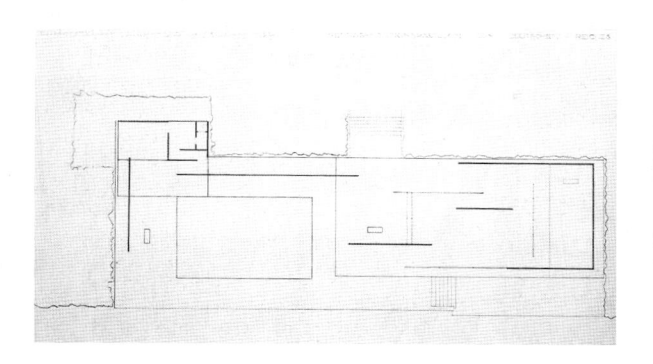

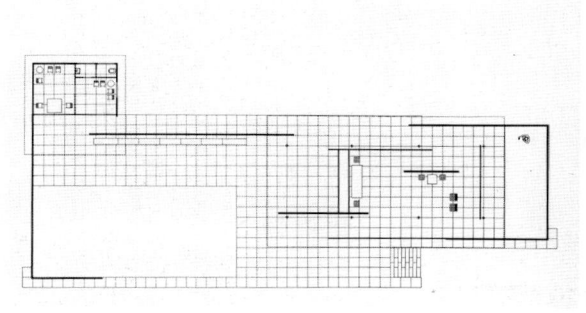

"objective" point of view, exemplified by the axonometric. Mies departed from any such objective working procedure by studying his pavilion not in plan, elevation, or axonometric view but in a physical model. This consisted of a plasticine base on which he manipulated planes of celluloid and cardboard covered with Japanese paper, simulating the pavilion's material qualities, to capture the perceptual character of the spatial sequence.[12] Mies accorded primacy to the temporal experience in three dimensions, rather than to any unified understanding of the building.

Mies's choice of site also reflects his interest in overcoming the static quality of a picturesque object terminating a vista. He rejected his original site, the indented corner of the Palace of Alfonso XIII to one side of the exposition's main axis, in favor of one that ends its major transverse axis and lies along the primary route to the Spanish Village, a popular exposition tourist attraction. Thus the pavilion acts as a threshold between the formal layout of the exposition grounds and a picturesque pastiche of Spanish vernacular house types. Accentuating this liminal role was a line of freestanding columns that originally framed the site, testimony to a prior historicist impulse. The Ionic colonnade was an essential element of the sequence, a portent of the discontinuities that lay within.

Mies's interest in manipulating the visual sequence, evident in his preliminary sketches, was to remain the pavilion's spatial leitmotif. The site offered the possibility of an extended view in only one direction, that of the approach, yet Mies thwarted any such extension by devising a series of nonaligned transverse walls in order to limit visual extension to the pavilion's longitudinal dimension, which he bracketed with end walls. For Mies, the walls were the primary agents in the spatial sequence, unlike Le Corbusier, whose concept of the free plan relied on the structural and

(left) Aerial view of the Barcelona International Exposition, 1929, with Mies's Barcelona Pavilion in lower right and the Spanish Village in center right. *Mies van der Rohe's German Pavilion in Barcelona, 1929–1986,* Mies van der Rohe Foundation, Barcelona, 1987.

(right) View of the Barcelona Pavilion from the Palace of Alfonso XIII. *Carrer de la Cuitat.*

THE BARCELONA PAVILION 49

conceptual primacy of the columns. Mies's columns, introduced at a later stage in the design, remained structurally ambiguous.[13] His later recollection of this project reflects this difference: "One evening as I was working late on the building I made a sketch of a free-standing wall and I got a shock. I knew it was a new principle."[14]

The distinction between "object" and "system" at the Barcelona Pavilion is relative, as there is no overriding geometric system. The cruciform columns delimit only approximate squares in plan. Furthermore, Mies used the paving grid to provide visual rather than mathematical order, adjusting the dimensions of the travertine blocks to align with the joints in the pavilion's vertical surfaces. The spatial continuity is perceptual; the result is not "universal space," but space as a palpable entity—a conceit that relies on separation rather than unity.[15] While classical space results from the unified, hierarchical treatment of architectural elements, Mies gave priority neither to space nor to the elements, calling to mind Sidney Robinson's distinction between (classical) system and picturesque "connection":

> System, of course, clearly sets the terms for the connection of constituent parts. Discovering the rule explains everything. Picturesque "connection" is always in the process of being discovered. Saying what it is, finally, is not quite possible without reference to a level of abstraction which strikes one as begging the issue.[16]

The podium and columnar grid are frequently cited as evidence of Mies's tendency to resort to classicism.[17] Yet neither is perceived as a whole; the end walls and reflecting pools interrupt the podium surface, while the spurious reading of the columns as a classical colonnade is possible only in plan. As José Quetlas notes, each column exists in a distinct spatial context.[18] Mies's shimmering cruciform columns support a similar contradiction; their formal precision dissolves under the visual distortion of their polished steel surfaces. Rather than refer to some external reality, these elements all serve, like the partitions or roof slab, as mute testimony to the symbolic essence of architecture.

In its silence Mies's architecture is cacophonous.[19] The pavilion is a montage of independent systems: travertine slab and plaster ceiling, chromium columns and marble partitions (of travertine, Tinian, verd antique, and onyx dorée), together with various tints of glass (brown, green, milk, light blue, and black), all colliding visually in its polished reflective surfaces. The precision of the materials contrasts their perceptual instability.

Unlike the type of optical device popular in the eighteenth century, which provided an illusion of control over nature, the reflective surfaces of Mies's pavilion simulate the temporal flux of nature.

Mies subjected all natural elements in the pavilion to architectural control. Vines are captured in a continuous planter atop the travertine wall terminating the entry court, while the lustrous green Tinian marble in the inner court echoes the cluster of trees beyond, affirming the distance between architecture and elements of nature. The rear garden, a semicircular plane of grass level with the podium, was conceived of as an extension of the pavilion; its origin is in architecture rather than in nature. "Nature" exists by virtue of architecture, a human construction, inverting Schinkel's famous dictum: "Architecture is the continuation of nature in her constructive activity."[20]

Water was for Mies a material comparable to marble or steel. The pavilion's inner pool, originally lined with black glass tiles, created the paradoxical illusion of limitless depth in the solid earth, in contrast to the outer pool, tiled in light-blue glass, which appeared shallow and reflected the infinite sky. Glass was a material of similar paradoxes. Not simply a transparent medium, it was a means to condition perception and shape space, as Mies demonstrated with his Project for a Glass Skyscraper of 1922 and his Glass Room for the Stuttgart Werkbund Exhibition of 1927. In a propagandist statement written for the Union of Plate Glass Manufacturers, he extolled its material properties: "Only now can we give shape to space, open it, and link it to the landscape, thereby satisfying man's spatial needs."[21] Recent interpretations of Mies's use of glass vary from that of

Interior views of the Barcelona Pavilion. Collection of the Ludwig Mies van der Rohe Archive, Museum of Modern Art, New York.

THE BARCELONA PAVILION 51

(left) Outer court of the Barcelona Pavilion with reflecting pool lined in light-blue mirrored tile. Collection of the Ludwig Mies van der Rohe Archive, Museum of Modern Art, New York.

(right) Inner court of the pavilion as reconstructed in 1986, with pool painted faux marble rather than lined in the black mirrored tile of the original.

Tegethoff, who considers it "the single, absolute prerequisite for a new conception of space . . . by means of which space-defining walls may be reduced to a mere transparent membrane," to that of Manfredo Tafuri and Francesco Dal Co, who see it as "an insuperable boundary."[22] Although glass could be regarded as the modern equivalent of the ha-ha, Mies was concerned primarily with its phenomenal qualities. Describing his Friedrichstrasse Skyscraper of 1921, he explained, "I discovered by working with actual glass models that the important thing is the play of reflections and not the effect of light and shadow as in ordinary buildings."[23] His use of tinted glass in the Barcelona Pavilion—particularly the distinction between the green tinted glass facing the inner court and the brown tint to that facing the front and back—is a reminder that knowledge is contingent on perception. Such "insoluble dichotomies" ground the pavilion in reality and open it to creative interpretation.[24]

Mies's realism derives from his concept of order, which distances him from the utopian aspirations of the Modern Movement. In his inaugural address at the Armour Institute of Technology (1938), he argued: "The idealistic principle of order . . . with its overemphasis on the ideal and the formal, satisfies neither our interest in simple reality nor our practical sense. So we shall emphasize the organic principle of order as a means of achieving the successful relationship of the parts to each other and to the whole."[25] This celebrates difference rather than imposing similarity, as he later elaborated: "The real order is what St. Augustine said about the disposition of equal and unequal things according to their nature."[26]

Three elements fall outside this limited systemic treatment: the onyx wall, the luminous wall, and Georg Kolbe's statue *Morning*. The onyx wall is the pavilion's only interior partition and the only one of this material, one of the world's rarest and costliest marbles. Its numinous quality derives from its distinctive color rather than from its material treatment, which links it with other elements of the pavilion's "inner sanctum." Contrary to the claim, put forward by some critics, that the size of the onyx block determined the planning module for the structure, it merely determined the pavilion's height and the length of the wall itself, which varies somewhat in Mies's early plan studies. Indeed, he was careful to avoid precise mathematical correspondences among the pavilion's components.[27]

In a deliberate departure from conventional ideas of shelter, the onyx wall marks the only relative point of repose in the composition. The wall clings to the jet-black carpet at its base, as if by magnetic force. This is an attraction of opposites, for the carpet is a visual abyss, denying the possibility of inhabitation. This double paradox is underscored by its function as a dais for the white leather "thrones" that Mies designed for the king and queen of Spain, who were to participate in the pavilion's opening ceremonies. The implied stasis of the onyx wall is further disrupted by its horizontal seam at eye level, which splits the partition in half. It recalls the horizon, reinforcing the reading of the pavilion interior as a landscape, and evokes a passage that Mies underlined in his copy of Oswald Spengler's *Decline of the West*: "In analogizing the horizon with the future, our age identifies itself with the third dimension of experienced space."[28]

Critics have long interpreted the onyx wall as the heart of the composition. Curiously, however, there has been little mention of an equally significant phenomenon: the luminous volume that lies closer to the pavilion's geometric center. It appears only peripherally in original published

(left) Reception space of the Barcelona Pavilion with onyx wall. *Cahiers d'Art* 4, nos. 8/9 (1929).

(right) Rear of the Barcelona Pavilion showing glass court lit at night. Wolf Tegethoff, *Mies van der Rohe: Die Villen und Landshausprojekte*, 1981.

photographs; moreover, its sensual qualities seem to elude photographic representation. This inaccessible void bounded by translucent glass was the only element in the pavilion that Mies adjusted to conform to the paving grid. He originally conceived of it as a thin, wall-like element, but ultimately realized it as a volume of light, artificially lit from within.[29] It has attributes of a courtyard but, like the entry court and the inner sculpture court, can be occupied only in the imagination. A comparable luminosity emanating from the inner court (continually bathed in sunlight during daylight hours) is visible on mounting the podium, serving to draw the spectator into the inner sanctum. In contrast, the ineffable qualities of the luminous wall are perceived only from within. Its end walls, of verd antique marble and black glass, respectively, render it invisible from the pavilion's entry or rear garden, while sunlight in the outer court counteracts its visual presence from that direction.

There is a precedent in Mies's work for this "garden of light." In his Glass Room for the Werkbund Exhibition, he included two inaccessible spaces: a sculpture court and a garden court. The first of these, bounded by glass walls and housing a female torso by the sculptor Wilhelm Lehmbruck, accentuated the simultaneous reflective and transparent properties of plate glass. The statue is entombed in a world removed from human occupation. The second court, containing three ungainly potted plants, was the only space in Mies's exhibition not bounded by glass or capped by stretched muslin. While it provided a suggestion of open air within the enclosed volume of the exposition hall, it was remote from any natural source of light or air, rendering this "garden court" a lifeless relic, its natural elements framed and isolated for the purpose of contemplation.

In contrast, the luminous court of the Barcelona Pavilion has an ineffable quality. Its light seems to emanate magically from within, like the autonomous light source of a cubist painting. "Nature" is rendered as light within an architectural frame of steel and glass, a garden in the machine. The luminous court alludes to the spiritual otherness of nature, its objectification, in contrast to the naive aspiration for communion with nature associated with Modern Movement ideals. For Mies architecture was a vehicle for nature to reveal itself to humankind.

Kolbe's statue is the pavilion's only anthropomorphic element. Axially aligned within the innermost court, it dominates a space denied to human occupation. Rather than providing a goal in the sequence, it stands for the absent spectator. Like the contrived, scenographic effects of the picturesque landscape garden, Mies's architecture renders the spectator an active participant in the scene; yet here the stage remains empty, the actor/spectator distanced. Mies's client Grete Tugendhat used related terms to describe the effects of his architecture: "For just as one sees each flower in this room in quite an uncommon way, and every piece of art seems more expressive (for example, a piece of sculpture standing in front of the onyx wall), so too a person appears, both to himself and to others, to be more clearly set off from his surroundings."[30] Despite its overwhelming interiority, the Barcelona Pavilion resists inhabitation. The role of the spectator is fleeting, transitory. The reflective surfaces of glass, polished marble, and chromium-plated steel absorb any human presence, casting doubt even on the body's own substance, just as the pavilion's architectural language denies its metaphoric presence. The self merges with the other as fleeting ephemera in the cumulative layers of reflection.

Unlike the tendency of the picturesque landscape to miniaturize its architectural elements, Kolbe's statue expands the pavilion's apparent scale. A visitor, measuring him- or herself against the oversized figure, is humbled. This experience of the statue within the labyrinthine configuration augments the pavilion's material presence to overcome its seeming limitation of size. Mies's structure rivals the massive Palace of Alfonso XIII on the hill directly above, yet it does so through anticlassical means—denial of its object status and of symbolic references to man or nature.

The luminous court, the wall of onyx dorée, and Kolbe's statue are unique elements in the pavilion; all participate in its hierarchical "center."

Mies van der Rohe and King Alfonso XIII at the opening ceremony of the Barcelona Pavilion, 1929, with Georg Kolbe's statue *Morning. Carrer de la Cuitat.*

They refer, respectively, to the metaphysical realm, the material realm, and the realm of human inhabitation, reflecting the paradoxical means by which Mies strove "to bring Nature, man and architecture together in a higher unity"—by asserting their mutual distance.[31]

Just as each element asserts its independent status, so the pavilion asserts its independence from the context to which it is inextricably bound. Approached from the exposition's symmetrical transverse axis, the podium establishes a caesura with the classical space of the exposition grounds, creating the world anew and celebrating architecture as a human construct. The podium is a boundary, a *templum* of space hewn out of the surrounding landscape, replacing the garden wall. Mies denied it any classical reference to the earth or to its axial approach; instead, the end walls ground the pavilion in the earth, and its entrance is displaced to one side. To the rear of the pavilion, Mies reversed this arrangement by raising the ground to the level of the podium and reestablishing the symmetry of the approach. In the transverse direction, travertine walls in the outer court echo the base of the adjoining palace, while walls of green Tinian marble in the inner court reflect the canopy of surrounding trees. The pavilion arises from the particular circumstances of its site yet remains distanced from the neoclassical conditions of its context. It is both a critical reinterpretation of its worldly situation and an affirmation of reality. Irreducibly architectural, the pavilion was a means for Mies to dismantle the dialectic opposition of city and country and recompose a continuum conceived in terms of landscape.

Mies's experience as a youth of assisting in the family marble atelier in Aachen, as well as his early admiration for the work of Schinkel and Hendrik Petrus Berlage, undoubtedly contributed to his obsession with the visual properties of materials. A more direct influence, however, was his period of collaboration during the 1920s and 1930s with Lilly Reich, a textile and fashion designer and a fellow member of the Deutscher Werkbund, with whom he designed a number of exhibition installations, including that in Barcelona. Their Velvet and Silk Café at the 1927 Berlin Mode der Dame exhibition, which celebrated the fluid, diaphanous, and reflective properties of these fabrics, was a significant precursor to the Barcelona Pavilion, where Mies achieved similar effects with the solidity of marble, steel, and glass. Yet this concern with materials also had a deeper philosophical basis, for Spengler's *Decline of the West* had inspired Mies to attempt to transcend the "material" implications of post-Enlightenment "civilization" by reinstating the "spiritual" dimension of "culture."

The material qualities of the Barcelona Pavilion also parallel those of an element of the early picturesque garden—the grotto, such as that of circa 1724 in the base of Alexander Pope's house in Twickenham.[32] Pope's grotto, incorporating an elaborate display of the poet's extensive collection of mineral specimens, was modeled on the type of Italian grotto that eighteenth-century British visitors described as a cabinet of curiosities, an antecedent of the modern museum. Indeed, Pope proclaimed his grotto a "Musaeum," or home of the muses.[33] Moreover, his concern with visual effects is reflected in the optical devices incorporated in his grotto, which enabled it to operate both as a "perspective glass" through which to view the river from the Shell Temple that stood in the garden opposite and as a sort of camera obscura, projecting images of the outside world upon its reflective interior surfaces.[34] These devices contributed to the grotto's power, like the garden itself, to both signify a world apart and act as a mirror of the larger world. A visitor of 1747 described its effects in terms that are startlingly evocative of the Barcelona Pavilion:

> To multiply this Diversity, and still more increase the Delight, Mr. *Pope's* poetic Genius has introduced a kind of Machinery, which performs the same part in the Grotto that supernal Powers and incorporeal Beings act in the heroick Species of Poetry: This is effected by disposing Plates of Looking glass in the obscure parts of the Roof and Sides of the Cave, where sufficient Force of Light is wanting to discover the Deception, while the other parts, the Rills, Fountains, Flints, Pebbles, etc., being

(left) Velvet and Silk Café at the Mode der Dame exhibition, Berlin, by Lilly Reich and Mies van der Rohe, 1927. Collection of the Ludwig Mies van der Rohe Archive, Museum of Modern Art, New York.

(right) Watercolor study of Alexander Pope in his grotto, attributed to Lady Burlington, c. 1730s. Copyright Devonshire Collection, Chatsworth. Reproduced by permission of Chatsworth Settlement Trustees.

duly illuminated, are so reflected by the various posited Mirrors, as without exposing the Cause, every object is multiplied, and its position represented by a surprising Diversity. . . . Thus, by a fine taste and happy management of Nature, you are presented with an undistinguishable Mixture of Realities and Imagery.[35]

It is well known that Pope and his circle, which included Lord Burlington and William Kent, intended that their gardens should serve a larger aim, that of embodying on English soil a classical civilization emulating that of the ancients. Unlike its antique counterparts, however, Pope's grotto—like the Barcelona Pavilion—incorporated no allusions to literature or mythology. Its effects were conveyed primarily through an appeal to the individual imagination. As John Dixon Hunt has argued, Pope's vision was distinguished by "this very awareness of what could not be achieved, except in the mind's eye."[36]

In the Barcelona Pavilion Mies deployed a similar tactic. Charged with designing a German *Repräsentationsraum,* with implications for serving formal or ceremonial rather than utilitarian purposes, he rejected emblematic motifs or signs. The architecture alone reflects the pavilion's role as a symbol of the modern, progressive state of Germany, represented internationally for the first time in Barcelona. Two flags flanking its entry facade were its sole representational devices.

There is a further, more immediate parallel to Mies's use of materials: the Italian grotto as a conspectus of natural and artificial wonders had a counterpart in the *Wunderkammer,* or cabinet of curiosities.[37] The collection it housed was understood as a metaphor of the world. Its underlying order, like that for the Barcelona Pavilion, was based on aesthetic rather than scientific criteria, with objects grouped according to material, for example. The Barcelona Pavilion shares with the *Wunderkammer* the aim of epitomizing a sense of mystery and wonder, rather than offering rational explication. Just as the cabinet of curiosities originated in response to the crisis of values following the breakdown of Renaissance certainty, so Mies's pavilion reflects a comparable phenomenon during the post-Enlightenment era.

Historically, the garden has been an essential form of expression—a reflection of humankind's relationship to nature and a reconstitution of the world in microcosm. That role was largely abrogated in the twentieth century. As Paul Kristeller has argued, once the art of gardening began to dissociate itself from architecture and ally itself with landscape, it attained its greatest cultural significance, yet simultaneously initiated its decline as a fine art.[38] Like the historic garden, the Barcelona Pavilion is a pure instrument of meaning; it represents a break with reality, constituted historically, yet posits itself as an alternate reality. Mies revealed the possibility of transcending the decorative and sentimental limits of the modern garden and recovering its intrinsic value, without resorting to mimesis, by reinstating its architectural essence. He created an architecture analogous to the fleeting understanding of a world where absolutes are no longer possible. His affirmation of the power of architecture to embody a fragmented, fractured worldview is indebted to the reversal of the traditional hierarchy of architecture and landscape that took place in the eighteenth century. As David Watkin has argued, rather than conceive of landscape as an extension of architecture, the picturesque provided the inspiration to conceive of architecture as landscape.[39] Mies's work transcends the eighteenth-century distinction between a rationalized and a representational view of nature, a formal debate that has only recently subsided. The distinction between the geometric garden and the "natural" garden was itself a product of the picturesque emphasis on formal values. Each is contrived, the product of human action; each was inspired by the dialectic between formal and informal that existed in the gardens of antiquity and Renaissance Italy. The differences lie primarily in diverging attitudes toward nature and toward humankind's role in the natural world. Mies rejected the myth of raw nature as pure datum, independent of human action, promoted by certain advocates of the Modern Movement. In his Barcelona Pavilion "nature" is a cultural phenomenon that exists only by virtue of being interpreted. By conceiving of his pavilion in terms of landscape, Mies overcame the pictorial limitations of the picturesque. Transcending the appearance of nature, he affirmed the power of architecture to achieve the status of nature.

Mies's fleeting accomplishment depended on the idea of nature as something that is physically remote. With the conservatories of the Tugendhat House and the Nolde House, the gardens of the court houses, and the scenic views from the Resor House and the Farnsworth House, he reverted to a pictorial treatment of nature. Nature was again enframed, its eighteenth-century status restored. For Mies the contemplation of nature from afar was superior to experiencing it directly: "When you see nature through the glass walls of the Farnsworth House, it gets a deeper meaning than [from the] outside. More is asked for from nature, because it becomes part of a larger whole."[40]

In Barcelona Mies transformed the picturesque dichotomy between stasis and motion into a dichotomy of form and perception, thereby disallowing any stable interpretation. Meaning is initiated rather than imposed, recalling the idea of the picturesque circuit as a route to knowledge. If the picturesque introduced the element of doubt, Mies recognized the potential for creative interpretation that accompanies a modern perception of the limitations of knowledge. With the Barcelona Pavilion he modified our understanding of the picturesque to invest it with a generative importance it previously lacked, exemplifying the aim of modernism not simply to break with the historical past but "to attempt to equal its highest achievements under new and difficult conditions."[41] The Barcelona Pavilion fulfills Mies's dictum that "architecture is the will of an epoch, translated into space: living, changing, new."[42] Its shifting nuances of meaning reflect "the central problem of our time—the intensification of life."[43] Schinkel put it less succinctly: "Striving, budding, crystallizing, unfolding, driving, splitting, fitting, drifting, floating, pulling, pressing, bending, bearing, placing, vibrating, connecting, holding, lying and resting . . . these are the ways in which architecture must manifest life."[44]

THREE

THE URBAN LANDSCAPES OF ERIK GUNNAR ASPLUND
Architecture between "Nature" and the City

Little critical attention has been devoted to Erik Gunnar Asplund's contributions to the modern landscape, apart from the Woodland Cemetery (1915–40), on which he collaborated with Sigurd Lewerentz between 1915 and 1935. Of the two architects, Lewerentz was more renowned for his expertise in cemetery design, while Asplund's efforts were directed to broader issues of landscape design in the public realm. Despite pronounced stylistic shifts in his architecture—from his early enthusiasm for Nordic classicism, exemplified by his Stockholm Public Library (1926–31), to his espousal of "functionalism," manifested in his designs for the Stockholm Exhibition (1930)—Asplund maintained a consistent attitude toward landscape. It derived equally from Social Democratic political ideology and the avant-garde ambition to reintegrate art and life. Under the Social Democrats, who enjoyed a majority in the Swedish parliament beginning in 1917, the functionalist ambition of improving the quality of daily life through architecture became a reality that extended equally to landscape design.[1]

For his first public building commission, the European Secondary School in Karlshamn (1912–18), sited on a steep promontory that overlooks the sea at the edge of a small town in southeastern Sweden, Asplund devised an irregular distribution of volumes to mediate between the building's internal spatial logic and the conditions of the broader context. A sequence of semienclosed courts accommodates entry, a play area, and a botanical garden, while a loggia at the highest point provides an outlook to the sea. This volumetric fragmentation serves larger ends: the architecture is a vehicle for passage from city to landscape. The complex gestures beyond itself in every direction. This apparent primacy of landscape over building volume was to surface again and again in Asplund's work as he probed physiological and psychological thresholds of inhabitation and use.

Asplund's concept of establishing psychological connections to the urban landscape through fragmentation of the architectural sequence received perhaps its most eloquent elaboration in an unrealized proposal for the Stockholm Royal Chancellery competition that he submitted with Ture Ryberg in 1922. The irregular site in Stockholm's Old Town lies between two baroque palaces, the Royal Palace and the Bonde Palace, and is divided by a street that links these buildings with certain vestiges of medieval Stockholm.[2] Rather than emulate the monumental scale of these neighboring buildings, as did the winning competition entrants, Asplund

Site plan/ground floor plan of the European Secondary School at Karlshamn by Erik Gunnar Asplund, 1912. From the collections at the Swedish Museum of Architecture; photographer Thomas Hjertén.

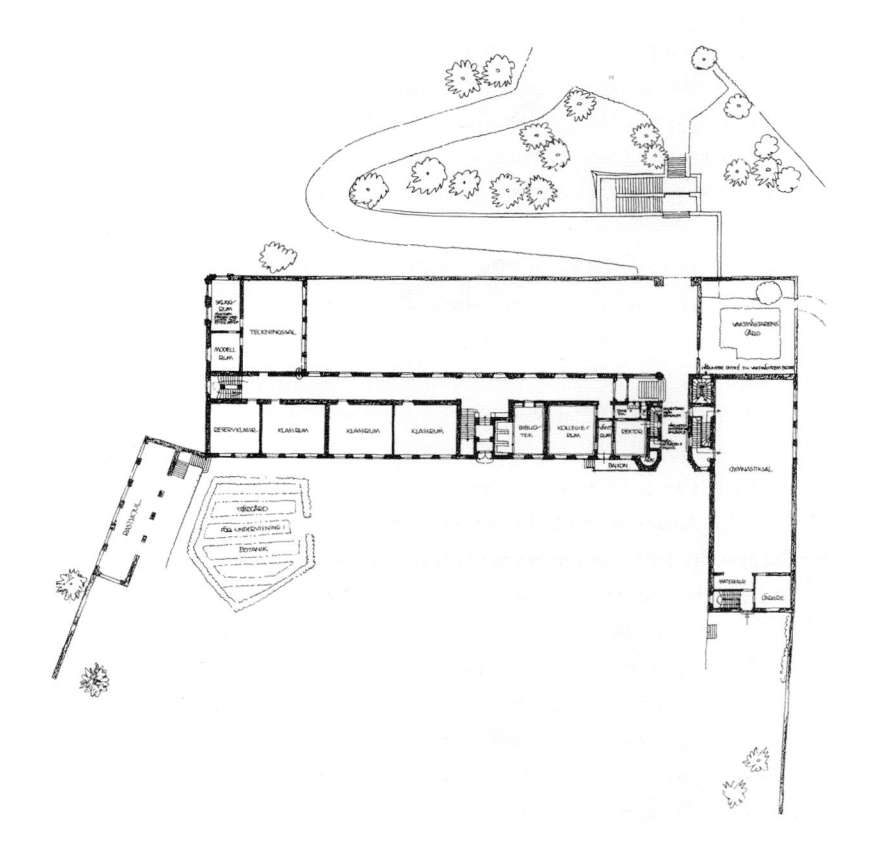

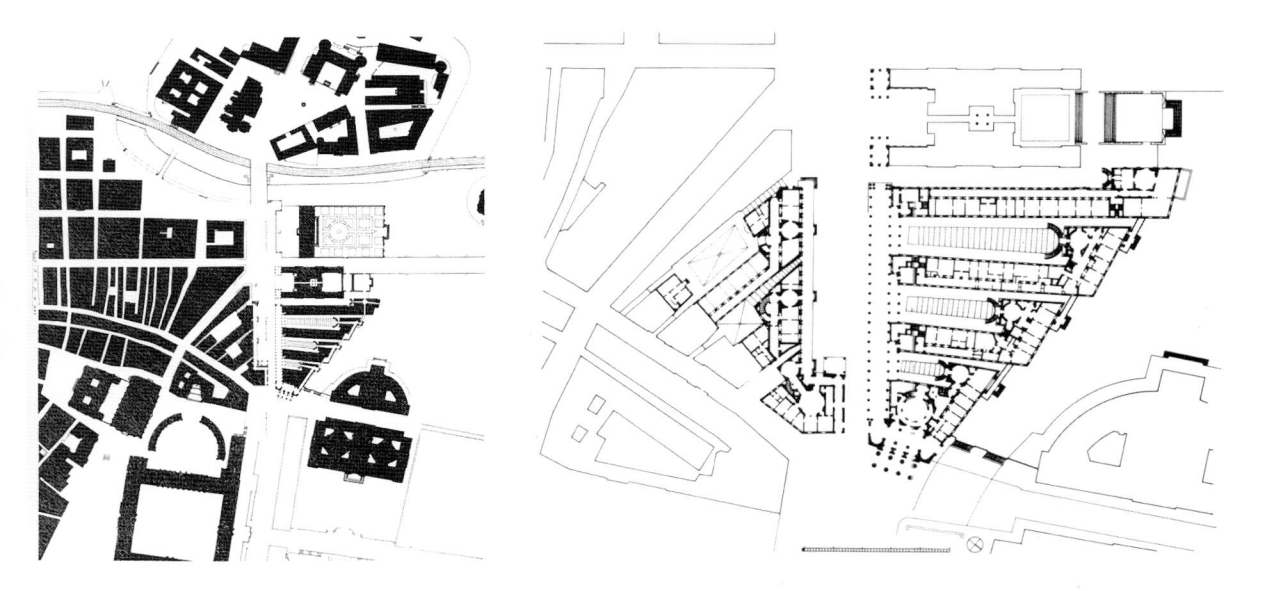

and Ryberg were inspired by the narrow passages and modest courtyards of the vicinity's more anonymous structures to distribute the chancellery offices among five narrow, L-shaped wings. The complex establishes a series of entrances to the city. Dominating the series of narrow courts are broad ramps that lead from Lake Malaren up to Myntgatan, the street that divides the complex and, in turn, connects the Royal Palace with the thirteenth-century Ruddarholm Church. By interweaving the building program with a hierarchical network of waterways, roads, and pedestrian passages that emulate the adjoining medieval street network, Asplund and Ryberg subjected the disparate site conditions to a systematic internal order while simultaneously celebrating linkages between the city's system of public spaces and its natural setting.[3]

With the park that he designed for the Stockholm Public Library (1918–30), Asplund made his most significant contribution to the urban landscape. In 1920, when he was awarded the commission for the library building, Asplund was already involved in formulating a master plan for the area of Observatory Hill, which the city had designated as the site for its first public library. Critical evaluation of Asplund's library has focused primarily on its stylistic qualities rather than on its role in the cultural life of the city, and thus its civic implications. Yet from 1918, when he was appointed to the Library Committee, until after the building opened to the public in 1928, Asplund studied a series of strategies for the prominent

(left) Site plan of the Stockholm Royal Chancellery competition entry by Erik Gunnar Asplund and Ture Ryberg, 1922. From the collections at the Swedish Museum of Architecture; photographer Thomas Hjertén.

(right) Corresponding ground floor plan. Stuart Wrede, *The Architecture of Erik Gunnar Asplund*, figure 68; copyright 1980 Massachusetts Institute of Technology; reprinted by permission of The MIT Press.

site that manifest his broader cultural aims.[4] The structure lies at the intersection of two main streets at the base of Observatory Hill, a steep natural promontory that is a remnant of deposits left by retreating ice floes—a vivid reminder of the city's archaic past. Asplund's numerous site studies, including his proposals for the adjoining public park, situate the library design in a broader discussion of issues central to his architecture—"the relationship between space and man, between object and man, between nature and man"—issues made more poignant by the site's dramatic juxtaposition of urban and natural conditions.[5]

The idea of creating a public library for Stockholm was an outgrowth of the Enlightenment project of social and urban reform that led European nations to create public institutions—including museums and educational facilities as well as libraries and parks—out of resources that were once the exclusive domain of the aristocracy. Yet by limiting analysis of the relationship between Asplund's library and its park to a reliance on formal distinctions between "natural" and "geometric" forms, scholars have overlooked the internal consistencies in his design approach as well as the ideological impulses underlying both his architecture and his landscape designs.

The building campaign had a protracted history. The Stockholm City Council formed a Public Library Committee in 1910 to implement an idea that had been under discussion for some time. The committee's initial proposal of 1912 was modest, reflecting the limited funding then available.[6] In 1918 the project was revitalized by a generous grant from the Wallenberg banking family, supplemented by Forsgren Foundation funds. That same year city officials donated the site at the foot of Observatory Hill for the building and invited Asplund to join the Library Committee to help determine programmatic requirements and prepare a competition brief. His initial planning proposal for the area was unveiled to a great deal of publicity in February 1920, stimulating public discussion about the project. The following August, Asplund and head librarian Fredrik Hjelmqvist embarked on a fact-finding tour of library facilities in the United States, where the broadest public library systems proliferated. Asplund's notes for this trip indicate his interest in every aspect of contemporary library design, ranging from furniture and equipment to planning strategies. Upon his return, rather than proceed with the competition (the usual practice for developing public buildings in Sweden), the Library Committee awarded Asplund the commission to take advantage of his intimate familiarity with the nuances of the site and program.

The library was to serve a dual purpose in the civic life of Stockholm. As a monumental testament to the acquisition of knowledge it should have a vital symbolic presence, while as a sanctuary for learning it should be functionally isolated from the daily life of the city. Compounding these conflicting requirements was the challenge posed by its dramatic setting: to relate the building to the natural conditions of Observatory Hill while satisfying the programmatic requirements for a controlled internalized volume. Throughout his site studies, Asplund addressed these issues by conceiving of the building as a compact volume, thereby asserting its presence against the imposing mass of the hill, while also distinguishing its massing from the relative continuity of the adjoining urban fabric.

Asplund's earliest sketches demonstrate his concern with imparting a monumentality, befitting its civic role, to the library's relatively modest volume, which he included amid a sequence of buildings lining the streets and surmounting the hill. In several studies made early in 1919 he sited the lending hall, a cylindrical volume with tall, narrow windows and surmounted by a lantern, at the street intersection, attached to the closed end of a U-shaped block. The distinctive volume of the lending hall terminates a series of apartment slabs that step up the hill along Odengatan, oriented perpendicular to the street. In these early studies, Asplund left the street corner relatively open, providing a view to the summit from the intersection while adhering strictly to the city planning guidelines of

(left) Asplund's sketch study for the Stockholm Public Library, 1918, including site plans (at different scales and orientations) and perspective study of library from street corner. From the collections at the Swedish Museum of Architecture; photographer Thomas Hjertén.

(right) Asplund's plan proposal of 1919 for Observatory Hill, including the Stockholm Public Library at the street corner *(lower right)*. From the collections at the Swedish Museum of Architecture; photographer Thomas Hjertén.

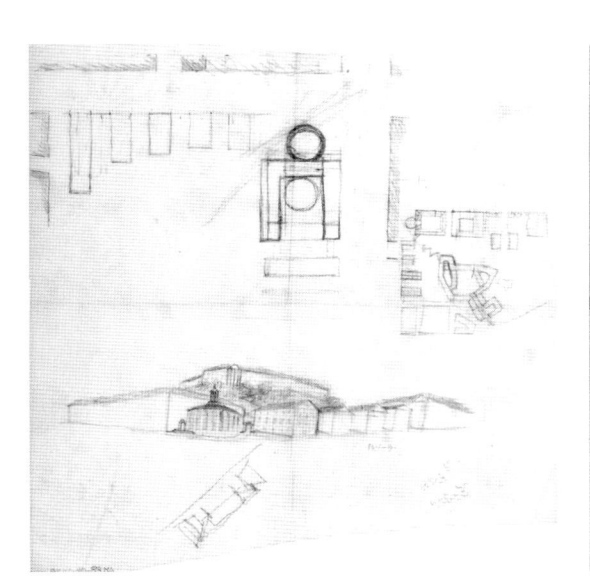

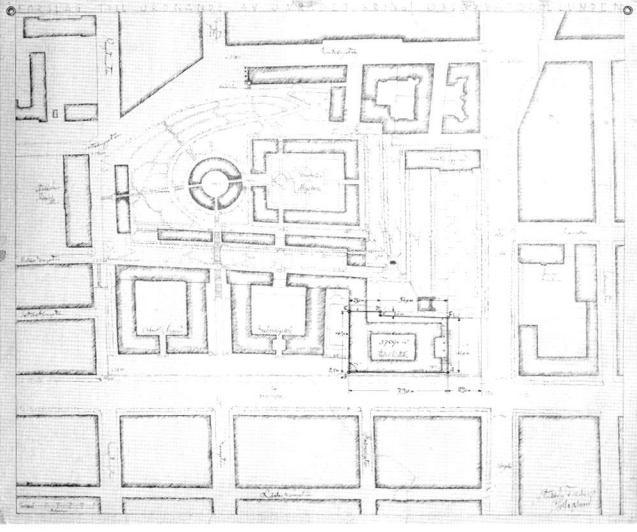

1915, which called for public buildings along Sveavägen and apartment blocks along Odengatan.

In his planning proposal for the area, made public in February 1920 and represented in a site plan and model, Asplund conceived of the locale as an acropolis for scholarship. Using geometric means to control the entire block, he transformed the hill into a series of rectilinear terraces, densely built up with university facilities along Sveavägen, a formal garden that steps up the hill along Odengatan, and an imposing complex of university buildings dominating the crest.[7] He imparted monumental expression to the university buildings along Sveavägen, befitting the avenue's eighteenth-century origins, when King Gustav II had it created to link the Royal Palace in the Old City directly with Haga, the royal estate to the north that he intended to rival Versailles. Asplund reinforced the overriding geometry of his proposal by establishing a pair of pedestrian cross axes that link the university buildings on the avenue with those on the summit, where he positioned a round courtyard building to culminate the sequence; the latter structure would have replaced the historic observatory, designed by Carl Hårleman in 1748–53, as its oblique orientation was incompatible with the overriding geometry of Asplund's solution. This was the most extreme of his site proposals, subordinating any natural expression to architectural control.

Although the scheme was to undergo radical changes, this early study contains the kernel of Asplund's design strategy, in which he conceived of the library as a compact, rectilinear structure with a protruding lending hall, set within a public landscape. The library faces Odengatan across a small plaza and adjoins sculptor Carl Milles's massive monument to Swedish regent Sten Sture.[8] Asplund's concern with the vista from the street corner, manifested in these early site studies, is evident in a striking model photograph in which Milles's monument and the university buildings crowning the summit overshadow the library volume. Despite the liberties Asplund took with the city's planning guidelines—substituting a formal park for the requisite residential buildings along Odengatan—criticism of the scheme's overwhelming urban character led planning officials to revise their intentions for the area, affording him greater freedom to exploit the site's natural amenities. Subsequently he explored various means to develop the interrelationship of architecture and landscape.

Asplund's voyage to America later that year gave him an opportunity to investigate the pragmatics of library accommodations. When he was awarded the commission upon his return, Asplund was able to approach the design from a fresh point of view. In his first official proposal as architect of the building, submitted in 1921, the library is a taut, cubic volume with a central hemispherical lending room, surrounded on four sides by reading rooms and stacks. Asplund now positioned his lending hall on an upper level, culminating a dramatic approach sequence, an idea inspired by the public libraries of Boston (McKim, Mead and White, 1887–95) and New York City (Carrère and Hastings, 1897–1911), as well as Harvard University's Widener Memorial Library (Horace Trumbauer, 1915), all of which he had visited during his American travels. The central position of the lending hall and the dramatic use of light, ideas nascent in Asplund's early sketches, are also indebted to Albert Kahn's library for the University of Michigan, which was completed in the year before Asplund's visit to the United States.

With this iteration, Asplund began to envision the library as a focal element in a more extensive public landscape. Articulating Observatory Hill as a series of garden terraces that provide a backdrop for the architectural ensemble, he lined the streets with a formal sequence of buildings and gardens. This site strategy—a simplified version of his proposal of 1920—gives the library greater prominence. Asplund set it off from the street corner by a public square from which formal terraced gardens step up the hill along Odengatan; the structure terminates a pair of university buildings along Sveavägen, including the proposed Faculty of Economics and Business Administration.[9] As with his site plan of 1920, Asplund drew attention to the library's civic presence by giving it a distinctive form and projecting it forward of the university buildings, while simultaneously

Asplund's proposal of 1921 for the Stockholm Public Library: site plan *(left)* and entry facade and section through lending hall. From the collections at the Swedish Museum of Architecture; photographer Thomas Hjertén.

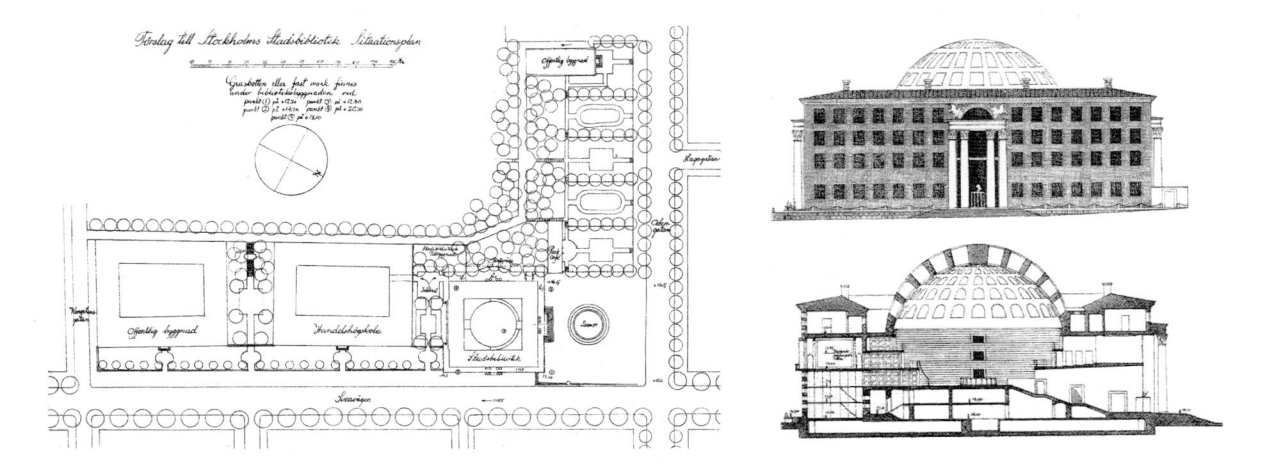

asserting its independence by orienting it away from them and toward the plaza at the urban intersection. In subsequent proposals, he struggled to reintegrate the dichotomous realms of "nature" and the city.

By 1923 Asplund had shifted the library to face Sveavägen, again oriented toward a plaza at the intersection. This reorientation was critical, establishing the library as an element in a sequence of monumental civic buildings that line the primary avenue, thereby transforming this segment of the royal processional route into an urban locale serving the broader citizenry. To reinforce the significance of this gesture, Asplund sited the Economics Faculty at the opposite end of the block, where it was soon realized to the design of Ivar Tengbom (1925–26), along with Erik Lallerstadt's adjoining Faculty of Law and Humanities along Norrtullsgatan. To mediate between the library plaza at the primary intersection and the park on the hill above, Asplund inserted a walled garden along the avenue; while formally related to the plaza, this garden is materially affiliated with the park. Taking greater advantage of the site's natural amenities, Asplund now limited his landscape interventions to a series of garden terraces in the midblock segments along each street and a monumental podium at the summit, which accommodates both the old observatory and an imposing new rectilinear courtyard building. To negotiate the irregular terrain between the lower and upper terraces, he combined meandering paths with straight runs of stairs, an idea he would reiterate in his prizewinning entry to a civic design competition of 1926. Asplund initially set the library on a low platform overlooking the plaza at the intersection; significantly, the complex seems to be part of the hill rather than of the urban fabric, from which it is subtly removed. He ultimately raised the platform to accommodate shops at the street level and subtly shifted the library's orientation from that of its podium, thereby augmenting both its monumentality and its distance from the space of the city.

By 1924 Asplund's building design achieved its final definition, and construction began. He articulated the central lending hall as a cylindrical volume and surrounded it on three sides by reading rooms and book storage. He also planned the fourth side, originally open toward the hill, to accommodate an extension, which was realized in 1932. A monumental ramped stair rising from the sidewalk to the podium echoes the dramatic internal ascent to the library's main lending hall. Historians have noted the building's multiple historic references.[10] The Egyptian influence of the hieroglyphs that ring the drum and the neoclassicism of the outsized doorways, inspired by Gottlieb Bindesbøll's Thorvaldsen Museum in

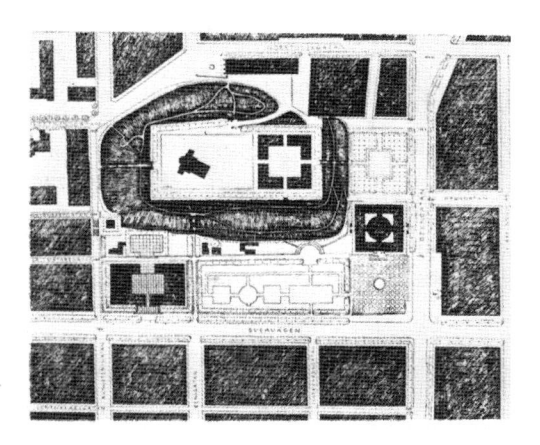

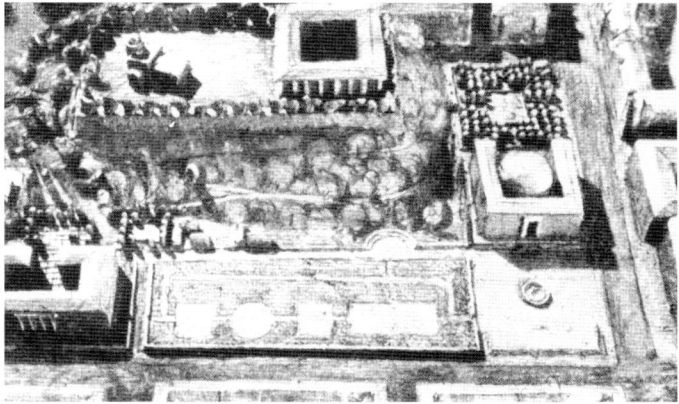

Copenhagen (1839–48), extend to Ivar Johnsson's shallow reliefs in the entry hall depicting scenes from the *Iliad*. The volumetric purity of the cylindrical lending room may have been inspired by Claude-Nicolas Ledoux's Barrière de la Villette (1785–89), as well as by local neoclassical works by Nicodemus Tessin the Younger and Erik Palmstedt. Seeking a new yet timeless mode of expression, Asplund merged ideas from such diverse historic sources into a cohesive architectural statement.

While the library was under construction, Asplund continued to explore the possibilities for developing the adjoining terrain as a public park. In 1926 he submitted proposals for the park sites along Sveavägen and Odengatan to a competition organized to solicit suggestions for civic improvements. His prizewinning scheme for the site along Sveavägen underwent significant modifications before it was realized, beginning in 1929. In his competition proposal, Asplund limited geometric interventions to the uppermost and lowest segments of the site and the narrow cross paths linking them, thereby emphasizing the contrast between architecture and "nature." He controlled the water welling out of a spring beneath the rocky outcrop in a geometric fashion. It rushes down the steep incline in a straight narrow channel and passes through a platform at the level of the library, where it is traversed by a pedestrian footbridge. From this point, the pedestrian path parallels the descent of the water, which cascades down a chute bounded by stairs to a small pool lined with a grove of trees. The water then flows down a broad stair to a shallow reflecting pool at the base of the hill. The rectilinear geometry of the reflecting pool is echoed in a low-walled precinct at the top of the hill, bracketing the hillside between horizontal planes.

Asplund's proposal for Observatory Hill of 1923 as seen in site plan and model, with the library reoriented to face Sveavägen. From the collections at the Swedish Museum of Architecture; photographer Thomas Hjertén.

Asplund's definitive scheme of 1924 for the Stockholm Public Library: entry facade *(above)* and section through lending hall. From the collections at the Swedish Museum of Architecture; photographer Thomas Hjertén.

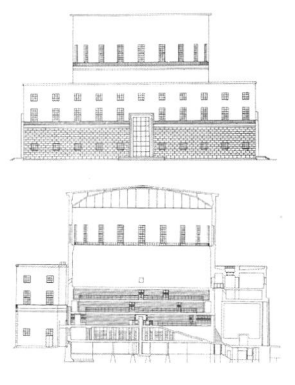

URBAN LANDSCAPES OF ERIK GUNNAR ASPLUND   69

In his calculated control of the water that surges out of the hill down the steep incline, then is progressively brought to a state of calm, Asplund may have derived inspiration from certain sixteenth-century Italian villas, particularly the Villa Lante at Bagnaia and the Villa d'Este at Tivoli, both of which he visited during his Italian sojourn of 1913–14.[11] In both gardens the water progresses via architectural means from an evocation of a "natural" condition to a geometric form, from a state of motion to one of stasis, while evoking mythological iconographic themes. The influence of Sigurd Lewerentz is also suggested by certain parallels with the Woodland Cemetery, their collaborative project of 1915 to 1935 in which Lewerentz had primary responsibility for landscape development.[12] The chute of water plunging straight down the hill bears comparison with the Way of the Seven Wells, a long straight path that traverses the cemetery's pine forest. The grove of trees at its base not only recalls the precinct that Asplund created for the family tomb of Prince Bernadotte (1921) but can also be seen as a forerunner to the cemetery's Meditation Grove (c. 1934).

Both park and library are set off from the space of the city. A line of trees along the far end of the pool screens Tengbom's Economics Faculty from view, while a high wall separating sidewalk from reflecting pool forms a distinct boundary between the urban realm and that of the park. The pedestrian route through the site's steep irregular topography provides a varied experience for the ascent to the platform at the summit, where Asplund regained control over the natural terrain through geometric means.

Asplund's related competition proposal for the scarred site of a former gravel pit along Odengatan, published in *Byggmästaren* in 1926,

(left) Plan and section of Asplund's Library Park proposal, submitted to the Stockholm Civic Improvement Competition of 1926. *Byggmästaren,* July 1926.

(right) Asplund's coeval perspective drawing of the Odenhall, intended for the area immediately behind the Stockholm Public Library. *Byggmästaren,* August 1926.

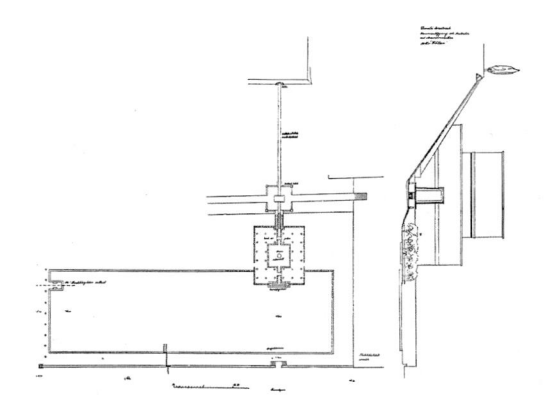

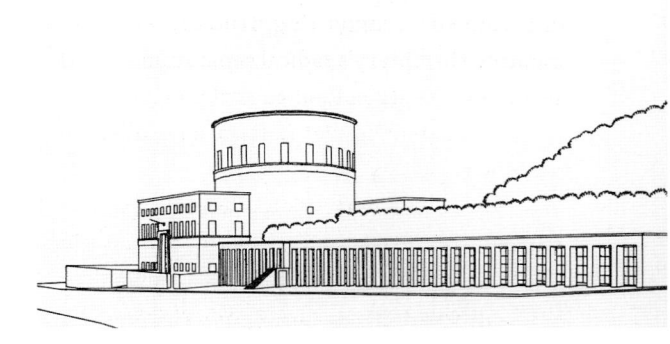

was a significant precursor to his ultimate site strategy for the library building. The Odenhall, a linear structure that consists of an open loggia fronting a series of market stalls, serves as the base to a garden terrace at the rear of the library. The simple rectilinear platform on the summit that Asplund now proposed as the setting for the observatory is lined with a ring of trees, echoing the neoclassicism of the market hall below. Breaking through this upper colonnade of trees, a run of stairs descends straight to Asplund's garden terrace below in a manner that parallels the water chute on the adjacent incline, while meandering paths negotiate the irregular intermediate terrain.

Asplund's market hall was never realized; instead, beginning in 1929, the city erected three administrative buildings perpendicular to the street, in accordance with its revised planning guidelines. While the spaces between these structures were carefully landscaped, no attempt was made to link these intermediary spaces to the park, as Asplund intended in his earliest site studies. His Odenhall plan is significant, however, as it marks the first clear graphic indication that Asplund had subtly shifted the orientation of the library, then under construction, from that of its platform and park terraces, which align with the urban grid. The decision to position the building in this manner was seminal, indicating Asplund's desire to isolate the library further from its urban context, reinforcing the impact of its podium. While his propensity for subtle oblique angles as an appeal to architecture's psychological and experiential dimensions is often noted, Asplund usually used this device to establish connections rather than disrupt them. He subsequently realized the full implications of this gesture by integrating it with his revised conception for the park.

In 1928, the year the library opened to the public, Asplund proposed a second dramatic change: inserting an abstract base with broad expanses of glass directly beneath the library's massive podium. This pair of revisions—in which he first shifted the library's orientation and then visually undermined its supporting structure—are related critical operations, augmenting the library's radical separation from the urban intersection. They seemingly freed Asplund to envision a different strategy for the park, no less formally manipulated than his earlier proposals but far less reliant on geometry.

In his final park layout, developed late in 1930 or early the following year, Asplund made further significant changes. He now ringed the library and pool with trees in an effort to mitigate the contrast between architecture and elements of nature. Moreover, by making both pedestrian path and watercourse irregular, he caused building and park to inflect toward each other in a unity that transcends differences between architecture and landscape. This subtle gesture to the dramatic irruption of a natural outcrop within the urban fabric augments the library's distance from the space of the city, an idea reiterated in the delicate transparency of its base.

Although planting of some of the park's trees and sowing of its lawn had begun by 1929, an intermediate park plan, dated August 1930, demonstrates Asplund's ongoing concern with every detail of the landscape, including its furnishings, surface materials, and planting. Here the water originates in a square pool at the top of the hill and meanders toward the reflecting pool in a freer fashion, while a pedestrian path winds up to a grove of clipped trees that juts out from the northeast corner of the upper terrace. In this version, Asplund eliminated the wall along Sveavägen, opening the park directly to the urban avenue. This exposure reinforces visual affinities between the glass facades of his library platform and the shimmering surface of the reflecting pool, both fully visible from the street, providing a further point of contrast with the massive library volume, isolated atop its platform of shops.

Inspired by Sigurd Lewerentz's contributions to the Woodland Cemetery landscape, Asplund used plant materials selectively. He admired Lewerentz's propensity for choosing specific species for their formal and symbolic attributes and grouping them so they play a particular role in the ensemble. Asplund selected plant materials based on their olfactory and emotive power as well as their form, and he positioned them to reinforce

(left) Asplund's definitive site plan of 1930 for the Stockholm Library Park. From the collections at the Swedish Museum of Architecture; photographer Thomas Hjertén.

(right) Asplund's perspective of 1928 of the Stockholm Public Library atop its modernist base. From the collections at the Swedish Museum of Architecture; photographer Thomas Hjertén.

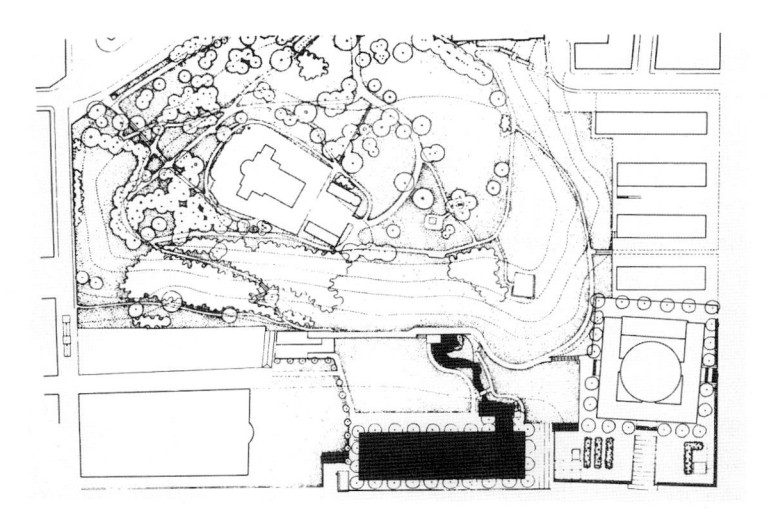

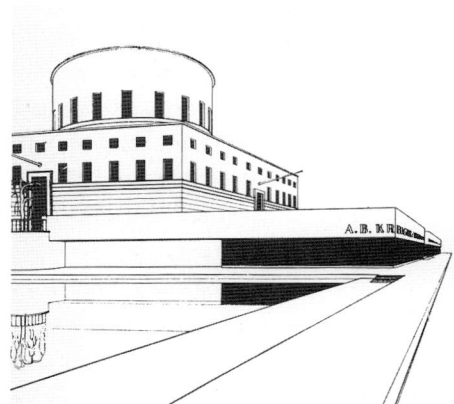

his spatial intentions for the park. Willow trees envelop the reflecting pool, while a U-shaped grove of poplars rises at the juncture between the watercourse and the pool. The area near the stream is planted with spirea and salix, interspersed with park roses and shaded by a single oak tree, while lilies and a pair of willows mark the juncture of the stream and a small footbridge. Asplund intended the grassy lawn to overhang the retaining walls that he placed to the south and west of the pool and lined with benches. To the south a rectilinear "theater" of maples with parallel rows of seats overlooks the pool across a bed of perennials.

To strengthen the freer organization of his final park plan dated later that year, Asplund reincorporated certain aspects of his competition proposal of 1926. The water again issues directly from a hillside spring, from which it flows in a sharply meandering sequence to a low dam, thence falling in sheets to the reflecting pool. The wall separating the sidewalk from the park has reappeared as a distinct boundary, and the pool precinct is lined with a protective ring of weeping willows.[13] To the south Asplund added a small open-air pavilion marking entry to the park and a line of poplars to screen Tengbom's Economics Faculty from view. He also proposed to simplify the pathway leading to the northern crest of the hill, although this portion of the scheme was never carried out. The spring, streambed, and reflecting pool were completed between 1931 and 1933, and the surrounding area was planted in 1934 and 1935, essentially as Asplund proposed in his detailed site plan of 1930.

Asplund used sculpture within the park to accentuate liminal conditions. He originally intended to position Nils Molleberg's 1934 figure *Youth* adjacent to the children's library entry from the park, but in 1937 it was placed in the open-air pavilion that terminates the pool. He used Ivar Johnsson's sculpture *Dancing Youths,* installed that same year, to mark the transition between the rushing watercourse and the tranquil reflecting pool. Sigrid Fridman's bronze *Centaur* was added in 1939 at the corner of the hilltop platform, where its dramatic profile is visible from the lower part of the site, signaling the threshold between earth and sky.

Recent critics have deemed the naturalism of Asplund's final park design regressive. In his groundbreaking monograph on Asplund, Stuart Wrede argues about his competition plan of 1926: "This severely rectilinear but rich landscape plan remained the basis for the park, but both the stream and the small square were unfortunately modified into a more naturalistic solution."[14] Lars Olof Larsson provides a more pointed critique of the park's overt romanticism:

Asplund made the slope of the hill with its little brook look like an untouched, romantic piece of nature. Thus, . . . the abstract, perfect volume of the library is embedded in a pseudo-archaic landscape, reminding us of the typical setting of many utopian projects of the decades around 1800.[15]

Such interpretations are more indicative of their authors' formal preoccupations than of the significance of Asplund's design. Indeed, a coeval project for the Stockholm Exhibition (1930) on which Asplund collaborated with Sigurd Lewerentz provides further insight into Asplund's broader social and cultural aspirations for Observatory Hill.

Asplund's site strategy for the Stockholm Exhibition, heralded as the onset of Swedish functionalism, exemplifies his interest in improving the quality of urban life by drawing upon the natural attributes of the environs. While the style of his temporary exhibition buildings derives from international strains of the so-called Modern Movement, his organizational layout draws upon the particular qualities of the Stockholm landscape. A broad watercourse, Djurgårdsbrunnsviken, splits the site into two primary segments. Concentrating his exhibition layout at the water's edge, Asplund directed entry from the city to an open plaza and lined its inland side with pavilions oriented at right angles to form a series of culs-de-sac. This hierarchical system of open spaces oriented toward the waterfront recalls his strategy for the Royal Chancellery competition. A pedestrian footbridge at the end of this sequence leads to further attractions on the island of Djurgården, a royal hunting park that had been devoted to public recreation since the eighteenth century and served as the site for the Stockholm Exhibition of 1897. Just as Asplund intended his pavilions to provide neutral settings for the items on display, so he conceived of them as subsidiary to the site itself.[16] He used light construction methods, based on a modular system of open wooden frames enclosed in canvas and glass, to give the exhibition a transitory appearance that was enhanced by a plethora of billowing flags and an advertising mast, designed by Lewerentz, that rose over the main plaza. While such a festive atmosphere was unprecedented in contemporary European architecture, it was essential to Asplund's avant-garde ambition of reintegrating art and life.

Although roughly half of the exhibition area was devoted to housing, Asplund left this aspect of the design to his contemporaries, leading certain of his Swedish colleagues to question his commitment to the

Aerial perspective of the Stockholm Exhibition of 1930 in a gouache by Max Söderhold, 1929. From the collections at the Swedish Museum of Architecture; photographer Thomas Hjertén.

reform potential of modern architecture. They failed to see the social relevance of his site layout or pavilion designs, as they deemed the provision of housing a more urgent priority.[17] Just as his contemporaries directed their further comments to the stylistic aspects of his buildings rather than their implicit social value, a similar focus on the formal qualities of Asplund's architecture has diverted historians from considering his contributions to the urban landscape.

Like his library park, Asplund's Stockholm Exhibition reflects his interest in integrating the urban fabric of Stockholm with its unique natural heritage for the direct benefit of the citizenry. Although he carried out both projects under the auspices of the Stockholm Parks Department, that organization's efforts in this direction were initially sporadic. In 1936, under the direction of architect Osvald Almqvist, the Parks Department began to formulate a more cohesive set of objectives for the city's open spaces, drawing upon the region's natural attributes. Refining these goals, Almqvist's successor, Holgar Blom, who served as parks director from 1938 to 1971, created a systematic network of parks that contributed to neighborhood identification while linking broader segments of the city. Asplund's efforts to revitalize neglected open spaces in the city were important precursors to this more methodical transformation of the Stockholm park system during the department's heyday in the 1940s and 1950s.

Just as the American institution of public libraries provided an important precedent for the Stockholm Public Library, so the systematic development of American urban parks by Frederick Law Olmsted and his successors influenced the subsequent transformation of the Stockholm landscape.[18] Rejecting the relatively consistent visual appearance that Olmsted utilized in his parks throughout the United States, however, Swedish landscape architects embraced a more regional approach, drawing upon and enhancing the particular qualities of individual locales as they adapted the city's undeveloped areas for public use.

At the Stockholm Public Library, as with his numerous interventions in the local urban landscape, Asplund fused a monumental architectural conception with a monumentalization of the natural terrain, seeking to further communal edification and public memory through his park design, just as was the case for his library building. This is not the picturesque element in a landscape garden that some critics have claimed; rather, it reflects Asplund's efforts to endow his architecture with the timeless spirit of the classical through new expressive means—not through recourse to symbolic qualities, but through a direct appeal to fundamental experiences. Such resolution extends to his landscape strategy, wherein Asplund posited architecture as a middle ground between "nature" and the city.

Postcard from the late 1930s of the Stockholm Public Library, looking across the reflecting pool toward the café in the library base. Photograph by Axel Eliasson. From the collections at the Swedish Museum of Architecture; photographer Thomas Hjertén.

FOUR

TOWARD A SPIRITUAL LANDSCAPE
The Woodland Cemetery
and Swedish Burial Reform

In their collaborative design for the Woodland Cemetery in Stock-holm's southern outskirts of Enskede (1915–35), architects Erik Gunnar Asplund and Sigurd Lewerentz rejected traditional European prototypes for the cemetery—the city of the dead or paradise garden—as well as nineteenth-century secularized forms based on the English landscape garden.[1] They sought to imbue their memorial ground with greater cultural relevance by drawing upon the ritual capacity of landscape. Their starting point was the site itself, a wooded tract within agricultural environs that was punctuated by a granite ridge and scarred by quarrying operations. Transcending the limitations of conventional Christian iconography, they relied primarily on enhancing attributes of the site—ridge and valley, earth and sky, forest and clearing, meadow and marsh—to evoke associations of death and rebirth in a landscape of spiritual dimension. Such amplification of the landscape's spiritual potential has significant social implications. The cemetery is a site of communal remembrance.

While the Woodland Cemetery has been widely analyzed in terms of its buildings, viewed as embodiments of the stylistic transition from Nordic classicism to modernism during the early decades of the twentieth century, scholars have rarely considered the cemetery as a whole, including its landscape.[2] From this vantage point, a different account emerges. Despite obvious stylistic differences, the cemetery buildings contribute to a larger unity comprising architecture and landscape. This integrity extends to a consistency of purpose in both the social and psychological dimensions. Such coherence is grounded in the architects' conscious efforts to counteract the modern eschewal of death.

The Woodland Cemetery evolved in reaction against nineteenth-century reforms that replaced the thousand-year-old custom of burying the dead under the aegis of the church with a secular approach to death. In response to widespread sanctions against burial within city limits, owing to sanitary and aesthetic concerns, a popular form of cemetery emerged during the early nineteenth century in northern Europe and the United States. Based on the English landscape garden, this new form of cemetery appropriated a private, secular garden typology for burial on a civic scale. In Sweden, after King Gustavus III prohibited the sale of burial sites within urban churchyards for hygienic reasons in 1783 (anticipating a similar Napoleonic decree of 1804), responsibility for burial reverted to the state. Stockholm's North Cemetery (1815–27) exemplifies the large municipal cemeteries that resulted from this legislation, situated outside the cities and envisioned as parks to reflect their hygienic intent. The garden cemetery's formal association with leisure activity only facilitated the symbolic avoidance of death intrinsic to its extraurban location.

The Woodland Cemetery was the first of a series of cemeteries developed in Sweden during the first half of the twentieth century as part of a concerted public initiative for burial reform. This reconception of the cemetery is a complex and seminal exploration of the modern landscape and its symbolic potential, undertaken by architects who allowed the particular qualities of each site and general issues of landscape design to inform and shape their work. Asplund and Lewerentz were individually responsible for the most significant examples; their collaborative Stockholm cemetery was the first to address burial reform at the scale of landscape. The Woodland Cemetery rarely served as a formal model for subsequent Swedish cemetery development, however, as such densely wooded locales were rarely utilized in this manner. Adapting their social, psychological, and spiritual aims to diverse geographic situations throughout the country, Asplund and Lewerentz countered the modern tendency toward secularization in extraurban municipal cemeteries with an affirmation of the sacred value of landscape. They infused the profane and generalized infinite space of modernism with the spirit of the concentrated and particular *locus sacer* of antiquity, amplifying the cemetery's symbolic resonance through a direct appeal to essential experiences.

Planned on an unprecedented scale, these new Swedish cemeteries had few sources from which to draw inspiration. The stimulus for innovation came from Germany, where the idea of a woodland burial ground, or *Waldfriedhof,* originated. Hans Grässel, council architect for Munich, developed the type in opposition to the prevailing model of the cemetery as a metropolitan park or place of leisure. To overcome the symbolic limitations of the garden cemetery and impart the explicit character of a burial ground, Grässel adopted references to early Christian and Byzantine architecture in his funeral chapels and service buildings. To avoid monotony and foster intimacy, he subdivided the flat, wooded site of the Munich Waldfriedhof (1907) into a number of burial quadrants, which he differentiated according to planting and memorial type, while drawing upon the physical continuity of the forest to provide a sense of unity. Rather than rely on the individual memorial to link the worlds of the living and the dead, Grässel thus effected a more universal, symbolic liaison between nature and death. Because the forest serves to obscure the presence of a burial ground, the site retains the pervasive salutary atmosphere of a garden cemetery. Grässel's conception thus remains a formal variation on an established cemetery type, rather than something radically new. In Stockholm Asplund and Lewerentz would invest the forest with greater symbolic overtones by situating it within a processional sequence that accommodates both public and private acts of mourning.

The Swedish movement for burial reform was given new impetus by Gustav Schlyter, town commissioner of Helsingborg, whose interest in reanimating the practice of cremation led to his appointment in 1911 as secretary of the Cremation Society of Sweden. The motto "To death—to life" that he devised for the society's pavilion at the Baltic Exhibition held in Malmö in 1914 summarizes Schlyter's primary ambition: to renew attitudes toward life by encouraging a more positive outlook on death. As he affirmed in a letter to Torsten Stubelius, his architect for the Helsingborg Crematorium, "It is for the living that we work."[3]

Schlyter's efforts on behalf of cremation had significant architectural ramifications. In light of the movement's hygienic and practical basis, he recognized the need to enhance the aesthetic and psychological aspects of cremation in order to sway public opinion in its favor. His architectural program called for a ritual sequence leading from a dark and somber funeral chamber—the Vault of the Dead—to a tall, brightly lit Hall of Life. To encourage those in mourning to confront their loss in order to approach acceptance of the parting, he advocated a processional route in which mourners would not retrace their steps. Toward this end, Schlyter specified an appropriate treatment of the crematorium landscape in which all memorials are subordinated to their immediate milieu. This idea of a ritualized sequence directed toward the emotional impact of bereavement was Schlyter's most important contribution to Swedish funerary landscapes and architecture.

In 1911 Schlyter enlisted Torsten Stubelius to design a crematorium for a hillside setting in Helsingborg. For Sigurd Lewerentz, working in partnership with Stubelius at the time, this commission initiated a lifelong inquiry into issues of cemetery design. The architects conceived of their site plan and spatial sequencing to fulfill ritual aims. They positioned the chapel to one end of the site in a gesture that appears to transform it through contours manipulated to conform to an overall architectural order. Water flowing along the bottom of the site in the remains of an old moat lined with willows drifts slowly toward an irregular pool near the attenuated slab of the funeral chapel. Channeled into a vaulted arch at the base of the chapel, the water emerges on the chapel's far side transformed by an existing cascade into the turbulent waters of life. The dual themes of death and rebirth suggested by the flow of water also govern the processional route; entry into a dimly lit funeral chamber at one end of the chapel is followed by ascent to a lofty Hall of Life. From here the route emerges into an arcaded cloister lined with urns, which leads to an adjoining memorial grove overlooking terraced burial grounds that descend the layered contours of the hill. In their unrealized design, Lewerentz and Stubelius expanded upon the themes that Schlyter set out in his program, subordinating individual grave markers to an overall architectural order and assimilating the landscape into the ritualized sequence.

Schlyter's ideas provided an important starting point for the Woodland Cemetery, influencing both the architecture and its relationship to the cemetery grounds. Asplund and Lewerentz included a variation on the Helsingborg chapel in their competition proposal. In their subsequent development of the funeral chapels they pursued the architectural ramifications of Schlyter's program, demonstrating its potential for inspiring formal variations. The architects' greater contribution, however, was in building upon the landscape's symbolic and ritual possibilities, a challenge on a vastly different scale.

In their competition proposal the idea of a ritual sequence—from dark to light, from sorrow to expiation, from the fear of death to the promise of life everlasting—pervades the cemetery landscape and its architecture: the Way of the Cross as well as the chapel's processional route to the Hall of Life. Although the chapel complex is prominently situated at the crest of a ridge, only its bell tower is visible from the cemetery entrance, beckoning those in mourning to embark on the slow ascent along the dimly lit forest path. The Way of the Cross, lined with neoclassical tombs, is a Via Appia in the forest. By setting tombs of neoclassical provenance amid the pine trees, Asplund and Lewerentz endowed the landscape with the same sense of profundity and salubrious melancholy that Schlyter intended for the crematorium architecture, a spirit derived not only from the cemetery's ritualistic basis but also from Nordic attitudes toward nature.

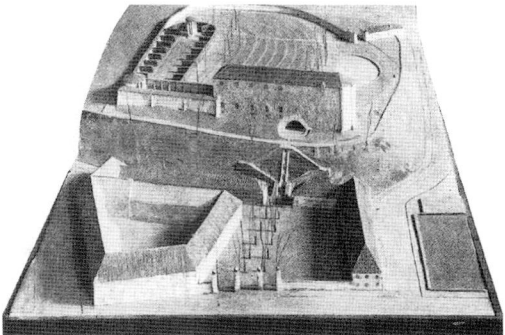

By recourse to images that are simultaneously pagan and biblical, Nordic and classical, the architects sought to augment the spiritual qualities of the processional sequence in a manner directly accessible to the emotions. The tilted wooden cross marking the beginning of the pedestrian path has pagan as well as Christian implications. An element with rustic German origins, such a cross was used in romantic eighteenth-century parks of Swedish and Danish country houses as a symbol of the reintegration with nature that the aristocracy sought in country living. The competition submission also incorporates more obscure references: the numerological and biblical significance of the number seven, for example, in its sequence of seven gardens, seven wells, seven terraces, and seven clearings. A brief musical passage from Edvard Grieg's tone poem "The Death of Åse," positioned beneath the proposal's title, also alludes to the underlying symbolism. Lacking any citation, it provides the initiated with an enigmatic suggestion of the project's thematic grounding in the mysteries of nature.

Between 1916 and 1935 Asplund and Lewerentz gradually refined their initial conception, seeking deeper levels of meaning in the visible world to express ideas about the invisible. The site's capacity for meaning grew more pronounced as the architects brought selected landscape elements to prominence, clarifying their relationship to the ritual sequence.

(left) Model of the Helsingborg Crematorium by Sigurd Lewerentz and Torsten Stubelius, 1911–14, with view overlooking canal and ritual entry landscape. From the collections at the Swedish Museum of Architecture; photographer Thomas Hjertén.

(right) View of model showing waterfall at rear of chapel. *Teknisk Tidskrift: Arkitektur,* 1914.

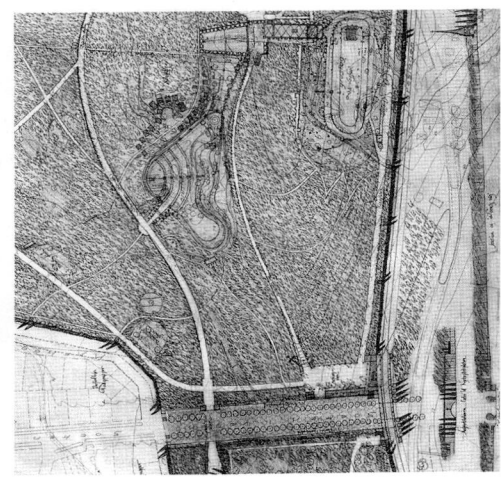

(left) Competition model of Erik Gunnar Asplund and Sigurd Lewerentz's winning entry for the Stockholm South Cemetery Competition, 1915. From the collections at the Swedish Museum of Architecture; photographer Thomas Hjertén.

(right) Corresponding portion of the competition plan. From the collections at the Swedish Museum of Architecture; photographer Mats Widén.

Whereas their original proposal relied on a mythical spatial understanding, elaborating specific qualities of place in an ensemble of thematically linked individual episodes, the architects ultimately incorporated a sense of continuity and a suggestion of the infinite to ground the cemetery landscape in a more modern spatial conception. They also transformed the cemetery's spatial content. Their initial proposal was melancholic, even foreboding in tone, relying on a melodramatic contrast of darkness and light to address the mourners' sense of loss during bereavement. They ultimately articulated the cemetery landscape in a more affirmative psychological manner, imparting a sense of serenity in the face of death through reconciliation with nature. To accommodate the increasing demand for equality in burial practice, they gradually subsumed individual expression in memorial design to the greater significance of the whole. Rather than serving as a backdrop for vainglorious attempts to memorialize the individual, the cemetery assumed a broader moral function: to symbolize the equality we share in death and to invest the conduct of our daily lives with that communal consciousness. The cemetery's resonance of meaning arises from its appeal to the emotional impact of death rather than through recourse to external symbolism. In their search for a corresponding expressive means, the architects relied increasingly on the mediating potential of landscape.

While the realized Woodland Cemetery differs from the architects' initial conception, it sustains and elaborates upon the theme of a ritual journey postulated in the competition proposal. Formal allées of pollarded lime trees line a broad suburban avenue, screened by high stone walls that obscure any inward view. To the south a grassy forecourt, semicircular in form and bounded by retaining walls of dressed stone, interrupts the sequence, providing access to the cemetery within. Surmounting the curved entry walls, Swedish whitebeams profiled against the internal pine forest effect a transition from built to natural, reiterated in distinctions among the ashlar surfaces of the entry walls, the rougher texture of the walls facing the avenue, and the turf-capped fieldstone of the walls surrounding the cemetery precinct.

The bold semicircular form of the cemetery forecourt draws the visitor toward a clearing punctuated by a large granite cross that is visible through the break of the entry drive. From the forecourt, the cross is the only object to interrupt the horizon—the boundary between earth and sky, visible and invisible. The entry route is channeled between retaining walls of ashlar masonry where a fountain to one side—a fieldstone wall bathed in a steady trickle of water and screened by a Doric colonnade—suggests eternity as well as tears of mourning. This wall of tears marks the gateway to the sacred enclosure, while the gradual ascent of the entry drive reinforces a sense of departure from the realm of the living.

Within the cemetery the architects transmuted this celebration of boundary to the relationship of earth to sky. The open lawn viewed upon entry is free of burial markers, imparting serenity to the setting. Asplund and Lewerentz originally envisioned this entry landscape as covered with

View into the open entry landscape of the Woodland Cemetery, with the Way of the Cross and Chapel of the Holy Cross (Woodland Crematorium) visible in the distance.

pine trees and dotted with graves. They realized its potential as an open expanse only while construction was in progress, when they filled in its rocky escarpments and covered the ground with a smooth lawn to give it a more reassuring sculpted appearance. This grassy expanse provides a view of the cemetery's broader organization and choice of route. To the east, a broad walk of rough paving stones leads through the carpet of grass; in a gradual ascent it passes the cross and a series of chapels, culminating in a monumental porch as it extends to the horizon. To the west, a long segmented flight of stairs ascends a steep earthen mound to a low-walled precinct, where a grove of weeping elms is dramatically profiled against the sky.

This grass-covered knoll topped by a meditation grove draws upon a variety of sources. It recalls ancient Swedish burial mounds, such as those of the Swedish kings at Old Uppsala, dating from the fifth to the seventh century, as well as garden mounts depicted in Eric Dahlberg's *Svecia antiqua e hodierna* of the late seventeenth century. While the hill's massive form suggests the difficulties of the mourner's task, the ascent comprises successive flights of steps that decrease in height to ease the approach to the summit. The Meditation Grove crowning the hill is paired with the chapel porch, known as Monument Hall; the shape of the loggia echoes the disposition of trees in the grove, and the pillars recall the tree trunks. Delicate branches of weeping ash bend toward the earth, while a sculptural Monument to the Resurrection reaches toward an opening to the sky. Near the main chapel, a sweep of paving stones set in the open lawn culminates in a low mound surmounted by a catafalque, marking an outdoor setting for funeral rites. A lily pond at the crest of the hill is deliberately isolated from any natural source of water. Singled out to reinforce its

(left) The Way of the Cross leading to Asplund's Woodland Crematorium complex of 1935–40.

(right) The Way of the Seven Wells leading to the Meditation Grove.

84 TOWARD A SPIRITUAL LANDSCAPE

symbolic reference to the eternal cycles of life and death, the pool serves as a backdrop to the open-air ceremonial plaza.

To the south, a birch grove marks the forest edge, providing a colonnade to the burial grounds that lie within the pine forest beyond. The architects had the forest thinned to create a visual continuum, eliminating deciduous trees to enhance the impression of uniformity. Toward this end they had the undergrowth cleared and the ground plane planted with grass, modifications that distinguish this wooded landscape as a human construct and thus a symbolic act. A unified aesthetic also characterizes the treatment of the grave markers; their subordination to the effect of the whole is ensured by dimensional restrictions as well as by a mandatory design review process. The uniform carpet of grass dotted with simple grave markers differs from the characteristic demarcation of family burial plots with curbs and fences in traditional Swedish cemeteries. At Enskede the ground plane is communal, its continuity broken only by modest memorials of stone, iron, or wood, oriented with the chapels toward the setting sun.

A long straight path pierces the forest as it extends from the Meditation Grove to the airy columnar forehall of a small solitary chapel. Lined with spruce trees and pressed into the forest floor, this footpath suggestively simulates descent into the earth and gradual reemergence on approaching the chapel. A crosswalk leads through the pine forest to a second individual chapel within a low-walled precinct: a microcosm of the cemetery landscape. To one side of the chapel a rectangular area sunk into the earth is dotted with small memorials dedicated to children, beyond

(left) The lily pond, outdoor ceremonial plaza, and Meditation Grove viewed from the Chapel of the Holy Cross.

(right) The Way of the Seven Wells leading to Lewerentz's Resurrection Chapel of 1921–25.

The Woodland Cemetery burial ground, with its modest grave markers aligned with the path of the setting sun.

which a low circular mound lined with miniature willows provides a tranquil respite from the burial grounds.

This ritualized landscape communicates with little recourse to religious iconography. Except for the cross and the Resurrection Monument, sheltered in the porch of the main crematory chapel, the cemetery's meaning does not rely on the intermediary authority of the church; instead, it builds upon the common private experience of mourning to convey a sense of oneness with humankind and with nature. Such an elevated view of human destiny and notion of community with the living imparts a spirituality reflected in the Swedish word *stämning*. As Leo Spitzer has noted about its untranslatable German equivalent:

> What is missing in the main European languages is a term that would express the unity of feelings experienced by man face to face with his environment (a landscape, nature, one's fellow man), and would comprehend and weld together the objective (factual) and the subjective

(psychological) into one harmonious unity. . . . for a German, *Stimmung* is fused with landscape, which in turn is animated by the feelings of men—it is an indissoluble unit into which man and nature are integrated.[4]

Ingrid Lilienberg's probing commentary on the Stockholm South Cemetery Competition, published in the journal *Arkitektur* (1915), both anticipated the spirit of Asplund and Lewerentz's design modifications and established the conceptual framework for subsequent Swedish cemetery design. Questioning the nature of a meaningful expression for such a site, Lilienberg speculated: "Should the cemetery be subordinate to the forest or the forest the cemetery—or how should the overall relationship between them be formed?" Characterizing the premiated design as "nothing more than a piece of nature with beautiful graves in it," she argued that the Stockholm competition entrants failed to address the latter riskier and more difficult question. "First and foremost," she elaborated, "from beginning to end it should have an entirely specific cemetery atmosphere [*stämning*], which only man's molding and forming hand can provide. Further, the orientation must be clear. The cemetery's size and form must be perceptible in the planning. Its scale and atmosphere [*stämning*] should fulfill the destiny of an urban population."[5]

The objectives for the Malmö Eastern Cemetery, the subject of a national design competition held in 1916, reflect the import of Lilienberg's challenge. The program stipulated: "Great weight is placed on the area acquiring the pervasive dignified character befitting a cemetery."[6] The open site, affording a broad outlook over the rich agricultural landscape of Skåne, consisted of a grassy plain culminating in a sandy ridge, punctuated

(left) The Way of the Seven Wells subtly depressed into the earth as it leads to Lewerentz's Resurrection Chapel of 1921–25.

(right) Asplund's Woodland Chapel of 1918–22, crowned by Carl Milles's *Angel of Death*, 1921.

by a Bronze Age burial mound. Arguing that it would be unnatural to transform the site into a woodland or a park and that a geometric treatment would also sacrifice the site's inherent character, the jury imposed a further qualification: "It is first and foremost a requirement that the ridge's natural monumentality be exploited and reinforced, and that it be used as a basis for orientation in the design."[7]

In his prizewinning proposal "Ridge," Lewerentz built upon the site's existing features, using the ridge as a natural boundary to a zone of burial precincts subdivided by hedges. He later articulated the ridge more architectonically by lining it with chapels, mausoleums, and a crematorium. Ultimately, however, he preserved its original character as a grassy expanse, free of burial markers, where ashes of the deceased could be freely distributed. Here Lewerentz's own ashes were scattered upon his death in 1975. He initially intended the large chapel, based on his Helsingborg Crematorium, to dominate the ridge and loom over the burial precincts. Lewerentz ultimately submerged the entire complex, including associated mortuary chambers, within the ridge. Only the monumental entry loggia of the Chapel of St. Birgitta is visible on approach, imparting greater significance to both the ridge and the adjoining burial grounds.

Throughout the cemetery's development Lewerentz maintained the ritual character of his competition proposal while subordinating the architectural elements to the symbolically ordered landscape. To emphasize the main circulation route at the base of the ridge he imposed a series of subtle misalignments on the geometrically ordered burial precincts, disengaging the precincts from one another. He relied on the ridge's visual prominence to enhance the mourner's sense of orientation, directing movement to secondary circulation routes within the cemetery. Ultimately Lewerentz

Sigurd Lewerentz's Malmö Eastern Cemetery of 1916–70: ridge with the Chapel of St. Birgitta, 1926 *(left)*; burial quadrants viewed from the ridge.

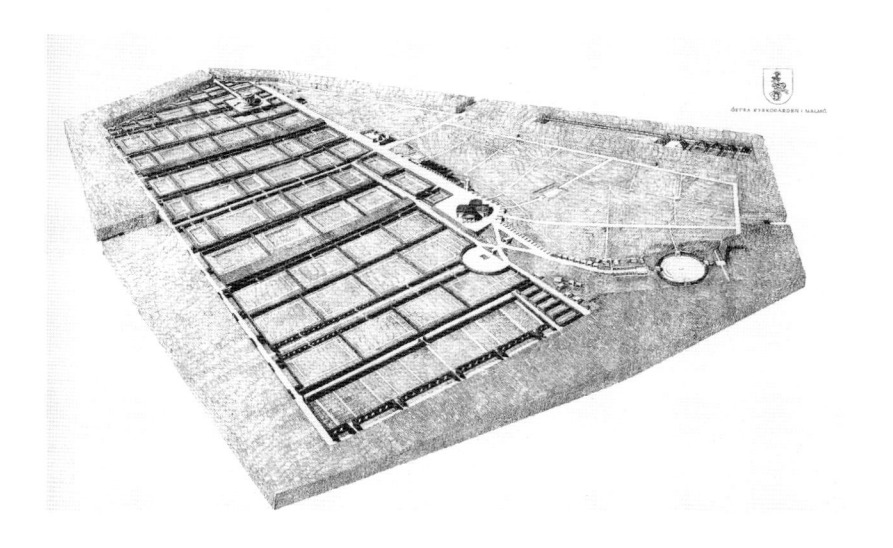

(left) Aerial perspective of the Malmö Eastern Cemetery, c. 1923, including a round outdoor ceremonial plaza and irregularly aligned burial quadrants essentially as realized. From the collections at the Swedish Museum of Architecture; photographer Thomas Hjertén.

(right) Chapels of St. Gertrud and St. Knut of 1936–43, viewed from the burial grounds.

amplified the ridge's symbolic import by modeling its contours and planting it with wheat.

In 1943, when he added the twin chapels of St. Gertrud and St. Knut in the burial grounds to the south, Lewerentz planted additional blocks of trees to screen the newer volumes from view. Suggesting affinities with Skanian farms, the tree-lined crematorium complex affords a requisite sense of privacy while ensuring the visual dominance of landscape. Successive layers of planting—1.6-meter-high hedges subdividing the burial precincts and a wall of beech trees separating the cemetery from its agricultural environs—contribute to a feeling of removal from the realm of daily life. Lewerentz's manipulation of this regional landscape to augment the site's spiritual dimension provides a fitting response to Lilienberg's charge "to fulfill the destiny of an urban population."[8]

Although acclaim for the Woodland Cemetery afforded both architects opportunities for further cemetery commissions, Lewerentz was more renowned for his expertise in cemetery design. With each proposal he gave detailed instructions for the disposition of graves, always subordinating the individual memorial to the effect of the whole. If such restrictions constituted a prerequisite for preserving both the communal character of the burial ground and its symbolic ordering of nature, they also remained controversial.[9] During the 1930s Lewerentz began taking these principles to new extremes. Arguing that upright memorial stones interrupt the peace and solemnity of a cemetery landscape, he proposed horizontal memorial stones for the area around the chapel in his entry to the Kviberg Cemetery competition, restricting standing monuments to the peripheral hillside areas. As he elaborated in 1939, in an unpublished essay on cemeteries: "An upright monument characterizes more the struggle and competition between individuals that life implies than the inference of a memorial slab concerning the life of perhaps a more peaceable human being." He sought a more unified expression of communal values through the symbolic ordering of nature: "The large cemetery must as a rule endure as a fragment of nature with suitable character of land and vegetation. Grave monuments constitute an architectural addition which should work with, rather than disturb, the lines of the terrain."[10]

During the late 1950s, when the Stockholm Cemetery Authority again solicited his expertise on elements of the Woodland Cemetery landscape, Lewerentz broadened his vision of a burial environment undisturbed by memorials with his most experimental proposal: a Memorial Ground atop the ridge west of the main entrance. According to regulations for cremation issued in November 1957, ashes could be distributed in unmarked ground, either strewn upon its surface or buried without urns. The Stockholm Cemetery Authority, confronting a shortage of adequate burial space, was eager to ensure the popularity of this most economic form of interment. The authority envisaged "a monumental construction of some sort" to enhance the visibility of this new form of common grave.[11] Using minimal gestures to mark the area reserved for depositing ashes, Lewerentz countered the Cemetery Authority's request for architectural monumentality with a visionary evocation of the forest's inherent power. By arranging layers of elm trees along the edge of the pine forest, he clarified the relationship between the main cemetery entrance and the pedestrian ascent along the eastern face of the ridge. Throughout the pine forest at the summit, ashes could be spread over the forest floor, which Lewerentz preserved in its natural state, covered with heather and wild blueberry. Immediately to the south he provided a grassy clearing in which ashes could be buried without urns. He limited memorial flowers to a zone along the pedestrian route where he provided inset stones as a subtle indication of the precinct's boundaries. The unobtrusive character of his Memorial Ground underscores the inherent theme of bodily reconciliation with nature.

Despite its pagan ramifications, Lewerentz's idea represents a modern response to the fear of bodily decay, enabling a return to fundamental Old Testament precepts that emphasize death as a natural event: ashes to ashes and dust to dust. The value of cremation is in honoring the life of the human spirit over the degradation of the body in traditional burial. Lewerentz sought an appropriate expression for this conception of death. While his renunciation of architectural means defies heroic visions of modernism, it reflects aspirations for humility, equality, and deference to nature that are deeply rooted in contemporary Swedish culture.

Whereas twentieth-century adherents of the artistic avant-garde strove to achieve the unity of art and life, Swedish architects of the period formed a more complex understanding of the total work of art. In the modern cemetery, they aspired to fuse art with nature, death with life. Landscape's very indeterminacy made it a salient vehicle to reanimate the social dimension of art. By severing familiar correspondences between form and content, Modern Movement architects laid bare the question of meaning, an issue made more poignant in cemetery design by the breakdown of traditional religious values. If the nineteenth-century suburban cemetery conceived of as a parklike urban adjunct reflected the void engendered by that spiritual crisis, early twentieth-century Swedish architects responded by imbuing their cemeteries with a more fundamental spiritual content that was grounded in psychological realities and experiential rituals rather than doctrinal symbolism. The history of Asplund and Lewerentz's collaborative efforts at the Woodland Cemetery reveals their persistent suppression of the competition proposal's overt symbolism—its primordial forest teeming with burial mounds of pagan inspiration and tombs of neoclassical provenance—in favor of using palpable experience in support of the ineffable and the imagined. Such amplification of the symbolic through recourse to ritualized experience characterizes the most

Sigurd Lewerentz's Memorial Ground at the Woodland Cemetery of 1958–61: entry route past stone threshold for depositing flowers *(left)*; route along the crest of the ridge adjoining the woodland for depositing ashes.

significant of Asplund's and Lewerentz's cemeteries, in which landscape is sensed as much as it is viewed.

While the search for the spiritual and the ineffable that arose during the early decades of the twentieth century in opposition to positivist and materialist philosophies was an influential force in modern painting, its effect on landscape design has been relatively unacknowledged. For certain proponents of the architectural avant-garde, the spiritual was a device for empowerment, authorizing the artist/architect as the privileged interpreter of the modern world.[12] Swedish architects of the period were more humble in their aspirations. Focusing on the *humane* as well as the human, they made their appeal to the inner being, seeking to enhance the spiritual essence of daily life. As the Swedish poet Gunnar Ekelöf has argued: "One of the most important things in all art: Leave a respectable part up to the reader, the observer, the listener, the participant. There shall be an empty setting at the ready-laid table. It is his."[13]

FIVE

A LANDSCAPE "FIT FOR A DEMOCRACY"
Jože Plečnik at Prague Castle

> I don't want anything great, I want things small; these I will make great.
>
> —Jože Plečnik

Seeking to transform Prague Castle from a symbol of Habsburg domination into a reflection of its role as the seat of a democratic government, in 1920 Tomáš Garrigue Masaryk, president of the newly created democratic republic of Czechoslovakia, appointed Slovenian architect Jože Plečnik to serve as castle architect. His protracted search for architectural forms capable of embodying the cultural spirit of his fellow Slavs led Plečnik to transform the landscape of Prague Castle during the years following World War I in an idiosyncratic manner—one that is unique in twentieth-century architecture. Despite a conscious evocation of the milieu's cultural history in his designs, Plečnik encountered considerable opposition to his work in Prague Castle that ultimately led him to resign from his post. Examination of the social and political motivations underlying the interventions Plečnik made in Prague Castle between 1920 and 1935 suggests reasons for the resistance that this work sustained during both the early democratic and succeeding communist eras in Czechoslovakia, which stemmed from his recourse to figuration as the means to a more open, "democratic" approach to symbolism and meaning.[1]

Plečnik's architecture is difficult to classify. Like many of his Modern Movement contemporaries, he sought forms that were new yet grounded in human experience and cultural memory. Unlike his functionalist counterparts in Prague, Plečnik anticipated the dangers of severing architecture from the nourishment of the past; he sought an organic relationship with history, whereby historic forms would continue to have meaning, albeit transformed, in the present. His method of incorporating historical references is largely without precedent. While eschewing established formal means, Plečnik produced elements that rely on specificity rather than abstraction. He based the unity in his work on discontinuities rather than connections; inverting the expectations of classical architecture to embody the whole in the part, he posited a new relationship of part to whole wherein an individual form, while complete in itself, is understood as an element of an incomplete and implied whole. Starting from the symbolic potential of an architectural fragment, he initiated a process of reconstruction, a means to an end rather than an end in itself. This expanded power of the individual architectural gesture facilitated Masaryk's cultural aspirations—the construction of a national identity for the new democratic Czechoslovak Republic.

From Vienna to Prague, 1894–1921

Plečnik's interest in his Slavic heritage was nourished both in his native Ljubljana and in Vienna, where he undertook his professional training and launched his independent architectural practice during the final decades of the Austro-Hungarian Empire. Pan-Slavism was particularly intense in fin de siècle Vienna owing to the minority status afforded the Slavs after Emperor Francis Joseph granted the Hungarian majority greater autonomy in 1867 to avoid splitting the empire. Although he carried out several important commissions in the Austrian capital, including the Zacherlhaus (1903–5) and Church of the Holy Spirit (1908–13), Plečnik accepted the post of professor of architectural composition at Prague's School of Applied Arts in 1911, a position he held until 1921. Official opposition may have prompted the architect to abandon Vienna and its rising tenor of German nationalism in favor of Prague, where, in a more liberal political climate, critics looked favorably upon his work as a creative individual and a Slav.

To avoid competing with Czech architects, Plečnik initially undertook only minor design commissions and devoted himself primarily to teaching, using the long vacations of the academic year to further his research into Slavic art. This fruitful period of contemplation stimulated his belief in the Slav mission. Just as he encouraged his students to value their cultural roots, Plečnik made frequent visits to his native Ljubljana to probe the distinctive aspects of his own Slovenian heritage. Plečnik's Slavic self-consciousness proved provident for his architectural ambitions. The murder of Archduke Francis Ferdinand in June 1914 and the subsequent collapse of the Austro-Hungarian Empire at the end of World War I led to the unification of Czechs, Slovaks, Germans, Ruthenes, and Magyars in the democratic republic of Czechoslovakia, with Tomáš Garrigue Masaryk as president. The arbitrary nature of this political alliance led Masaryk to a self-conscious search for a new national identity capable of surmounting cultural differences.

Prague Castle (Hradčany), 1920–35

After a competition held in 1920 for the reorganization of Prague Castle's Southern Ramparts Garden failed to elicit any promising proposals, the organizing committee, on which Plečnik served, asked him to submit a design for the western portion of the site, known as the Paradise Garden. While developing a proposal that related to both the castle complex and its immediate environs, Plečnik met President Masaryk, who appointed him castle architect. Plečnik's Slovenian roots were initially regarded as an attribute, as Chancellor Přemysl Sámal subsequently argued:

> He has the respect of the entire Czech artistic community, itself a guarantee that the building works might proceed without controversy. Had the works been entrusted to a Czech architect we would, given the well-known tendency of the art world to bicker, have unleashed a frightful welter of contradictory opinion, and we should not have got as far as we have today.[2]

In Plečnik, Masaryk sought an architect capable of expressing in architectural form those values that he associated with the new Czechoslovak state, delineated in his aims for the castle complex:

> The purpose of this project is to render the Castle a seat of a democratic president. The complete reconstruction of the Castle's exterior and interior must be simple but artistically regal, symbolizing the notion of the state's independence and democracy. The nation looks upon the Castle as a national seat and therefore, in order that the Castle be transformed from an edifice conceived and executed in the spirit of the monarchy to that of a democratic castle, not only the President but also his government must be mindful of the changes.[3]

In this transformation Masaryk sought a pan-national acropolis embodying a new Slavic style, capable of fulfilling ceremonial as well as symbolic requirements:

> This is where the artistic making of a democratic State symbolism and ceremony comes in. . . . [It] is necessary to think of a democratic garden and park, etc.—all these are problems, and serious ones at that, which should involve the highest intelligences in the field of art. Ceremony is the expression of an idea to be received by the eye and the senses in general, and thus very important from the viewpoint of instruction and education.[4]

While President Masaryk envisioned an architecture capable of engaging the citizenry in self-education, he did not limit his vision to modifying the castle complex; he also sought to integrate the castle with its rural and urban environs, as he professed in March 1920:

> I frequently observe with what reverence and loving devotion people come to the castle to see the thousand years of our architectural history. So immediately after my return from abroad I made arrangements for the necessary repairs to be carried out and for the various parts of the castle to be properly surveyed. My aim is to make the castle a worthy monument to our past. On the Letná, as on the northern and southwestern part of the Petrín, I wish to lay out parks. . . . To avoid continuing the irregular communication of the old city without a plan and for the future, I believe it is necessary to solve the problem of the regulation of and communications in the venerable part of Prague.[5]

This declaration became a manifesto for Plečnik, who accepted the appointment as castle architect in November of that year.

The existing architectural milieu was replete with political overtones. A feudal seat founded in 884–85 by the Přemysl ruler Bořivoj, Prague Castle came to embody the political, religious, and cultural history of the emerging Czech state. During the fourteenth century Charles IV, German emperor and king of Bohemia, transformed Prague into a seat of the Holy Roman Empire and began construction of the Gothic cathedral. Because the major building campaigns undertaken by Habsburg kings Ferdinand I and Rudolf II failed to give the castle the grandeur of comparable monarchic seats in Vienna or Paris, Empress Maria Theresa (reigned 1740–80) engaged court architect Niccolo Pacassi to transform the medieval castle, a fortified city with its piecemeal baroque development, into a

Prague Castle viewed from Charles Bridge by Petr Parlér of Gmünd (from 1357).

palace—an embodiment of Austro-Hungarian domination. Despite its extensive physical embellishment, the castle became an empty symbol under the Habsburgs, who used it infrequently and only for ceremonial purposes. The complex thus fell into a period of decline that extended until the end of the Austro-Hungarian Empire.

In pursuit of a "democratic" means of expression, Plečnik sought to counteract certain manifestations of Habsburg rule. Through a relatively modest series of interventions carried out incrementally, he amended the castle's imperial overtones by forging new connections, internally as well as externally, with the city and surrounding countryside. As a result of these changes, Prague Castle came to reflect the spirit of Charles Bridge (from 1357), which operated both as an extended threshold removed from the space of the city and as a monumental roadway linking Prague's Lesser Quarter, at the base of Hradčany (the rocky promontory on which Prague Castle is situated), with the Old Town across the Vltava River. Plečnik's concern with issues of access and visibility was simultaneously physical and historic in nature. He countered a set of specific historic forms, with their attendant iconography, with elements that were equally precise in form, although smaller in scale and more ambiguous in meaning. To modify the imperial overtones of the eighteenth-century additions, he made frequent reference to the castle's prior history. His modifications to the first courtyard demonstrate his selective attitude toward that history.

First Castle Court, 1921–25

The form of the first court as a *cour d'honneur* opening to Hradčany Square emanated from Niccolo Pacassi's additions of 1763 to 1771. The space is dominated by the Matthias Gate (1614), a ceremonial entrance that originally overlooked the castle's western moat. To provide an antechamber for the presidential reception suite, Plečnik proposed to close the gateway and fill its upper zone with glass. To counteract this subversion of its historic role, he bracketed the gate with a pair of flagstaffs that extend twenty-five meters in height, each cut from a single tree.[6] These rustic wooden flagstaffs with their gilded bases and tops are important indications of Plečnik's intentions. Historians trace their forms from such diverse examples as the pylons of Egyptian temple complexes and the flagpoles in Venice's Piazza San Marco.[7] Such recourse to multiple precedents was a hallmark of Plečnik's work in Prague Castle; it was a means to imbue the complex with broader cultural relevance. Framing a rusticated facade

(left) The First Castle Court, with the Matthias Gate of 1614, facades renovated by Niccolo Pacassi in 1763–71, and Jože Plečnik's rustic wooden flagstaffs of 1921–25. Prague Castle Archive, fond SDSsPH, inv.č. 1176.

(right) Jože Plečnik's Columned Hall of 1927–28, opening directly to the first and second courts (since modified). Prague Castle Archive, fond SDSsPH, inv.č. 670.

98   A LANDSCAPE "FIT FOR A DEMOCRACY"

of stone, the flagstaffs combine rustic simplicity and formal sophistication, thereby satisfying Plečnik's aim of overcoming distinctions between "popular" and "high" cultures.

Plečnik's courtyard paving reflects his intended entry sequence. He restructured the presidential entry route by inserting an open passage to the right of the Matthias Gate, while redirecting visitors through his Columned Hall to the left of the historic portal. He created this lofty volume in the manner of a peristyle court by boldly opening up three stories of the eighteenth-century structure that formerly housed the kitchens. This hall, since modified, originally opened directly to both the first and the second courts.[8] Plečnik lined the hall's plaster walls with false colonnades of gray stone and sheathed its ceiling in copper, held in place with a grid of brass tacks. Through its formal autonomy the Columned Hall provided a hiatus in the continuity of the Theresian complex, a threshold capable of preserving the entry court's historic appearance while simultaneously altering its processional sequence.

As the Matthias Gate's vitreous enclosure was never built, Plečnik's interventions in the first court had the force he intended only following Masaryk's death, when the Renaissance gateway was draped in black so that the public filed directly into the Columned Hall to observe the president's body lying in state.[9] Plečnik's proposal to close the gate would have diminished the hierarchical value of the first court, yet this gesture was consistent with his broader aim of providing a variety of approaches to the complex to enhance accessibility while granting greater primacy to the third castle court as a ceremonial anteroom for state functions. Although the incomplete state of these modifications led to misunderstandings concerning his intentions, the creation of thresholds out of boundaries remained an important tactic for transforming the castle from a symbol of Habsburg domination into a more democratic form of expression.

Third Castle Court, 1927–32

Plečnik's transformation of the castle's third court was prompted by an archaeological survey undertaken as part of Masaryk's broader initiative to acquire a systematic understanding of the castle's early history. As the president subsequently argued: "Only if we respect the heritage of our forefathers will we find our own path toward freedom and continuous development."[10] The courtyard's existing structures are replete with historic significance: the Bishop's Palace, its oldest extant structure and seat of the bishops of Prague from the tenth to the twelfth centuries; St. Vitus Cathedral, begun by Matthew of Arras in 1344, with its historically dominant Golden Portal (1385–99), created for Charles IV by Petr Parlér of Gmünd; the Royal Palace, with ninth-century origins, enlarged under Charles IV (from 1333) and Vladislav Jagiello (from 1483); and the subsequent additions of the Summer Palace of Rudolf II (1583) and presidential offices, resheathed in Pacassi's eighteenth-century facades. A wall separating the court's two primary levels was surmounted by the St. George Fountain (1373), which marked the site of an early source of water for the complex.

To enhance the third court's spatial continuity without sacrificing the integrity of its existing buildings, Plečnik devised a warped ground plane capable of linking their diverse levels. He lowered the northern portion of the courtyard, exposing the foundations of an earlier basilica, while raising the segment to the east, revealing its original level in the Eagle Fountain that he created at the entry to the Royal Palace. To preserve access to the archaeological remains, he covered the excavations with a structure of reinforced concrete that left those foundations nearest the cathedral exposed to view. His adjustments to the numerous doors that open onto the third court attest to the site's prior complexity, while his ramp descending to the adjoining Royal Palace court enables the diverse historic layers to be perceived with a new simultaneity. To reinforce the

(left) The third castle court viewed from the tower of St. Vitus Cathedral, showing Plečnik's gridded paving pattern of 1927–32. Prague Castle Archive, fond SDSsPH, inv.č. 1255.

(right) The St. George Fountain atop Plečnik's new base of 1929–30 and his obelisk, erected in 1928, both aligned with the paving grid.

resulting spatial continuity, Plečnik gave the courtyard surface a gridded paving pattern the geometry of which both originates with the entry to the governmental offices and aligns with the St. George Fountain, which he elevated on a new base at its former site (1929–30).[11]

Plečnik also used the grid to rationalize the position of an obelisk that he introduced to draw the visitor into the third court from its western gateway. The obelisk was a major theme in his reorganization of Prague Castle. Masaryk originated the idea of erecting a monument to the Czech legionaries killed in World War I for another site in the castle grounds. After the solid granite shaft broke during transport to the site, the broken remnant sat unused for three years before the disconsolate Plečnik could adapt it to a different purpose. In 1928, to commemorate the tenth anniversary of the founding of the Czechoslovak Republic, he gave its broken end a suggestive shirred profile and erected the monolith on a concrete base in the third court. Recalling the president's original impetus for the memorial, Plečnik sited the monument over a pre-Romanesque burial ground, where the tomb of a noble warrior had been excavated in July of that year.[12] Unlike its historic antecedents that terminate axial vistas, thereby controlling vision, Plečnik's obelisk deflects attention to the court's historic components. Like his many contributions to the castle complex, the monument destabilizes meaning to ground it in the interpretive powers of the individual imagination.

Protruding from the southeastern corner of the third court is the threshold to a stair that Plečnik created in 1929–31 to connect the third courtyard with the Southern Ramparts Garden. In its design and siting the stair combines references to the castle's mythic origins and early history with a novel means of access and visibility. Plečnik placed his stair near a Romanesque tower, one of three tenth-century castle approaches that originally provided access from the city to both the Royal Palace and the cathedral's dominant southern portal. This role had been undermined when the tower's rectangular form was embedded in palace extensions of the fifteenth century.[13] Rather than emulate the closed defensive form of the historic tower, he created an open stair within a caesura that he excised from Pacassi's eighteenth-century facades. Plečnik oriented the descent to a view of Vyšehrad, a rocky outcrop overlooking the Vltava that was traditionally (though mistakenly) interpreted as the site of Prague's earliest settlement. In a gesture that affirms the moral and religious foundations of Masaryk's humanistic socialism, the stair also aligns with the cathedral's southern portal, which served as its primary entrance until the

Plečnik's threshold to the "Bull Stair" of 1929-31 (leading from the third castle court to the Southern Ramparts Garden), adorned with Damian Pešan's figures of Queen Libuše and her consort, the peasant farmer Přemysl.

nave and facade were completed in 1929. This axis marks the medieval site for the coronation of Czech kings, a ceremony that evoked the mythic origins of Hradčany under the founders of the Přemysl dynasty, Queen Libuše and her consort, the peasant farmer Přemysl. Plečnik's threshold projects into the third court, its form evoking these mythic foundations.

According to the early twelfth-century chronicles of Cosmas, from a site on Vyšehrad Libuše envisioned "a town the glory of which will reach to the stars" on a site where her subjects would find a man building a threshold (in Czech, *práh*) for his cottage.[14] He was duly found on Hradčany, and the city was named Praha. Plečnik created four columns, representing the mythic doorsill, surmounted by four bulls that allude to the labors of the farmer Přemysl. Plečnik sought broader connotations for such forms; in addition to their association with Minoan iconography, the bulls have both classical Athenian and vernacular Slovakian antecedents.[15] Damian Pešan's sculptural reliefs crowning the threshold reaffirm its association with the local myth; incised in gold on the exposed ends of the wooden roof beams, the figures of Queen Libuše and her consort soar in a trance-like state, holding aloft the clothlike copper roof.

Prague Castle Gardens: Paradise Garden (Rajská Zahrada), 1920-25

Plečnik's strategy of forging new spatial connections to augment consciousness of the nation's history derives from his first undertaking for Prague Castle, the redesign of the Paradise Garden that lay just below the wing that he converted to house the presidential offices and apartments. The Paradise Garden originated in the mid-sixteenth century as a walled appendage to the Summer Palace built for Archduke Ferdinand of Tyrol; it was the first of a series of baroque gardens developed atop a former rubbish heap along the steep southern slopes of Hradčany. This self-contained and private enclave took the form of a Renaissance *giardino segreto* (secret garden) adapted to the sloping site. It included a circular gazebo built in 1617 for the Emperor Matthias on the exposed corner of the precinct wall; this was the first structure within the castle gardens to take advantage of the urban prospect, an important theme in Plečnik's modifications.[16]

Vestiges of a pair of monumental stairs uncovered beneath the garden's terminal segment in 1919 prompted Plečnik's design, which includes a broad staircase rising from a grassy sward to a gate that he inserted in the fortification wall.[17] To reinforce this transgression of the garden's historic boundary, he projected the stair's uppermost landing beyond the

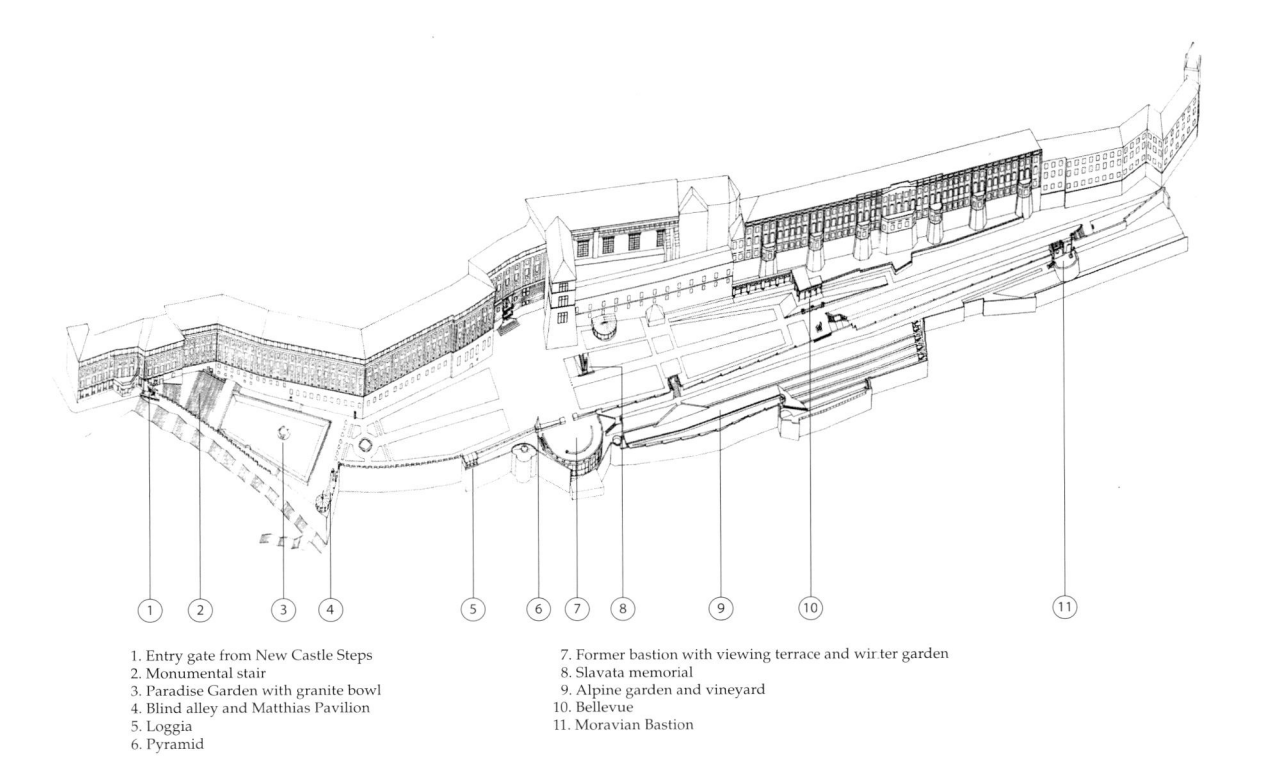

1. Entry gate from New Castle Steps
2. Monumental stair
3. Paradise Garden with granite bowl
4. Blind alley and Matthias Pavilion
5. Loggia
6. Pyramid
7. Former bastion with viewing terrace and winter garden
8. Slavata memorial
9. Alpine garden and vineyard
10. Bellevue
11. Moravian Bastion

Axonometric of the Paradise Garden and Southern Ramparts Garden. Drawing by E. Herbert. From *Josip Plečnik: An Architect of Prague Castle*, Zdeněk Lukeš, Damjan Prelovšek, and Tomáš Valena, eds., 1996.

precinct wall so that it extends into the New Castle Steps that ascend from Prague's Lesser Quarter. The central column separating the dual gateway is a characteristic feature of Plečnik's architecture; it serves both to thwart axial vistas and to engage the visitor in acts of interpretation. On the central landing of his stair Plečnik intended to place the obelisk that Masaryk envisioned as a memorial to the soldiers lost in World War I, its form seemingly extruded from the palace wall, which it resembled in profile.[18] Near the top of the shaft was to be an eternal flame befitting its memorial purpose, with Jan Štursa's sculpture of the Czech lion and Slovak cross rising above the flames. After the monolith was damaged in transport to the site, Plečnik devised a second, hollow version with an internal stair. He ultimately abandoned the idea of including an obelisk in this portion of the castle precinct after this second attempt resulted in the shaft's being broken in removal from the quarry. For the garden's opening ceremonies he marked its intended site with a black cube crowned with a wreath, a memorial to a lost memorial. Set on the edge of the stair landing, the cube *(left)* Plečnik's gate leading from the New Castle Steps to the Paradise Garden, 1924–25.

(right) View from inside the gate to the Paradise Garden, with a black cube on the stair landing marking the site intended for Plečnik's unrealized obelisk. Damjan Prelovšek, *Jože Plečnik, 1872–1957: Architectura Perennis*, 1997.

served as a temporary war memorial while simultaneously commemorating the obelisk's ill fate.

The Paradise Garden at the base of these stairs represents a radical interpretation of a traditional theme. To emulate the historical evocation of paradise in the medieval cloister garden, Plečnik created a curbed sweep of lawn dominated by a monolithic granite basin, which hovers on a minimal support of two rectangular blocks and marks the historic site of the baths of Ferdinand II.[19] Just as the obelisk was seemingly freed from the wall, so the basin, with its protruding bottom surface, is assertively free of the ground—a geometrically pure center suspended over a reflective marble surface and set in a grassy carpet. Rather than terminate the garden sequence in the literal verticality of an obelisk, Plečnik used the basin's more suggestive form to transmute the dominant horizontal focus of the Southern Ramparts Garden to a vertical orientation. The basin's exceptional size (4.3-meter diameter) operates together with the viewing distance imposed by the lawn to discourage any complete grasp of its volume; one can see into it only from the presidential offices and reception suite above. Plečnik reinforced the basin's association with the office of the president by aligning it with the doorway to the official reception rooms, which he elaborated with delicate gilt symbols of the Czechs and Slovaks (1922). This substitution of the role of a democratic elected official for the watchful eye of god in the traditional Paradise Garden conforms with Plečnik's vision of the president as the Christian Good Shepherd watching over his flock. He refrained from idealizing this representation of paradise by shifting the stone curbing that edges the grassy sward to accommodate an existing yew, the oldest specimen in the castle gardens. Rather than reinterpret the garden's historic form, Plečnik contemplated the problem anew, representing paradise as an inaccessible ideal while deforming its edges to accommodate an element of nature.

Although a wall originally separated the Paradise Garden from the adjoining garden on the ramparts, at the time Plečnik took on the problem of revitalizing this segment of the castle precinct the neglect of the intervening period had mitigated the formal contrasts between them. To unify the garden sequence further, he destroyed the wall, leaving three baroque piers as remnants of the historic boundary, which he transformed into a spatial entity by aligning them with a row of conically trimmed hornbeams. Terminating this threshold is a "blind" alley that he excised from the constructed terrain adjoining a projecting segment of the rampart surmounted by the Matthias Pavilion. Here Plečnik provided visitors an opportunity to withdraw from the garden sequence, drawn to the vista afforded by this "passage" with no other destination. Like the Columned Hall of the first courtyard and the "Bull Stair" descending from the second, this blind alley is a further example of a threshold forged from a historic boundary.

The Paradise Garden with Plečnik's granite basin of 1923-25 and overlook to Prague's Mala Strana (Lesser Quarter) *(left)*; the "blind" alley at the threshold between the Paradise Garden and Southern Ramparts Garden, terminating in the Matthias Pavilion of 1617.

Southern Ramparts Garden (Na Valech), 1921-27

As with his modifications to the courtyard sequence, Plečnik's modifications to the Southern Ramparts Garden lying immediately east of the Paradise Garden concern issues of access and visibility that are both physical and historic in nature. Originally planted as a vineyard, the terrain atop the southern ramparts had been developed after 1860 as an English park, with a series of paths that meandered amid an irregular layout of trees. Plečnik began his reorganization of the Ramparts Garden by extending a path straight from a baroque fountain (1703), which he repositioned below the Paradise Garden, to the ramparts' eastern gate. While giving the garden a certain unity, comparable to Pacassi's eighteenth-century facades, this walkway provided a foundation for the architect's numerous interventions along its length.

Plečnik's letters to his assistant Otto Rothmayer indicate his concern for the multiple vistas available from each addition to the garden sequence. Rejecting the picturesque focus on a sequence of static vantage points, Plečnik structured circulation through the garden to take advantage of the myriad "eye-catchers" available in the urban panorama. He sculpted the ground plane to provide a variety of routes, while maintaining the large trees on the site, originally planted according to a picturesque concept of order, as they contrast his more geometric treatment of the terrain. To enhance visual connections with the city below, he selectively diminished the height of the rampart wall and created a series of overlooks and descents to the garden's lower levels. Few of these elements were completely new; in addition to the blind alley, Plečnik added a bellevue (1924) at the garden's highest point and a loggia (1926–27) atop the lowered rampart wall.

In his modifications to the Southern Ramparts Garden, Plečnik encountered a new set of challenges to the castle's intended democratic appearance. Reflecting the site's historic role of defense, the rampart walls countered the image of democratic accessibility to which Masaryk aspired; by isolating the castle visually, moreover, they emphasized the precinct's monumentality. Although both the Paradise and the Southern Ramparts Gardens originated during the Renaissance, when this narrow strip of land was created atop the debris from a fire that devastated the castle in 1541, their bounding walls bore differing cultural associations. Unlike the walls that originally lined the Renaissance garden, built to ensure privacy rather than to provide military protection, the southern ramparts were erected following the revolution of 1848, when the Prague citizenry sought to turn the Habsburg Empire into a constitutional monarchy.[20] In contrast to his treatment of the Renaissance walls, which Plečnik shored up and preserved, he reconfigured the Theresian ramparts by lowering their height and punctuating the linear sequence with a variety of elements, including granite spheres recalling those in the sixteenth-century Royal Garden across Stag Moat.

The bastions posed a further provocation to the garden's intended ambience of openness and accessibility. Plečnik sought to overcome their defensive character by transgressing their historic bounding walls and using them to enhance visual relationships with the city. He differentiated between that adjoining the Theresian wing of the Royal Palace, which emanated from the period of Charles IV, and the pair of nineteenth-century bastions that lined the ramparts, associated with the hated period of Habsburg domination. Transforming the earlier bastion into an aviary (1924), he drew attention to its historic roots through a stair that descends to its Přemyslid foundations.[21] While maintaining selected components of the Habsburg bastions, he sought to transform their significance. The first became a semicircular viewing platform above a winter garden, which Plečnik sheathed in glass to obviate the wall's defensive appearance (1923–24).[22] He lowered the height of the Moravian Bastion and covered it in brick to create a second viewing platform (1922–23). He added a slender obelisk topped by an Ionic capital and golden orb to mark its presence from afar; streaks of lightning bursting from this gleaming sphere allude to a line from the former Slovak national anthem. An altarlike table shielded by a pergola provides a respite from the castle grounds. A pair of mottoes inscribed on the table base accentuate the humility that Masaryk brought to the

(*left*) Viewing platform atop the winter garden (no longer extant) that Plečnik created in 1924 from the first bastion of the Southern Ramparts Garden. Prague Castle Archive, fond SDSsPH, inv.č. 1363.

(*right*) Plečnik's transformation of the Moravian Bastion of 1922–23, with an obelisk topped by a golden orb emitting streaks of lightning. Prague Castle Archive, fond SDSsPH, inv.č. 1352.

office of president: "A majority of people can be helpful to a single man, rather than an individual to the majority" and "Four eyes see more than two."[23]

Reiterating these transgressions of the Habsburg bastions, Plečnik embellished an existing stair to a lower garden by opening up its lateral walls and inserting central columns in the openings. Damian Pešan's evocative sculpture of a female head that Plečnik placed over the threshold (1924–25) may be a further reference to the legendary Queen Libuše; such recourse to elusive iconography remained a hallmark of his work in Prague Castle. This sirenlike figure beckons visitors to descend below the ramparts, where Plečnik organized the sloping terrain as a series of terraces, linked with diagonal ramps and planted as a vineyard to reflect the site's prior history. Boulders strewn about the segment nearest the winter garden give the vineyard the rustic qualities of an "alpine" garden, reiterating the thematic dialogue of primitive and classical by which he sought to make the castle's complex history palpable.

Despite the linear form of the Southern Ramparts Garden, Plečnik offered visitors a variety of routes along its four hundred–meter length while amplifying its cross axes. In the vicinity of the castle's historic southern portal, he created a monumental stair overlooking the Ramparts Garden; its form contrasts the more intimate "Bull" canopy in the third court to which it leads. He reinforced this threshold's Minoan allusions by including tapered columns in the stair landings, modeled after those at the Palace of Minos in Knossos. Plečnik reiterated the stair's visual links with the city's purported ancient origins by placing a pyramid astride the lowered rampart wall (a reference to Rome's Pyramid of Cestius on the

(left) The boulder-strewn Alpine Garden below the Southern Ramparts Garden.

(right) The reconfigured terrain around the Slavata Monument, exposing the historic level of the site where the king's governor landed when he was jettisoned from the tower of the Royal Palace in 1618. Prague Castle Archive, fond SDSsPH, inv.č. 1368.

Aurelian wall) that successively obscures and reframes views of Vyšehrad during descent to the garden below. While such recourse to Mediterranean imagery remained controversial, it provided an effective counterpoint to the castle's Germanic aspects, furthering Masaryk's vision of a Slavic acropolis.

In his modifications to existing garden elements Plečnik stressed ideological affinities between Masaryk's democratic ideals and early Czech history. He elevated the existing "Hercules" fountain on a new base that he decorated with symbols of the unification and concordance of the Czechs and the Slovaks, an issue associated with the region's first legendary rulers that was also fundamental to Masaryk's political philosophy.[24] Two obelisks commemorating the second defenestration of Prague mark the spots where the king's governors landed when they were jettisoned from the windows of the Royal Palace by Protestant noblemen in 1618, provoking the uprising of the Czech Estates against the Habsburgs in the Thirty Years' War. To enhance awareness of the first memorial, dedicated to Jaroslav Bořita and visually obscured in a reentrant angle of the palace, Plečnik lowered the ground under the second obelisk, commemorating Vilém Slavata, to reveal the site's historic level. He reinforced the religious significance of this historic event in a number of ways. Beside the Slavata Monument he added a giant balustrade, oval in section, in a form reminiscent of an altar rail. Together the obelisk and the balustrade form a cross, like those Plečnik added atop both historic monuments, reflecting the Catholic triumph in the Thirty Years' War as well as the religious foundation of Masaryk's humanistic socialism.

New Bastion Garden (Na Baště), 1927–32

Plečnik's garden atop the new bastion recalls certain problems he confronted in the third castle courtyard. The site consisted of two segments at different levels: the castle's fourth courtyard, bounded by two wings of Theresian origin, and an extension to the earlier fortification, where a horse ramp provided access to the seventeenth-century Spanish Hall. Rather than unify the bastion's discrete levels, which were separated by a brick palisade, Plečnik drew upon their differences to heighten visual links with the adjoining Stag Moat, a natural ravine that reinforced the castle's defensive bulwarks when Rudolf II had it enclosed to create a deer park. To mark the limits of the earlier fortification, Plečnik inserted a low stone wall traversed by a variation on Bramante's Belvedere staircase in

The New Bastion Garden of 1930–32, with its historic segments joined by a stair inspired by Bramante *(left)*; concrete retaining wall and stair of cyclopean masonry terminating the New Bastion Garden and leading to Stag Moat, 1932–35. Prague Castle Archive, fond SDSsPH, inv.č. 1422/1418.

the Vatican. He reiterated this historic division by further subdividing the garden into three main areas: a paved terrace in the lower court, a gravel upper terrace planted with a columnar grid of cypress trees, and a grassy lawn with a ramped stair leading to the Spanish Hall. Plečnik's paving in the lowest level—where granite strips marking rectangular subdivisions frame pebbles set in grout—is a rustic variation of that in his third court. This geometric order contrasts with the segment of lawn adjoining the Spanish Hall, where remnants of a fortification wall from the period of Přemysl Otakar II (ruled 1253–78) were discovered while construction was in progress. Plečnik distributed those rough stones in an irregular pattern around a primitive stone-and-wood pergola, which he created to shelter the historic remains. Such archaism was not only consistent with his additions to the other castle courts and gardens—the fir flagstaffs in the first court, the "Bull Stair" in the third, and the alpinetum below the Southern Ramparts Garden—but it also provided a visual transition from the castle's paved inner courts to the rough "wilderness" of Stag Moat. Plečnik reiterated this primitive gesture in the far corner of the garden, where his stair of rough cyclopean masonry descending to the ravine of Stag Moat contrasts both the smooth stuccoed arcade of his retaining wall and the precise profiles of its urnlike stone balusters.

To augment access to this remote segment of the castle sequence, Plečnik created internal passages linking the New Bastion Garden with the first and second courts as well as a pedestrian footbridge leading to a vehicular bridge that crosses Stag Moat. This footbridge was intended as part of an unrealized circulation route by which he proposed to link the entire castle perimeter, transforming the precinct's formerly defensive perimeter into an open circulation zone.

Bastion Overlooking Stag Moat, 1922–24

Outside the castle bulwarks, beyond Stag Moat, is a series of gardens and pavilions begun in the mid-sixteenth century by Ferdinand I. Calling this part of the castle complex "the most beautiful architectonic poem of central Europe," Plečnik argued, "There is no greater task than that of adapting them."[25] In conjunction with his schemes for restructuring the vehicular approach to Prague Castle, he made numerous proposals for this segment of the castle landscape.[26] Although few of his suggestions for revitalizing the Royal Garden were carried out, Plečnik made a significant contribution to a more remote site on this far side of Stag Moat.[27] On an isolated spot that afforded a magnificent view back to the castle, President Masaryk had placed a simple bench beneath a linden tree, where he could seek respite from his official duties. Plečnik amplified the inherent isolation of this presidential vantage point by erecting a low bastion around the tree. He elaborated its access route to enhance his patron's sense of removal from daily concerns within the castle precinct. After penetrating a wall that prohibits any outward prospect, the president would encounter a sequence of terraces lined with grapevines and linked by a flight of steps that rise on axis with the linden, which Plečnik created to restore the view gradually. The architect used the tree as he would a central column, to deflect a dominant visual axis and engage the visitor in myriad vistas. The manner in which his bastion elaborates upon this simple presidential ritual exemplifies Plečnik's architectural objective: "I don't want anything great, I want things small; these I will make great."[28] The effectiveness of his piecemeal interventions in Prague Castle derives not only from their historic grounding but also from his ability to apply such logic at scales ranging from the detail to the broader landscape.

The Politics of Interpretation

In his efforts to revitalize Prague Castle as a historic construct, Plečnik dissolved Theresian surface continuities with great precision in order to posit a new reality. Suspending those elements that once embodied a unified

Access route to the presidential bastion of 1922–24, flanked by a grape arbor *(left)*; view from the presidential bastion across Stag Moat to Prague Castle. Prague Castle Archive, fond SDSsPH, inv.č. 1515 01/02.

concept of power, he introduced pauses, silences, intervals, suspensions. Although his tactic of providing new access to the past by opening historic sites up to reinterpretation and thereby giving them new life in the present was concordant with the most progressive reconstruction theories of the day, the risks involved in such an approach were considerable. If the resulting experience is analogous to the visual simultaneity of an archaeological plan, the significance of these gestures also relies on historic memory, which the communists sought to eradicate during their political control of the Czech lands between 1945 and 1989. Both the association of Plečnik's contribution with the democratic period and the castle's heightened openness and visual accessibility countered communist aims.

Whereas the communist apparatchiks viewed Plečnik's work as a threat to their totalitarian aims, many of his Czech contemporaries looked upon his contributions with equal disdain. Pavel Janák, a devoted admirer who succeeded Plečnik as castle architect, summed up the differences between Plečnik's architectural approach and that espoused by his functionalist counterparts:

> Down below, the struggle for a way of thinking and building, the search for a single, universally valid conception that can be imposed and defended against all other possibilities, that would be applicable everywhere, that would be beyond questioning. Up here [in Prague Castle] an artist who simply builds, as if he had not the slightest doubt as to what he was doing.... Down below they are interested only in necessity and in justification.... Here we have an art full of modesty and devotion.[29]

Although the effectiveness of Plečnik's piecemeal interventions in Prague Castle derives in large part from his understanding of their broader urban implications, he encountered virulent opposition to his proposals for creating a monumental approach from the north. Local architects branded Plečnik a "barbarian," condemning his lack of sympathy for the city's history in his plans for restructuring the ascent to Prague Castle. Sparked by opposition to his proposals to demolish components of the city's historic districts, they attacked Masaryk as Plečnik's sponsor.

While the reasons for such opposition are complex, two factors stand out: it reflects an ongoing reaction against Alfred Hartig's late nineteenth-century modifications to Prague's Old Town, which impeded subsequent urban reorganization efforts throughout the city, as well as conflicts in values with Antonin Engel, planner for the district of Dejvice to the north, who prioritized traffic requirements over issues of state symbolism and ceremony. Complaints from the Society of Friends of Old Prague—whose approach to designing in a historic context was consistent with that of both Plečnik and his successor—ultimately prompted the Slovenian to resign from his position.[30] The argument published in the society's newsletter conveys ethnic prejudice as well as professional jealousy:

> We have so many excellent Czech architects who would lovingly and patriotically take charge of the necessary adaptations without harming the monument left to us by our ancestors. We are now allowing a foreign architect, using a foreign style, and with neither love nor sensitivity for our historical monuments, to do what the former hostile government did not do. The women of the Czech Republic beg of you: Save our Castle.[31]

We are faced here with a paradox of conflicting interpretations. Whereas Plečnik's affiliation with Masaryk's democratic administration led the communists to censure his contributions to Prague Castle (and the resulting lack of access hindered local architects from appreciating his work), the idiosyncratic nature of his forms blinded many of his contemporaries to their ideological implications. Although the restoration efforts undertaken by President Václav Havel undoubtedly enhanced awareness of Plečnik's remarkable contributions to Prague Castle, comprehension of their historic relevance continues to elude the castle's record numbers of visitors. This is because Plečnik favored the profundity of the unspoken to the clarity of the spoken. Although such repudiation of the conclusive is customarily associated with abstraction, he belied this conventional wisdom through the figurative essence of his forms. That their meaning should remain open and elusive yet simultaneously historically grounded constitutes the essence of his democratic approach.[32]

SIX

COLLABORATIVE FRUITS
Garrett Eckbo's
Communal Landscapes

In his address to the annual meeting of the American Society of Landscape Architects (ASLA) in 1941, Edwin Bergstrom, president of the American Institute of Architects (AIA), stressed the importance of collaboration for the various professions involved in the building arts. Yet by limiting the professional expertise of landscape architects to "knowledge of soils and of trees and shrubs and planting and all that makes them thrive" and the role of the designed landscape to providing "a satisfying setting for the building," Bergstrom implied that the role of the landscape architect is subordinate to that of the architect, that landscape architecture is, in effect, a service profession to be valued—like engineering—primarily for its technical contribution to the design process.[1]

Ten years earlier, during the depths of the Great Depression, Henry Hubbard, editor of *Landscape Architecture,* anticipated a more significant role for his fellow landscape architects:

> We now think of ourselves as a force worth considering in the affairs of the country. We believe that we have opportunities of which we have not as yet availed ourselves, duties which we have not yet performed. We are willing to spend time and money in order to begin our honest part in many matters not local and emphatically not confined within the boundaries of the garden or of the private estate.[2]

Within three years, 90 percent of Hubbard's previously unemployed colleagues from the ASLA had abandoned aspirations for private garden commissions in favor of landscape work in the public domain, reflecting the professional impact of the collective ideology of New Deal programs.[3] In the analysis of landscape historian Phoebe Cutler, this shift was to the detriment of landscape architecture as a "fine art," as it reinforced the technical and practical, rather than the aesthetic, contributions of the profession.[4] Although her assessment is consistent with Alexis de Tocqueville's insight that "democratic nations . . . cultivate those arts that enhance the convenience of life rather than those whose purpose is to embellish it," the collaborative projects carried out by the Farm Security Administration's western division transcend the polarities of Cutler's evaluative criteria.[5] Indeed, American landscape journals consistently welcomed the profession's expanded role under the New Deal, which architectural historian Turpin Bannister attributed to the social idealism evident in both the garden city movement and the impetus to create public parks.[6]

In the aftermath of World War II, however, the executive committee report of the first congress of the Union of International Architects, meeting in Lausanne, Switzerland, in June 1948, asserted the merits of a hierarchical relationship among the disciplines in collaborative undertakings. Describing the architect as "one who has extensive knowledge, a sense of coordination, and a vision of harmony in space and time," the UIA reasoned that the architect alone is capable of directing the teams of technical experts needed to address the physical and social devastation wreaked upon the war-torn regions of Europe. Accordingly, among the responsibilities its report delegated to architects was "the development of green spaces."[7]

Lamenting the norm of such a professional hierarchy, American landscape architect Garrett Eckbo strove throughout his career for the "ultimate integration of architecture and landscape," which he achieved through collaborative undertakings with a number of architects, engineers, and planners on projects at diverse scales. Yet, as he ultimately acknowledged, "in actual practice this integration rarely happens through direct, one-time, equal basis collaboration. Usually architecture/construction is there first—actually, conceptually, or economically." As a consequence of this reality Eckbo reasoned:

> The landscape elements must adapt to, grow from, and extend the architectural/structural concepts (whether or not they seem to lend themselves to that), and establish connections or separations between

the project and the surrounding neighborhood and region. The environment is littered with impossible tangles that have resulted from the absence of foresight that such an end product would emerge from each development project. The environmental art of the future will be kept busy trying to untangle such messes. The occasional one-to-one collaboration between architect and landscape architect serves as guide and beacon.[8]

In his ongoing efforts to heal this professional rift, Eckbo affirmed the inherent conceptual links between building and site development, arguing in his first book, *Landscape for Living* (1950): "The site only exists in its visual and spatial relation to people, through the introduction of the building which establishes a permanent relation between people and site. The building and the site are one in fact and in use."[9] Decrying the ongoing focus of landscape architects on the elitist private garden, Eckbo sought to shift professional attention to addressing the social needs of the emerging mass society, asserting: "Smaller gardens, and the landscaping of public buildings and parks, are more directly relevant to the problems of our physical environment."[10] Basing this premise on a series of collaborative projects he had undertaken over the prior decade, Eckbo sought to instill in his American counterparts the social ethos of the European avant-garde.

Late in his career Eckbo regarded the decline of the landscape profession in the United States as part of a broader cultural phenomenon, citing Denise Scott Brown's contention that contemporary design trends challenged the status of design disciplines associated with the built environment: "The decline of planning . . . The death of urban design . . . The trivialization of landscape architecture."[11] Yet Eckbo failed to mention Scott Brown's related premise—"The demise of social concerns"—an issue equally germane to his professional philosophy. To Eckbo collaboration was not merely a tactic for enhancing the status of his profession; it was, more significantly, a viable means to address the era's rapidly changing social conditions in environmental terms. His experiences working on migrant labor camps with the Farm Security Administration (FSA) beginning in the late 1930s, and on cooperative housing projects with architect Gregory Ain a decade later, led Eckbo to view the process of collaboration—like the governing process of the housing cooperative—as an instance in miniature of participatory democracy in action. Although his designs for these collaborative projects appear to challenge the hierarchical relationship of the disciplines, in each case the "democratic" essence of the project was thwarted by a combination of factors, including federal policies that implicitly or explicitly fostered economic and racial segregation.

Collaborative Roots

Eckbo began his quest to integrate architecture and landscape while pursuing graduate studies in landscape architecture at Harvard University (1936–38), where Dean Joseph Hudnut had just merged the faculties of architecture, landscape architecture, and city planning into the Graduate School of Design (GSD). In an independent student project, "Small Gardens in the City," published in the architecture journal *Pencil Points* (1937), Eckbo developed formal variations on residential gardens for a hypothetical urban block.[12] He followed this proposal with a combination of individual and collective landscapes in his thesis project, "Contempoville" (1938), a suburban subdivision associated with a World's Fair he imagined to take place in Los Angeles in 1945. His site plan, inspired by Clarence Stein and Henry Wright's layout for Radburn, New Jersey (1929), features curved streets and single-family houses with individual gardens organized around a central "superblock park." In plan drawings for both projects, Eckbo gave the architecture specific elaboration, indicating his early interest in the conceptual concordance of the disciplines. To accomplish this integration in his thesis project, he borrowed liberally from known architectural examples, utilizing house layouts from published contemporary sources.[13] He also incorporated Mies van der Rohe's Barcelona Pavilion of 1929 in his park design, reinterpreting its form as a community swimming pool and shelter. Eckbo subsequently commented on this deliberate usurpation: "The Barcelona Pavilion achieves (or descends to) functional community use," wryly implying that the artistic value of the original would be either augmented or diminished by imparting practical, day-to-day functions to the minimal aesthetic of the original.[14] The spatial gradations afforded by Mies's breakdown of boundaries between outdoors and indoors provided ongoing inspiration for Eckbo's work, particularly in the nuances of the public/private interface that he explored in his numerous housing proposals. If the collaborative aspect of these student projects was covert, in his professional housing commissions it would become explicit.[15]

Social Stirrings: Farm Security Administration Projects

Although Eckbo rejected the Beaux-Arts basis of his Harvard design education, his experience at the GSD kindled an interest in the social motivations that Hudnut brought to the curriculum when he appointed Walter Gropius to chair the Architecture Department in 1937.[16] Eckbo's social awakening burgeoned as a result of his early professional experiences. Upon graduating from Harvard, he worked briefly for the U.S. Housing Authority, where he developed hypothetical recreation spaces for public housing projects. Later that year he returned to California to work for the western division of the Farm Security Administration, headed by architects Burton Cairns (1937–39) and Vernon DeMars (1939–43). This latter experience was seminal to Eckbo's career, as he subsequently noted: "My work with the Farm Security Administration politicized me and gave my imagination a chance to flower."[17] Working collaboratively on projects that addressed urgent social needs provided Eckbo the opportunity to respond to practical concerns without an accompanying sacrifice of artistry.

The western division of the FSA was established to combat the economic plight of hordes of midwesterners who streamed into the American Southwest in search of employment after being displaced from their family farms by the Dust Bowl drought of the 1930s—a predicament memorably captured in the work of FSA photographer Dorothea Lange as well as John Steinbeck's novel *The Grapes of Wrath* (1939).[18] In residential camps designed for migrant, semipermanent, and permanent agricultural workers in California, Arizona, and Texas, Eckbo and his colleagues sought to foster communal interaction while affording a measure of privacy for the individual household, resulting in a conception that was "not merely shelter but rather the creation of a new pattern of community life," in the estimation of architectural historian Talbot Hamlin.[19]

In these projects Eckbo was primarily responsible for landscape development rather than overall site planning, which was largely carried out by his predecessor, Francis Violich, in collaboration with FSA engineers.[20] Eckbo sought to provide the inhabitants with humane living environments, unlike public housing efforts, in which, he subsequently argued, "the vicious practice of developing minimum standards based on income strata, rather than optimum standards based on bio-technic needs, are too apt to produce the slums of tomorrow." He countered the regimented and repetitious geometric layouts of the FSA building complexes through formal variations in his planting schemes. Focusing on the sociospatial potential of landscape rather than its pictorial value, Eckbo sought to mitigate the limited volumes of the residential units by extending spaces pertinent to daily life to the outdoors. Advocating "the use of plants as space-organizing elements rather than as decoration," he subdivided the sites with foliage that afforded visual extension in the communal zones and enhanced privacy for the dwelling units.[21] By introducing subtle layers of native trees and shrubs to generate these spatial effects while respecting existing vegetation and topography, he fostered a distinctive sense of place in each camp.

Eckbo's landscape proposals manifest his concern with practical considerations: providing much-needed shade and windbreaks to control erosion and dust, as well as distinct outdoor areas for recreation, drying yards, and individual garden plots. Nevertheless, in assessing these migrant labor camps, architect William Wurster stressed their artistic merits, arguing: "Minimum shelter for human beings became 'architecture.' The design of buildings emerged as social art, and I hope it will never be placed exclusively on the luxury shelf again."[22] Similarly focusing on the architectural aspects of these projects, Hamlin echoed Wurster's positive appraisal: "The extraordinary achievement has been to make this effort, despite the necessary pressure of time, despite the tremendous need for unit economy, nevertheless true architecture."[23] Contending that "it is in the variety and character of the house types that the originality and independence of the designers is best shown," Hamlin commended the combination of aesthetic and practical qualities in the site planning and planting, but failed to acknowledge the extent to which the artistic merits of these projects hinged on their qualities as designed landscapes.[24] In overcoming the supposed

The Farm Security Administration's migrant labor camp, Tulare Basin, San Joaquin Valley: aerial view of tents for migrant workers in hexagonal layout, with semipermanent housing units above *(left)*; Garrett Eckbo's planting plan for hexagonal zone with central utility building *(middle)*; detail planting plan of central space, 1941 *(right)*. Garrett Eckbo Collection (1990-1), Environmental Design Archives, University of California, Berkeley.

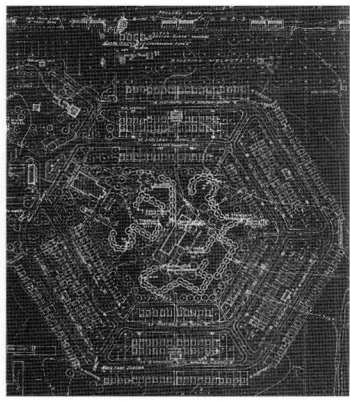

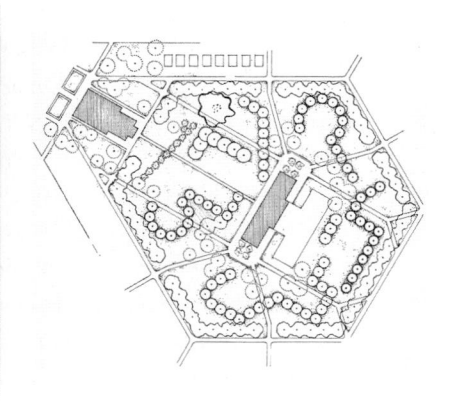

120   COLLABORATIVE FRUITS

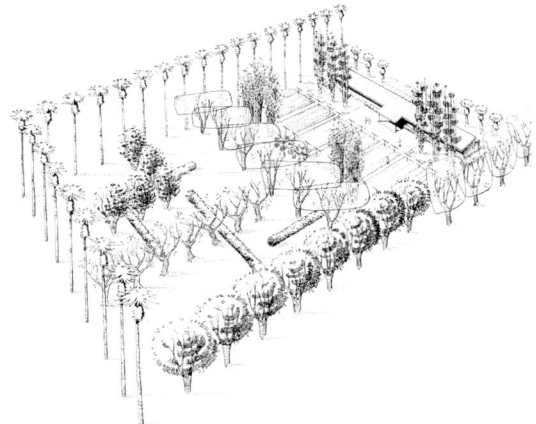

schism between the artistic and practical aspects of these FSA settlements, Eckbo and his colleagues belied the aesthetic deficiency that Cutler attributes to landscapes created under New Deal programs.

Despite the constraint of working with limited resources to provide an affirmative living environment for their inhabitants, these early projects afforded Eckbo a degree of freedom that made them among the most satisfying of his career, which he later attributed to "the combination of large open site[s] without intensive demands beyond the already existing natural character and the social function."[25] Working in a team that included some thirty engineers and twenty architects, as well as three landscape architects, he viewed as his most rewarding experience of interdisciplinary collaboration.[26]

In contrast to the affirmative evaluations of these FSA projects by Eckbo and his architectural contemporaries, historians have produced a more complex and troubling account. Labor historian Cletus Daniel reminds us that farming in the Southwest differed substantially in its scale and priorities from the family farm advocated by Thomas Jefferson as a foundation of democratic values. By the end of the nineteenth century vast tracts of land amassed under the colonial land policies of Spain and Mexico, which yielded "feudalistic patterns of ownership and control," had become agricultural "factories" that exemplified the commercial ethic of modern industrial America.[27] The economic motivation of these large-scale enterprises, in which labor was viewed as a factor of production, contrasted sharply with the civic virtues of a classless rural society, which Jefferson associated with the small-scale family farm. Despite idealistic efforts on

(left) Laundry facilities and steel housing units at FSA migrant labor camp in Westley, San Joaquin Valley, California, February 1939. Photograph by Dorothea Lange. Library of Congress, Prints and Photographs Division, FSA/OWI Collection [LC-DIG-fsa-8b32823].

(right) Garrett Eckbo's aerial perspective of community center park at FSA migrant labor camp in Harlingen, Texas, 1940. Garrett Eckbo Collection (1990-1), Environmental Design Archives, University of California, Berkeley.

Large-scale farming operations near Meloland in California's Imperial Valley. Photograph by Dorothea Lange, February 1939. Library of Congress, Prints and Photographs Division, FSA/OWI Collection [LC-DIG-fsa-8b33207].

the part of agrarian reformers to shift the scale of farming in the American Southwest to one more compatible with the country's Jeffersonian roots and values, family farming remained largely an abstract dream in that part of the country.[28]

The vast scale of these farm enterprises necessitated employing large numbers of harvesters at disparate times of the year, resulting in a migratory labor force that initially consisted primarily of immigrants of Mexican and Filipino extraction, along with a small percentage of Chinese. Despite the flagrant abuses that growers repeatedly imposed on these minority laborers, government intervention in the migrant housing crisis was initiated primarily in response to the stream of white farmworkers and their families—the "Okies"—who flowed into the American Southwest in search of employment throughout the 1930s. In her evocative account of bearing witness to this mass migration in California, Dorothea Lange alluded to the invisibility of those destitute Americans:

> All of that day, driving for the next maybe two hundred miles—no, three or four hundred miles, I saw these people. And I couldn't wait. I photographed it. That was the beginning of the first day of the landslide that cut this continent and it's still going on. . . . I could have been like all the other people on that highway and not seen it. But this I discovered myself. This thing they call social erosion. I saw it.[29]

In response, the growers, whose solid economic base provided them with considerable political clout in the region, largely resisted the creation of government-sponsored migrant labor camps, which they anticipated would lead the workers to unionize.[30]

Further complicating this conflict between farm owners and workers was the fundamental antiunion bias of the New Deal approach to the agricultural workforce, which contradicted the paternalistic philosophy underlying the New Deal.[31] Despite contemporary efforts to draw attention to the predicament of farmworkers by Carey McWilliams, chief of the California Division of Immigration and Housing (1938–42), and by the public hearings of the La Follette subcommittee of the Senate Committee on Education and Labor held in 1939, which concluded that "the economic and social plight of California's agricultural labor is miserable beyond belief," farm laborers continued to be denied rights guaranteed to workers in other industries.[32]

Such conflicts between owners and laborers contributed to a tension, evident in the camp layouts, between the need to operate either as self-sufficient communities, protecting their inhabitants from external threats of vigilantism, or as fragments of a broader network of social services and civic functions. In effect, the FSA migrant settlements had to do both. Thus landscaped buffer zones isolated the residential quarters from the immediate environs, while limited educational and medical facilities were generally sited along roadways to serve the broader populace. The earliest settlements provided only meager sanitary facilities and tent platforms in the manner of a campground, centered on a provisional communal structure; they ultimately included more permanent forms of housing and meeting spaces as well as schools and health clinics.[33] Many of these service structures were added at the suggestion of camp managers, who lived near the entrance to each site in order to monitor internal relations while supervising links with the immediate environs. In projects that incorporated a range of housing types (which varied according to length of occupancy), the units were segregated according to type, thus acceding to the functional logic that motivated contemporary planning strategies. To encourage long-term settlement, certain FSA developments included fields for subsistence farming that adjoined the most permanent forms of housing. These units were often grouped at the farthest extremes of the sites, in contrast to the temporary dwelling units, which were located nearest the communal facilities and resident managers, in the belief that short-term occupants would be most in need of social support as well as mechanisms of control. The migrant camp layouts thus served as relatively explicit diagrams of intended social relations, reifying distinctions of power, class, and, ultimately, race.

Inspired by the communitarian and socialist theories of Charles Fourier and Robert Owen, who advocated decentralized, self-sufficient

(left) Aerial view of FSA migrant labor camp, Yuba City, Sacramento Valley, 1939, with permanent multifamily housing in foreground, double hexagon of temporary housing (tents) in background, and semipermanent housing units to the right. Vernon DeMars Collection (2005–13), Environmental Design Archives, University of California, Berkeley.

(right) Aerial view of Tulare Camp, San Joaquin Valley, 1937–42, with permanent multifamily housing in foreground and hexagonal array of temporary housing in background. Marc Treib and Dorothée Imbert, *Garrett Eckbo: Modern Landscapes for Living*, 1997.

COLLABORATIVE FRUITS   123

communities combining agriculture and industry,[34] the FSA conceived its migrant labor camps not only to provide sanitary housing and communal facilities for the laborers but also to achieve explicit social and political ends, as historian Walter Stein elaborates:

> At the camps, the Okies were to be schooled in the FSA's concept of American democracy; "rugged individualists" were to be given their first exposure to the idea of community. Under the direction of their camp managers, the Okies would be taught to subordinate private goals to the welfare of the group. In short, the FSA camps strove to reconcile two sides of a dilemma that was centuries old. "Liberty" would be taught to coexist with the New Dealers' version of fraternity.[35]

To foster these "democratic" social objectives, the camps were governed by a "constitution" drawn up by FSA officials and modeled on the American Constitution; it granted legislative powers to a Community Council—an elected body of camp residents—and judicial powers to a court designated by the council. Yet the rights vested in these bodies were limited by the executive power conferred upon the camp manager, who held veto power over council decisions, resulting in what Stein calls "an experiment in 'guided democracy.'"[36] Moreover, an unofficial practice of racial segregation, consistent with the social values of the Dust Bowl transplants and achieved through the assignment of different races to different segments of the camps, ultimately became policy.[37]

In practice the FSA migrant labor camps functioned more as subsidies for the growers, relieving them of responsibilities for providing workers with housing, social services, or even minimal wages, than as instigators of a new form of communal life. At best they provided temporary solutions to a pressing economic problem. The FSA was ultimately unable to achieve its utopian social objective—to transform residents into "ideal citizens of an ideal republic," as Stein terms it.[38] This failure derives less from the group's ideological premises or the forms of its migrant settlements, which were explicitly conceived to advance certain collective principles, than from the underlying naïveté of the reformers' approach to addressing social problems in which they assumed an explicit correlation between built form and social form.

The FSA sought to promote an impression of social harmony in the agricultural landscape of the American Southwest, yet this image operated to conceal underlying social realities, as Carey McWilliams pointed out in *Factories in the Field,* his attempt to reveal the "hidden history" lurking beneath the "surface placidity [of] the great inland farm valleys of California."[39] Writing in 1939, McWilliams contended: "The migratory camps are not a solution: They are merely demonstrations of what might be accomplished." Yet his remedy for the farm-labor problem—"the organization of farm workers" together with "the substitution of collective agriculture for the present monopolistically owned and controlled system"—was doomed to failure on political grounds.[40] With hindsight Daniel argued that, inasmuch as federal agencies such as the FSA sought "to assist agricultural wage earners, . . . it was to relieve the most visible symptoms of their powerlessness rather than to alter the one-sided relationship between them and their employers."[41] In addition, the FSA's collectivist ideology made it susceptible to accusations of harboring communist sympathies.[42]

With the United States' entry into World War II, the FSA shifted its emphasis to defense housing, for which Eckbo employed design strategies similar to those he developed for the migrant labor camps, using landscape to mediate between the abstract geometric layouts of the housing sectors and the more complex spatiality implied by the social realities of daily life. The occupants of these projects, in which forms inspired by European avant-garde architecture were adapted to local climate and topography, deemed them far less successful than the migrant camps had been.[43] Moreover, with these more permanent housing projects, governmental policies officially sanctioned racial segregation, thus establishing on the West Coast "the culture of postwar white suburbia and the development of publicly supported black city neighborhoods," in the analysis of Marilynn Johnson.[44]

The darkest period of FSA history began in 1942, when the western division was ordered to develop assembly centers for Japanese American residents of West Coast communities, who were subsequently confined to more permanent internment camps for the duration of the war. Although Eckbo opposed this overtly racist policy in principle, he advised on the design of several camps in California's Owens Valley, where the FSA was transforming facilities developed for migrant farmworkers into assembly posts for Japanese American "evacuees."[45] The need for supervision in these assembly centers differed only in degree from that in the migrant labor camps. The hexagonal layout of dwelling units around a central utility building at Tulare, for example, was easily adapted to more assertive mechanisms of control with the addition of barbed-wire fencing at the perimeter, guarded by military personnel.[46] Despite this shift from an aesthetic of social "improvement" to one of social restraint, Eckbo continued to employ the spatial strategies he developed in his earlier work for the FSA, countering the overt geometric rigidity of the building layouts through layers of irregular planting intended to support the projects' more redemptive social aims. He subsequently rationalized this approach to accommodating temporary farmworkers as means "not just for providing shelter, but also for developing [the inhabitants'] fundamental potential dignity."[47] For the Japanese Americans held in these centers, however, such dignity was possible only through temporary release from custody, which was granted for individuals to attend college, to enlist in the military, or, more likely, to work as seasonal laborers in the region's agricultural fields.

If the regimented building layouts in the FSA's camps for migrant and semipermanent agricultural workers reflect the paternalistic imposition of an idealized collective order, Eckbo sought to mitigate that effect in his landscape designs by introducing a spatiality he imagined to be more in keeping with the inhabitants' daily lives, affording them limited opportunities for privacy and for relief from the specter of overt mechanisms of control. Talbot Hamlin claimed that Eckbo and his colleagues were successful at the deepest psychological levels: "These communities are human and attractive because their designers understood people and their needs and insisted that all of those needs—intellectual and emotional as well as physical—should be taken care of."[48] Yet the minimal physical adaptation involved in the shift from a landscape of social betterment to one of social control suggests significant parallels in the predicaments of the two types of inhabitants. Despite the best intentions of the FSA, the occupants of its migrant labor camps were effectively as restrained in their daily lives as were the Japanese Americans, confined within barbed-wire fences.

Independent of direct supervision from its Washington, D.C., superiors, the western division of the FSA succeeded in developing some forty permanent camps and fifteen mobile facilities for agricultural workers. Adapting a limited range of building types and site layouts to diverse topographic conditions ultimately enabled the team to ready each camp for occupation within six months of its site purchase. Yet these efforts could not dispel the essential duplicity of the landscapes in which the FSA operated, as Ann Copperman observed in a postwar issue of *Task* devoted to the West Coast, for which Eckbo served as a guest editor:

> *The Grapes of Wrath* shocked the nation, for the "factories in the fields" are well shrouded by their magnificent setting. It is only with effort that the observer can wrench himself from the overwhelming distraction of

scenery, and, in so doing, he runs the risk of accepting the Western scene as wholly agricultural. The setting conceals far more than the West Coast's rural misery, it conceals its oil refineries, its banks, its utilities.[49]

Despite the extreme limitations in its scope and economic impact, as well as the naïveté of its social ambitions, the FSA program for farm laborers instilled a strong social ethos in the minds of its team members. It was this philosophy that Eckbo would bring to the series of cooperative housing developments he undertook a decade later, in which he aspired to a more transparent relationship between ideology and form—and with entirely different implications for the communal potential of landscape.

Telesis

A direct outgrowth of the social idealism inherent to the FSA experience was Telesis, an organization Eckbo described as "of, by and for progressive planning technicians (planners, architects, landscape architects, industrial designers) in the San Francisco Bay region."[50] The name Telesis refers to a theory of planned social progress employing scientific research methods to direct the evolution of human society, formulated in the late nineteenth century by the prominent American sociologist Lester Frank Ward. The San Francisco group, founded in 1939 by FSA colleagues DeMars, Cairns, and Eckbo with former FSA landscape architect and planner Francis Violich, advocated rational interdisciplinary planning of the environment at scales ranging from region to dwelling. In Violich's account, the members of Telesis aspired "to present to the average man the equipment for the new social order, for the better, more abundant life."[51] Eckbo associated the group's primary efforts with "struggling with the arbitrary separation of the professions that existed in this kind of formalistic structure of work which was not really related to the nature of the problems that, as they developed, were seen to be continuous interlocking problems."[52]

Describing Telesis as a "movement toward architectural cooperation and away from professional competition," architect Serge Chermayeff cited its credo: "(Who) We, as designers of the new environment [that] cannot be effectively designed by isolated individual efforts, have organized in the spirit of cooperation and personal anonymity so that by collaboration in our efforts we may encourage scientifically significant work."[53] The Telesis statement of beliefs stressed the social and economic implications of such planning efforts, as well as their cooperative essence: "(Why) We recognize that there are basic social and economic forces at work in bringing about a new environment and believe that it is our duty to thoroughly understand these forces that we may intelligently interpret their significance in planning man's environment."[54] To counter suspicions of "'mass' thinking . . . generally conceded to be un-American," the statement emphasized the rational and technical basis of planning:

> There is nothing mysterious or totalitarian about this planning. It is in essence foresight based on study and experience. . . . People and the Land make up the environment which has four distinct parts—a place to Live, Work, Play and the Services which integrate these and make them operate. These components must be integrated into the community and urban region through rational planning, and through the use of modern building technology.[55]

Consistent with its insistence on rational logic as a means to forge new possibilities for the contemporary urban environment, the group derived these functional categories from the fourth meeting of the Congrès Internationaux d'Architecture Moderne (International Congresses of Modern Architecture, or CIAM), held in 1933 and devoted to "The Functional City."[56] In addition to forming working groups to investigate such topics as urban rehabilitation, housing, and transportation, Telesis members disseminated their findings through an exhibition on contemporary architecture and planning, displayed at the San Francisco and Seattle Museums of Art.

Although Eckbo welcomed the nonhierarchical interdisciplinary spirit of Telesis, his own design philosophy relied less on scientific and technological rationalization and more on the ethical aspects of the group's aspirations, which he directed toward enhancing the social potential of landscape so that it might serve as an active locus of daily life—in both an individual and a collective sense. Despite the group's emphasis on the social impact of environmental design, Eckbo noted: "The war caught Telesis flat-footed. Its failure, as a group, to consider political and economic backgrounds left it unable to analyze and understand the real nature of the forces involved." In response, he explained, a subgroup was formed "to develop truly democratic environmental standards" by studying issues of "housing, work space and recreation."[57] Exploring the implications of "democratic" standards for housing and recreational landscapes would motivate the series of cooperative housing projects Eckbo worked on during the late 1940s with Los Angeles architect Gregory Ain.

Communitarian Ethos

Through collaborative projects undertaken in a variety of circumstances, Eckbo sought to balance individual and collective needs—issues inherent to the democratic condition—in the designed landscape. He identified two points of divergence within landscape design: the stylistic split between formal and informal design and the ideological split between socially motivated and artistically motivated design. Challenging such categorical distinctions, Eckbo asserted: "Classical (formal) design can be socially oriented and social design may be art. Regardless of form concepts, the basic question may be: is design for people, or are people a vehicle for design?"[58] Theorizing potential affinities between landscape form and social form, he argued that the goal of site planning is "to produce the best possible physical pattern within which a group of people can develop a good social pattern."[59] This is neither the aesthetic imperative associated with nineteenth-century urban parks, intended to ameliorate urban living conditions, nor the functional imperative that motivated the widespread development of recreational parks and playgrounds in American cities and towns during the early twentieth century; it is closer to philosopher John Dewey's more open-ended concept of participatory democracy—a community in which opportunities and resources are available to enable every individual to participate fully in political, social, and cultural life.[60]

Eckbo's most significant effort to develop the ramifications of landscape design as a social art was Community Homes, a cooperative housing proposal that he developed with his good friend architect Gregory Ain after moving to Los Angeles to open a second office of Eckbo, Royston and Williams in 1946.[61] The timing of Eckbo's relocation was propitious; seeking to fulfill his ambition "to house the masses," Ain had recently reoriented his practice from its prewar focus on small-scale private houses by forming an association with Joseph Johnson and Alfred Day to address the region's postwar housing shortage.[62] Ain's long-standing commitment to social reform through architecture—stemming from his socialist upbringing in a vibrant, ethnically diverse neighborhood of Los Angeles, interrupted by a one-year interlude at the experimental farming cooperative Llano del Rio (1914), his affiliations with members of the American Communist Party, and his experiences working in the offices of socially progressive architects Rudolph Schindler and Richard Neutra—complemented Eckbo's burgeoning interest in the communal potential of landscape design.[63]

Like Eckbo, Ain strove to overcome the Kantian distinction between aesthetic value and use value in his designs. Although he approached architecture as a problem-solving activity, Ain was equally adamant that it was "once primarily an art—a very vital art . . . the very focus of public pride," as he asserted during the mid-1960s.[64] He believed the design process should engage rigorous interdisciplinary research combined with a solid technical foundation in material properties and construction processes, as well as artistry—all of which require a suspension of the individual ego in favor of collaboration.[65] Frustrated by the "rampant individualism" and "compulsive expressionism" that he associated with the decline of his profession, with its "continued deprivation . . . of a real, tangible value which it has been architecture's traditional function to provide," Ain asserted: "We must reaffirm the truism that architecture is a social art, and that its aesthetic power must be derived from a social ethos."[66]

In addition to Community Homes, designed for a group of cartoonists, screenwriters, and other Hollywood guild members, Eckbo collaborated on two additional cooperative housing developments with the firm of Ain, Johnson and Day: Park Planned Homes in Altadena (1945–47) and Mar Vista in West Los Angeles (1946–48). Owing to restrictions the Federal Housing Administration placed on its mortgage guarantees in cases of racially integrated housing developments, however, the Community Homes cooperative was ultimately forced to abandon its project and sell off the land; for similar reasons only a portion of the other developments was completed, albeit through recourse to individual financing.[67]

Community Homes, 1946–49

Of the three cooperative housing projects that stemmed from this collaboration, the unrealized proposal for Community Homes was Eckbo's most sophisticated attempt to address the public/private interface inherent to suburban housing. In *The Art of Home Landscaping* (1956) he elaborated on this issue, contending that

> the relations between each private home and its neighborhood involve continuous choices between social and private living, sociability and privacy, community services and self-sufficient labor, what portions of life can best be handled individually and what portions can best be handled through some form of cooperation with the community.[68]

Seeking to encourage public appreciation of the benefits of forethought in landscape design and planning, as well as the social advantages of a communitarian approach to such planning, Eckbo directed this book to a lay public rather than to a professional audience.[69] His social idealism, cultivated by his experience at the FSA, flourished as a result of his working with, and ultimately joining, the Community Homes cooperative.

The project for Community Homes was launched in January 1946 when fifteen members of the cartoonists' union met to form a housing cooperative and engaged Ain to serve as their architect; within weeks 88 families had subscribed. Membership eventually grew to 280 households, a majority of whom were members of Hollywood unions or had related leftist political affiliations. The cooperative thus exemplified Alexis de Tocqueville's premise of the political origins of civic associations:

> It is through political associations that . . . [l]arge numbers of people thus see and speak to one another, come to a common understanding, and inspire one another in all sorts of joint ventures. Later, they take the lessons they learn this way and carry them over into civil life, where they put them to a thousand uses.[70]

Moreover, the cooperative membership involved a broad ethnic mix, as Ruth Jaffee, executive secretary of Community Homes, explained to California's congressional representative Helen Gahagan Douglas, who sought to assist the cooperative members in their efforts to obtain federal support for their project:

> Our development, as you know, is to be an interracial housing project. Represented in our membership of 280 families are: 11 Negroes; 1 Chinese-American; 1 Japanese-American; 1 Filipino; 1 Indonesian. This constitutes a 6% racial minority. Half of our development, or 140 families, are veterans. All of our members are American citizens.[71]

The basis of the group's cohesion was thus ideological and professional rather than racial or cultural.

The site organization for Community Homes, developed by Simon Eisner, a planner with the City of Los Angeles Housing Authority, was already in place when Eckbo joined the project team to develop the landscape design. Like his work with the FSA, this exemplified the sort of undertaking Eckbo was referring to when he argued: "Usually architecture/construction is there first—actually, conceptually, or economically. The landscape elements must adapt to, grow from, and extend the architectural/structural concepts."[72] Nevertheless, Eckbo's design for Community Homes appears to circumvent the prevailing disciplinary hierarchy, bringing landscape design to a state of parity with architecture and planning.

He accomplished this ostensible challenge to the norm of architectural dominance by adhering to advice he offered to architects in an essay published when he was still working with the FSA: "It will be well to think of the open space as the skeleton and controlling form of the site plan, rather than as a byproduct of the building and roadway arrangement." Transcending the spatial extremes of solid and void inherent to the diagrammatic figure–ground reversals subsequently espoused by Colin Rowe and his followers, Eckbo sought to activate the social potential of open space, arguing, "A physical pattern derives life and vitality only from its relation to the social pattern which it environs [sic]."[73]

Eisner's layout for 280 single-family houses on a flat, hundred-acre site in the San Fernando Valley prioritizes communal spaces and separates pedestrian from vehicular traffic in a manner inspired by Sunnyside Gardens (1924–28) and Radburn (1929) by Clarence Stein, Henry Wright, and Marjorie Cautley, as well as the local example of Baldwin Hills Village (Los Angeles, 1940–42), by Reginald Johnson and Robert Alexander.[74] In these

(left) Simon Eisner's site plan for Community Homes, Reseda, California, 17 March 1948. Gregory Ain papers, Architecture and Design Collection, University Art Museum, University of California, Santa Barbara [Collection no. 1978.104].

(right) Garrett Eckbo's corresponding landscape development plan, c. 1948–49. Garrett Eckbo Collection (1990-1), Environmental Design Archives, University of California, Berkeley.

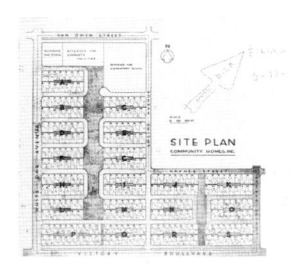

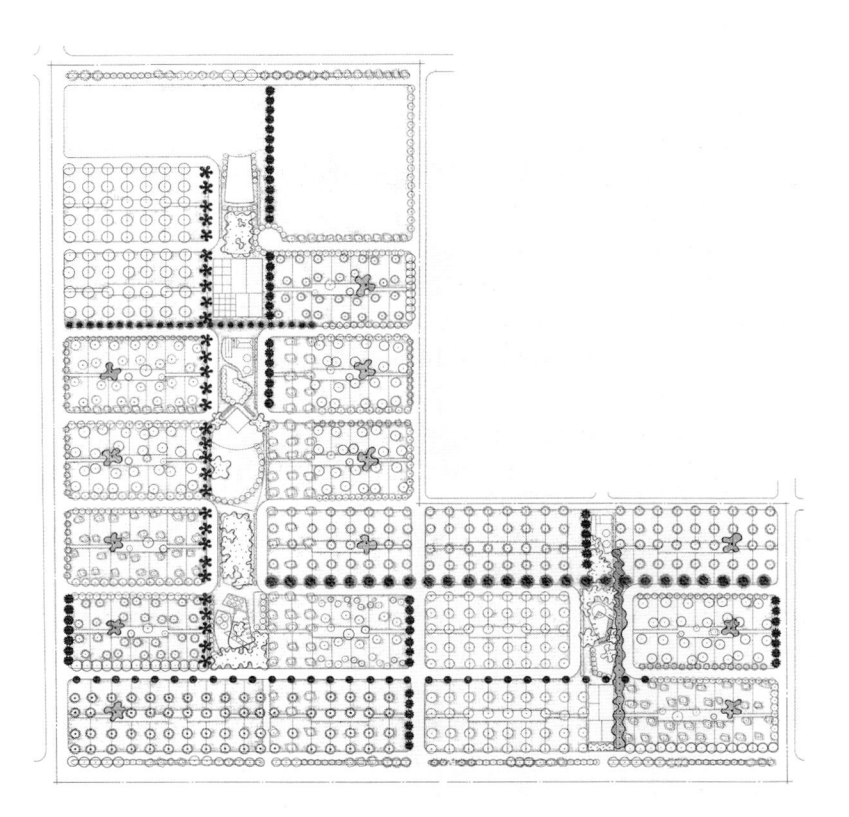

examples, as in Community Homes, the primary domain of social interaction is shifted from the street front to the block interior. Eisner synchronized his system of loop streets with the gridded road network of the broader suburban environs, while accommodating pedestrian circulation primarily in strip parks and finger parks, around which he clustered the housing units, and only secondarily in sidewalks.

This layout not only won swift approval from the local planning commission but also prompted enthusiastic praise from one commission member, who proclaimed, "In my opinion, this sub-division is the finest example of land planning for individual home ownership which has ever been presented to the Planning Commission for approval."[75] It compensates for what Jürgen Habermas laments as the loss of clear distinctions between public and private spheres resulting from streets being overtaken by the requirements of traffic flow. In Habermas's terms, Eisner's site strategy affords both "a spatially protected private sphere" and a "free space for public contacts and communications that could bring private people together to form a public."[76]

Rather than deviate from the rigid geometry of Eisner's site plan, Eckbo brought it to life, using differentiated layers of planting to impart a sense of continuity to the neighborhood while avoiding monotonous repetition in the residential streets. He subsequently argued that he derived formal inspiration for his landscape strategy from Ain's architecture, and indeed their design strategies are intrinsically related. To avoid architectural monotony while affording a degree of economic efficiency, Ain created six basic house types, each capable of being reversed, together with specific possibilities for expansion, resulting in twenty-six alternatives. His note on an undated drawing emphasizes the integral relationship between the units and their immediate sites: "All houses have protected living gardens . . . away from the entrance side. Garages are paired at alternate lot side lines, for minimum interruption of continuous front landscaping. All kitchens open to east service yards. No house has windows towards windows of an adjacent house."[77] As Eckbo explained his own process: "In all of these Ain projects the houses had a repetitive clarity with subtle variations. They challenged me to exploit variations in garden design for smaller spaces, and variations in street front treatment within overall unity."[78]

A further point of inspiration came from Eckbo's observations, gleaned while he was working for the FSA, of the rural landscape—"those regions where man and nature have met, mingled, but seldom completely dominated one another":

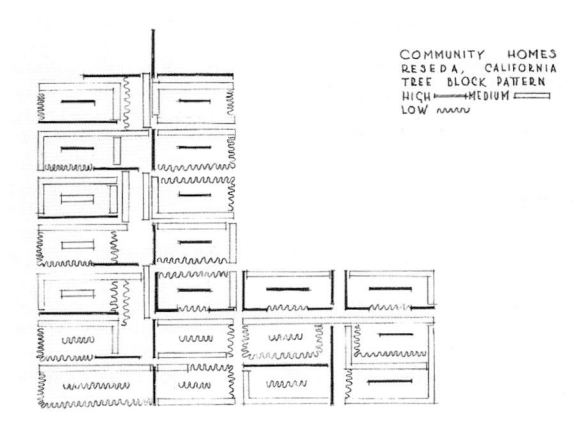

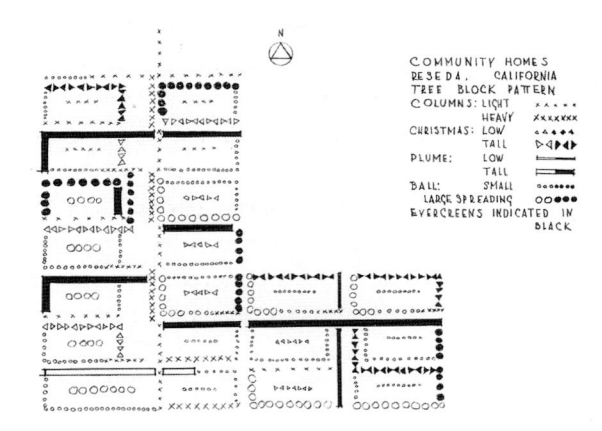

Eckbo's tree block pattern diagrams for Community Homes, c. 1948–49. Garrett Eckbo Collection (1990-1), Environmental Design Archives, University of California, Berkeley.

There we do find innumerable definite three-dimensional space forms produced with both structural and natural materials: rectangular or polygonal fields cut from solid natural wildwoods; trees in rows or belts forming planes; the regularity of orchards; straight lines of untrimmed hedges and mixed hedgerows, and of fences and old stone walls, grown up with natural plants; free-standing clumps of trees forming natural pavilions; intersecting planes of these lines of trees and hedges and walls forming a fragmentary organization of space.

In this essay Eckbo acknowledged the relative advantages of landscape as a medium:

> The forms and proportions given to outdoor space can vary a great deal more than those found in buildings, because they are not so completely tied to structural economies and necessities, but rather are concerned with the establishment of relation between human beings and the natural scale of the site.[79]

This freedom enabled him to apply his succinct inventory of landscape forms to migrant labor camps and cooperative housing developments alike, providing the means to address social aspirations inherent to both types of community—involuntary as well as voluntary.

In Reseda, Eisner devoted sixteen of the site's one hundred acres to communal space, which Eckbo developed as parkland, recreation areas, playgrounds, and finger parks between the housing clusters. His site plan, indicating only landscape elements and curb cuts, conveys the basis of the individual/communal interface while anticipating the addition of architecture. Landscape elements simultaneously unite and differentiate the streetscapes, house sites, and parks, establishing the terms for communal expression, an idea that Eckbo subsequently articulated: "The overall pattern of trees in a neighborhood of detached houses is the single most important visual element. It can integrate the neighborhood, give it identity and character and a sense of unity." He countered the potential threat to individual expression involved in coordinating and planning "an entire street, block by block, including both private front yards and the public right of way" with an appeal to "democratic processes," as he elaborated:

> The great fear which this idea is apt to invoke in the breast of the average American is that it may involve placing limitations on his personal freedom of expression. The only answer to this fear is the maintenance of democratic processes, through which no such limitations can be established until the agreement of the majority of those directly affected has been secured. . . . It is not a question of choosing either planning or individuality. . . . Planning in groups, and individualism, are

Eckbo's aerial perspective of Community Homes landscape, c. 1948–49. Garrett Eckbo Collection (1990-1), Environmental Design Archives, University of California, Berkeley.

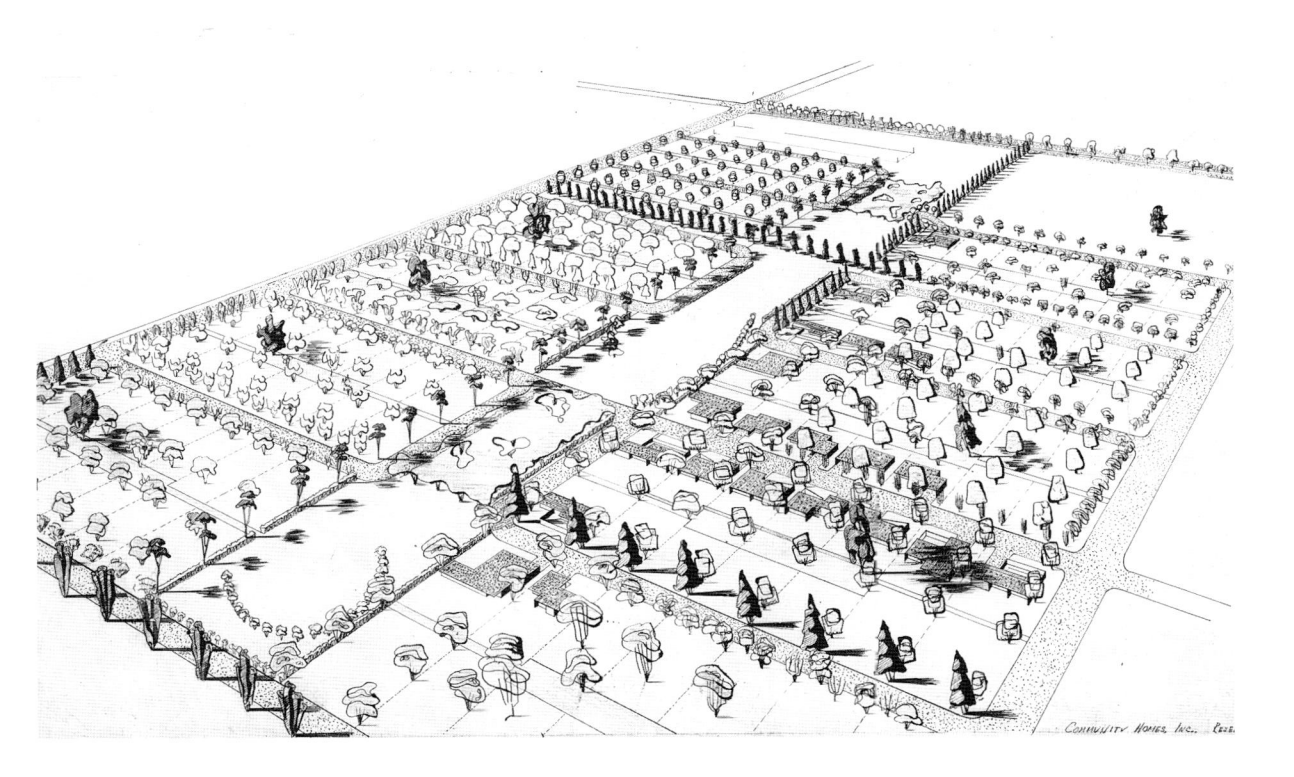

COLLABORATIVE FRUITS 135

not incompatible. They actually help each other if basic democratic processes of full information, open discussion, and majority agreement are maintained.[80]

While such an open process directed Eckbo's development of the Community Homes streetscape, parks, and recreation spaces, his design strategy also provided the basis for individual expression in private gardens, numerous variants of which he developed in explicit response to Ain's unit designs. The opportunity to work with home owners to address their individual landscaping needs and proclivities within the framework of the communal landscape of streets and parks enabled Eckbo to correlate his private garden designs with his broader strategy for the development. Articulating the boundaries of each residential plot with various combinations of hedges and garden walls in the backyards, where privacy was most important, he developed a looser relationship between boundary and physical form along the street front; the front yards, while differentiated, would also contribute to the continuity of the streetscape. Moreover, because the immediate surroundings were only in their initial stages of development, these design parameters could potentially be implemented at a broader scale, so as not to mark clear distinctions between Community Homes and future housing projects in the environs, for the cooperative did not conceive of itself in isolation.[81]

Plans for two of Garrett Eckbo and Gregory Ain's collaborative house and garden designs for Community Homes, c. 1949. Garrett Eckbo Collection (1990-1), Environmental Design Archives, University of California, Berkeley.

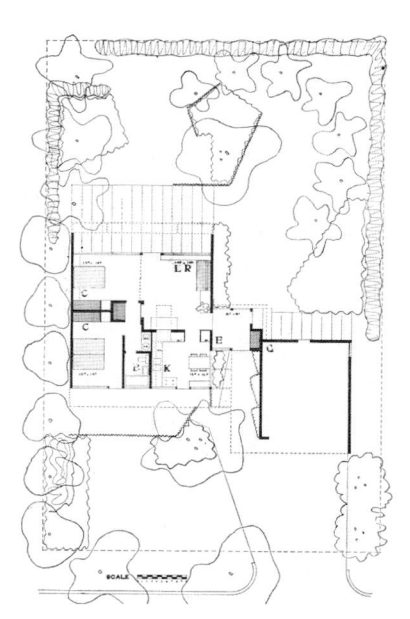

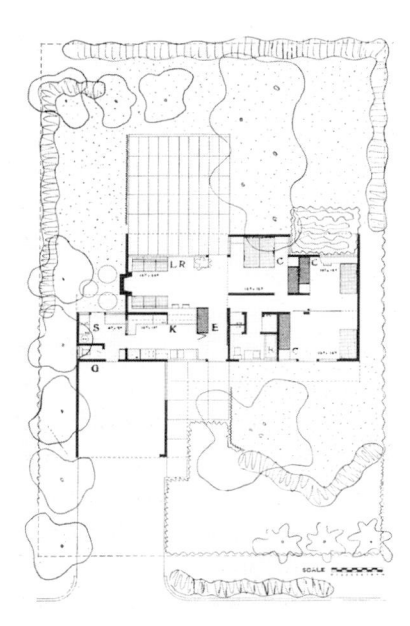

Eckbo viewed the neighborhood as the "minimal home unit" for rational planning and advised his students to avoid endless suburbanization by seeking to control neighborhood planning through democratic participation.[82] In this light the Community Homes Corporation included an ambitious range of civic responsibilities among its purposes: "To own and operate schools, churches, libraries, hospitals, places of entertainment, playgrounds, auditoriums, parks, and places of assembly." Such extensive facilities could not be accommodated on the segment at the northern edge of the site that Eisner set aside for stores, community facilities, and an elementary school, suggesting that the cooperative viewed itself as a fragment of a broader neighborhood. Consistent with these civic ambitions, the Community Homes Articles of Incorporation stipulated a range of social responsibilities, including "facilities for housing, feeding, transporting, maintaining and providing professional care, education and means of communication for its members and others and otherwise to provide for the welfare and accommodation of its members and others."[83] The principle of cooperation thus extended from the community's physical amenities—its communal landscape and on-site facilities—to the daily interactions among its residents and their neighbors.

The communal facilities accommodated in the Community Homes site layout are consistent with advice offered in a broad range of inter- and postwar publications stressing the value of thinking at a neighborhood scale to address the nation's severe housing shortages. In *The Art of Home Landscaping,* Eckbo cited one such source: an argument made by architects Oscar Stonorov and Louis Kahn in their pamphlet *You and Your Neighborhood* (1944), produced by Revere Copper and Brass to promote citizen participation in the planning process. Evoking a familiar historic analogy, Eckbo reasoned, "Neighborhoods must re-create the spirit of the New England town meeting to obtain citizen participation, and citizen support for action."[84] Eckbo's partner Robert Royston considered a second booklet, *Planning the Neighborhood* (1948), issued by a North American committee of the League of Nations, especially useful. It defined a neighborhood in terms of access to services and social activities in the vicinity of an elementary school (within a walking scale of one-fourth mile), which would both determine the neighborhood's scale and serve as a meeting place.[85] More significantly, it viewed the neighborhood as part of a suburban network, stressing the need for access to community facilities, work sites, and commercial enterprises. Consistent with the policies endorsed in these publications, the Community Homes cooperative envisioned its neighborhood school and adjoining commercial and communal facilities as the social nexus for a broad range of participants.

In contrast to the cooperative emphasis of these booklets, most federal government publications focused on quantitative economic and programmatic means to address the nation's housing shortages, endorsing restrictive covenants to maintain property values as well as the importance of the neighborhood elementary school as the focus of a residential development.[86] Eckbo was frustrated by the limited advice proffered in these federal publications:

> We are told that the individual family is the democratic social [module], and we are told that the desirable neighborhood unit is of a size sufficient to support an elementary school. But there is little indication of what [sort] of cellular breakdown between these two sizes is desirable socially, in conditions of rural decentralization and urban centralization.[87]

In response, Eckbo sought in his cooperative housing proposals to engage the intermediate scales of landscape that he deemed essential to establishing a suitable living environment for a democratic society.

There is another notable difference between these government-sponsored publications and their counterparts emanating from other public and private sources. Whereas the U.S. government envisioned the architect as the mastermind, controlling all aspects of a residential development, *You and Your Neighborhood* encouraged citizen participation from the outset of the planning process, while *Planning the Neighborhood* stressed the importance of involving a landscape architect during the earliest phases of the work.[88] In contrast, a booklet that the National Housing Agency put together in 1947 to advise veterans on organizing cooperative housing associations not only promoted engaging an architect early in the process but also assumed that he—the male architect—would be responsible for site planning:

> In planning a project to suit a particular site the architect must seek to achieve the greatest possible privacy for the occupants of the units, protection of the project from adverse influences, attractiveness of site and structural design, and the lowest possible costs compatible with good construction and operation. Here again, consultation with an architect experienced in this field and the advice and aid of the FHA technicians may result in appreciable savings in time and cost.[89]

This advice is curious, given that several of these issues involve areas of expertise other than those associated with architecture.

In an essay addressed to an architectural audience, published while he was working with the FSA, Eckbo elaborated upon professional spheres of competence, not to claim priority for landscape architecture, but to insist on the value of collaboration:

> Site planning is the one field which points out, clearly and unmistakably, the futility and obsolescence of the present carefully established and maintained professional boundaries. No single kind of professional designer can do a completely good job of site planning all by himself. It requires collaboration between architects, engineers and landscape architects on smaller jobs, with the addition of professional town planners on larger ones.

To reinforce his understanding of the integrative value of site planning, Eckbo disparaged the objectives of each profession when approached in isolation:

> Site planning is the arrangement of environments for PEOPLE. Its primary objective is not engineering convenience, or mechanical efficiency, or esthetic delight, or a monument for posterity, or good camera angles, or speculative profits. It is to produce the best possible physical locations within which a group of people can develop a good social pattern.[90]

Housing activist Catherine Bauer had asserted such a correlation between social form and environmental form in describing "real architecture" as "the clear and consistent expression of a social order that people can make out of their physical environment, for their own satisfaction."[91] In an essay prompted by the racism associated with New Deal housing policies—an issue that contributed to the ultimate dissolution of the Community Homes cooperative—Bauer challenged academics from the political and social sciences to engage the more profound social implications of thinking at the neighborhood scale, including "the critical question of class and race relations in a democracy; . . . the creation of new opportunities for citizen participation and responsibility in civic development to prevent the overgrowth of a governmental paternalism that could be as dangerous in its own way as private monopoly."[92] The issue of agency—that is, the potential for inhabitants to act on their freedoms versus living as subjects—is paramount; it differentiates Eckbo's notion of

Community Homes as a "democratic" landscape from the work he carried out with the FSA.

No less idealized than Eckbo's communal aspirations for the migrant labor camps, the Community Homes layout reflects a parallel attempt to forge a society in miniature. Yet, as New Deal historian Paul Conkin elaborates on the plight of the agricultural worker:

> When a simple farmer, wide-eyed with wonder and expectancy . . . moved into a glittering new subsistence homestead or resettlement community, he was entering a social show window. Willingly or unwillingly, knowingly or unknowingly, he was a human mannequin in a great exhibit, for the many architects of the New Deal communities, despite varying philosophies, were all striving to create, within the conducive environment of their planned villages, a new society with altered values and new institutions.[93]

Whereas the inhabitants of the migrant labor camps were unwitting participants in a social experiment, the prospective occupants of Community Homes were willing accomplices in theirs. Accordingly, the designs for the migrant labor camps, in their recourse to highly programmed landscapes as vehicles of social change, bear comparison with the Social Democratic housing projects developed in Germany under the Weimar Republic, while the issue of an explicit correlation between social form and environmental form in Community Homes remains more open and contingent. Not only was its communal landscape less programmatically determined, but its social and physical and boundaries were also less circumscribed than those of the camps; participation in the cooperative's many cultural opportunities was voluntary and open to the broader community.

Its organizational structure was also more flexible, with governance delegated to a fifteen-member board of directors that was charged with carrying out all cooperative business, including the administration of land held in common. Elected by and from the active cooperative membership to serve limited one-year terms, the members of the board were in turn responsible for designating officers with specified duties. One position, that of the chief administrator, or "manager," was to be "chosen by the Board of Directors solely on the basis of his executive and administrative qualifications" and need not be an active member of the cooperative, but could be removed "at will."[94] Thus, although the bylaws established an administrative hierarchy, the limited temporality of board appointments facilitated equitable consideration of the interests of all cooperative members.

To maintain the aesthetic unity of the cooperative while fostering a degree of individual expression in the dwellings, the Committee on Architecture, a standing committee elected by the board of directors, was delegated responsibility for "approving designs, supervising structures, determining and adjusting free-spaces and set-backs, and determining and adjusting uses."[95] Cooperative restrictions also included a vague attempt to impose architectural standards, without regard to style.[96] Although the Federal Housing Administration endorsed such aesthetic restrictions for their potential to enhance property values, the cooperative encountered resistance when it sought financial backing from that agency.

Established by the National Housing Act of 1934, the FHA fostered private ownership of single-family houses by providing insurance to financial institutions to guarantee 80 percent of mortgage loans against the risk of default by home owners. Whereas New Deal policies toward agricultural workers reflected a conflicted attitude that combined an aspiration for social betterment with benign neglect, federal housing policies fostered a more explicit two-tiered system that supported home ownership in racially exclusive suburban neighborhoods for members of the working classes, as distinct from housing assistance for the poor. Either implicitly or explicitly, such policies sanctioned economic as well as racial segregation.[97]

Claiming that its principle of encouraging restrictive covenants merely reflected market conditions, the FHA specified in its *Underwriting Manual* of 1936 that the "presence of incompatible racial elements results in a lowering of the rating, often to the point of rejection."[98] Despite revisions to the *Underwriting Manual* of 1947 eliminating such specific references to race, the Housing Act of 1937 endowed local authorities with the power to determine issues of racial occupancy, so that the principle of basing mortgage protection decisions on so-called market conditions continued to prevail in FHA policies.[99] Despite a U.S. Supreme Court ruling of 1948 that determined racially restrictive covenants to be unconstitutional, racial barriers in federal housing policies continued unabated under various guises—including those of maintaining "professional standards" or ceding responsibility for such decisions to local jurisdictions—until 1962, when John Kennedy issued a presidential order banning such policies from federal housing initiatives.[100]

Among the stipulations the FHA variously insisted upon during its prolonged deliberations with the Community Homes cooperative was the addition of restrictive covenants to all but twenty residential lots; the members found this proviso unacceptable.[101] The FHA also required that the area covered by finger parks be associated with individual ownership (in the manner of Sunnyside Gardens), contributing to further delays in the approval process.[102] Although ongoing financing difficulties led to a serious decline in cooperative membership, a core group persisted in their efforts to see the project through, so that by July 1949 site improvement was under way, with sewers installed and grading completed. Yet after more than three years of active planning, the Community Homes cooperative was ultimately forced to dissolve, having failed to secure mortgage protection from either the FHA or other public and private agencies.

A series of essays challenging federal policies of racial segregation appeared in the winter 1944–45 West Coast issue of *Task*, for which Eckbo served as a guest editor for Telesis. These included a refutation of the government's repeated assertions that racial integration compromises real estate values and urged architects and planners to involve themselves directly in issues of housing integration.[103] While working with the FSA, Eckbo had argued unequivocally against differentiating living standards on the basis of "race, creed or economic status":

> **People** *must be considered because the project is for them. One must not only have a sense of and sympathy for the way they live, work and play; one must have a basic faith in the potential goodness, decency, and dignity of every human being, a complete lack of snobbery, condescension, benevolent paternalism or authoritarianism, and a realization that race, creed or economic status have no real relevance to the determination of living standards for people as individuals, families, or larger social groups.*[104]

He was apparently unable to discern the paternalism inherent to the FSA approach to its migrant labor camps, yet the experience of engaging social issues in those federal projects inspired Eckbo's work for Community Homes, where the prospective residents were united in their communal aspirations.

Although historians have generally cited the interracial character of Community Homes as the primary reason for the FHA's rejection, broader political biases undoubtedly contributed in part to this decision; at the time the FHA was ill equipped to consider mortgage protection for housing developments under cooperative ownership. An FHA official acknowledged that his agency was "ideologically unfit" to consider such applications; in the words of one cooperative member, "They thought we were all crazy radicals."[105] In his evaluation of three cooperative housing projects realized in the Los Angeles area during the 1940s (Baldwin Hills Village, Mar Vista, and Crestwood Hills), George Rand traces the "ignominous [sic] end" of such planning efforts in 1951 to "a fury of McCarthy-era accusations that socially planned projects were nothing more than a communist conspiracy to take over the city housing authority." Archival records provide evidence of communist sympathies among various individuals associated with both the FSA and the cooperative housing initiatives in which Eckbo participated, yet, as Rand argues, such projects "remain planning landmarks" in their subordination of individual expression to the interrelationship of the housing units with each other and with the broader landscape.[106]

The period when Community Homes was being conceived, designed, and deliberated over by various funding agencies coincides with what historians Larry Ceplair and Steven Englund term the years of the "grand liberal-radical" alliance in Hollywood.[107] Amplified by the economic impact of the Great Depression, the humanitarian principles of racial equality and antifascism underlying Communist Party ideology appealed to progressives, liberals, radicals, and socialists alike, contributing to its disproportionate influence on the American left. Nevertheless, the American Communist Party shared contradictions inherent to political radicalism in the United States between its egalitarian aims and its espousal of violent upheaval and between the middle-class roots of its membership and the revolutionary fervor of its rhetoric. Like many members of the American Communist Party affiliated with Hollywood's motion picture industry, the Community Homes participants consisted of middle-class professionals rooted in the bourgeois culture of upward mobility and class fluidity. Just as cooperative members with Communist Party affiliations undoubtedly viewed communism as a principal symbol of social justice, fully compatible with democratic values, so they envisioned the cooperative organization as a primary vehicle for living out those ideals. Immediately following the dissolution of the Community Homes cooperative, however, the Soviet Union signed a nonaggression pact with Nazi Germany, exposing the totalitarian essence of Soviet communism, bringing such contradictions to the fore, and depleting the membership ranks of the American Communist Party as well as its political power.[108]

Following the demise of Community Homes, Title 213 of the 1950 Housing Act established a section of the FHA with responsibility for fostering cooperative ownership and building, yet economic principles continued to prevail in federal housing policies, augmenting the trend toward racial and economic segregation that had characterized governmental efforts to address housing shortages since the Great Depression.[109] As Joseph Hudnut argued: "Whatever else it may be the housing project is an act of segregation. It defines, separates and establishes economic and, to some extent, social stratifications."[110] Nevertheless, Eckbo's social idealism remained intact, as he asserted in an interview in 1993: "The good society is not stratified, except as a result of democratic processes. Still a dream. The need for strong leadership is only a measure of the weakness or inadequacy of the membership. The ideal organization functions without leaders."[111] His assertion could be taken as an idealization of collaborative practice as well as cooperative modes of living.

In *Town Planning in Practice* (1909), British planner Raymond Unwin had lauded such a participatory process in cooperative residential developments, which he imagined would facilitate a correspondence between external communal form and inner social reality.[112] Reflecting on the potential reciprocity between the human environment and a democratic way of life, Eckbo contended:

> Democracy isn't kept alive on a diet of free ballots alone—it requires something more solid and balanced, plus a physical pattern in which it can operate. The chaotic surroundings within which 98 per cent of our social and economic activities attempt to function is an inhibitor of democratic processes, a propagator of political and commercial exploitation, and a direct expression of an age in which human dignity is of only minor importance.[113]

He assumed a correlation between the formal order implied by "something more solid and balanced" and the more open question of "a physical pattern in which [democracy] can operate." As the tension between these two conditions remains a fundamental aspect of environments directed to enhancing a democratic way of life, Eckbo sought to bring a sense of transparency between formal attributes and social aspirations to the Community Homes landscape. In theory such legibility would not only benefit residents of the cooperative but also open the group to productive dialogue with neighboring constituencies, as political theorist Nancy Fraser argues:

> [In] self-managed [organizations such as] residential communities, internal institutionalized public spheres could be arenas of both opinion formation and decision making. . . . this would leave open the relationship between such internal public spheres-cum-decision-making-bodies and those external publics to which they might also be deemed accountable.[114]

Fraser envisions a process—precluded by New Deal housing policies—in which minority voices would be taken into consideration, a process accountable to external and potentially weaker publics, including economic as well as racial minorities.

A contemporary article on the Mutual Housing Association in Crestwood Hills—a cooperative subsequently formed by several former members of Community Homes for which Eckbo also served as landscape architect—stressed the role of dissent as a crucial component of a malleable democratic process: "When issues are real, membership will exercise its control rights and protect the democratic process which is responsible for the life or death of the venture."[115] Yet in order to receive financing assurance from the FHA, the Crestwood Hills cooperative adopted restrictive covenants that limited membership to whites, thereby eliminating the issue of race as a point of contention. Participants who endorsed this capitulation reasoned that, owing to the impending Supreme Court decision, such restrictions would have no practical significance. Following that decision, which precluded racial discrimination in federal housing initiatives, however, the Mutual Housing Association rejected applications for membership from minority families, thus maintaining the development's racial homogeneity.[116] Racial segregation prevailed in the development, with two hundred houses realized, all with white ownership.

Ruth Jaffee described the aim of Community Homes as a "struggle for better housing in a truly democratic community."[117] Although the democratic aspirations of the cooperative members were undoubtedly heartfelt, the project's democratic essence remained an open question, as Vernon DeMars acknowledged. While lauding such efforts to create housing cooperatives, which he termed "a healthy new kind of democratic building activity," he questioned the social implications of the members' narrow range of occupations and income levels. Citing the combination of cooperation and individualism in the American pioneer spirit, DeMars contended:

> A wider cross-section of interests will result in a healthier community life later on. And while a spread of income ranges is not in accord with recent real estate practices, it does not run counter to American tradition or the democratic ideal. This leads inevitably to the next question. Co-operatives have traditionally insisted on nondiscrimination as to race, creed and color, a rather academic consideration in England or Scandinavia, and one presenting no difficulty in running a consumer's

grocery store in the United States. Housing is something else again, and co-operatives should abandon not idealism but naïveté. Better housing is, in itself, a crusade—so is the co-operative way.[118]

Community Homes reflects only a step toward such an ideal; its membership exemplified political unanimity and economic parity as well as racial heterogeneity, assuring a level of social conformity that contrasts the diversity of opinion and economic status inherent to a participatory democracy. It thus exemplifies what political philosopher Michael Sandel refers to as an "'instrumental' community . . . in which individuals with their previously defined interests and identity enter in view of furthering those interests."[119] Moreover, because the FHA's property evaluation criteria discouraged economic as well as racial diversity in housing, the type of development DeMars was endorsing—a "constitutive" community in Sandel's terms—was essentially precluded in the American political context of the 1940s and early 1950s.[120] Citing the federal government as both "the co-operatives' best hope and greatest disappointment," DeMars concluded: "What was achieved by Peninsula Housing Association at Ladera . . . and by Mutual Housing Association came only through continuous disheartening struggle. The results give some idea, however, of what might have been, and what might yet be done with a change in heart toward co-operatives."[121]

Just as Eckbo's efforts in cooperative housing developments reflect the limitations of realizing a "truly democratic community," so his crusade to promote interdisciplinary collaboration under conditions of professional parity proved to be an elusive goal. He envisioned potential affinities between the collaborative design process and cooperative living, a correspondence noted in the aforementioned article on the Mutual Housing Association: "The cooperative spirit is as much a part of the design process as it is a part of administration and control."[122] Throughout his career, moreover, Eckbo strove to reach an architectural audience and foster mutual disciplinary understanding by contributing to professional architectural journals. These contributions far outnumbered his essays published in related landscape publications. He derided the elitist thinking he associated with contemporary landscape theorizing:

> Is art for art's sake, or for people? If the latter, is it for a majority or a minority? If the latter, which minority? If it is true that "landscape design can be truly appreciated only through the eye and mind which are trained to see and understand," how and by whom is appropriate

> training provided for our clientele? Is it only the individual private clients who get this training? How about the majority who experience our park designs? Do they require a course of training before they can enjoy them? Or do we preserve the finer concepts for the more understanding private clientele, and design down to the broad masses? And so on—each question begets another.

Instead he sought to make his landscapes meaningful on their own terms, as essential facets of daily life, concluding: "Our work is done for people, to provide settings for their life and activities."[123]

Central to Eckbo's argument was his understanding of the "skills or bodies of knowledge" intrinsic to his discipline—"Design (including planning); Natural factors; Social factors." He cited these categories to distinguish landscape architecture from other disciplines associated with the built environment:

> In each discipline the relative emphasis and manipulation varies, as does the approach to each specific area. Planning tends to be utilitarian and socio-economic oriented. Engineering, architecture, and most other design fields tend to see natural factors as elements which can be shaped and rearranged as man may desire. Only landscape architecture as a field sees the need for balanced organic influence from both natural and social factors in planning and design decision[s].[124]

Despite persistent efforts by Eckbo and others to develop a collaborative spirit in which they could operate in parity with other design professionals, the profession of landscape architecture continued to operate at a disadvantage.

In 1865 architect Calvert Vaux had opined in a letter to his Central Park collaborator Frederick Law Olmsted that landscape architecture was emerging as a "better" field than architecture in terms of its ability to "supply a public need," yet a century later the disciplines' professional organizations were engaged in ongoing disputes concerning the relative hierarchy and scope of their respective contributions to the built environment.[125] A report by the AIA Special Committee on Education in 1963 sought an expanded leadership role for the architect "to encompass those professional services necessary for the creation of environmental forms and spaces." The report proposed to subsume under its disciplinary purview "architectural design, urban planning, landscape design, urban socialeconomic planning, administration and the fine arts."[126] In response, the

ASLA countered: "We must strengthen our numbers; we must broaden our training; we must continue to lead the way in this, our traditional area of concern," which it identified as "the preservation and proper development of our American landscape on a new regional and national scale." Seeking to avoid professional rivalry, the ASLA report stressed the need for "a *team* approach" to the built environment, while reasserting its disciplinary expertise: "In the areas of physical and land planning the most knowledgeable and able men are *landscape architects*."[127] In 1972, however, the society responded more vehemently to the AIA's challenge. Lamenting the reality that "landscape architects are unlikely to function in a situation in which their professional authority can be exercised without question," the ASLA sought means to invert the prevailing disciplinary hierarchy.[128]

Eckbo never sought such a position of preeminence for his discipline. Instead he asserted, "I have always felt that the two chief sources of inspiration for landscape design were architecture and nature, and that the most interesting and exciting things took place, by conscious design, in the interface areas where they meet." Nevertheless, as he observed in 1970, "the gulf between architecture and landscape seems wider than ever."[129] Moreover, despite his efforts to forge "a truly democratic community" in Community Homes, the potential for creating a "democratic" landscape remained an open question.

SEVEN

FROM THE VIRGILIAN DREAM TO CHANDIGARH
Le Corbusier and the Modern Landscape

Le Corbusier's contribution to the modern landscape has drawn little critical attention, since landscape was not a primary concern either of Modern Movement theorizing or of his particular theoretical position.[1] Indeed, in many respects his approach to landscape seems anachronistic: his interpretation of nature as both an original condition and an emblem of rational order; the reduction of landscape in his idealized urban propositions to a mute ground plane, lacking in topographic character or scale, and the corresponding failure to invest such collective zones with formal or programmatic content to activate their social potential; the "timeless" aspiration of his quest, in contrast to the temporal aspect of landscape that has risen to theoretical prominence among architects and landscape architects in recent decades. These notions, stemming largely from the theoretical foundations of Le Corbusier's design approach, reflect a fundamental difference between architectural and landscape theory; as Elizabeth Meyer explains, the latter is situational and contingent, rather than abstract and universal.[2] Nevertheless, Le Corbusier's design for the capital complex at Chandigarh is convincing testimony to his evolving interest in integrating architecture and landscape. At Chandigarh Le Corbusier brought his regard for the particularities of the regional landscape and its cultural significance to bear on his broader theoretical insights, infusing modern spatiality with mythopoetic content in a landscape that extends its purview to the horizon.

If in his architecture Le Corbusier sought to avoid overt historical references, in the landscape of the capital complex he made explicit use of symbolism associated with the traditional Mughal paradise garden, abstracting its forms and adapting its spatial qualities so as to forge meaningful connections between aspects of local culture and what he regarded as immutable truths. There he recovered a spirit of inquiry that architects have pursued only intermittently since the late nineteenth century, when architecture and landscape design began to emerge as separate disciplines.

Le Corbusier did not explicitly seek to reintegrate the two domains; indeed, his polemical theories tended to disrupt the traditional connections between them. Rather, his persistent desire to reconcile man, nature, and cosmos through architecture ultimately led to his broader concern for the designed landscape. This aspect of Le Corbusier's work exemplifies a current within modernism that falls outside its polemical boundaries yet evolves out of its utopian aspirations.

Le Corbusier rarely wrote about landscape. Moreover, his interest in assimilating traditional landscape principles in a manner appropriate to the new age, evident in his early Purist buildings, is often belied by the images he used to publicize them. Such discrepancies between his polemics and his built work, often pointed out in criticism, have obscured the role of landscape in Le Corbusier's work.[3] He ultimately achieved the reconciliation of architecture and landscape through his designs rather than through his polemical writings.

His attitude toward landscape developed in no single, consistent line. Rather than start from a set of rules that invert historic principles, as he claimed of his architecture, Le Corbusier often appropriated historic landscape techniques directly, questioning them only in later projects. If his architecture derived from a priori theoretical concerns, his attitude toward the landscape evolved a posteriori from practice. Though his treatment of the landscape was initially eclectic and schematic, it evolved to encompass a symbolic dimension. Only after his architecture transcended its seeming negation of history and his landscape its diagrammatic relationship to history could the two domains meet in conceptual unity.

Nature as Ideal

In Le Corbusier's writings, nature is a prevalent theme, often imbued with semireligious overtones. His understanding of nature was complex and often contradictory. Sometimes he invoked it as a force antithetical to the works of man, equivalent to chaos or the romantic notion of the sublime. Yet he conceived of nature in its essence as a system of which man is part and as an embodiment of order—an analogue of modern engineering, the beauty of which derives from adherence to natural laws: "The objects of nature and the results of calculation are clearly and cleanly formed; they are organized without ambiguity. It is because *we see clearly* that we can read, learn and feel their harmony."[4] This dual interpretation of nature, as original condition and emblem of rational order, is one of many polarities Le Corbusier sought to integrate within his architecture.

The theme of nature was also central to his social aims. He considered nature an agent for the moral regeneration of humankind, capable of rekindling humanitarian values lost to industrialized society: "Man is a product of nature. He has been created according to the laws of nature. If he is sufficiently aware of those laws, if he obeys them and harmonizes his life with the perpetual flux of nature, then he will obtain (for himself) a conscious sensation of harmony that will be beneficial to him."[5] In evoking a state of consciousness that was simultaneously primordial and millennial, Le Corbusier infused modern rationality with a primeval mythos. He thereby sought to endow his architecture with universal and eternal validity: "There is no such thing as primitive man; there are primitive resources. The idea is constant, in full sway from the beginning."[6] This modernist conflation of a radical starting point with the quest for universal truths implied a return to nature and the natural landscape as essential points of departure.

For Le Corbusier, the source of man's alienation from human nature and from nature itself was the city. By merging the natural environment with the city, he hoped to relieve the ills of traditional urbanism without sacrificing its cultural possibilities. His utopian urban proposals dissolve the polarity of city and country, merging the density of the former with the "*soleil, espace, verdure*" of the latter. He sought to elevate the quality of modern life by providing a setting conducive to creative thought, encouraging both collective interaction and solitude through a combination of density and proximity to the natural environment.[7] Yet his urban proposals, with their Virgilian overtones, fail to conceptualize adequately the designed landscape, which remains more diagrammatic than aesthetic, more eclectic than symbolic.[8]

Le Corbusier's interest in the natural landscape as integral to an architectural idea is evident in his early travel sketches.[9] He was particularly awed by the Acropolis, which he claimed to have visited every day of his four-week stay in Athens. He extolled the way "the Acropolis extends its effect right to the horizon," as he elaborated: "The Greeks on the Acropolis set up temples which are animated by a single thought, drawing around them the desolate landscape and gathering it into the composition. Thus, on every point of the horizon, the thought is single. It is on this account that there are no other architectural works on this scale of grandeur."[10] This image of the Acropolis remained embedded in his imagination, profoundly affecting the spatial and symbolic role of landscape in his work.

An obsession with the horizon pervades Le Corbusier's architecture, whether intensified through the geometric contrast of the Villa Savoye or through the more analogous plastic expression of Ronchamp. The horizon is a visible embodiment of the cosmological unity Le Corbusier sought in architecture, as he reiterated shortly before his death: "We must rediscover man. We must rediscover the straight line wedding the axis of fundamental laws: biology, nature, cosmos. Inflexible straight line like the horizon of the sea."[11]

Architecture and Landscape

The search for a modern architectural language initially diverted Le Corbusier from these metaphysical aims. His theoretical principles, conceived in reaction to Beaux-Arts academicism, inverted the traditional relationship of building to landscape. Instead of using a rusticated base, thematically linking building and ground, Le Corbusier proposed to elevate buildings on *pilotis* to preserve the continuity of the ground plane. The landscape, thereby isolated from the building volume, became an object for contemplation from within the architectural frame. He transferred the

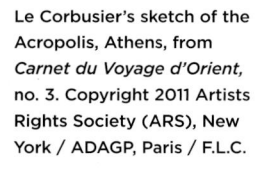

Le Corbusier's sketch of the Acropolis, Athens, from *Carnet du Voyage d'Orient,* no. 3. Copyright 2011 Artists Rights Society (ARS), New York / ADAGP, Paris / F.L.C.

landscape as finite figure to the roof garden, domesticating nature in a room open to the sky.[12] Le Corbusier's dramatic roof gardens imbue his urban dwellings with the isolated quality of rural villas. They are compelling explorations into the designed landscape, demonstrating the quest for primordial values that led him to transcend his radical theoretical methods and ground his approach to landscape design in a more evocative, symbolic manner of expression.

In his first significant garden, a roof terrace overlooking the Champs-Elysées for Charles de Beistegui (1931), Le Corbusier was inspired by his eccentric client to use architectural forms to surreal ends.[13] Through this pictorial device, he expanded the expressive possibilities of the architectural landscape beyond the dialectical opposition of human-made and natural that characterizes his early Purist villas. On the penthouse roof he accentuated the rupture between garden and nature through formal manipulation: reflective glass paving stones set in a carpet of grass stand for water, hedge walls in mechanically operable trays act as draperies to control the view, and a fireplace in the parapet of the upper terrace transforms sky into ceiling, supported by columnar trees. The hedge wall is a tilted ground plane elevating the horizon, on which the Arc de Triomphe appears as an isolated element in a continuous landscape. The uneasy equation of fireplace and urban monument suspends the ordinary scalar understanding of space and enhances the sense of withdrawal from the space of the city, which is underscored by a periscope entombed on the

Terrace of Le Corbusier's Beistegui roof terrace, Paris, of 1931, with the Arc de Triomphe seen in the distance. Copyright 2011 Artists Rights Society (ARS), New York / ADAGP, Paris / F.L.C.

lower terrace. While detachment from the urban condition was to remain a prevalent theme in his work, Le Corbusier later rejected such overt surrealist tactics, since the language of the Beistegui garden countered his aim of reintegrating man and nature.

Instead, on the roof of the Unité d'Habitation at Marseille (1946–52), he evoked archaic values with primal natural forms, the deliberate ambiguity of which amplifies the mythopoetic potential of the rooftop landscape. Totemic exhaust stacks denote a human presence, while an irregular cooling tower suggests more natural sources of inspiration. A ramped plane along the rooftop parapet, understood simultaneously as ground and wall, is allied visually with the distant mountains, a parallel that Le Corbusier endowed with a related ambiguity; despite their physical properties as uplifted ground, the mountains appear from the Unité roof terrace as a vertical backdrop against the sky. The rooftop parapet, like that of the Beistegui penthouse, blocks the city from view to become a substitute horizon, collapsing foreground and background. By visually eliminating the middle ground, Le Corbusier effected an isolation from the immediate urban environs to recover the spirit of integration with the horizon that he admired in the Acropolis.[14]

Le Corbusier's shift during the mid-1940s, from an idealistic preoccupation with prismatic solids contrasted with elements of natural origin to a more poetic concern for an architectural synthesis with natural forms,

The Unité d'Habitation, Marseille, of 1952: communal rooftop structures and rooftop parapet framing the distant mountains. Photograph by Lucien Hervé. Copyright 2011 Artists Rights Society (ARS), New York / ADAGP, Paris / F.L.C.

154   VIRGILIAN DREAM TO CHANDIGARH

had foundations in his early work.[15] Of the three housing prototypes he formulated by 1920, only the Maison Monol, with its traditional Catalan vault, was embedded in the earth.[16] Yet Le Corbusier began to exploit the Monol concept only as the designed landscape became more important to his architectural ideas. In the Maison de Weekend at La Celle St.-Cloud (1934–35), he made a pivotal attempt to unite building and site by combining the Monol system with a warped plane of sod that extended from garden to roof.

The warped ground plane derives from the ramp connecting roof terrace and ground that Le Corbusier first used in the Villa Savoye at Poissy (1929–31) to establish the conceptual and experiential continuity of the *promenade architecturale*. While the warped ground plane of the Maison de Weekend remains isolated from the internal processional sequence, the theme provided an important starting point for three later projects. At the Carpenter Center for the Visual Arts (1959–64), Le Corbusier initially conceived of a ramp descending from the roof as a landscape connecting the building's series of discrete roof gardens.[17] In his Congress Hall at Strasbourg (1964), an elongated ramp not only provides vehicular access to the building, distinct from its internal pedestrian routes, but also transforms both ground and roof planes, dramatically merging building and site. Finally, in the Church of Saint-Pierre in Firminy (1960–65), the warped ground plane achieves iconic significance.

The Firminy Church was commissioned in 1960 as the final component of Le Corbusier's complex incorporating a sports stadium and cultural center outside an undistinguished industrial town in the undulating landscape of the Massif Central. The scarred site, originally a surface mine, had been used as a municipal dump for many years. The church's distinctive volume sustains multiple nuances of meaning. Formally, it is a

Perspective sketches of the Maison de Weekend, La Celle St.-Cloud, 1934–35 *(left)*, and the Church of Saint-Pierre, Firminy, 1963. Copyright 2011 Artists Rights Society (ARS), New York / ADAGP, Paris / F.L.C.

synthesis of primary elements; the vertical transmutation from cube to pyramid to cone terminates in a skylight cut on an oblique, suggesting a dome.[18] Symbolically the structure appears as an isolated rock, an appropriate illusion for a church dedicated to Saint Peter. Situated at the bottom of a scarred valley, the compelling form "asserts the presence of a temple on an inverted and imploded Acropolis," in Anthony Eardley's analysis.[19] Yet the building also exists in dynamic equilibrium with its landscape: the attenuated spiral promenade of the entry sequence is transposed within the building volume to become seating for the sanctuary; on the exterior, in counterpoint, the ground plane is excised to provide for vehicular entry. This modest volume transforms the profane geology of its environs to a sacred dimension.

The Role of the Site

Although Le Corbusier claimed to base his architecture on a set of idealized assumptions, he always adjusted his formal principles to the particular circumstances of the setting. This attitude toward the broader milieu is frequently misunderstood because of his insistence on a theoretical starting point, which he reinforced through careful manipulation of the photographs used to illustrate his work.[20] He preferred closely cropped images to generalized overall views, and he often altered these to suit his aesthetic

Le Corbusier's mother's house, Vevey, Switzerland, viewed from Lake Geneva, 1924. Copyright 2011 Artists Rights Society (ARS), New York / ADAGP, Paris / F.L.C.

aims. Such propagandizing obscures the importance of the site as a challenge to his theoretical assumptions. Indeed, Le Corbusier advised architectural students: "The site is the nourishment offered by our eyes to our senses, to our intelligence, to our heart. The site is the base of the architectural composition."[21]

In the exceptional case of his mother's house in Vevey, Switzerland (1924), Le Corbusier claimed he first developed "a rigorous, functional and efficient plan and then sought an appropriate site on Lake Geneva for its realization."[22] This procedure led to the critical displacement of the modest structure by its garden elements, which Le Corbusier scaled to the vast alpine landscape. That the site be appropriate was also a condition for two projects realized in locations other than those for which they were originally designed, the Villa Shodan in Ahmedabad (1965) and the Maison des Jeunes in Firminy (1960–65), as well as the Firminy Church, which Le Corbusier contemplated building outside Bologna.[23] In 1961 he rejected the opportunity to design a church for La Chaux-de-Fonds because he found the intended location inappropriate to the symbolic program. In a letter to the pastor, Louis Secretan, he explained: "Had you said to me, 'Will you create a place open all the year, situated on the hilltops in the calm and the dignity, the nobleness of the beautiful Jura site?' the problem could have been considered. It was a problem of psychic nature, and, for me, of decisive value."[24]

More than any of his buildings, the pilgrimage chapel of Ronchamp (1950–54) was inspired by the spiritual qualities of its natural setting. Built in an ancient clearing *(rond champ)* on a hilltop used in pre-Christian times for ritual sun worship, the chapel is, in Le Corbusier's words, "a vessel of intense concentration and meditation." References to nature abound, from the abstract, geometric forms of the cistern to the alternative landscape of the roof, which he claimed was inspired by a clamshell. Le Corbusier rationalized his inspiration for the chapel's complex form: "One begins with the acoustics of the landscape, taking as a starting point the four horizons."[25] To interpret acoustical phenomena, he subsequently elaborated, was the privileged role of the artist, "a being sensitive to the things of the universe."[26]

If he first achieved such a fusion of architecture and "nature" in this religious building, it was probably because Le Corbusier endowed nature with a spiritual content that to him surpassed religious values.[27] In the capital complex at Chandigarh (1951–65), he extended that fusion with nature to the synthesis of architecture and the designed landscape. He accomplished this synthesis, influenced by the symbolically explicit model of the Mughal paradise garden, by transferring his mythopoetic treatment of the rooftop landscape back to the ground plane.

Chandigarh: The Designed Landscape

The need for a new capital city for the Punjab arose as a result of events following India's independence from British rule in 1947. In the partition that was a condition of that independence, the state of Punjab was divided and its old capital, Lahore, became part of Muslim-ruled Pakistan. Chandigarh was created to fulfill practical, political, and spiritual aims: to satisfy the need for a new capital after partition, to accommodate resettlement of the west Punjab Hindus, and to fulfill the aspiration for a national identity following the prolonged period of colonial rule. Le Corbusier was called in as planning adviser and architect of the capital complex following the sudden death of Matthew Nowicki, his former collaborator and original architect of the capital. Le Corbusier was initially skeptical, since he was required to adopt the master plan conceived by the American planner Albert Mayer, and he felt the chances for realization of the project were slim. The progressive, utopian aspects of the undertaking—as a symbol of Prime Minister Jawaharlal Nehru's modern India—ultimately attracted Le Corbusier, affording him the opportunity to test his architectural ideas on an unprecedented scale.

At Chandigarh he distinguished three scales of landscape: the pragmatic landscape of the residential city, the monumental landscape of the capital complex, and the more intensely symbolic landscape of the governor's palace. His master plan of 1952 retains the primary organizational features of Mayer's proposal of 1949, in which broad boulevards divide the city into housing and business sectors, with a central commercial zone and a separate government center at its head. Le Corbusier quickly transformed Mayer's organic layout into a regularized grid of boulevards that contrast with curved lateral streets and meandering strips of public parkland threading through the internal segments of the blocks. Despite the colonial associations of the plan's monumental, axial qualities—reminiscent of Sir Edwin Lutyens's layout for New Delhi, which replaced Calcutta as the capital of British-ruled India—Le Corbusier's plan corresponded to Nehru's aspirations for the city. The revisions met with quick approval, allowing Le Corbusier to focus his attention on the more symbolically charged capital complex.

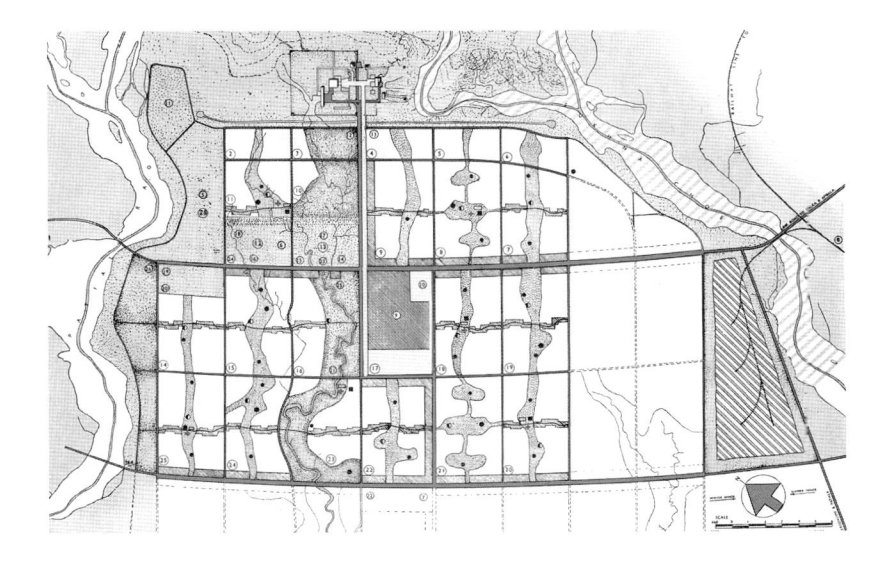

The government center is set in a vast plain against the dramatic backdrop of the Himalayan foothills. Le Corbusier separated it from the rest of the city with a roadway, a canal, and a series of artificial mounds to effect in the flat landscape of the Punjab an isolation reminiscent of the Athenian Acropolis.[28] This disjuncture from the more mundane sectors of the city, reiterated by the monumental character of his governmental buildings, is accompanied by a corresponding synthesis with the landscape. The fusion is both spatial and symbolic, as Le Corbusier elaborated: "The site united with the inexpressible, the imperceptible, the inexplicable. . . . Finally . . . I was able to erect an architecture which fulfills the day-to-day functions but which leads to jubilation."[29]

Le Corbusier's studies of boundaries for the capital complex reveal the historical origins of his spatial ideas. On the city side he proposed "a continuous *glacis* [consisting of] a horizontal embankment."[30] Viewed from the city, it resembles the outer ramparts of a Renaissance fortification, its folds and crevices intensifying both the separation and the continuity of natural and urban landscapes. From within, the embankment would operate much like his rooftop parapets, blocking the city from view while bringing the distant landscape into focus.[31] Elsewhere he proposed a ha-ha to preserve unobstructed views of the Himalayas and exclude the grazing animals.[32]

Le Corbusier's ultimate delineation of boundaries within the capital precinct was more radical. He established corner posts or obelisks to

(left) Le Corbusier's master plan for Chandigarh of May 1952, adhering to the same programmatic distribution as found in Albert Mayer's plan of 1949. Copyright 2011 Artists Rights Society (ARS), New York / ADAGP, Paris / F.L.C.

(right) Albert Mayer's master plan for Chandigarh of 1949, with the capital complex at the head of the organization, business and commercial facilities at the center of the residential area, and industrial zone to the southeast. Norma Evenson, *Chandigarh*, 1966. Courtesy Norma Evenson.

VIRGILIAN DREAM TO CHANDIGARH 159

mark its limits and to demarcate 400- and 800-meter-square subdivisions within.[33] Despite parallels he noted between the dimension of 800 meters and certain monumental distances in Paris, Le Corbusier's spatial order deviates sharply from that of the traditional city.[34] He associated the dimension of 400 meters with the mind rather than the eye: "Though the eye does not encompass a distance of 400 meters, the mind does conceive distances of 400 meters, 200 meters, and thence, the multiples of 800, 1200, etc., which automatically imply concepts of time."[35] The obelisks delimit overlapping squares in plan, derived from the Modulor as well as from traditional Mughal gardens, in which the square is equated with the ordered universe. The buildings are positioned within geometric fields. In contrast to the classical origins of Le Corbusier's initial layout, the modified symmetries of his final version increase the dynamism among the buildings and their integration with the broader landscape. Space, rather than object, is the primary datum.

These boundary markers are abstract points on the ground plane, disconnected visually. Their meaning is revealed only in the conceptual

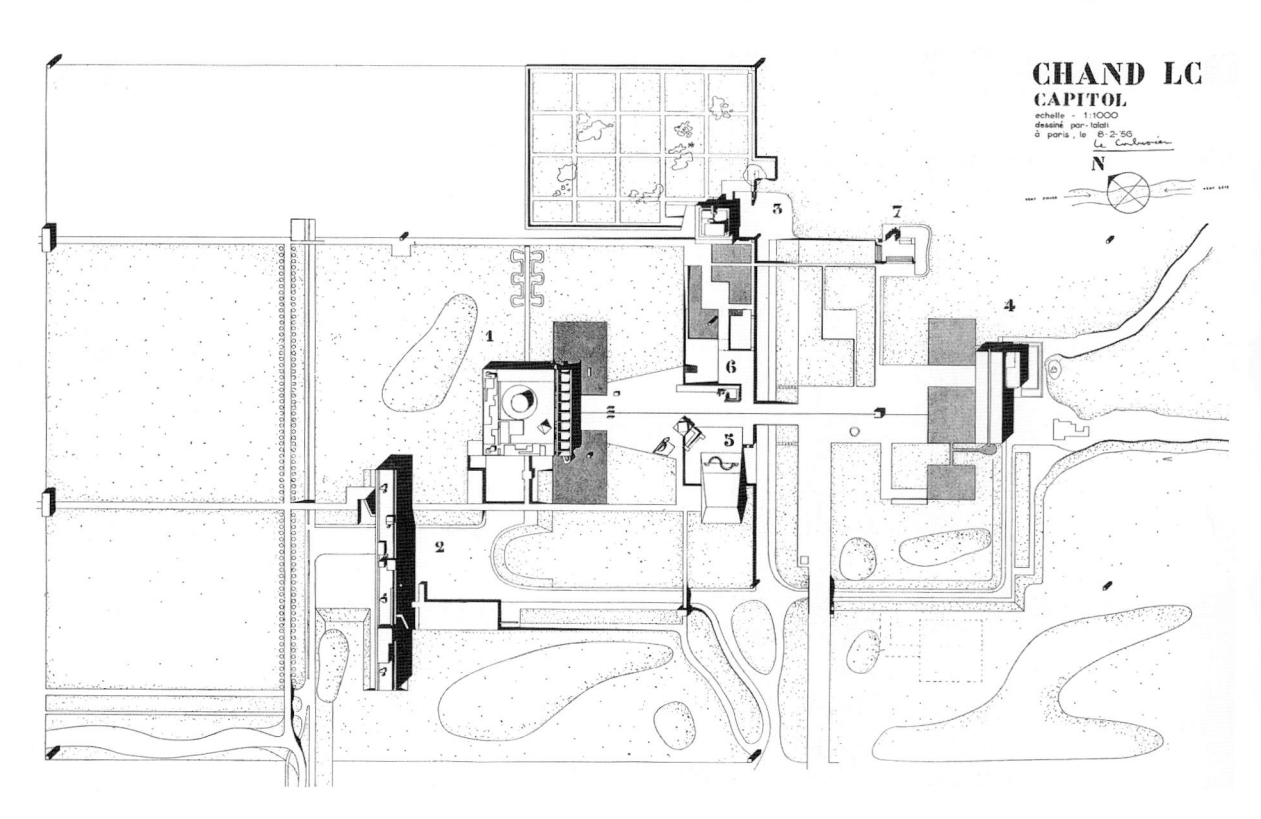

Le Corbusier's final layout of August 1956 for the capital complex, Chandigarh. Copyright 2011 Artists Rights Society (ARS), New York / ADAGP, Paris / F.L.C.

overview of the plan; no buildings are to transgress the imaginary lines connecting these points.[36] The boundary between the landscape of the capital complex and the natural landscape is rendered imperceptible. The obelisks, while providing a modern counterpart to the ha-ha, also delimit precincts within the landscape—reinstating the garden within the domain of architecture. They enable Le Corbusier to resolve the inherent conflict between traditional notions of boundary and the modern spatial continuum. Although Le Corbusier never resolved their formal or material properties, the obelisks had an experiential purpose as well: providing a standard by which to measure the vastness of the Punjabi plain.

Le Corbusier's spatial vision was profoundly affected by modern aviation. The airplane expanded perceptual possibilities, providing humankind an experience that could previously only be imagined—the bird's-eye view—thus transcending the limitations of humanist perspective to achieve a new legibility that he associated with the cosmic: "But we have left the ground in an aeroplane and acquired the eyes of a bird. We see, in actuality, that which hitherto was only seen by the spirit. The whole spirit of our plans will be illuminated and amplified by this new point of view."[37] He was conscious of the difficulty in reconciling the spatial potential of the "fifth facade" viewed from above with the experiential implications of his plan: "December 15, 1957. Moving through the space between the lake (the dam) and the Capital . . . I discover Asiatic space. My palaces 1500 [meters] away fill the horizon better than at 650 meters. The scale is nobler and grander from a distance."[38]

Chandigarh Secretariat and Assembly viewed from across a reflecting pool. Copyright 2011 Artists Rights Society (ARS), New York / ADAGP, Paris / F.L.C.

Le Corbusier sought to transcend this difference by infusing modern spatiality with mythopoetic content. The vast pedestrian plaza linking the Assembly and the High Court was inspired in spirit and detail by airport runways, while reflecting pools to reduce the visual distance derive from Mughal garden precedents.[39] The shifted ground plane, with its artificial mounds, reflecting pools, and sunken courts, represents a sacred landscape created ex nihilo. Large earthen mounds, positioned to enhance the perceptual sequence, allude to the distant mountains and contribute to the primal imagery. These landscape elements and the monuments intended to populate the plaza suggest myriad nuances of meaning, as if to amplify their spatial significance.

Throughout the capital complex Le Corbusier used cosmic references to affirm the unity of nature and human consciousness. Many of its monuments and hieroglyphs cast in their concrete surfaces refer to the sun, its daily path and its radiance. He considered the sun a primal force ruling all life, an emblem of harmony between man and nature.[40] He invoked this theme in the Tower of Shadows, a lofty volume for meditation at the heart of the government complex, oriented to the path of the sun and the axis of the earth. Le Corbusier intended the monumental inclined plane of the adjoining Trench of Consideration to be inscribed with the path of the sun and the play of the two solstices, while he incised his symbols of proportional laws, the harmonic spiral and the Modulor, in the pedestrian plaza. He associated the Monument of the Open Hand, set to the east of the Governor's Palace amid irregular groves of sacred mango trees, with the forces of nature; it was designed to rotate with the winds.[41]

Le Corbusier often infused such natural references with ritual intent. The ceremonial door to the Assembly building is enameled with various

(left) Chandigarh capital complex model with plaza monuments and Governor's Palace. Photograph by Lucien Hervé. Copyright 2011 Artists Rights Society (ARS), New York / ADAGP, Paris / F.L.C.

(right) Le Corbusier's sketch of the Monument of the Open Hand, c. 1952. Copyright 2011 Artists Rights Society (ARS), New York / ADAGP, Paris / F.L.C.

cosmic symbols, including the sun in its diurnal revolution, the pyramid/ mountain, and the tree of life. It is used only once a year, on Republic Day, to admit the governor for the opening of Parliament, when the skylight over the assembly hall casts a beam of sunlight on the speaker's platform, in the spirit of the celestial observatories at Jaipur and Delhi. On the Assembly rooftop, the truncated tower and pyramid duplicate at a monumental scale the primal elements of the Ronchamp cistern, while the elements intersecting its skylight symbolize the crescent moon and the path of the sun. Le Corbusier elaborated: "This framework will lend itself to possible solar festivals recalling to men, once a year, that they are children of the sun (entirely forgotten in our unfettered civilization, crushed by absurdities, particularly in architecture and city planning)."[42] Through such cosmic references the Assembly roofscape is the psychological culmination of the *promenade architecturale* rather than a substitute garden. Ritual and symbolic functions here supersede the more visual qualities of Le Corbusier's earliest roof terraces; it is a space of psychic as well as physical occupation, challenging the observer to engage in its interpretation.

Le Corbusier's success at Chandigarh in uniting a mythopoetic conception of space with a modern expression of the spatial continuum was ultimately limited. He reflected on the unprecedented nature of the task:

> There was anxiety and anguish in taking decisions on that vast, limitless ground. . . . The problem was no longer one of reasoning but of sensation. Chandigarh is not a city of lords, princes or kings confined within walls, crowded in by neighbors. It was a matter of occupying a plain. The geometric event was, in truth, a sculpture of the intellect. . . . It was a

(left) Le Corbusier's enameled mural on the Assembly building's monumental entry portal.

(right) The assembly building's ritual roofscape. Copyright 2011 Artists Rights Society (ARS), New York / ADAGP, Paris / F.L.C.

battle of space, fought with the mind. Arithmetic, texturique, geometrics: it would all be there when the whole was finished.[43]

Indeed, as many critics have noted, Le Corbusier was unable to accommodate the monumental scale that he associated with the aspirations of modern India to the realities of perceptual experience. Furthermore, his vision for the capital complex was significantly altered in execution. His landscaping scheme was never realized, and the existing planting has not been adequately maintained. Of the series of monuments that he designed for the esplanade, only the Monument to the Martyrs of the Indian Partition was completed during his lifetime. Plans for the Governor's Palace and adjoining garden that were to crown the complex were abandoned because Nehru considered their inclusion with the governmental buildings unsuited to a democracy. These omissions significantly compromise the symbolic and spatial substance of the whole.

The Architectural Landscape

For the Governor's Palace precinct, Le Corbusier proposed an architectural landscape to mediate between the monumental scale of his government buildings and the more modest volume of the palace. In his sketchbook he noted, "Capital garden must be a miracle!"[44] His use of a garden is particularly appropriate because the name Chandigarh (Hindi for "fortress of the war goddess") and the word *garden* derive from the same Indo-European root: *gher,* meaning "a place set apart, walled off."[45]

Instead of using traditional garden walls, Le Corbusier conceived of a dramatic drop in the flat terrain to render the palace forecourt sacred. In this way he achieved the bounded quality of a garden without interrupting the spatial continuum. This transformation of the ground plane through changes in level and scale is reinforced by the formal imagery. Mock mountains are created through selective excising of the ground plane, a procedure that also yields a totemic column, a watercourse, and a reflecting pool. Rather than mimicking architectural forms, as he did in the Beistegui roof garden, Le Corbusier evoked natural forms and man himself in this garden.

The imagery is accessible to interpretation on many levels; its roots are culturally diverse. In an early sketch the garden and crowning Governor's Palace are evocative of an aircraft carrier. Like the cruise ship, the aircraft carrier was for Le Corbusier an important symbol of the modern

Le Corbusier's sketches of the Governor's Palace and garden, 12 April 1952, and of an aircraft carrier, which he posited as an analogous structure. Copyright 2011 Artists Rights Society (ARS), New York / ADAGP, Paris / F.L.C.

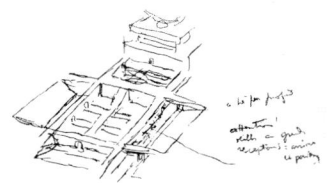

age; both served as paradigms of the engineer's aesthetic and the autonomous communal structure. Unlike the cruise ship, the aircraft carrier is analogous to a landscape; it symbolizes the integration of nature and the machine.[46] On a more primitive level, the garden evokes the sacred landscape of an Egyptian temple complex; the stepped contour of the palace resembles a pyramid, denoting the axis of the universe and the cosmic mountain linking earth and sky.[47] These diverse sources reflect Le Corbusier's desire to endow his work with universal significance, yet the spirit of this garden also reflects its more immediate heritage: the sixteenth- and seventeenth-century gardens of Mughal India. In 1951 Le Corbusier visited two of these gardens, the seventeenth-century Pinjore gardens near

Terraced lake garden outside Amber Fort, near Jaipur, one of many sixteenth-century Mughal gardens Le Corbusier visited during his repeated trips to India.

Chandigarh and the Baradari gardens in Petaia. For the roof terrace of the Ahmedabad Museum (1951–56) he created an abstracted version of a Mughal garden, using a geometric arrangement of flowers, shrubs, and forty-five reflecting pools. For the Governor's Palace, Le Corbusier evoked the essence of the Mughal garden rather than reiterating its form.

The *charbagh*, or paradise garden, was the distinctive creation of nomadic Mughal tribes, built to serve in lieu of buildings as an open-air palace. The *charbagh* (literally "four gardens") was divided into four quadrants by water channels, representing the four rivers of life, and terraced to correspond to the Koran's description of paradise. At the Governor's Palace Le Corbusier transformed the geometric structure of the Mughal garden, adapting the formal precision of the original to the ambiguities of modern spatial expression. Intersecting walkways at grade suggest the paradigmatic four subdivisions, displaced by shifting geometries based on the square and the golden section. In place of lush vegetation he substituted paved terraces, which he deemed more appropriate to the arid climate, yet he retained the traditional iconographic elements of the *charbagh*: terraced levels, watercourses, mountain of paradise, and the cosmologically sacred tree, symbol of regeneration, immortality, and ascent to heaven.

Mughal gardens were spaces for contemplation, sensual delight, and retreat from the intense heat, rather than for appreciation through three-dimensional experience. Walkways were raised to allow for irrigation of the planted areas, which varied in depth to enable the tops of plants and walkways to align, thus creating the effect of a Persian carpet, the patterns of which often reflected paradisiacal garden plans.[48] By keeping his walkways at grade while sinking the reflecting pools and terraced courts, Le Corbusier brought a modern spatiality to traditional Mughal motifs. The contemplative qualities of his garden are revealed through the perceptual sequence. Upon descent to the lower level, the constructed landscape would supersede the natural horizon and frame the palace, in turn preceded by its own reflection in a pool of water. This oscillation between foreground and background suggests a tension between traditional space, understood through perspective, and modernist space, which is collapsed and rendered ambiguous to engage the mind as well as the eye.

The approach sequence dramatizes the role of the Governor's Palace, which crowns the composition volumetrically and in plan. Its form recalls the silken awnings set on platforms that provided temporary enclosure in the earliest Mughal gardens. While the palace is the smallest building Le Corbusier proposed for the capital complex, it would command attention through its distinctive profile and integral relationship to its garden, capturing the essence of the Mughal *charbagh*. The direct connection of interior and exterior in the traditional garden is appropriated in the palace's free plan organization and massing. Its stepped terraces, alternating solid and void, also suggest the ritual levels of self-discovery on the Hindu path to unity with the divine.[49] These culminate in an upturned crescent on the roof, silhouetted against the Himalayan foothills, which serves as a viewing platform, shading device, and trough to catch the monsoon rains. The singularity of this form contrasts with its deliberate ambiguity of meaning: it cradles the sky, simultaneously evoking the crescent moon, mountain, and the horns of the sacred ox, yet it also refers to Le Corbusier's favorite symbol of Chandigarh, the Open Hand. Just after he sent his final design for the palace to India, Le Corbusier spotted a similar form—a brick kiln atop a hill—in Bogotá, Colombia, confirming for him the universality of the gesture.[50]

The complex is steeped in a monumental tradition that links East and West. The garden, a haven from the hostile forces of nature, commonly symbolizes the creative potential of life and the reconciliation of humankind with the profusion of nature. The form of the Mughal garden, derived from the mythological structure of the world, connotes the universe in microcosm. The crossing of its two major axes, creating the four-part subdivision, is a cosmic form associated with the Hindu yantra as well as the Buddhist mandala; it is related to the ritually conceived pattern of ancient Indian towns as well as the founding rites of the ancient Roman town. In India the crossing of the major streets traditionally marked the elders' meeting place and the quarters of the highest caste, while in

Le Corbusier's sketch of May 1953 of the Governor's Palace and gardens *(left)*; sketch of May 1951 of a brick kiln at Bogotá, viewed from an airplane. Copyright 2011 Artists Rights Society (ARS), New York / ADAGP, Paris / F.L.C.

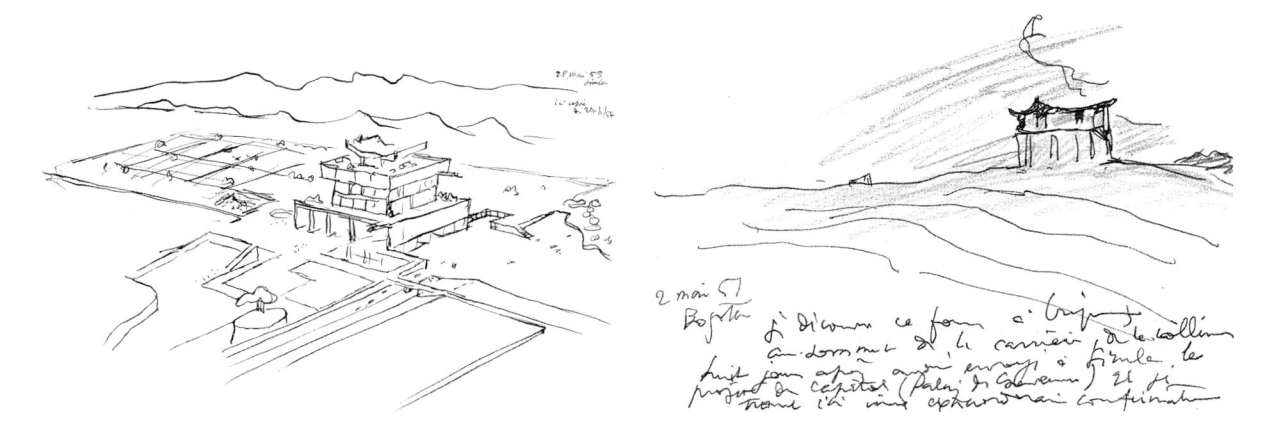

VIRGILIAN DREAM TO CHANDIGARH 167

Sketch integrating diverse scales of landscape at Chandigarh. Copyright 2011 Artists Rights Society (ARS), New York / ADAGP, Paris / F.L.C.

ancient Rome it was the site of the forum.[51] At Chandigarh Le Corbusier transformed this paradigmatic structure to relate three distinct scales of landscape: the garden of the Governor's Palace, the pedestrian plaza of the capital complex, and the organization of the city.

By fusing Mughal symbols with primal imagery, imperial ritualistic space with classical architectural principles, Le Corbusier sought to conflate the traditional Indian concept of the sacred with a modern metaphysic, the cultural with the universal. He noted the congruence of his ideals with the aims of Hindu philosophy: "fraternity between the cosmos and living beings."[52] In addressing fundamental human concerns—the relationship of humankind to nature and of architecture to landscape—he employed a degree of abstraction that transcends the iconographic roots of any particular element. Ultimately the significance of the capital complex rests not on its formal iconography but on "the highly structured, ambiguous union of form and content" by which Le Corbusier sought to render its meaning universal.[53]

The significance of the Governor's Palace garden is both universal and particular; the garden unfolds as a microcosm of the Indian landscape. By separating out a discrete landscape from the general spatial continuum, Le Corbusier rendered meanings more intensely, while in the vast landscape of the capital city such symbolism is diffuse. The effect recalls his description of the Acropolis; the architecture extends its influence to the horizon. In a fitting final tribute, at his last rites the Greek architects deposited a portion of earth from the Acropolis on his grave, while those from India offered water from the Ganges.[54]

EIGHT

HILBERSEIMER AND CALDWELL
Intersecting Ideologies
in Lafayette Park

> This decentralized city would combine the advantages of a small town with those of a metropolis. The metropolis can be located in the landscape. With its parks and gardens it can, indeed, become part of the landscape—*urbs in horto*—the city set in a garden—Chicago's old motto could become reality again.
> —Ludwig Hilberseimer, *The New Regional Pattern* (1949)

> The garden cities of tomorrow could be the rediscovery of America. Then it would be [a] nation of ten or twenty million small farms and of productive parks and vegetable gardens in the parks, of sun-filled houses and sun-filled apartments—and all as one continuous part of the living landscape—the new city, the city of the future which could be now.
> —Alfred Caldwell, *Architecture and Nature* (1984)

Lafayette Park (1955–63) is a paradox—an indication of both the potential of the modern city conceived as an open landscape and the limitations of such a vision. The development is situated within a few blocks of Detroit's downtown core, yet it is profoundly suburban in character. Although widely regarded as one of the most successful examples of urban renewal in the United States, it remains an island of relative affluence amid the sea of empty lots and abandoned buildings that has come to characterize metropolitan Detroit.

Lafayette Park is best known for its buildings, designed by Ludwig Mies van der Rohe, yet the project's most prominent feature is its landscape. The collaborative endeavors of Ludwig Hilberseimer and Alfred Caldwell that culminated in the overall layout and landscape design of

Lafayette Park began in 1940, shortly after Hilberseimer immigrated to the United States. Certain mutual interests undoubtedly contributed to this unlikely alliance between a German architect associated with the *Neue Bauen* and an American landscape architect affiliated with Chicago's Prairie School of landscape design. Both rejected the chaos of the modern metropolis, seeking to achieve a simpler lifestyle by avoiding the deleterious social and health effects of the industrial city; both espoused "organic" design principles and endorsed planning as a route to social reform. Hilberseimer's propensity to rationalize his building volumes and layouts to optimize solar impact and natural ventilation led him to formulate a system of settlement units that prioritized open space. This idea had its formal counterpart in the rolling prairies of the American Midwest, which Caldwell sought to emulate in his landscape designs. Both associated this spatial openness with democratic principles.

Despite their common responses to the "evils" of the industrial city, however, the two designers approached form making from radically different perspectives. Whereas Hilberseimer advocated a modern vernacular architecture that would have broad relevance for the industrialized world, Caldwell developed landscapes arising from and suited to their particular locale. Hilberseimer rationalized every aspect of his proposals, basing his urban propositions on his analysis of major components of contemporary urban life and their interrelationship, while Caldwell rejected any scientific basis for planning and valued beauty for its own sake. Moreover, the underlying political and social implications of Hilberseimer's and Caldwell's visions for the new city differed in several key respects.

Just as Lafayette Park represents an effort to adapt European housing innovations to the American social and political context, so its open landscape reflects the merging of the designers' disparate ideologies as they sought a middle ground between socialism and capitalism. This approach is rooted in garden city ideals as they influenced urban development in Germany and the United States.

The Role of Landscape in Hilberseimer's Settlement Unit

By 1938, when Hilberseimer arrived in the United States to teach at the Armour Institute of Technology (later Illinois Institute of Technology, or IIT), he had already established the foundations for his urban ideas that found their most succinct embodiment in Lafayette Park. Hilberseimer's urban thinking is grounded in the concept of the settlement unit, a semiautonomous entity at pedestrian scale in which discrete building typologies are isolated from one another and linked via an open landscape. The settlement unit incorporates proximity of home to work, separation of automobile and pedestrian traffic, and ease of access to elementary school, public transport, cultural amenities, and parkland, which is productive (i.e., farmed) as well as recreational.

Despite the centrality of landscape to this concept, it was not a component of Hilberseimer's initial urban speculations, as he subsequently argued about his utopian proposal "Highrise City" (1924): "The repetition of the blocks resulted in too much uniformity. Every natural thing was excluded: no tree or grassy area broke the monotony . . . the result was more a necropolis than a metropolis, a sterile landscape of asphalt and cement, inhuman in every aspect."[1] By 1930 Hilberseimer rectified this situation in his mixed-height housing development *(Mischbebauung)*, in which landscape replaced asphalt as the dominant surface. Integrating high-rise apartment slabs with low-rise single-family housing, he aligned the buildings north–south and proportioned the spaces around them to provide comparable solar access for each building type, using scientific logic to regulate housing density.

Hilberseimer's insistence on isolating pedestrian from vehicular traffic also contributed to the dominance of open space in these early proposals. Whereas he initially confined automobile traffic to deep canyons and elevated pedestrian routes in the air, with his mixed-height development Hilberseimer no longer segregated circulation routes through sectional displacement, but limited vehicular access to the perimeter of superblocks composed of distinct housing types spaced to optimize solar

(left) Lafayette Pavilion Apartments, townhouses, and garden walls of court-house units at Lafayette Park, Detroit, by Mies van der Rohe, Ludwig Hilberseimer, and Alfred Caldwell. Photograph by Hedrich Blessing, August 1959. Chicago Historical Society [HB #22688-M].

(right) Ludwig Hilberseimer's perspective view of "Highrise City" of 1924, as published in *Groszstadtarchitektur,* 1927. Archival Image Collection, Ryerson and Burnham Archives, The Art Institute of Chicago. Copyright The Art Institute of Chicago.

impact on their respective volumes. Despite the plethora of landscape in such a system, it would hardly liberate residents in their use of outdoor space, because pathways within the blocks would limit pedestrian access to neighbors living in the same building type—unmarried individuals in high-rise slabs and families in row houses.

Hilberseimer overcame this relative isolation by adapting the cul-de-sac, which Henry Wright and Clarence Stein employed in Radburn, New Jersey (1928), to his next hypothetical layout, the "Fish Spine" scheme (1931–34), in which he first articulated his settlement unit principles. The programmatic distribution also resembles that for Radburn. Civic and cultural facilities, including elementary school, library, community center, and exhibition space, occupy the parks that separate spines containing housing and work spaces, while shops line the highways that connect the culs-de-sac. With the Fish Spine scheme, Hilberseimer abandoned the rigid orthogonal organization that characterized his earlier proposals, suggesting a more integral relationship between rectilinear buildings and an undulating, irregular landscape. Landscape not only links the various programmatic elements of the settlement unit but is also fundamental to its social foundations.

Hilberseimer's approach to open space in these early utopian propositions, comprising allotment gardens, public parks, and recreational areas, drew upon Ebenezer Howard's garden city principles as realized in the *Siedlung* housing settlements of Weimar Germany, in which garden reform was associated with democratic ideals as well as domestic reform. Hilberseimer was familiar with Leberecht Migge's appeals for land reform that would enable cities to break their economic dependence on the countryside, as well as similar arguments published in *Sozialistische Monatshefte* (Socialist monthly bulletins), a series to which he contributed between 1919 and 1922.[2] The model of economic self-sufficiency inherent to the allotment garden was part of a larger effort to address Germany's dire social and economic plight by forging a "third way" between capitalism and socialism. The *Siedlung* landscape was thus intended not only to improve the health and moral fiber of workers and their families but also to play a significant role in the economic plan for the reform of German society.

In his settlement unit, Hilberseimer extended the logic inherent to the *Zeilenbau* housing configuration to metropolitan and regional scales. Conceived in reaction to the unhealthy conditions associated with low-income housing in European industrialized cities, the *Zeilenbau* formation consisted of parallel rows of housing oriented north–south to optimize solar orientation, natural ventilation, and relationship to open space. After initially directing such rationalization to the internal organization of housing units as well as building volumes and orientation, Hilberseimer began to focus on issues of planning—that is, the relationship between the building volumes and their spatial milieu—that he ultimately extended to a regional scale. Because neither the settlement unit nor the *Zeilenbau* configuration was tied to existing patterns of urban settlement, either system could theoretically be expanded indefinitely to form the new city. In addition to offering economic benefits from standardization and health benefits from solar orientation, both models bore the promise of social egalitarianism.[3]

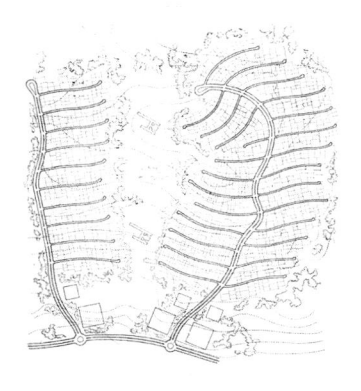

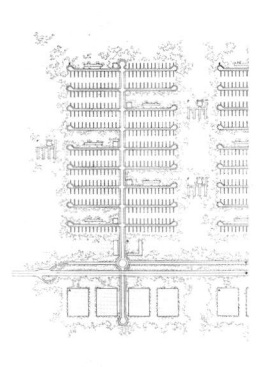

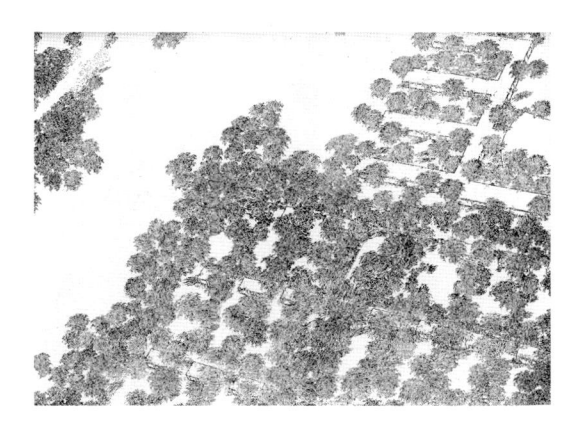

The social organization of the settlement unit is that of an economically self-sufficient medieval village: work space and dwelling are integrated, while ample space for gardens and farms fosters interdependence of village and landscape. In Hilberseimer's idealized interpretation of medieval cities, "free labor becomes the source of economic as well as political freedom. Here was true democracy based on economic equality and independence."[4] Hilberseimer attributed the decline of American cities to the forces of capitalism—the profit motive, unchallenged speculation—as well as a general lack of understanding of the use of technology.[5] By emulating the medieval village in his settlement unit, Hilberseimer sought a return to the qualities of *Gemeinschaft,* Ferdinand Tönnies's sociological category denoting a social order bound by a unity of wills—a quality lost in the fragmentation of modern technological society.[6]

These proposals contain the kernel of Hilberseimer's urban ideas, which he applied to the American midwestern city in general and to Chicago

(left) Hilberseimer's "Fish-Spine" site plan, or "Residential Unit Adapted to the Topography," c. 1931–34, an important basis of his subsequent urban propositions. Siedlungseinheit, der Topographie angepaßt (page 40, illustration 28), *Enfaltung Einer Planungsidee* (Berlin: Ullstein, 1963). Ludwig Karl Hilberseimer papers, Ryerson and Burnham Archives, The Art Institute of Chicago. Copyright The Art Institute of Chicago.

(middle) Hilberseimer's settlement unit plan from *The New City,* 1944. A new settlement unit, 1944. Ludwig Karl Hilberseimer, Archival Image Collection, Ryerson and Burnham Archives, The Art Institute of Chicago. Copyright The Art Institute of Chicago.

(right) Alfred Caldwell's aerial perspective of a settlement unit. Ludwig Hilberseimer, *The New City,* 1944.

in particular upon his immigration to the United States in 1938. Chicago was an opportune destination for Hilberseimer, who cited it as a model for the new city in early drafts of *Groszstadtarchitektur* (1916–18, published 1927).[7] His aspiration to merge city and landscape parallels the motto established at Chicago's founding: "*Urbs in horto*—a city set in a garden," which may in turn have inspired Howard's garden city ideals.[8] Moreover, the spatial aspirations of Ossian Cole Simonds, Jens Jensen, and other adherents of the Prairie School of landscape architecture provided an appropriate counterpart to the spatial openness of Hilberseimer's urban proposals.

Encountering the Prairie Landscape

The seemingly unbounded expanse afforded by the prairie landscape of the American Midwest had a significant impact on European immigrants such as Hilberseimer and Mies, who brought Hilberseimer to Chicago to teach. As Caldwell subsequently argued in a letter to Hilberseimer: "Space in Mies van der Rohe's buildings and the landscape space in the cities you make . . . have a profound relationship to Chicago. Chicago is in the middle of the country, on the tremendous flat prairies of America. These prairies are like the floor of the world with a sense of freedom and space without end."[9] According to Wilhelm Miller, an outspoken advocate for the Prairie School of landscape gardening, the prairie landscape is "the most characteristic scenery on the American continent" and the prairie horizon "the strongest line in the western hemisphere."[10] For Caldwell's mentor and former employer Jens Jensen, the attraction of the prairie was analogous to that of the sea:

> There is . . . great similarity in the vastness expressed in the open expanses of the prairies and that of the sea. The sea has a distinct power of drawing one out, of arousing one's curiosity to investigate what is beyond the horizon. . . . The prairies, too, have mystery. They too, have a horizon that calls. . . . However, the prairies give a far more secure feeling than the sea. The prairies are inhabited; they are human. Like oases the homes of man are scattered over them. . . . They are the Mid-American empire, the heart and moving force of our great country.[11]

The open prairie landscape provided Hilberseimer an ideal milieu in which to both test and expand upon his settlement unit principles.

Hilberseimer's adaptation to this new environment was facilitated by his collaboration with Caldwell, which began in 1939 when the latter was taking courses at the Armour Institute in preparation for his architectural registration exam. Caldwell was steeped in Prairie School principles, having worked with Jensen in the years before the Great Depression. He absorbed principles of ecology from his mentor and learned to appreciate the particular qualities of the midwestern landscape by responding directly to each site and using indigenous plant materials. His antiurban attitude also derives from Jensen, who contrasted the "prison-like" conditions of life in the city with the open spirit of the plains: "The plains speak of freedom—earth and sky meet on the far horizon. There is nothing to intercept the vision from the infinite."[12]

Another significant influence on Caldwell was Frank Lloyd Wright, whom the landscape architect visited at Taliesin East. Caldwell assimilated many lessons from Wright, particularly "the feeling of architecture that floats in space"—a primary affinity between Wright and Mies.[13] Wright's influence on Caldwell is evident in the pronounced horizontality of his buildings at Eagle Point Park in Dubuque, Iowa (1936), elaborated through shallow-pitched roofs, deep overhanging eaves, and stratified walls of natural stone—qualities associated with the architect's Prairie Style houses. Drawing on a principle that Frederick Law Olmsted utilized in his plan for New York's Central Park (from 1858, with Calvert Vaux), Caldwell also separated pedestrian and vehicular routes at Eagle Point Park, as Hilberseimer was then advocating.

Caldwell's landscape experience, drawing skills, and engaging lecture style were all useful to Hilberseimer, who enlisted the student to make drawings for his forthcoming book, *The New City* (1944). Caldwell taught at IIT (1945–60 and 1981–96). He frequently served as a stand-in on the lecture circuit for Hilberseimer and Mies, who were uncertain of their English proficiency, and his writings soon began to resemble those of Hilberseimer.[14] As a result of this interaction, Caldwell's architecture shifted from Wrightian structures in wood and stone to Miesian proposals in steel and glass. Despite this stylistic about-face, Caldwell's description of his buildings at Eagle Point Park could apply equally to his intentions for Lafayette Park: "the merging of Nature and Architecture, resulting in a kind of mysterious continuum of light and shadow, a wavering of reality, of a world glimpsed and undefinable, uncertain and mesmerizing."[15]

Hilberseimer also influenced Caldwell's theoretical approach. In 1948 Caldwell received his master of science degree in city planning from IIT with a thesis titled "A City in the Landscape: A Preface for Planning," carried out under Hilberseimer. He based the written portion on the idea of eliminating poverty by integrating industry and agriculture, town and country, an idea borrowed from Peter Kropotkin's *Fields, Factories, and Workshops* (1898) and Henry Ford's *My Life and Work* (1922). In *The New City* Hilberseimer endorsed the social and economic benefits of this idea, arguing that it would promote self-sustainable communities, reduce both infrastructure and unemployment, and promote a healthy lifestyle.[16] The integration of industry and agriculture was also a precept of Wright's Broadacre City, which Hilberseimer cited as an example of "how city and country can be connected and become a unit."[17] Like Broadacre City, the settlement unit features land distribution as an inevitable consequence of industrial innovation. This protoecological argument implied a changed attitude toward the exploitation of natural resources, although Wright's democratic individualism ran counter to Hilberseimer's communitarian principles.

The collaboration in turn had a marked effect on Hilberseimer. The ecological perspective latent in Hilberseimer's urban ideas had its landscape counterpart in Caldwell's work. Ecology became a prominent aspect of Hilberseimer's writings, as his concept of the organic evolved from visible notions of order to those encompassing underlying processes and the scale of his concerns expanded to encompass regional dimensions.[18] The drawings that Caldwell made for *The New City* and *The New Regional Pattern* (1949) reflect the increasing role of landscape in Hilberseimer's urban thinking: "The New Regional Pattern will be determined by the character of the landscape: its geographical and topographical features, its natural resources; by the use of land, the methods of agriculture and industry, their decentralization and integration; and by human activities, individual and social, in all their diversity."[19]

(left) Hilberseimer's proposed replanning of Chicago, 1940. "City of Chicago. A Diagram of Its Proposed Replanning, 1940," Chicago, Illinois, 1940. Ludwig Karl Hilberseimer, Archival Image Collection, Ryerson and Burnham Archives, The Art Institute of Chicago. Copyright The Art Institute of Chicago.

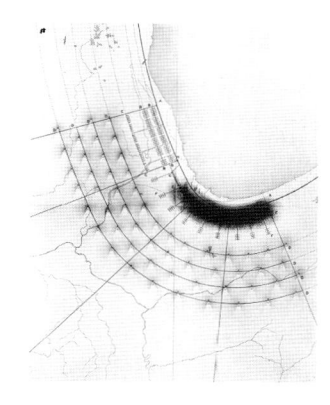

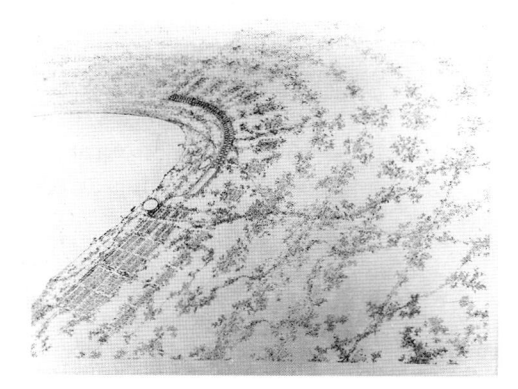

(right) Alfred Caldwell's aerial perspective of the replanned city of Chicago, from *The New City*, 1944. City of Chicago, Replanned, Chicago, Illinois, 1944. Ludwig Karl Hilberseimer, Archival Image Collection, Ryerson and Burnham Archives, The Art Institute of Chicago. Copyright The Art Institute of Chicago.

In these plans and aerial perspectives, architecture recedes from view under the camouflage of landscape, as Hilberseimer envisioned the new city: "Just as the house fuses with the landscape, the room with the garden, the interior with the exterior, so also the city itself can merge with the landscape and the landscape can come within the city."[20] The aerial perspective dislocates the viewer from the space of the city. It privileges the modern conception of space as a continuum without prior accents of meaning, rather than space as an occupiable, palpable domain. It displaces the human subject from the space of the city, countering the organic communal qualities of *Gemeinschaft* that Hilberseimer imagined would arise within his settlement unit. This contrast between Hilberseimer's view of space as a continuum and Caldwell's concept of space as a palpable entity is grounded in their respective interpretations of organic design principles.

Organic Principles and Democratic Ideals

Both Caldwell and Hilberseimer espoused organic logic as a means to establish relationships among the parts of a composition, although their design approaches differed in fundamental respects. For Caldwell, as for Wright, the organic is grounded in the natural world, an anticlassical stance in which organic architecture, like organic society, resists all external impositions. As Wright argued, such architecture "proceeded from the ground and . . . somehow the terrain, the native industrial conditions, the nature of materials and the purpose of the building, must inevitably determine the form and character of any good building." Borrowing an expression from Lao-Tzu, he elaborated that organic architecture "consisted not in the four walls and the roof but inhered in the space to live in."[21] Caldwell's design approach was similarly based in notions of landscape as a lived milieu, the effects and significance of which accrue through active engagement over time.

In contrast, for Hilberseimer, as for Mies, the organic comprised an autonomous structural logic capable of resolving oppositions between art and technology, nature and culture, inner essence and outer form, into a new unity regulated by natural laws of self-generation:

> Order is not, like organization, a mechanical addition of parts, or a pattern superimposed upon an object. Order grows out of the nature of things, seeks harmony, relates parts to the whole and the whole to the parts, and gives each part and every activity its place according to its

value and function. Order creates a balance between the individual and society as well as between the forces of matter and spirit. Order provides the medium in which everything can grow and unfold organically.[22]

Hilberseimer's sense of the organic thus arises from human logic, from geometric principles of economy, efficiency, and organization—a classical understanding of order capable in turn of being adapted to specific settings.

As early as 1929, Hilberseimer endorsed organic planning as a means to address the cultural destabilization brought about by modernization.[23] In a passage highly indebted to Mies, he subsequently argued:

> The organic order is autonomous; its guiding principle is that each part must develop according to its own law, that each part must have its due place, according to its importance and function, within the whole. It means, as St. Augustine said, "the disposition of equal and unequal things, attributing to each its proper place." Organic planning aims to find the pattern and form adequate to a city's location and function. It deals also with the forms and means of life and strives to establish a balance between things material and things spiritual. It provides the conditions in which all things can grow and unfold.[24]

To Hilberseimer, this organic/mechanistic paradigm was capable of imparting order to the chaotic phenomena of urban growth in the United States. Moreover, it posited the inseparability of housing and planning, architecture and landscape—a premise fundamental to Lafayette Park.

Like Ebenezer Howard, Hilberseimer was less interested in the physical form of the new city than in its social processes.[25] His writings and the images he used to illustrate his ideas reflect the possibilities of what life might be like in this future environment, rather than rules for its design and construction. The fact that his settlement unit comprised a limited number of functions was less important than that its form embodied a particular organizational logic. Moreover, his planning strategy is not authoritarian but capable of accommodating changing circumstances over time. He applied an incremental approach to urban redevelopment in his studies of several Chicago neighborhoods. By intermittently interrupting the regular street grid to insert linear parks and automobile culs-de-sac, he gradually transformed the typical system of urban blocks to conform to his settlement unit principles, thus adapting them to the existing infrastructure without the devastation wreaked upon American cities by urban renewal. Through such successive acts of erasure Hilberseimer imagined that the contemporary metropolis could evolve into his vision of the new city.[26] This planning strategy was a vehicle for the progressive reconstruction of capitalist society into cooperative communities, as Hilberseimer argued:

> City planning is not merely the expression of changing social patterns; it is also a positive force in the development of those patterns. It is a social and an economic task. It may thus function creatively to build the structure of the future in which the economic philosophy is based not on arbitrariness but on the necessities of life for men—a structure in which people and nations and regions may find complete development within a world-wide federation.[27]

In his vision of the new city, the organic comprises a new nature, of human origin, linked to the construction of a new humanity: a classless society with inherent new freedoms.

Caldwell ultimately sought to reconcile their diverse interpretations of the organic by rationalizing nature in a manner similar to Hilberseimer and Mies: "Nature is structure. Nature is not a shape; it is not a sentiment; it is not a prerogative. Nature is ultimate reality. Nature is that which must be. Therefore nature is fate." Deriving his view of nature from human logic, Caldwell drew analogies between nature and architecture: "Every structure—like nature—has its own innate law."[28]

Both Caldwell and Hilberseimer equated their organic notions of order with democratic principles, although these were rooted in different concepts of political organization as well as landownership and access rights. Both endorsed land redistribution to further their social agendas, yet Caldwell assumed distinctions between private and public space such as exist throughout the United States, whereas Hilberseimer operated with assumptions of public access to the land, such as exist in Germany and England.

Hilberseimer argued: "The pattern of free cities is of an organic order. It reflects the community spirit of cities self-ruled and based on a voluntary coalition of citizens."[29] He associated this democratic character with both the scale of the settlement and its prevalence of open space:

> Any settlement, to be effective, should be large enough to provide for variety and diversity and to make possible the maintenance of communal hygiene and cultural institutions as well as to furnish proper arrangements for the distribution of goods. But it should also be small enough to maintain an organic community life, so that democracy can prevail and each individual be a participant in community activities.[30]

Hilberseimer equated open space with freedom of choice and hence with democratic values: "Today our spatial feeling tends to openness: so does our city structure. Different forces tend to dissipate the confinement of the city, to liberate the house, and with it, man; and to link man to nature once again."[31] He reasoned that the democratic spirit of his proposals would derive from the settlement unit parkland, a significant component in his aim to balance individual and collective needs.

Despite his leftist political leanings, Caldwell considered private ownership of land to be a fundamental American value.[32] He associated his democratic vision with the Jeffersonian ideal of the yeoman farmer—the rural citizen as an active and effective participant in the political life of his community: "The living landscape could give back the freedom, security and independence implicit in the Jeffersonian principle, upon which the Republic was originally founded."[33] Caldwell considered himself a pioneer in Hilberseimer's new city; he included his farm in Bristol, Wisconsin, in an aerial perspective of the Chicago region that he drew for Hilberseimer in 1942:

> Thousands of city plans have been made for the cities of America. But not one—even the most timorous—has ever been followed. They only gather dust in the vaults' shelves. However this particular plan is unique. In a manner of speaking, it is actually under construction. This architect—turned city planner—purchased 40 acres of an 80-acre tract, and began to build the city on his own.[34]

The forty-acre tract had its origins in the Land Ordinance of 1785, passed at Thomas Jefferson's urging, which furthered the agricultural basis of the American economy by subdividing the land into square-mile units, irrespective of natural boundaries, to encourage settlement. Caldwell associated his farm/villa with Jeffersonian values, which he in turn equated with American values.[35]

As a result of their collaboration, Hilberseimer also came to embrace certain Jeffersonian ideals. In *The Nature of Cities* he reasoned that, should his vision of urban resettlement come to pass,

> human beings, no longer regarded as means to an end, could again be able to seek that self-improvement which might, at last, replace the ideal of material progress with the ethical ideal of human welfare. Egotistic self-interest might become secondary, in such a world, to the altruistic concept of the welfare of others and of the community as a whole.[36]

These qualities of self-improvement and community involvement through working the land emerged most forcefully in his examination of various types and sizes of farms in *The New Regional Pattern,* where he argued the merits not only of landownership but also of farming: "Everyone who wished to, could have land of his own to till and with it the personal independence that only land can give."[37] Hilberseimer imagined that this variegated farmland, fully integrated with industrial uses, would constitute an organic unity related to that of his settlement unit: "The cultivated landscape, like the natural, can be an organic unit, a living entity whose parts are coordinated and supported by each other, whose usefulness and conservation are identical, whose varied and sound functioning makes possible a good and lasting life for those who dwell within it."[38] His vision of the new city thus involved a transformation of the entire American landscape, urban and rural. Although he believed that the settlement unit could accommodate growth without sacrificing the clarity or humanizing aspects of its urban structure, this presumes an infinite expanse of land available for settlement, a romantic conceit that harks back to the American wilderness as an unlimited resource to be exploited. His proposal for Lafayette Park treats the evacuated city of Detroit as an untapped resource, similar to the midwestern prairie, its limits confined only by its suburban outposts.

Because Hilberseimer deplored the emptiness of the material way of life, he proposed a new urban form of greater asceticism and simplicity, arguing that the "only possibility of emerging from this chaos [is] the most extreme economy of form, the most extreme primitiveness."[39] He based his emphatic rejection of the modern metropolis on the assumption that the success of historic cities resulted from their clear organizing structure: "To solve so complex a problem we must go back to fundamentals. We must learn to see the intricate simply, even naively. We must disentangle the chaos of our conceptions. We must define our purposes. Only then can we plan and build our cities to our satisfaction."[40] The influence of Fordism on this type of design rationalization made Detroit a fitting milieu for Hilberseimer to test his urban preoccupations.

The Lafayette Park Landscape

Despite Hilberseimer's objections to urban renewal, the clearance of 120 acres in Detroit's Lower East Side between 1950 and 1953, financed in part by the Federal Housing Act of 1949, paved the way for the most complete embodiment of his settlement unit.[41] The characteristic pattern of urban redevelopment in the United States—a superblock comprising low-density groups of apartments or row houses, realized through a combination of private and public initiatives—had begun in 1932 with the Hoover administration under the influence of Henry Wright, first consultant to the Housing Division of the Public Works Administration.[42] The form emanated from Wright's interest in adapting European housing innovations to the American social and political context. The provisions of the 1949 Housing Act radically altered the social and economic program for urban revitalization, however, by placing responsibility for redevelopment in the hands of private developers.[43] After the 1954 plan of Oscar Stonorov, Minoru Yamasaki, and Victor Gruen for the Gratiot Redevelopment Project (subsequently known as Lafayette Park) failed to arouse interest among developers, the Citizens Redevelopment Committee solicited Chicago developer Herbert Greenwald to submit a proposal. Greenwald in turn enlisted a design from Mies and Hilberseimer, who replaced the previous group's grand avenue bounded by housing clusters with a central linear park, in conformance with settlement unit principles.

Hilberseimer's superblock strategy was consistent with the Detroit Plan of 1949, which called for a development of low- and high-rise housing interspersed with public green space, commercial space along Lafayette Boulevard, and a school adjoining the park. Rather than locate high-rise dwelling units along the major traffic arteries bounding the site, he initially dispersed them amid the low-rise units, linking the diverse housing

(left) Hilberseimer's site plan sketch for the Gratiot Redevelopment Project (Lafayette Park), c. 1956. Richard Pommer et al., *In the Shadow of Mies: Ludwig Hilberseimer, Architect, Educator, and Urban Planner,* 1988.

(right) Plan of Lafayette Park as built, c. 1963, indicating site of proposed school at the bottom of the park, housing zones sold off to other developers in upper right, and site for a neighborhood shopping center in lower right. Lafayette Park, Pavilion Apartments and Townhouses, Detroit, Michigan, c. 1958–65. Ludwig Mies van der Rohe, Archival Image Collection, Ryerson and Burnham Archives, The Art Institute of Chicago. Copyright The Art Institute of Chicago.

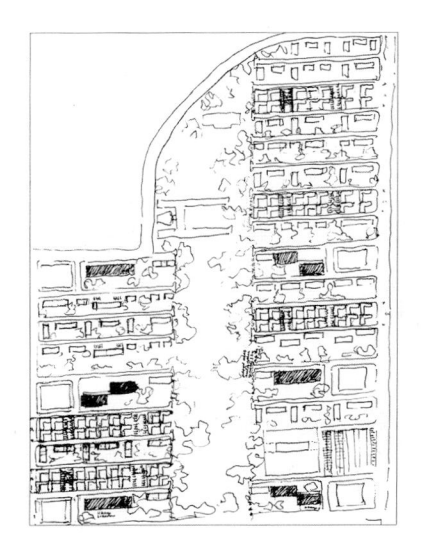

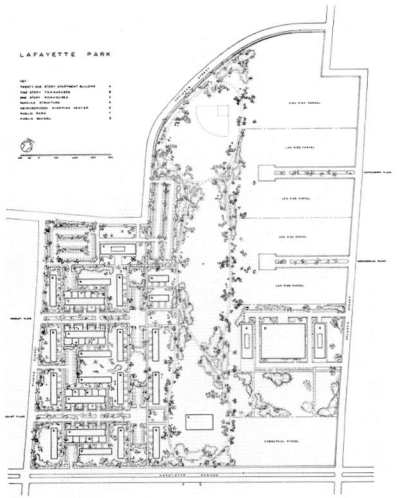

types both directly and via the park. Although his layout was consistent with prevalent urban planning theories of the day, the project was oppositional in many senses. The housing stock in Detroit consisted primarily of single-family houses; apartment buildings were rare, and only a single cooperative project existed at the time Lafayette Park was built. The superblock concept, a component of all three plans, interrupted the existing pattern and scale of the urban infrastructure.

By the time Hilberseimer was given the task of providing a layout or the site, its buildings had been demolished, but its street grid remained. He argued successfully to have these remnants of the nineteenth-century city eliminated, converting the site to a tabula rasa that was interrupted only by the specimen trees that the design team took care to preserve. Thus he made no reference to the site's prior variegated grid of avenues, roads, and service alleys, or even to its preurban configuration as linear farms lining the Detroit River, but determined the positions of culs-de-sac internally, in accordance with the modular character of Mies's housing units.[44]

In his various layouts for the Gratiot Redevelopment Project, Hilberseimer oriented his buildings to the urban street grid rather than in strict alignment with the solar path, despite both his insistence on the importance of solar orientation and his desire to eliminate all signs of the site's previous infrastructure. Moreover, he alternately oriented the low-rise housing *either* approximately east–west *or* north–south, while consistently maintaining a dominant southern orientation for the high-rise housing slabs. (The ultimate shift in orientation of Lafayette Towers to east–west may have resulted from his desire to avoid north-facing units.) Nevertheless, his site strategy, in which housing types were strictly aligned, differed significantly from the approach taken by Mies.

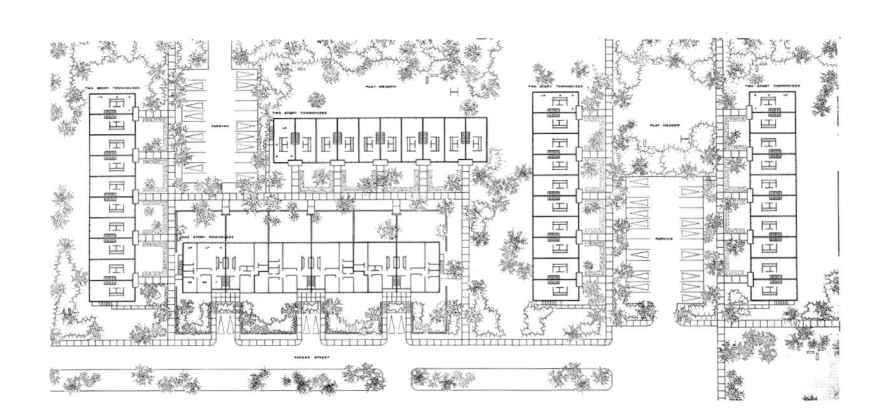

Ludwig Mies van der Rohe's detail plan of townhouses and court houses, Lafayette Park. Photograph by Hedrich Blessing. Chicago Historical Society [HB #23315a].

Whereas Hilberseimer considered open space itself a virtue, Mies recognized the advantages of formal tensions within the space, so he reoriented certain low-rise housing units east–west to augment the exterior spatial hierarchy. If Caldwell's landscaping reflects an attempt to soften the abstract rigors of such a layout, then the subtle variations in Mies's unit plans and dramatic shifts in building orientation do the same for the area's open spaces. Caldwell's inflected ground plane has a more pronounced effect, however—that of "correcting" the disembodied qualities of Miesian space. Yet the subtle berms and dense vegetation at the edges of the low-rise housing complex set this zone apart from its urban environs and demarcate it as a semipublic realm, in direct conflict with Hilberseimer's notion of open democratic space—a difference also reflected in the depressed parking areas that keep automobiles out of direct view of the dwelling units. The insular nature of this housing sector is echoed in the single-story row houses wherein social space centers on private courtyards. In these courtyard units, only the outer facades of floor-to-ceiling glass maintain the inhabitants' sense of presence in the community.

Early photos of Lafayette Park, in which the planting is immature and sparse, differ markedly from the heavily vegetated landscape one sees today. Because Greenwald was hesitant to spend the money to create the layered landscape that Caldwell envisioned for the site, the landscape architect maintained his intended amount of planting by resorting to young seedlings rather than using more developed specimens. An understory of flowering crabapple, dogwood, lilac, and viburnum reinforces the spatial variety of the building layout within a unifying canopy of honey locusts along the culs-de-sac and parking areas, while hawthorn hedges demarcate segments of lawn fronting the two-story units and screen views of the interiors.

Alfred Caldwell's manipulation of the flat site at Lafayette Park as seen in a berm at the development border and a depressed parking area.

Such is not the case with the public park, where construction was funded by the city and severe budgetary restrictions prevented Caldwell's conception—a long narrow clearing bounded by thick groves of trees and shrubs—from being realized. In keeping with Prairie School principles, Caldwell sought to simulate the effect of a midwestern prairie by maintaining a long view through the park, which in the opinion of Wilhelm Miller was more suited to daily life than the broad prairie view, which could not be achieved on such a constricted urban site.[45] Instead, isolated trees distributed randomly throughout the park supplemented the mature specimens preserved during site demolition. Moreover, Caldwell never realized his usual practice of staking out his landscape design directly on the site; Greenwald's firm enlisted John Heinrich to supervise the landscape installation, using plants from a bankrupt local nursery.

The landscape of Lafayette Park differs radically from the productive working landscape of Hilberseimer's settlement unit.[46] It is closer to the domesticated natural environment that Frederick Law Olmsted espoused to tame the tensions and contradictions of the industrial city. Like Olmsted, Hilberseimer and Caldwell associated their park with social reform; they conceived of it as a democratic social integrator, capable of serving the aesthetic education of the urban populace through the suggestion rather than the imitation of natural beauty. Unlike Olmsted, Caldwell sought to evoke the specific spirit of the midwestern landscape by relying heavily on native species and by fully integrating buildings and landscape features. The result was no less artificial than an Olmsted park, but contrived to different ends: to suggest the open expanses of the prairie within the confines of a flat urban site.

(left) Early view of the Lafayette Park landscape. Photograph by Hedrich Blessing, August 1959. Chicago Historical Society [HB #22688-C].

(right) Comparable view of Lafayette Park from 2009.

The public park at Lafayette Park.

Caldwell's description of his proposal for Chicago's Columbus Park provides a sense of his intentions for Lafayette Park:

> This park interprets the spirit of the native landscape. Like the landscape, it too is an organism, and the sense of the whole is evident in all the parts. Columbus Park is a creation, a conscious imaginative work of art, and not a duplication of nature. It is a structure created by the working of organized principles . . . based on an idea of life and space. That sense of space rejects the tyranny of closure. It repudiates the sterile masonry terrain of cities today that are as prisons, spaceless and visionless. It asserts the rights of man to the wide green earth. In this park an island of forest stands free on the edge of the prairie, and the prairie space between the free-standing forest and forest background is like a broad pathway to a world unseen. It possesses a mystical quality of infinite space, like the premonition of some irrational dimension. This quality of other-worldliness is a spirit and beyond definition. Columbus Park is a landscape located in the universe.[47]

At Lafayette Park, as in Columbus Park, Caldwell drew upon Jensen's antiurban bias as well as Olmsted's view of the urban park as the antithesis of the city.

Other aspects of Lafayette Park reflect ideas that were nascent in the American landscape. A sales brochure for the project proclaims: "Live in the Suburbs in a City . . . live in the City in a Suburb." The suburban character of Lafayette Park derives primarily from its single-use character and its parklike setting—its promise of life in harmony with nature within a close-knit, stable community. Greenery is used to segregate the residential community from Detroit's urban core. Like suburbia, Lafayette Park excludes all industry and commercial uses that do not directly serve the vicinity's residential areas.[48] Although racially integrated, the development is effectively a middle-class ghetto that turns its back on its more disadvantaged neighbors. Moreover, it lacks the ties to mass transit systems that Hilberseimer deemed essential to the settlement unit; the residents of Lafayette Park are dependent on the automobile.

Like Frank Lloyd Wright, Hilberseimer viewed technology as a positive force in shaping his vision of the new city: "Recent technical achievements—electricity and the automobile—are tending to decentralize urban settlements just as the railroad and steam power formerly tended to centralize and concentrate them."[49] To accommodate the automobile without interfering with pedestrian routes at Lafayette Park, he provided the low-rise housing units with surface parking lots, which Caldwell depressed into the ground to minimize their visual impact. Mies's parking structure for the apartment slabs is not only partially sunken below grade but also topped by a garden/recreation space, thus ensuring that automobiles are kept discreetly out of sight of the apartment units.

Because Hilberseimer reasoned that the automobile and the spatial openness of the modern city had invalidated traditional loci of public space, he sought new forms for community life and values in the landscape. At Lafayette Park, however, little attention was given to communal facilities. Instead, it was assumed that social benefits would accrue from living in proximity to nature. For Hilberseimer, as for Olmsted, nature was an antidote to the insalubrious conditions prevailing in industrial cities. For the hypothetical inhabitants of his settlement unit, gardening was to be a source of financial security as well as physical and moral health, recalling the rationale for the *Siedlung* landscapes of Weimar Germany. Yet residents of Lafayette Park lack individual control over their natural environs, save the few feet of ground immediately adjacent to the two-story row houses or within private courtyards of the single-story units. Thus, although Hilberseimer recognized the need to accommodate the private automobile, facilitating travel to the broader urban environs, he made few concessions to the rugged individualism of the American psyche. The hierarchy of ownership is a major factor in access to and control of this "democratic" landscape. Whereas the occupants of the high-rise rental units are limited to visual exposure to the park from on high or indirect access for recreational purposes, but have no say concerning its possible improvement, owners of the cooperative row-house and court-house units have direct contact with their individual yards and the broader landscape, as well as limited control (through co-op boards) over its specific character.

Lafayette Park is neither a transformation of the previous urban structure nor a complete realization of Hilberseimer's settlement unit. Although the development includes three types of housing, an elementary school, and a small shopping center, it lacks the integration of living and work space and proximity to public transportation networks that Hilberseimer deemed essential to the new city. By siting the school between the major boulevard and the park, moreover, Hilberseimer and Mies effectively isolated the park visually from the public space of the city. In addition, Greenwald's death in an airplane crash in 1959 led to the piecemeal development of the broader site, with the result that the adjoining high-rise apartment buildings and low-rise housing clusters designed by other architects occupy discrete parcels, disrupting Hilberseimer's intended spatial continuity. Subsequent development of surrounding parcels in the Gratiot Redevelopment area has followed a similar pattern, resulting in a series of insular middle-class condominium developments linked by parks that appear to be semiprivate. If Lafayette Park is one of the most successful examples of urban redevelopment in the United States, then it has also sealed "the ultimate fate of Detroit as a suburb of its own suburbs."[50]

An image of a Nazi rally that Hilberseimer included in his book *The New Regional Pattern* provides an indication of his formal proclivities and associated social assumptions. He paired this image, captioned "formed masses," with an overhead view of a randomly organized, anonymous crowd, captioned "unformed masses."[51] As he had no allegiance to the Nazi Party, Hilberseimer's rally citation provides an insight into the extreme formal measures he deemed necessary for reordering the American landscape in the aftermath of World War II. Equating the open ground plane of Lafayette Park with democratic freedom, he envisioned its featureless surface as inscribed with the social patterns of a classless society imbued with new liberties. Yet Hilberseimer's socialist vision reflects a top-down system of governance, rather than the open essence of a participatory democracy.

Hilberseimer traced the inadequacies of contemporary cities to three principal deficiencies stemming from rapid, unplanned growth: insoluble traffic problems causing danger to pedestrians and motorists, lack of sunlight and access to recreational space in residential areas, and lack of zoning that would regulate industry in relation to housing and integrate housing and work.[52] Many of the public health and sanitation issues that Hilberseimer addressed are no longer relevant: pedestrian safety is not a primary concern, the demand for adjacent green space is low, and proximity of home and work is devalued by those who seek greater choices among work places and dwelling places. Thus whatever interest remains in Hilberseimer's urban propositions seems to be for partial rather than comprehensive reasons.[53]

Assessments of his urban theories vary widely. Kim Halik praises their "proto-ecological" qualities.[54] David Spaeth calls Lafayette Park "nothing less than a working model for future urbanization, predicated on human values and needs, accommodating but not dominated by the automobile," while Albert Pope deems the settlement unit "a machine for the elimination of choice—the censuring of urban activity."[55] Paul Thomas argues: "In the end we may have to work out Hilberseimer's diagrams and ideas and restructure our cities and regions, although things may have to fall more terribly apart before we are ready to do so."[56] Pope counters: "By now it is clear that the dramatic spatial continuity of modern architecture sponsors the closed urban ghetto more than it sponsors any liberating openness of universal urban space."[57]

Despite its obvious theoretical flaws, Hilberseimer's vision of the new city—based on both a Jeffersonian sense of the inherent worth of the individual and a balance between individual and community, humans and nature—has little resonance with the landscape of Lafayette Park. His radical planning approach was ultimately tempered by Mies's modifications to the housing layout and Caldwell's landscape elaboration and subtle modulations of the ground plane. The development is a manifesto of European communitarian ideals combined with enticements directed toward American middle-class aspirations for leisure time. Yet apart from its semipublic recreational facilities—children's swings and sliding boards within the low-rise housing precinct and a swimming pool atop the garage for the high-rise apartment slabs—the Lafayette Park landscape is experienced in a passive manner. It lacks the type of synesthetic, cognitive experiences that would enable residents to interrelate and forge a collective sense of place through active engagement. Contrary to the social aims of both Caldwell and Hilberseimer, it is a reification of the pastoral vision that characterizes the suburban American dream.

NINE

THE ONCE AND FUTURE PARK
From Central Park
to OMA's Parc de la Villette

During the early 1980s disciplinary distinctions between architecture and landscape design were challenged by an international competition for a public park in Paris in which the most significant proposals came from architects. With their entries for the Parc de la Villette competition of 1982–83, Bernard Tschumi and Rem Koolhaas (with his collaborative practice OMA, the Office for Metropolitan Architecture), respectively, avoided predetermined architectural solutions by adopting open-ended design strategies intended to yield unanticipated results. While sharing certain aesthetic affinities with an ecological approach to landscape design, such cross-disciplinary means also pointed to significant distinctions between the professions. Despite parallels in the architects' theoretical accounts of these projects, moreover, their approaches to the problem differed substantially, leading in the case of Tschumi's premiated scheme to a construction that is formally definitive, while Koolhaas's proposal would have enabled the park's formal and programmatic resolution to remain open and socially contingent.

Conceived as a vehicle for both speculation about and realization of "a new model for an urban park," the Parc de la Villette competition raised implicit provocations about the evocation of power relations in a plural democracy as well as explicit questions concerning the form such an innovative landscape might take.[1] Koolhaas's proposal is atavistic, fostering modes of urban experience that were suppressed in nineteenth- and early twentieth-century efforts to infuse order into the historic city and provide a means of escape from its insalubrious conditions. His tactic contrasts with traditional public park design in several significant ways: it encourages social engagement that is potentially conflictual, rather than fostering social betterment or control; it imbues the park with the frenetic qualities of metropolitan existence, rather than positing an alternative to that condition; it embraces impermanence and malleability rather than permanence or stability; it acknowledges the status of nature as a cultural construct and the concomitant artificiality of introducing natural elements into an urban setting, rather than resorting to picturesque methods; it affirms the notion of reality as an imaginary construct, rather than an autonomous condition. In lieu of the novel typology envisioned in the competition brief, Koolhaas proposed an innovative approach to the park's development, which, by engaging the citizenry in the ongoing process of its formal and programmatic definition, has significant implications for a revitalized social sphere.

As a critique of the Western public park tradition, Koolhaas's proposal draws explicitly on that heritage, as well as on avant-garde approaches to architecture and urbanism dating from the 1950s and 1960s, to advance a park concept that is radically new. Its significance thus emerges in comparison not only with its more immediate twentieth-century sources of inspiration but also with New York's Central Park, which established the terms for public park design in the United States, as well as its most direct Parisian precursor, the neighboring Parc des Buttes Chaumont, realized as part of the urban transformations that Baron Georges-Eugène Haussmann, prefect of the Seine from 1853 to 1870, administered for Emperor Napoleon Bonaparte III.[2] The Parc de la Villette site had been a significant component of Haussmann's efforts to impose a new order on the city: a hygienic operation intended to make it more immune to social disruption by relocating undesirable elements to the urban periphery. Koolhaas rejected the authoritarian formal approach associated with Haussmann's urban interventions as well as with President François Mitterrand's *Grands Projets*, instigated to celebrate the bicentennial of the French Revolution, of which the Parc de la Villette was the only landscape component. Instead Koolhaas advanced a tactical proposal for a park that was ideologically less duplicitous than its historic antecedents and more appropriate to the inclusive framework of a contemporary democracy. While realization of Tschumi's proposal has made that scheme a focus of broad critical attention, Koolhaas's competition entry has greater bearing on contemporary issues of architecture and landscape design.

Landscapes of Democracy

The impetus to generate public landscapes in Europe and the United States during the mid-nineteenth century was an outgrowth of the Enlightenment project of reforming the urban environment by means of a series of innovative building types and urban spaces—theaters, marketplaces, museums, and educational institutions, as well as squares, boulevards, and parks—that provided the stage for new forms of civic life. Created in response to the democratizing forces that led European nations to forge public institutions out of resources that were once the exclusive domain of the aristocracy, these cultural institutions and civic spaces are both symbols of liberty and instruments for crafting an engaged, modern citizenry.

Thus, although the nineteenth-century urban park was conceived in part to serve as the "lungs" of the city—to ameliorate its insalubrious conditions by introducing open spaces replete with leafy vegetation—it was also one of several institutions intended to democratize the city by educating its citizens, providing them with opportunities for constructive leisure activities. Such reform initiatives, nominally intended to mitigate physical and psychological health concerns, were ultimately directed toward engineering social change. As British landscape architect Clough Williams-Ellis maintained in his report to the International Conference on Landscape Architecture (London, 1948): "It is our job . . . to see to it that the landscape not merely survives its new popularity and accessibility, but that it shall also be made to exert its civilizing influence on its teeming new public to the greatest possible effect—to the ultimate salvation of both—the solitudes and the multitudes."[3] Such reform measures have led one sociologist to claim that, under capitalism, "the direct producers are freed from the soil only to become trapped in a grid—one that includes not only the modern factory, but also the modern family, the school, the army, the prison system, the city and the national territory."[4] As Kenneth Robert Olwig argues, landscape is "integral to an ongoing 'hidden' discourse, underwriting the legitimacy of those who exercise power in society."[5] The relationship between democracy and landscape is accordingly problematized by landscape's implicit power relations.

Twentieth-century theoretical debates concerning landscape design center on issues long associated with democratic form—tensions between the notion of the democratic citizen as an informed and active contributor to the decision-making process and the fear of "mob rule" long thought to be implicit in universal suffrage, between individual liberty and political liberty, and thus between individual rights and communal well-being—as well as issues of citizen participation and democratic representation in a plural society.[6] If, as Robert Westbrook contends, "democracy is an 'essentially contested' concept whose definition is never neutral but always entangled in competing moral and political commitments," then the complex and open-ended relationship between public landscape design and a democratic way of life merits examination.[7] Such scrutiny reveals a contrast between the democratic rhetoric of openness and accessibility and the tacit exclusions that are ideologically imposed on the designed landscape. As Stephen Daniels acknowledges, "Landscape, the central concept of traditional cultural geography, does not easily accommodate political notions of power and conflict, indeed it tends to dissolve or conceal them."[8] Such lack of visibility results from the illusion of freedom inherent to "nature" as a purposefully manipulated medium of the designed landscape as well as the social constraints intrinsic to landscape design in the public realm.

In the legacy of social reform that adherents of the avant-garde inherited from the nineteenth century, architecture and landscape design were envisioned as significant instruments for societal change. Adrian Forty contends that it was a fundamental premise of European modernism that architecture should, through its use, "give expression to the collectivity of social existence, and, more instrumentally, improve the conditions of social life."[9] Thus, Roger Connah elaborates, in pursuit of its social aspirations Modern Movement ideology sought to transform not only the built environment but also its subjects: "The modern agenda assumed in the architects' enthusiastic program suggested it would not only produce social benefits, but it could define—in a strangely permanent way—what it would be like to live modern lives, in modern buildings, in modern cities," *and,* one might add, in modern landscapes.[10] Public landscapes developed under the auspices of liberal democracies and social welfare states alike thus reflect a tension between the ethic of social betterment and the authoritarian means deemed necessary to achieve such ameliorative ends.

The privileging of vision by many early twentieth-century landscape practitioners and theoreticians—a legacy of the picturesque landscape tradition in which the subject is detached from the complex realities of participation in the world—presented a fundamental contradiction to this assumption of design as a vehicle of social reform, leading to a theoretical focus on landscape in terms of style (geometric vs. irregular, architectural vs. "natural") or, alternatively, of function. As Anita Berrizbeitia argues, "Conceiving landscape as program, or ascribing functional value to parkland, is the first radical break from a pictorial conceptualization of landscape."[11] Yet the instrumentality of the functionalist paradigm did not preclude the possibility of a significant aesthetic component in efforts to address the avant-garde social agenda in landscape terms. While the social agency of the so-called Modern Movement has since been called into question, the reciprocal relationship between the form of the physical environment and its implications for social and political life remains a complex, but relevant, issue. Architecture and the designed landscape are not merely passive reflections of political, social, and economic institutions but active agents in the structuring of our daily lives and relations.

Efforts by avant-garde architects and landscape architects to engage the emerging mass society through planning strategies that encompass a significant landscape component range from those who accept disengagement from the land as an inherent result of industrialization to those who foster reengagement with the land, thus bridging the divide between *Landskap* and *Landschaft*: between landscape as a visual proposition, constituting the imposition of a new order on the built environment, and landscape as a component of quotidian experience. Stephen Daniels elaborates on this ideological difference:

> This tension between landscape as an élitist (and illusory) "way of seeing" and landscape as a vernacular (and realistic) "way of life" is rooted in the very complications of the idea of culture. . . . Landscape may be seen, as Adorno sees culture generally, as a "dialectical image," an ambiguous synthesis whose redemptive and manipulative aspects cannot finally be disentangled, which can neither be completely reified as an authentic object in the world nor thoroughly dissolved as an ideological mirage.[12]

Daniels concludes: "In Adorno's terms, the 'redemptive' and 'manipulative' dimensions of landscape should be kept in dialectical tension. . . . We should beware of attempts to define landscape, to resolve its contradictions; rather we should abide in its duplicity."[13] Probing the ideological issues inherent to the creation of public landscapes in the nineteenth century not only reveals their duplicitous essence but also elucidates the significance of Koolhaas's contribution to issues of park design in the context of late twentieth-century cultural issues and values.

Central Park, New York (1857–61)

In *Delirious New York* (1978), his retroactive manifesto in which the city of New York serves as a laboratory for the "Culture of Congestion," Koolhaas used the example of Central Park in a way that its creators, landscape architect Frederick Law Olmsted Sr. and architect Calvert Vaux, could not have anticipated: as the mark of a nascent paradigmatic shift from the public park as antithesis of the city to a constructed emblem of the metropolitan condition.[14]

> Central Park is not only the major recreational facility of Manhattan but also the record of its progress: a taxidermic preservation of nature that exhibits forever the drama of culture outdistancing nature.... If Central Park can be read as an operation of preservation, it is, even more, a series of manipulations and transformations performed on the nature "saved" by its designers. Its lakes are artificial, its trees (trans)planted, its accidents engineered, all its incidents supported by an invisible infrastructure that controls their assembly. A catalogue of natural elements is taken from its original context, reconstituted, and compressed into *a system of nature* that makes the rectilinearity of the Mall no more formal than the planned informality of the Ramble. Central Park is a synthetic Arcadian Carpet.[15]

Infrastructure construction for the New Reservoir in Central Park, New York, by Frederick Law Olmsted and Calvert Vaux. Photograph by Victor Prevost, September 1862. Rare Books Division, The New York Public Library, Astor, Lenox and Tilden Foundations.

Despite this acknowledgment of the infrastructural and constructed reality of Central Park, Koolhaas's account has closer affinities with his broader interpretation of Manhattan as a paradigmatic exemplar of metropolitan culture than with the reformist ideology underlying the park's creation. Yet a significant aspect of Koolhaas's La Villette proposal derives from its critique of the social and cultural issues inherent to Olmsted and Vaux's approach.

Whereas public landscapes of the late nineteenth and early twentieth centuries in Europe were often directed toward concrete social ends, and thus involved a high degree of programmatic specificity—including allotment gardens as well as cultural, educational, and recreational components—comparable examples in the United States were often relatively unprogrammed, an idea grounded in the social legacy of the American Transcendentalists. To Henry David Thoreau and Ralph Waldo Emerson, the experience of nature was a source of human betterment. For Olmsted, as for many social reformers of the nineteenth and early twentieth centuries, the presence of nature was a necessary corollary to urban life, as it played a strategic role in the quest for a more stable society. Public parks, Olmsted reasoned, had a spiritual as well as an aesthetic impact; they constituted a remedy for moral as well as bodily disease, promoting a virtuous life. American park planning of the mid-nineteenth century thus reflected the imposition of bourgeois values on the broader populace. Inherent to this approach was the idea that members of the working classes would benefit from exposure to elite values in the parks—versus the ascendant values of popular culture in a participatory democracy. Olmsted assumed that edification of the citizenry would be achieved primarily through the contemplation of nature, rather than through specific cultural and educational institutions (museums, zoos, and so on) or active recreation areas. While such government-sponsored parks suggested freedom and independence, they were also intended to control disruption and bolster the economic value of their urban environs.

Olmsted's sincere ambition to serve the less fortunate was in conflict with his determination to instill in them middle-class standards of behavior. He was wary of unsupervised citizens, particularly those of lower economic status, which he termed "the housekeeping class."[16] To stem undesirable conduct in New York's Central Park, Olmsted established rules regarding appropriate activities (picnicking and sitting on the grass were prohibited, for example) and trained a cadre of "keepers" to regulate public behavior.[17] He enthused about the result: "No one who has closely observed the conduct of the people who visit the Park, can doubt that it exercises a distinctly harmonizing and refining influence upon the most unfortunate and most lawless classes of the city—an influence favorable to courtesy, self-control, and temperance." Olmsted's vision of the park as a democratic social integrator—a place where "the prospect of coming together, all classes, largely represented, with a common purpose, . . . all helping to the greater happiness of each"—was belied not only by the rules he established to control public behavior but also by the lack of adequate public transport from more remote parts of the city, which would enable lower-income groups to take advantage of the amenities it afforded.[18] As Roger Starr argues, Olmsted intended his urban parks not only as instruments for imposing a moral order on the city's poor but also as means for realizing his vision of "a democracy in which all would share the ideals of a genuine aristocracy."[19] Stephen Germic expands upon this paradox with his claim that, although "promoted as a species of cultural institution that would universalize and incorporate threatening differences in urban space," Central Park "functioned at once to produce or maintain *and* reveal social distinctions." He concludes: "The actual process of building a place like Central Park was both disruptive (evicting stable communities) and stabilizing (helping to relieve the anxieties of the more-or-less privileged), but it did nothing to make threatening social differences disappear, other than from view."[20] This phenomenon exemplifies "one of the principal ethical imperatives of bourgeois art" in Manfredo Tafuri's analysis: "to dispel anxiety by understanding and internalizing its causes."[21]

The invisibility of social forces at work in Central Park (recalling a prominent aspect of the picturesque landscape garden) is only one among many contradictions inherent to American reformist landscapes of the era. The Olmstedian park reflected a related tension between the solitary contemplation of nature it facilitated—by means of visual isolation from its urban milieu—and the communal sensibility it purported to foster.

Olmsted's notion of Central Park as a relatively unprogrammed evocation of a "natural" condition has, with the loosening of restrictions on the park's use, left much of its landscape open to territorial claims by diverse interest groups. For example, the sheep meadow, a symbolic component of the initial design—evoking certain cultural and functional origins of the New England town common—has given way to an open landscape accommodating assorted activities, ranging from family picnics to informal ball games. Such adaptability is a particularly salient issue with respect to the programmatic excess of the Parc de la Villette competition requirements, a surfeit associated with a phenomenon subsequently cited by a competition entrant as "fear of the void."[22] In his proposal for the Parc de la Villette, Koolhaas seemingly took a cue from this aspect of Central Park, drawing upon the positive potential of the programless "void" while simultaneously cultivating a "culture of congestion" to address the disparate and evolving needs of an economically and culturally diverse urban populace.

Parc des Buttes Chaumont, Paris (1861–67)

In divergent respects the Parisian Parc des Buttes Chaumont also represents a significant precursor to Koolhaas's Parc de la Villette. In comparison to Central Park, Buttes Chaumont is a more overtly infrastructural project, conceived as both an extension of the urban fabric and a means of escape for the district's working-class inhabitants; "nature" is no longer treated as the reflection of a primordial condition, but acknowledged as an artificial construct; the "reality" it posits thus makes a more explicit appeal to the visitor's imagination. At La Villette Koolhaas expanded upon these qualities, envisioning the park as an emblem of the metropolitan condition while rejecting the motivation of social benevolence associated with Buttes Chaumont as well as its related formal properties.

Unlike Central Park, Buttes Chaumont was not intended as a democratic social integrator. Rather, it was created to serve a particular social group—the artisan and laboring classes of the nineteenth arrondissement—providing a social counterpart to the public parks Haussmann crafted for the bourgeoisie from the formerly aristocratic properties of the Bois de Boulogne and the Parc Monceau. These public landscapes were developed under the administrative aegis of Adolphe Alphand, whose training as an engineer at the Ecole des Ponts et Chaussées prepared him for the bureaucratic efforts involved in overseeing their construction.[23] The derelict site of Buttes Chaumont, a former quarry and refuse dump for sanitary sewage in an industrial area of the nineteenth arrondissement, was increasingly seen as a dangerous void in the midst of ongoing residential development. Its milieu of train yards, factories, and slaughterhouses (the latter relocated to this district as part of Haussmann's hygienic urban operations) was being developed to house members of the working classes, deliberately dislocated from the city center by Haussmann's urban revitalization efforts, as well as immigrant laborers from the French countryside, who swelled the population of the French capital during the 1850s and 1860s, seeking employment opportunities afforded by the vast scale of these undertakings. Social stratification by district was thus a deliberate consequence of Haussmann's urban operations.

The transformation of the site—from a "desert" (according to an internal memo of Alphand's office of 1861) into a "paradise," a "delicious oasis" (according to a guidebook published at the park's opening in 1867)—was accomplished in the remarkable span of six years from conception to execution.[24] This feat was all the more surprising given substantive doubts concerning the project's feasibility, which largely stemmed from the site's barren character. Haussmann traced the name Chaumont to the contraction of *chauve-mont* (bald mountain), "because the soil and the subsoil, composed only of clay, compacted marl and gypsum, would not support any type of vegetation."[25] To satisfy Haussmann's charge "to embellish what I have made clean and healthful," Alphand had eight hundred thousand cubic meters of earth brought to the site so that its extant topography could be regraded and planted, an effort that constituted a major portion of the total project cost of more than 3.4 million francs.[26] He extolled the innovative virtues of Haussmann's urban transformations, proclaiming,

"Rather than carrying out works of fantasy and of vain pomp, as in antiquity, Paris has taken the initiative and set an example for the transformation of old cities by applying the achievements of science and art to the viability and safety of the large city."[27] But if the Parc des Buttes Chaumont represents a marriage of science and art, it is also a work of supreme fantasy, involving unprecedented labor and material resources in accomplishing the adaptation of such formerly inhospitable terrain to the park's dramatic topography, lush vegetation, and prominent water feature.

In his Paris guidebook of 1749, Antoine-Joseph Dezallier d'Argenville argued that Parisians who are "strangers in their own city" might attain cultural benefits analogous to those obtained through travel by studying their immediate environs.[28] Like the Exposition Universelle of 1867 with which it was affiliated, the Parc des Buttes Chaumont enlarged upon such possibilities, but in a more permanent way, enabling Parisians to experience a "foreign" landscape within their own city. Unlike Central Park, where Olmsted exaggerated the site's extant features to evoke qualities of the rolling terrain that could be experienced in the immediate extraurban environs, Alphand's more radical and imaginative transformation of this derelict Parisian site resulted in the dramatic topography of a mountainous region that has no counterpart in the French countryside.

Yet Buttes Chaumont is also more integrated with its metropolitan setting than Central Park; it incorporates a local boulevard at grade and a lower rail line, which remains deliberately exposed to view. Although these infrastructural components interrupt the park's spatial continuity, their presence was celebrated as they furthered the dual character of the park as both an extension of the city and a retreat from the urban milieu. Marie Luisa Marceca argues about Alphand's related approach to nature: "To correct nature, modify it, urbanize it by taking its naturalness to extremes, to

Work in progress on 20 April 1866 at the site of Parc des Buttes Chaumont, Paris, by Auguste Deroy *(left)*; comparable view of the completed park, c. 1870. Copyright Musée Carnavalet / Roger-Viollet / The Image Works.

make it exploitable in the urban setting, to replace it by technique; these are the goals which Alphand sets himself."[29] The patent artificiality of the park landscape is reiterated in its details, which include concrete benches, railings and stairway treads and risers in the shapes of logs and tree limbs, and false stalagmites and stalactites in its cascades.[30]

Alone among the public parks created under Haussmann, the Parc des Buttes Chaumont reflects a hyperreality, remote from the evocations of nature associated with the picturesque landscape tradition and more closely aligned with the technological impetus of the Exposition Universelle. Several factors account for this difference between Buttes Chaumont and other parks realized under Alphand's management, notably Buttes Chaumont's explicit affiliation with the exposition's educational and social mission, as well as the physical deficiencies of the site. Exposition organizers sought to address the deleterious social consequences of industrialization by drawing explicitly upon Saint-Simonian principles, educating the predominantly bourgeois visitors to the potential for industrialization to enhance workers' living standards through a combination of factory production, hand craftsmanship, and agriculture. In a speech delivered at the ritual prize-awarding ceremony—which Alphand orchestrated as a tribute to the emperor in a manner reminiscent of the Roman Empire—Napoleon III reinforced this "democratic" motivation when he claimed:

(left) Aerial view of Parc des Buttes Chaumont by Felix Benoist. Copyright Musée Carnavalet / Roger-Viollet / The Image Works.

(right) The concrete cascade, from Adolphe Alphand, *Les Promenades de Paris*, 1867–73. Special Collections Library, University of Michigan.

[The exposition] is universal because, aside from the wonders that wealth generates for a few, it is concerned with basic necessities for the majority. The interests of the working classes have never aroused such intense concern. Their moral and educational needs, their requirements for a minimal existence, and the most productive measures for social welfare have been the object of patient research and serious study.[31]

Accordingly the Parc des Buttes Chaumont reflects faith in the potential for technological means to contribute to social betterment. It was intended not only to provide healthful fresh air and access to a "natural" environment for the working-class inhabitants of the insalubrious districts of Belleville and La Villette but also to instill in them more refined standards of behavior and morality—to offer them experiences analogous to those afforded the bourgeoisie in the Bois de Boulogne and the Parc Monceau.

Through its very existence the Parc des Buttes Chaumont sustained social distinctions between the leisurely bourgeois *promeneurs* of the city's fashionable boulevards and parks, who evoked the poetic reverie associated with the *flâneurs* of the previous era, and the working-class *promeneurs* of the nineteenth arrondissement, whose leisure time was more pragmatically directed to recreational activities and generally limited to Sundays. The term *promenade* originally implied an excursion from one type of environment to another, specifically from the city to a private landscaped garden in the urban periphery.[32] By integrating the concept of promenade within the urban fabric, Alphand sought to democratize that elite experience, making it accessible to the broader populace.

For the Parisian bourgeoisie, the public park was an inherent aspect of the metropolitan condition—a place to parade in one's finery, to act out a social pageant, to "see and be seen," much like the Haussmannian boulevard or opera—as well as a place to escape from the frenetic qualities of that condition, to embark upon the solitary contemplation of "nature." It was a primary accomplishment of the Parc des Buttes Chaumont to involve the district's working classes, however provisionally, in the spectacle of metropolitan life. The visual display it afforded was integral to the process of public consumption that had been ongoing among the Parisian bourgeoisie throughout the nineteenth century. The features of the park's exaggerated and patently artificial landscape were analogous to the spectacular goods displayed in the shops that lined the city's fashionable boulevards, its "engineered nature" arrayed for aesthetic consumption by the district's working classes.

Extending the experience of metropolitan culture to the working classes was an essential component of Napoleon III's program of benevolent paternalism, intended to secure his hold on power by attempting to rectify conditions of social inequity. Yet Haussmann's urban interventions not only preserved the class distinctions of the previous decades but also spatialized them through physical segregation of the proletariat. If the engineered nature of the Parc des Buttes Chaumont provided the district's working-class inhabitants with a radical diversion from the tedium of their daily existence, it was more effective at keeping them out of sight than at ameliorating their economic situation or quality of life.

While rejecting the overt attempts at social betterment inherent to both Central Park and the Parc des Buttes Chaumont, Koolhaas embraced the infrastructural logic of both examples. In his proposal for Parc de la Villette, moreover, he expanded upon the qualities of nature as an artificial construct and the urban park as an extension of the metropolitan condition found in Buttes Chaumont to address the social and recreational needs of a more diverse metropolitan populace.

Although Koolhaas never cited the Parc des Buttes Chaumont in his extensive writings, the Parisian example could equally serve his process of retroaction, the tactic he employed in *Delirious New York* to reconceptualize historic precedents. Indeed, his retroactive analysis of Central Park, cited earlier, would more appropriately serve to describe the Parisian example. Whereas Koolhaas's proposal for La Villette involved engineered accents combined with "natural elements . . . reconstituted, and compressed into *a system of nature*," it was also more overtly infrastructural.[33]

Parc de la Villette Competition (1982–83)

François Mitterrand's *Grands Projets,* like Haussmann's urban interventions, were empowered by politicians and administrators and created by professionals—architects, planners, and landscape architects—in an effort to forge a new urban image and identity.[34] Haussmann had shifted the center of wealth to the west of Paris, isolating the working classes in the city's eastern sectors. As subsequent urban development did little to rectify this social imbalance, during the mid-1970s the decision was made to focus municipal resources on development in those eastern districts.

The international competition to design the Parc de la Villette emanated from this combination of initiatives.

As with Buttes Chaumont, the site for Parc de la Villette included the residue of prior industrial operations. These remnants of nineteenth- and twentieth-century efforts to improve the city's physical and economic health included major infrastructural elements: the Canal de l'Ourcq and the Bassin de la Villette, created in 1812 to provide fresh drinking water for the city; the St. Martin and St. Denis canals, subsequently dug to facilitate freight transport; and a disused local rail line leading through the Parc des Buttes Chaumont. A centralized complex of municipal meat markets and slaughterhouses—an essential component of Haussmann's broader strategy of hygienic urban improvements—was erected to the design of Victor Baltard during the 1860s on either side of the Canal de l'Ourcq.

From the moment in March 1974 when the city decommissioned the slaughterhouses and meat markets of La Villette and dispersed their functions to peripheral locales, the sociocultural potential of the fifty-hectare site, conceived primarily in programmatic terms, became a dominant political concern. An "ideas" competition of 1976 yielded a range of compositional proposals that played upon the philosophical opposition of "culture" and "nature." This same duality characterizes Adrien Fainsilber's entry to a building competition of 1980 that resulted in the transformation of the remaining meat market into the Cité des Sciences et de l'Industrie (completed 1986). Providing a learning environment based on interactive engagement, Fainsilber's project was the lone constructed outcome of this phase of the site's transformation. Embodying a challenge to the Enlightenment aim of objective scientific truth, it reflects a crucial step toward a rethinking of the nature/culture dialectic that was to inform the subsequent competition for the park.[35]

Although the brief for the definitive competition of 1982 exhorted prospective entrants "to turn the Park of La Villette into a new model for an urban park," its stipulations reflect a relatively conservative approach to public park design.[36] Envisioning the result as a new typology, analogous to "the Central Markets, the large department stores, the railway stations and the airports," the competition guidelines included an exhaustive list of programmatic requirements rooted in nineteenth- and early twentieth-century European park ideology, with an emphasis on social benefits deriving from education, health, and access to sun, space, and greenery.[37] Moreover, the document anticipated an enduring monumental expression grounded in compositional principles:

> The goal is a project significant not only in terms of use and the links established between the various activities, but by its form as such, independent of its use and the contingencies of its creation. This is what is meant by the term "composition," with all its implications as to an urban landmark, a source of recognition and identity, a force capable of enduring beyond our epoch and taking its place as a genealogy of the great Parisian compositions.[38]

The programmatic and aesthetic biases reflected in the competition brief thus explicitly countered its mandate for innovation.

Like Central Park, the Parc de la Villette was conceived of as an instrument of socialization; it was intended to mediate social and cultural differences, countering the ongoing process of class segregation that had motivated construction of the neighboring Parc des Buttes Chaumont. In its survey of historic Parisian parks, the Etablissement Public du Parc de la Villette (EPPV), founded in 1979 to develop the area, extolled the social vitality of traditional Parisian parks, which "played a part in the social life of the city: as an urban place [sic] of encounter and interchange, they were constantly visited by a miscellaneous public." Attributing this vitality in part to the plethora of "attractions" found in the public park, either "added or adapted over the years," the EPPV derided the shift during recent decades to the phenomenon of the empty "*espace vert*" as "a development characterized by an impoverishment of the social function." Determining program to be the primary means to address this lack in the Parc de la Villette, the report directed the park's programmatic substance to explicit social ends. The EPPV envisioned the new park as a means to mediate cultural differences, variously describing it as "a new cultural instrument; . . . a meeting point of cultures which have the right to express themselves individually; [and] . . . a park of reconciliation."[39] Although such an interpretation of "encounter and interchange" as potential means of social "reconciliation" has notable parallels with Olmsted's aspirations for Central Park, the reliance on programmatic elements to effect such change at La Villette differs radically from the method Olmsted espoused.

Taking La Villette (the little city)—the urban sector in which the park is situated—as inspiration for the qualities he deemed appropriate to the contemporary urban park, Koolhaas subsequently reasoned, "What La Villette finally suggested was the pure exploitation of the metropolitan condition: density without architecture, and a culture of 'invisible' congestion."[40] Inspired by the programmatic excess of the competition brief, he differentiated between the aims of conventional park design and those of his proposal, which he envisioned as an essential component of metropolitanism:

> The site of La Villette is too small, and the program for the Park de la Villette too large, to create a park in the recognizable sense of the word. A conventional park is a replica of nature serviced by a minimal number of facilities that ensure its enjoyment; the program of the Park de la Villette extends like a dense forest of social instruments across the site.[41]

Rejecting the ethic of social betterment associated with the modernist paradigm, Koolhaas directed these "social instruments" to radically different ends from those of the traditional urban park.

In contrast to Georg Simmel's analysis of the metropolitan condition of 1903, in which he challenged modern individuals to preserve their individuality while accommodating themselves to the explosive shock of metropolitan existence, Koolhaas celebrated the frenetic nature of late twentieth-century metropolitan life, imagining his park as a vital locus of such experience.[42] His proposal invokes the exhilarating sense of modernity that Charles Baudelaire described in 1863—in explicit reaction to Haussmann's efforts to achieve social stability through his extensive urban transformations:

> By "modernity" I mean the ephemeral, the fugitive, the contingent, the half of art whose other half is the eternal and the immutable. . . . In short, for any "modernity" to be worthy of one day taking its place as "antiquity," it is necessary for the mysterious beauty which human life accidentally put into it to be distilled from it.[43]

Walter Benjamin, in his appraisal of Baudelaire, cited a further attribute: "Modernity in Baudelaire is a conquest; it has an armature."[44] Reevaluating those aspects of metropolitan life that had inspired certain architects of preceding generations—namely, the idea that the experience of the modern city should be engaging, enriching, and liberating rather than inhibiting and/or controlling—Koolhaas posited an infrastructural armature for Parc de la Villette capable of supporting ongoing societal, programmatic, and physical transformations.

Koolhaas envisioned his park of the twenty-first century not as a means of escape from the metropolitan condition but as a means of immersion in its volatile, frenetic character. The park is no longer directed toward social betterment or social control through formal means, but is formally malleable and socially contingent, establishing conditions for its implementation without anticipating ultimate outcomes. Koolhaas's proposal accordingly defies the monumental expression inherent to Mitterrand's urban vision, exposing the contradictions between the French president's socialist political alignment and the authoritarian means used to effect such changes in the urban landscape—an issue equally germane to the regime of Napoleon III.

Interpreting the surfeit of requirements in the competition brief as an opportunity to pursue the potential of programmatic malleability, Koolhaas subsequently reasoned:

> The second La Villette competition (1982) seemed to offer the ingredients for a complete investigation of the potential for a European Culture of Congestion. Here was the *par excellence* metropolitan condition of Europe: a *terrain vague* between the historical city—itself raped by the greedy needs of the 20th century—and the plankton of the *banlieue*; on it, two pieces of history marooned like spaceships. It was one of those nothingnesses of still infinite potential that in this case could be preserved since its program could not be expressed in form, a program that insisted on its own instability.[45]

By maintaining the quality of the site in its suggestion of "one of those nothingnesses of still infinite potential," Koolhaas admitted the possibility for ascendant values of popular culture to be incorporated into the park's form, rather than imposing a predetermined form upon it. Envisioning "a kind of post-architectural city" in which emptiness is not a loss that can be filled or replaced by architecture, but something you can cultivate, Koolhaas anticipated a combination of emptiness and congestion for his park landscape.[46]

The infrastructural character of his proposal establishes requisite conditions for the park's physical development and evolution, as he explained:

> The underlying principle of programmatic indeterminacy as a basis of the formal concept allows any shift, modification, replacement, or substitution to occur without damaging the initial hypothesis. The essence of the competition becomes, therefore, how to orchestrate on a metropolitan field the most dynamic coexistence of x, y, and z activities and to generate through their mutual interference a chain reaction of new, unprecedented events, or how to design a Social Condenser, based on horizontal congestion that is the size of a park.[47]

In *Delirious New York,* Koolhaas interpreted the Manhattan grid as "the most courageous act of prediction in Western civilization: the land it divides, unoccupied; the population it describes, conjectural; the buildings it locates, phantoms; the activities it frames: nonexistent."[48] These terms apply equally to his proposal for Parc de la Villette: an infrastructure setting the terms for the relatively blank canvas of the ground plane, perchance to be filled to excess.

Koolhaas's site strategy minimizes the compositional aspect of his proposal while establishing an essential modicum of constraints on the park's future development. He subdivided the area into a series of parallel bands of varied standard widths, establishing fixed points for the infrastructure to facilitate replacement and change. These bands incorporate the major programmatic elements, including the existing Science Museum and Great Hall as well as the theme gardens and discovery gardens, the latter allocated either arbitrarily or according to existing site characteristics. Koolhaas randomly distributed a series of small-scale elements—"point grids or confetti"—throughout these bands by means of a mathematical equation, in explicit rejection of the precision and certainty normally associated with such a method. Moreover, he imagined that the individual character of these elements would potentially influence the host zone in which each was located, leading to accidental clusters. An erratic array of light sources deployed throughout the site reinforces this arbitrary distribution of elements.

Taking a cue from Haussmann, Koolhaas designated two primary circulation routes, a linear access Boulevard that intersects the programmatic strips and enables limited twenty-four-hour accessibility (a program requirement that countered Koolhaas's metropolitan ambitions for the park) and a meandering Promenade in the form of a figure eight that winds through and connects the plazas. Finally, he incorporated elements that were too large or unique to be located according to a mathematical system: a new circular forest and City of Music as well as the extant Science Museum and Great Hall.

Consistent with Koolhaas's denial of monumental means was his parallel refusal to create a designed landscape:

> We insist that at no time have we presumed to have produced a *designed* landscape. We have confined ourselves to devising a framework capable of absorbing an endless series of further meanings, extensions, or intentions, without entailing compromises, redundancies or contradictions. Our strategy is to confer on the simple the dimension of adventure.[49]

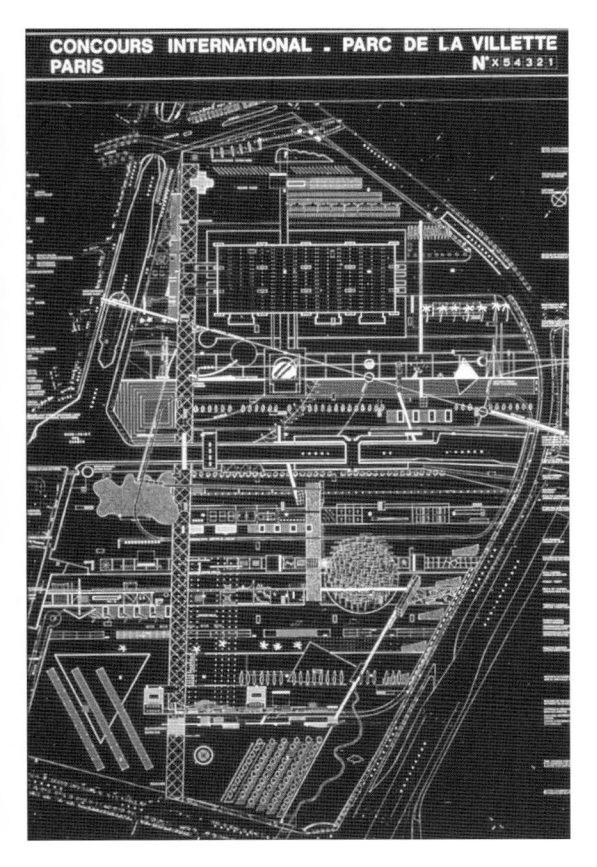

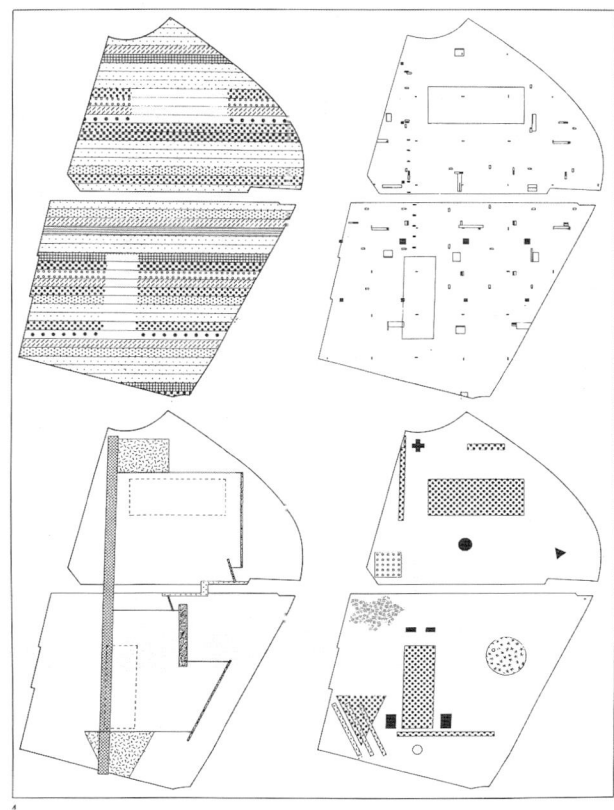

In collaboration with French landscape architects Claire and Michel Courajoud, Koolhaas developed the landscape components of his proposal for the second stage of the competition. He termed these components "anti-categorical elements"; they fulfill certain programmatic requirements (theme gardens, didactic gardens), constitute large-scale elements comparable to the existing buildings (a deciduous linear forest and an evergreen circular forest), or contribute to the spatial layering of the bands through variations in density and height. To reinforce the visual effect of this layering, the team proposed to vary the soil composition of the strips, thus amplifying the artificiality of the park's "natural" components and providing a further constraint on its future development. Koolhaas elaborated on the team's infrastructural approach to landscape: "In accordance with the principle of the utilitarian at the service of the poetic, the landscaping is conceived as the sum of the infrastructural interventions deemed necessary."[50]

(left) Rem Koolhaas/OMA Parc de la Villette competition plan of 1982. Photograph by Hans Werlemann. Copyright OMA.

(right) Rem Koolhaas/OMA Parc de la Villette plan diagrams. Clockwise from upper left: the strips; point grids or confetti; the final layer; access and circulation. Copyright OMA.

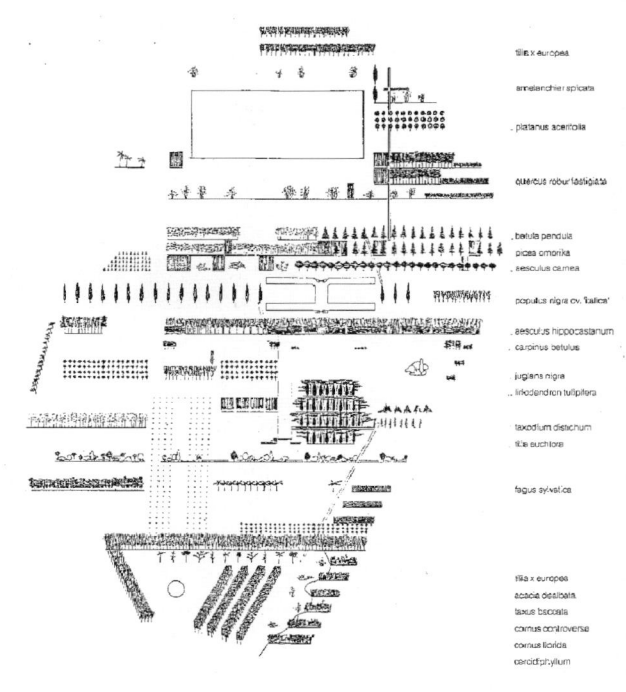

Parc de la Villette frontal axonometric showing landscape layers in a drawing by Alex Wall and planting scheme by OMA in collaboration with Claire and Michel Corajoud. Copyright OMA.

Inverting nineteenth-century efforts to reinstate aspects of "nature" within the city, Koolhaas's proposal affirms the artificiality of such an approach to nature while repudiating its picturesque status. Instead he embraced the notion of nature as a cultural construct, a product of technological forces and means: "The only stability was thus offered by the natural elements, the rows of trees and the Circular Forest—the forest machine—whose very growth insured their own instability."[51] At once stable and unstable, "nature" operates in dialectical tension with its programmatic milieu while simultaneously operating as a programmatic element. In this effacement of any distinction between real and manufactured natures, "nature" ceases to be an aesthetic commodity associated with the traditional park yet remains a vital component of the metropolitan spectacle.

Koolhaas's otherworldly images and model photographs produced for the second stage of the competition are suggestive of potential outcomes rather than concrete speculations about formal resolution. By means of a superimposed fluorescent ring the mirrored sphere of the Géode becomes Saturn, recontextualized as an element of the linear Astronomical Garden:

Along the cable car line, the planets of the solar system operate according to their respective distances from the sun. In this constellation, the semi-circular hall becomes Saturn and is therefore given fluorescent rings. The position of the sun coincides with the siting of the Mall and is indicated by a sundial at the end of the cable car line.[52]

Parc de la Villette model by Chiel van der Stelt and Hans Werlemann. Photograph by Hans Werlemann. Copyright OMA.

An Ariane rocket on its launching pad completes this futuristic illusion. In a further appropriation of the infrastructural context, Koolhaas proposed to engage the Boulevard Peripherique—a wall of sound—as an element of the metropolitan spectacle.

Toward an Architecture of Noncontrol

The mathematical basis of Koolhaas's park layout is indicative not of a desire to control through geometric means but of a proclivity toward immateriality. In a manner reminiscent of Le Corbusier's assertion that "*the architect is an organizer,* not a designer of objects," Koolhaas declares,

THE ONCE AND FUTURE PARK 211

"I'm interested in the essence of architecture; I'm trying to escape from architecture's entanglements and paraphernalia, and, in fact, from its entire physicality."[53] Rejecting the notion of the death of architecture that Manfredo Tafuri purportedly asserted in his essay "Toward a Critique of Architectural Ideology" (1969), where he cited this pronouncement by the Swiss architect, Koolhaas directed his critique to reanimating the discipline as an essential component of contemporary urban life.

The most provocative aspect of Koolhaas's park proposal—its refusal of formal resolution or control—reflects a reaction, common to the era, against the urban planning mentality that grew out of initiatives of the Congrès Internationaux d'Architecture Moderne (CIAM) in which social form was equated with physical form, as well as his appraisal of the limitations of contemporary architectural discourse: "I think that architecture is a desperate attempt to exercise control and urbanism is the failure of that attempt. And so therefore, I think that this gravitation toward architecture/urbanism as the same word that includes two different cores is the way that nostalgia for control is channeled towards almost forbidden domains."[54] Differentiating between the stability of architecture and the malleability of the contemporary city, he elaborated on this point: "The permanence built into the most frivolous of architecture and the instability of the metropolis are incompatible. In this conflict, the metropolis, by definition, will always win; in its pervasive reality architecture is reduced to the status of a plaything, tolerated as décor for the illusions of history and memory."[55] With his proposal for Parc de la Villette, Koolhaas drew upon the instability of the contemporary metropolis while simultaneously seeking to elevate architecture from its "status as a plaything" to one capable of reengaging the citizenry in a reconstituted social sphere. In positing the reciprocity of urban and park experience, in which the park is directed to urban residents of diverse ages and cultural backgrounds, Koolhaas suggests that the experience of such a landscape might foster new ways of utilizing and experiencing the contemporary city.

Koolhaas was familiar with a series of visionary architectural proposals dating from the 1950s to the early 1970s that reflect a related refusal of definitive formal resolution to facilitate novel modes of urban experience. In an essay published in the *Architectural Association Quarterly* when Koolhaas was a student at that institution, Robin Evans advocated such an approach in arguing for "anarchitecture," a term he devised to designate "the tectonics of non-control." Distinguishing between "the tendency to order in social systems and the tendency to order in the physical systems on which society relies," Evans espoused architecture capable of facilitating social action and interaction, while allowing for freedom of choice.[56] The idea had numerous precedents in European counterculture of the era, including Constant Nieuwenhuys's New Babylon of 1956–74 and the related theoretical output of the Situationist International (SI, 1957–72), whose renewed call for the reintegration of art and life involved the creation of "situations" in which the spaces of the city are reclaimed for public use; Yona Friedman's "Manifeste de l'architecture mobile" of 1956, where he proposed to limit the architect's role to the design of urban infrastructure, leaving the role of form giving to the urban inhabitants, and his associated Ville Spatiale proposals of 1958–62; various utopian urban propositions advanced by the members of Archigram, such as Peter Cook's Plug-In City, Dennis Compton's Computer City, or Ron Herron's Walking City (all of 1964); Cedric Price and Joan Littlewood's Fun Palace (c. 1962–76); Archizoom's No-Stop City (1969–72); and the concept of Non-plan espoused by Reyner Banham, Cedric Price, Peter Hall, and Paul Barker (1969).[57]

Such visionary formulations reflect reactions against the culture of alienation associated with the functionalist logic of the Modern Movement and its associated urban propositions, particularly those evolving out of CIAM proclamations such as the Athens Charter.[58] Notwithstanding their significant ideological differences, these examples all utilize physical malleability to afford a measure of spatial self-determination for urban inhabitants.[59] All envision novel forms of urban experience in which the postindustrial individual is immersed in a complex infrastructural web supporting flexible, ever-changing elements. All rely on emerging technologies and a faith in scientific progress. All are based on directing the unprecedented amount of leisure time presumably gained from technological advances toward creative undertakings. All are grounded in a search for new modes of architectural practice, de-privileging the role of architect as artist and reflecting a loss of faith in the capacity of the individual building, with its determinate immutable form, to foster culturally relevant means of individual and social engagement. All are politically motivated, reflecting a leftist turn to the ideal of participatory democracy during the late-1950s in reaction to the complacency promoted by the welfare state.[60]

Of these proposals only the Fun Palace by veteran theater director Joan Littlewood and architect Cedric Price was even remotely feasible for construction, although the project was ultimately never realized. Littlewood sought a "people's theater" capable of facilitating spontaneous, unscripted experiences.[61] Her concept, as Banham described it, could almost serve as a description of Koolhaas's agenda:

> a zone of total probability in which the possibility of participating in practically everything could be caused to exist, from political rallies to Greco-Roman wrestling, table tennis to choral song, dervish-dancing, model drag-racing or just goofing and fooling about, where even the simple business of walking around or finding where to go next would be rewarding or stimulating.[62]

Price responded with an open-air, multistory superstructure capable of supporting a variety of functional components, all suspended above the ground. He described his vision in a memorandum of 1964: "Its form and structure, resembling a large shipyard in which enclosures such as theatres, cinemas, restaurants, workshops, rally areas, can be assembled, moved, rearranged and scrapped continuously."[63] He variously termed the project a "mobile," "an anti-building," and "a kit of parts" with no fixed appearance.[64] Although such terms could potentially be applied to OMA's Parc de la Villette, Koolhaas rejected the overt technological expression inherent to Price's work.

Price and Littlewood conceived of their project in landscape terms, citing London's eighteenth-century public pleasure gardens at Vauxhall and Ranelagh, which reputedly served the city's broadest citizenry, as the only relevant precedents for their idea.[65] Moreover, they envisioned their scheme as affording a variation on the experience of a conventional urban park:

> We are going to create a university of the streets—not a "gracious" park but a foretaste of the pleasures of 1984. . . . The whole plan is open, but on many levels. So the greatest pleasure of traditional parks is preserved—the pleasure of strolling casually, looking in at one or other of these areas or (if this is preferred) settling down for several hours of work-play.[66]

Price and Littlewood thus directed their aim of fostering among the populace "the possibility of developing new experiences for themselves" toward educational as well as recreational ends, ambitions associated with public parks of the late nineteenth and early twentieth centuries.[67]

The desire to cultivate creative spontaneity implied ad hoc physical and programmatic mobility of the Fun Palace facilities in a limited time frame—measured in minutes or hours rather than weeks or months—

potentially leading to social anarchy rather than fostering constructive social encounters. Accordingly, Price and Littlewood enlisted Gordon Pask to serve as cybernetics consultant on the project team to incorporate in this "reactive and adaptive environment" a degree of predictability facilitated by computer analysis.[68] The feedback mechanisms afforded by cybernetics and game theory would theoretically enable the structure's systems to self-regulate and self-correct without an anticipated end result. Technology—the source of individual liberty—was thus envisioned as a source of systemic control.

Acknowledging the dual issues of facilitating liberty versus exercising a measure of social control, Pask argued, "[Architecture] perpetually interacts with its inhabitants, on the one hand serving them, and on the other controlling them." He envisioned cybernetic design as the means by which the architect could assume the role of social engineer:

> The structure of a city is not just the carapace of society. On the contrary, its structure acts as a symbolic control programme on a par with the ritual constraints which are known to regulate the behavior of various tribes and which render this behavior homeostatic rather than divergent. Hence, the architect is responsible for building conventions and shaping the development of traditions (this comment simply elevates the idea that a building controls its inhabitants to a higher level of organization).[69]

Like the visionary urban propositions of Archigram, Constant, and Friedman, the Fun Palace reflects an extension of the social programming associated with the Modern Movement as much as a reaction to it. Despite the lack of a definitive formal outcome in such schemes, design in the public realm continued to be conceived of as a means of social betterment, recalling the aims for the public parks of Olmsted and Alphand.

Such proposals embody a further discrepancy between the motivation to advance individual freedom of choice and the assumption of communal sensibility that would purportedly arise from such freedom. Banham, Constant, Friedman, and Price all associated the physical malleability of the megastructure with social engagement as well as individual liberty. As with the Modern Movement forebears of these fanciful proposals, social form is presumed to derive from physical organization. Nowhere is this more evident than in Archizoom's No-Stop City, a potentially limitless spatial continuum in which physical and social reality are theoretically undifferentiated.

As a speculation about the workings of the metropolitan condition without a comparable reliance on imagery, Koolhaas's Parc de la Villette both draws upon and formally inverts such examples. Inhabitants of these visionary megastructures would be immersed in artificial environments that are hoisted above the ground plane and intended to operate in dialogue with the extant urban terrain. Rejecting the hegemonic role of technological space in the English examples and of aesthetic space in New Babylon, Koolhaas adopted their topological approach to the city as a network of communications and junctions. At La Villette, he brought the transformative capability of the megastructure back to the ground plane while significantly altering its temporal dimension. Rather than relying on spontaneity as a means to foster creativity, as did Price and Littlewood and the members of the SI, Koolhaas sought a more gradual transformation of his park landscape in which change would come about through unspecified processes of social and political negotiation.

Despite its lack of formal resolution, Koolhaas's Parc de la Villette paradoxically celebrates the populist capabilities of modern architecture, its potential to be engaging and meaningful in nonelitist terms. Koolhaas interpreted the competition program "as a theme park with a strong social theme . . . anti-Disney," referring not only to its messy reality—versus Disney's explicit appeal to popular fantasy—but also to its lack of overt mechanisms of social control.[70] In *Delirious New York,* Koolhaas derived his concept of "Manhattanism," understood as the ability to support "an infinite number of superimposed and unpredictable activities on a single site," from his retroactive analysis of populist examples bypassed in normative histories of early twentieth-century architecture: Coney Island, the New York Athletic Club, Radio City Music Hall.[71] Just as he interpreted the United Nations Building as Le Corbusier's effort to export his concept of the Radiant City to New York, so Parc de la Villette represents Koolhaas's effort to export Manhattanism to Paris.

Koolhaas's analysis of Coney Island prefigures his approach to La Villette in significant ways—in its approach to nature, to technology, and to urban infrastructure:

> The total opposite of Nature, it has no choice but to counteract the artificiality of the new metropolis with its new Super-Natural. Instead of suspension of urban pressure, it offers intensification.
>
> The inordinate number of people assembling on the inadequate acreage, ostensibly seeking confrontation with the reality of the elements (sun,

wind, sand, water) *demands* the systematic conversion of nature into a technical service.

[The infrastructure of Luna Park] makes it square inch by square inch the most *modern* fragment of the world. Luna's infrastructure and communications network are more complex, elaborate, sophisticated and energy-consuming than those of most contemporary American cities.[72]

Moreover, Koolhaas interpreted Coney Island as a strategic source of emerging urban values: "At the junction of the nineteenth and twentieth centuries, Coney Island is the incubator for Manhattan's incipient themes and infant mythology. The strategies and mechanisms that later shape Manhattan are tested in the laboratory of Coney Island before they finally leap toward the larger island."[73] Just as Coney Island served in his analysis as a test case for the culture of Manhattanism, so the Parc de la Villette could serve Paris as the incubator of new means of civic engagement.

On his reason for writing *Delirious New York,* Koolhaas argued: "I wanted to construct—as a writer—a terrain where I could eventually work as an architect."[74] Indeed, it was Price's challenge to the architectural discipline, rather than his design strategies, that had the greatest impact on Koolhaas, who studied under Price at the Architectural Association.[75] Koolhaas rejects the "political operationality" of the discipline, its ideological basis as a humanist undertaking, with the associated objective of "improving bad and chaotic positions," yet the social dimension of architecture remains foremost among his concerns.[76] In an interview of 1998–99 he lamented the status of "'Architecture' as an endangered brand," arguing that he seeks "to reposition" the discipline by means of the "core of our activity—to reinvent a plausible relationship between the formal and the social."[77] His approach to societal issues is far more nuanced than those directions pursued by his twentieth-century predecessors.

Koolhaas's Parc de la Villette transforms the culture of the spectacle—the primary focus of SI resistance—into a mechanism for empowering the broader populace. While making use of available technologies, his tactic is no longer tied to technological notions of progress. The changes it anticipates are not so rapid as to lead to an experience of total disorientation.[78] His proposal is not an anarchic reaction to the bourgeois city but a means to extend the attributes of metropolitan culture to the full range of prospective urban inhabitants. Unlike the overt political action advocated by the SI, which operated in contrast to the city's dominant physical and institutional structures, Koolhaas proposed to use the territory of the park as a vehicle for direct social engagement and collective self-determination: a true public space, in accordance with Rosalyn Deutsche's understanding in which "public space, far from a pregiven entity created for users, is, rather, a space that only emerges from practices by users."[79] By participation, Koolhaas understands "a situation where it becomes impossible to say whose idea it really is, either the architect's or the user's." He elaborates that this is "a process in which the intelligence of others is mobilized," an assertion that reflects his own manner of working, liberally drawing upon a diverse array of sources in a critical manner to produce something that is radically new.[80] His proposal is not a call for renewed reliance on technology as a source of social betterment—an idea that had clearly run its course—but an appeal for understanding the social and ethical consequences of design decisions.

Although his Parc de la Villette shares aesthetic principles with an ecological approach to landscape design, Koolhaas did not conceive of its formal contingency from an ecological point of view. Concerning an ecological approach to the urban milieu, landscape theoretician Anne Whiston Spirn maintains:

> This is an aesthetic that celebrates motion and change, that encompasses dynamic processes rather than static objects, and that embraces multiple, rather than singular visions. This is not a timeless aesthetic, but one that recognizes both the flow of passing time and the singularity of the moment in time, that demands both continuity and revolution.[81]

To describe his urban vision, Koolhaas invoked similar terms of impermanence and open-ended processes:

> If there is to be a "new urbanism" it will not be based on the twin fantasies of order and omnipotence; it will be the staging of uncertainty; it will no longer be concerned with the arrangement of more or less permanent objects but with the irrigation of territories with potential; it will no longer aim for stable configurations but for the creation of enabling fields that accommodate processes that refuse to be crystallized into definitive form; it will no longer be about meticulous definition, the imposition of limits, but about expanding notions, denying boundaries, not about separating and identifying entities, but about discovering unnameable hybrids; it will no longer be obsessed with the city but with the manipulation of infrastructure for endless

intensifications and diversifications, shortcuts and redistributions—the reinvention of psychological space.[82]

Despite seeming parallels in their respective assertions, however, the disciplinary approaches of Spirn and Koolhaas differ radically. The malleability that Spirn describes derives from natural processes; that in Koolhaas's proposal emanates from human actions and interactions.[83] Although his tactic for Parc de la Villette engages numerous themes deriving from landscape theory—dynamic processes versus static outcomes, a stress on performance versus appearance—it uses ecological concepts metaphorically rather than taking the complexity of natural processes and systems into account. Instead, Koolhaas drew upon an inherent aspect of public space, postulating human agency as the instigating factor for his park proposal: "We have imagined, as a hypothesis, the coexistence on the site of La Villette of diverse human activities in a way that creates a park."[84] Yet ecology entails the inseparability of natural processes and human agency, suggesting not only that such divergent priorities need not be mutually exclusive but also that the disciplines have much to learn from each other. Although Koolhaas's Parc de la Villette constitutes a significant response to John Beardsley's plea that we "reclaim parks as part of our essential infrastructure, as key features in functioning social systems," it could potentially, given appropriate professional input, also operate as a component of functioning ecological systems.[85]

Koolhaas's approach to creating a site for unscripted social interaction in Parc de la Villette differs from the ethics of social betterment to which previous generations of architects, landscape architects, and planners aspired. Pointing to the disjunction between the share of the design problem affected by the designer (i.e., image production) and what he called "the real problem"—the benefit to society—Victor Papanek, an advocate of ecologically sound design principles, reasoned that the latter should have highest priority:

> [The designer's] social and moral judgment must be brought into play long *before* he begins to design, since he has to make a judgment, an a priori judgment at that, as to whether the products he is asked to design or redesign merit his attention at all. In other words, will his design be on the side of the social good or not.[86]

Eschewing any hegemonic determination as to what might constitute "the social good," Koolhaas sought to leave the park socially as well as formally open. Recognizing the limitations that any formal architectural solution would impose on such a site, he speculated: "Where there is nothing, everything is possible. Where there is architecture, nothing (else) is possible."[87]

Parc de la Villette: A Democratic Landscape?

The relationship between democracy and space is not inherent to physical form; rather, it depends on socially constructed and culturally mediated representations and prohibitions. Accepting the impossibility of any explicit correspondence between social space and political space, Richard Sennett maintains, "Were modern architects asked to design spaces that better promote democracy, they would lay down their pens."[88] This is because public/democratic space is always contingent, always in the process of realization; it is a contested zone of interaction and social discourse. As political geographer Edward Soja contends, "Space itself may be primordially given, but the organization, use, and meaning of space is a product of social translation, transformation, and experience."[89]

The issues inherent to a democratic landscape have been complicated by the shift during the course of the twentieth century from the concept of public space as open and accessible, yet protected from heterogeneity and conflict, to the notion of the public sphere as a site of contention among diverse interest groups—an approach that American philosopher John Dewey anticipated in his writings of the 1920s.[90] Accordingly, the public realm can no longer be considered a territory of shared values and beliefs; it is instead a site where difference can be revealed and negotiated, which political theorist Chantal Mouffe has termed an "agonistic" public sphere.[91] Indeed, as Rosalyn Deutsche argues in her investigations of connections among contemporary art, space, and political struggles, "Categories like 'the public' can, of course, be construed as naturally or fundamentally coherent only by disavowing the conflicts, particularity, heterogeneity, and uncertainty that constitute public life." In agreement with the propositions of Mouffe and other theorists of radical democracy, Deutsche maintains, "Conflict, far from the ruin of democratic public space, is the condition of its existence."[92]

In what sense can Koolhaas's proposal for the Parc de la Villette be interpreted as amenable to the open character of a contemporary plural democracy, inasmuch as its potential for physical transformation implies no direct social or political effects? As Deutsche declares, "To be democratic, society and public space must remain a question."[93] Yet the open-endedness underlying the OMA proposal ultimately led Koolhaas to lose the Parc de la Villette competition, as jury member Françoise Choay asserted in concluding that the verdict "was inspired by fear: —Fear of innovation and of the unpredictable, from the programmers who have been asking for it and refusing it at the same time. —Fear by lack of understanding, from the nonprofessional members of the jury. —Fear by too much understanding, from the same architects on the jury."[94]

The relevance of the OMA proposal for the diverse constituencies of a plural society would depend on unanswered questions concerning how the park's ongoing development would be administered and financed—that is, under what combination of public and bureaucratic processes its physical transformation might be carried out. In "Exodus, or the Voluntary Prisoners of Architecture" (1972, with Madelon Vriesendorp and Zoe Zenghelis), Koolhaas and Elia Zenghelis suggested one means by which such public engagement might be initiated.[95] Concerning the amateurs in the Reception Area, the zone through which the public would gain entry to their alternative urban proposition, the architects speculated:

> Through their busy dealings they are exercising an inspired state of political inventiveness, to which the architecture is the echo chamber: a volume of overwhelming sensuousness. The activities show that the sole concern of the participants is the present and future course of the strip: they propose architectural refinements, extensions, and strategies. Excited groups of different sizes elaborate the proposals in the special rooms built for this purpose, while others are continually engaged in making modifications to the model. The most contradictory programmes fuse without erosion.[96]

As this passage suggests, such a process of negotiation could be initiated through the inclusion of a related venue among multiple means to facilitate public participation in the development of OMA's Parc de la Villette.

Koolhaas's mandate for ongoing change in the park has inherent political implications. As François Barré argued in conjunction with the Parc de la Villette competition: "The creation of a park is first of all a political responsibility. Modelling [sic] the city, giving it breathing space and places for meeting, is a political choice."[97] Koolhaas envisioned the park as a site of public contestation and debate among diverse interest groups, as he elaborated: "The more the Park works, the more it will be in a state of revision."[98] Valorizing civic engagement as a means to both realize and continually transform the Parc de la Villette, his proposal draws upon the potential for the exercise of difference rather than adherence to preconceived social norms. Urban philosopher/sociologist Henri Lefebvre equates "the right to the city" with sites of heterogeneity and encounter with difference, qualities that Koolhaas associates with the European Union, which he characterizes as "the construction of a virtue out of difference."[99] In such terms his Parc de la Villette reflects a moment outside utopia where architecture, landscape, and the political could potentially overlap. Believing with Jürgen Habermas in modernity as "an incomplete project," Koolhaas seeks to reassert architecture as a viable mode of social praxis for a culturally diverse populace.[100] His proposal reflects an effort to transform the architectural landscape from an instrument of politics and/or socialization into a force for social and political action. It fosters reengagement with the land in the sense of giving the populace a voice in the park's development—as opposed to the physical and cultural identification associated with *Landschaft*—posing the possibility for a public landscape to operate simultaneously as a site of entertainment and as an "echo chamber" of the "inspired state of public inventiveness." It revels in the duplicity intrinsic to any act of design in the public realm—between the social restrictions such an operation imposes and its potential for endowing members of the public with agency in their use of space. Yet the risks involved in such an open-ended process are considerable. Without adequate provision for public involvement and appropriate administrative, political, and funding mechanisms (and their attendant constraints), the ultimate success of such a proposal would be severely limited.

    The bureaucratic decision-making process leading to the creation of recent Parisian parks is discouraging in this regard. The retrograde comments of Roland Castro, a politically militant French architect whose thought is inscribed with the national and political aspects of an urban architecture, are telling. When invited by President Nicolas Sarkozy to reflect on the future of Greater Paris, Castro endorsed civic beautification as a means to address the social isolation of the Parisian underclasses, citing one of Haussmann's urban interventions to substantiate his point: "To solve the problems of the suburbs—which the rest of the world learned of, stunned, during the spectacular riots of 2005—those ghettos should be generously improved by implementing squares in the manner of the city's Parc Monceau."[101] Castro's assessment only confirms Koolhaas's earlier indictment: "Paris can only become more Parisian—it is already on its way to becoming hyper-Paris, a polished caricature."[102]

Adolphe Alphand's transformation of the Parisian landscape under Haussmann satisfied the bourgeois interests of capitalism. It was, in Anthony Vidler's analysis, "the mechanism by which city became metropolis . . . adapting all of the forms of the picturesque in the service of artificial informality . . . making nature and the city interchangeable."[103] Resisting the commodification of nature inherent to such beautification efforts, wherein landscape is consumed by a detached public, Koolhaas exploited the potential for Parc de la Villette to initiate new social formations by fostering participation of an engaged citizenry. Inverting Alphand's process, he took the modus operandi of the city and inscribed it in the park, reflecting his effort to reinfuse metropolitan life within a city that had begun to stagnate under its own historical weight.

Postscript: It is unlikely that Koolhaas would approve of this interpretation of his submission to the Parc de la Villette competition. He made no claims for his proposal's "democratic" virtues. Moreover, he argues: "Every definition of our work clearly limits our freedoms. And if there's any consistency, in both our work and personalities, it involves a systematic search for freedoms."[104]

AFTERWORD

For many landscape architects, the results of the Parc de la Villette competition in Paris of 1982–83, in which the first- and second-place schemes were designed by architects Bernard Tschumi and Rem Koolhaas/OMA, respectively, served as a wake-up call to certain limitations of their disciplinary authority. Heralded as an inquiry into "the park of the future," the competition prompted disciplinary reevaluations that have had a significant bearing on architecture as well as on landscape architecture. Both proposals have been associated with the subsequent deflection from concerns with form and meaning to issues of "performativity" and "effect" associated with the postcritical—a distinction that seems as specious as the outmoded polarity of culture and nature. Moreover, they evoke such parallels in different ways. Whereas Tschumi's design, with its disjunctions among form, use, and social value, comprises directed fields in which the unstructured interplay among program, event, and activity would theoretically generate an array of potential uses by means of fixed architectural forms, Koolhaas's more tactical proposal anticipates the current emphasis on formal and social as well as programmatic malleability, facilitated in architectural terms by recent advances in digital technology. Although Koolhaas's competition entry was inspired by the architectural instability of the metropolitan condition, our current perception of urbanism—as entrenched in complex transformative processes of natural as well as human origin—is more indebted to an ecological perspective that derives from landscape architecture. Accordingly, there is general agreement among professionals of both disciplines that the contemporary metropolis is a multifaceted and ever-changing phenomenon for which new tools of analysis and creative thought are needed if we are to affect the shifting environmental circumstances of life on this planet.[1] Now, more than ever, it is imperative for design practices to address existing environmental, social, economic, and political frameworks in a critical manner—to challenge the institutional and political milieus in which design work is produced by advancing alternative models of practice capable of yielding new methodologies and results.[2]

Nevertheless, architects generally persist in using landscape concepts metaphorically, rather than engaging deeper ecological considerations.[3] They equate the malleability and open-ended qualities of landscape not only with design processes facilitated by digital technologies but also with the social malleability they presume will result from such open-ended methods. Landscape architects, on the other hand, often constrain themselves to either a scientific approach to ecological issues, associated with sustainability, or a purely aesthetic approach to design, a divide that James Corner and Chris Reed attempt to bridge in their writings and their work.[4] In stressing the creative and imaginative potential of ecological thought as much as its technical possibilities, they seek to affect the broader cultural significance of landscape design in the public realm.

The examples scrutinized in this book point to significant correlations among formal invention, new modes of conceptualization (including ecology), new technologies, and issues of social agency in design, and thus the importance of understanding the complex social, cultural, and political interrelationships implicated in any interventions in the built environment, whether derived from architecture, landscape architecture, or urban design and planning. Toward that end, it is crucial to imagine interdisciplinary modes of working that can enable the different types of form making emanating from architecture and landscape architecture to operate in concordance with evolving social processes as well as the formative, natural processes of landscape. Disciplinary empowerment can result only when architects and landscape architects understand and respect their distinct values, modes of operation, and areas of expertise, in addition to their potential spheres of convergence, and work collaboratively with the aim of engaging the cultural imaginary as well as having an impact on the built environment.[5]

NOTES

Preface

1. James Corner, "Eidetic Operations and New Landscapes," in *Recovering Landscape: Essays in Contemporary Landscape Architecture,* ed. James Corner (New York: Princeton Architectural Press, 1999), 153–54. For elaboration of the evolving concept of landscape inherent to these terms, see Denis Cosgrove, "Landscape and *Landschaft*," *German Historical Institute Bulletin* 35 (Fall 2004): 57–71.

2. Landscape has been classified as comprising three types of nature: "first nature," or unmediated nature (wilderness); "second nature," or nature that has been manipulated for practical ends, such as agriculture or infrastructure; and "third nature," or nature that has been symbolically ordered, that is, manipulated for artistic purposes. See John Dixon Hunt, response to "Most Important Questions," *Landscape Journal* 11, no. 2 (Fall 1992): 168.

Introduction

I am grateful to Karen M'Closkey, who provided feedback on an earlier version of this chapter.

1. W. J. T. Mitchell, "Introduction," in *Landscape and Power,* ed. W. J. T. Mitchell (Chicago: University of Chicago Press, 1994), 2.

2. Rachel Ziady DeLue, "Elusive Landscapes and Shifting Grounds," in *Landscape Theory,* ed. Rachel Zaidy DeLue and James Elkins (New York: Routledge, 2008), 11.

3. J. B. Jackson, "The Word Itself," in *Discovering the Vernacular Landscape* (New Haven, Conn.: Yale University Press, 1984), 8.

4. Denis Cosgrove, "Introductory Essay," in *Social Formation and Symbolic Landscape* (1984; repr., Madison: University of Wisconsin Press, 1998), xxvii. Although Cosgrove qualified this claim in his "Introductory Essay for the Paperback Edition" (1998) and provided a more nuanced interpretation in his subsequent essay "Landscape and *Landschaft*" (*German Historical Institute Bulletin,* no. 35 [Fall 2004]: 57–71), numerous authors have reiterated it. For example, associating the rise of landscape with European imperialism, W. J. T. Mitchell argues, "Landscape is an exhausted medium, no longer viable as a mode of artistic expression." Mitchell, "Imperial Landscape," in Mitchell, *Landscape and Power,* 5. For efforts to recuperate the dense political, cultural, and mythic associations of landscape, see Kenneth R. Olwig, "Recovering the Substantive Nature of Landscape," *Annals of the Association of American Geographers* 86, no. 4 (December 1996): 630–53; Olwig's *Landscape, Nature, and the Body Politic: From Britain's Renaissance to America's New World* (Madison: University of Wisconsin Press, 2002), 9–26; Simon Schama, *Landscape and Memory* (New York: Alfred A. Knopf, 1995); and John R. Stilgoe, *The Common Landscape of America, 1580–1845* (New Haven, Conn.: Yale University Press, 1982).

5. Cosgrove, *Social Formation,* 1–2. For a similar claim of decline of landscape as a fine art, see Paul O. Kristeller, "The Modern System of the Arts," in *Renaissance Thought and the Arts: Collected Essays* (Princeton, N.J.: Princeton University Press, 1980), 226.

6. John Barrell, *The Political Theory of Painting from Reynolds to Hazlitt: "The Body of the Public"* (New Haven, Conn.: Yale University Press, 1986), 29–39. Grounding his argument in the discourse of civic humanism in eighteenth-century British art criticism, Barrell traces the decline of the arts (including landscape) to the overtaking of public virtue by self-interested commercial forces, reflected in the rise of separate professions (ibid., 47). At the same time, he notes, the concept of "public" broadened from an aristocratic ruling class presumed to embody moral virtue to a more egalitarian but aggregate mercantile citizenry. Accordingly, he argues, John Ruskin associated the nineteenth-century preoccupation with landscape with a love of liberty that no longer finds satisfaction in civic life. See John Ruskin, *Modern Painters* (New York: E. P. Dutton, 1906), pt. 4, chap. 16.

7. See James Corner, "Recovering Landscape as a Critical Cultural Context," in *Recovering Landscape: Essays in Contemporary Landscape Architecture,* ed. James Corner (New York: Princeton Architectural Press, 1999), 1. Certain French scholars date the return of landscape in that country to 1973, the year that the Ecole Nationale du Paysage was established at Versailles under the leadership of Michel Corajoud and Alexandre Chemetoff; see Sébastien Marot, "The Return of

Landscape," and Manuel Delluc, "Michel Desvigne and Christine Dalnoky," in *Desvigne and Dalnoky: The Return of the Landscape* (New York: Whitney Library of Design, 1997), 6–9; 11.

8. I use the term *avant-garde* as a phenomenon of the early twentieth century, when aestheticism gave way to an attack on art as an autonomous institution (art for art's sake) in order to reinstitute the integral relationship between art and lived experience. It involves a social and economic critique of bourgeois culture, and thus implies the imposition of an alternative order on the landscape.

9. John Claudius Loudon first used the term *landscape architecture* in the title of his edition of the writings of Humphry Repton, *The landscape gardening and landscape architecture of the late Humphry Repton, esq.: Being his entire works on these subjects* (London: Longman, 1840). Loudon equates "landscape architecture" with landscape designed in relation to architecture—a concept landscape theorists subsequently termed the "architectural" or "architectonic" garden.

10. Charles W. Eliot, "The Need of Conserving the Beauty and Freedom of Nature in Modern Life," *National Geographic* 26, no. 1 (July 1914): 68. In 1900, under Eliot's presidency, Harvard University instituted the United States' first professional degree program in landscape architecture affiliated with the arts, rather than the scientific disciplines of botany or forestry. Eliot's son was the noted landscape architect Charles Eliot, who apprenticed in Frederick Law Olmsted's office and was a partner in the Olmsted firm from 1893 until his untimely death in 1897.

11. Frederick Law Olmsted, "Public Parks and the Enlargement of Towns," in *The Public Face of Architecture: Civic Culture and Public Spaces,* ed. Nathan Glazer and Mark Lilla (New York: Free Press, 1987), 241; originally published in *American Social Science Association* (Cambridge, Mass.: Riverside Press, 1870).

12. Martin Wagner, "Freiflächenpolitik," *Das neue Berlin* 1, no. 6 (1929): 110, cited by Ludovica Scarpa, "The Standards of Happiness in Socialdemocratic Berlin," *Lotus International* 30 (1981/I): 121; Achille Duchêne, *Les Jardins de l'avenir: Hier, aujourd'hui, demain* (Paris: Vincent, Fréal et Cie., 1935), 2.

13. Christopher Tunnard, "Modern Gardens for Modern Houses: Reflections on Current Trends in Landscape Design," *Landscape Architecture* 32, no. 2 (January 1942): 58. Walter Gropius, chair of the Architecture Department at the Graduate School of Design, Harvard University, brought Tunnard, a modern landscape theorist and practitioner, from England to teach at Harvard (1939–43). Tunnard also worked in Gropius's Cambridge, Massachusetts, office, The Architects Collaborative.

14. For discussions of ongoing efforts to qualify the discipline of landscape architecture and the issues that surround it in the American context, see "Monkeying with the Name: Divers Opinions as to the Term 'Landscape Architecture,'" *Landscape Architecture* 33, no. 1 (October 1942): 20–23; "Most Important Questions," *Landscape Journal* 11, no. 2 (Fall 1992): 160–81.

15. James Corner, "Landscape as Question," *Landscape Journal* 11, no. 2 (Fall 1992): 163–64. Associating "stewardship" with domination and control of nature, Elizabeth Meyer is critical of such terminology: "In the traditional view of culture versus nature, . . . man's relationship to land is one of stewardship rather than partnership." Elizabeth Meyer, "Landscape Architecture as Modern Other and Postmodern Ground" (lecture, EDGE 2 conference, Melbourne, 1992), quoted in Paula Dietz, "A Feminist View of Landscapes: A Partnership with Nature," *New York Times,* 29 April 1993. Carolyn Merchant, who articulated this concept of partnership in *The Death of Nature: Women, Ecology, and the Scientific Revolution* (New York: Harper & Row, 1980), subsequently elaborated: "A partnership ethic means that a human community is in a sustainable ecological relationship with its surrounding natural community." Carolyn Merchant, "Introduction," in *Key Concepts in Critical Theory: Ecology,* ed. Carolyn Merchant (Amherst, N.Y.: Humanity Books, 1999), 20. In response to ecofeminist critiques such as these, Corner qualified his earlier argument: "A good strategy . . . is more conversational and engaging than it is confrontational or assertive." James Corner, "Not Unlike Life Itself: Landscape Strategy Now," *Harvard Design Magazine* 21 (Fall/Winter 2004–5): 32. Merchant's logic echoes the earlier thoughts of Garrett Eckbo, who argued: "I object to the notion of land ethic or stewardship of the land as again too simple and too paternalistic. Who are we stewarding it for? The people who are too stupid to steward it for themselves? That is a blind alley." Garrett Eckbo, "Study of the Profession of Landscape Architecture: Answers to Questions for Consultants," in *A Study of the Profession of Landscape Architecture: Technical Report,* ed. Albert Fein (McLean, Va.: ASLA, 1972), sec. 6, 10. See Edward Relph's related concept of "environmental humility" in his *Rational Landscapes and Humanistic Geography* (London: Croom Helm, 1981).

16. For further elaboration of the design approaches of landscape architects, see Elizabeth Meyer, "Site Citations: The Grounds of Modern Landscape Architecture," in *Site Matters: Design Concepts, Histories, and Strategies,* ed. Carol Burns and Andrea Kahn (New York: Routledge, 2005), 93–129.

17. Elizabeth Kassler, *Modern Gardens and the Landscape* (New York: Museum of Modern Art, 1964), 8, 15. Accordingly, Kassler organized her book typologically, with sections on the outdoor room, parks and plazas, a view from above, gardens and flower gardens, gardens in a natural landscape, constructed landscapes, and buildings and the land. MoMA director René d'Harnoncourt commissioned this book independent of any museum exhibition. Kassler, a curator in MoMA's Department of Architecture and Design from 1938 to 1946, was the sister of housing expert Catherine Bauer, who was associated with MoMA from 1932 to 1942. Elizabeth Meyer reiterates Kassler's point in arguing that attempts to reduce distinctions between the professions in hybrid design practices of the 1950s diminished the concept of site planning from a "temporal, geological and ecological site

framework" to a "spatial, environmental, and functional one"—an approach codified in such publications as John Simonds's *Landscape Architecture* (New York: F. W. Dodge, 1961) and Kevin Lynch's *Site Planning* (Cambridge: MIT Press, 1962). Meyer, "Site Citations," 117.

18. Garrett Eckbo, "Is Landscape *Architecture*?" *Landscape Architecture* 73, no. 3 (May/June 1983): 64–65.

19. James C. Rose, "Integration: Design Expresses the Continuity of Living," *Pencil Points* 19, no. 12 (December 1938): 760. Note Rose's reference to disciplinary decline in his phrase "the stagnant era."

20. Garrett Eckbo's early essays addressed to an architectural audience include "Small Gardens in the City: A Study of Their Design Possibilities," *Pencil Points* 18, no. 9 (September 1937): 573–88; and "Site Planning," *Architectural Forum* 76, no. 5 (May 1942): 263–67. Those by James C. Rose include "Freedom in the Garden," *Pencil Points* 19, no. 10 (October 1938): 639–43; "Plants Dictate Garden Forms," *Pencil Points* 19, no. 11 (November 1938): 695–97; "Integration," *Pencil Points* 19, no. 12 (December 1938): 758–60; "Articulate Form in Landscape Design: People and Materials Defeat Preconceived Pattern," *Pencil Points* 20, no. 2 (February 1939): 98–99; "Plant Forms and Space," *Pencil Points* 20, no. 4 (April 1939): 226–28; "Landscape Models," *Pencil Points* 20, no. 7 (July 1939): 433–40; "Why Not Try Science," *Pencil Points* 20, no. 12 (December 1939): 777–79; "Gardens," *California Arts and Architecture* 57, no. 3 (May 1940): 20–30.

21. Garrett Eckbo, Daniel Kiley, and James C. Rose, "Landscape Design in the Urban Environment," *Architectural Record* 85, no. 5 (May 1939): 70–77; "Landscape Design in the Rural Environment," *Architectural Record* 86, no. 2 (August 1939): 68–74; "Landscape Design in the Primeval Environment," *Architectural Record* 87, no. 2 (February 1940): 74–79.

22. Pierre-Louis Flouquet, "L'Association Internationale des Architectes de Jardins Modernistes," *Bâtir* 7, no. 64 (1938): 130–33; see Dorothée Imbert, "Counting Trees and Flowers: The Reconstructed Landscapes of Belgium and France," in *The Architecture of Landscape, 1940–1960*, ed. Marc Treib (Philadelphia: University of Pennsylvania Press, 2002), 87. During the ensuing decade, as membership in the international landscape organization dwindled, certain AIAJM members joined forces with CIAM groups in their respective countries—albeit to little effect—until the demise of that organization in 1959.

23. Christopher Tunnard's essays in the *Architectural Review* (October 1937 to September 1938) constitute a serialized version of his book *Gardens in the Modern Landscape* (London: Architectural Press, 1938).

24. André Vera contributed an essay on contemporary garden design. "Une Phase nouvelle dans l'évolution de jardin," *L'Architecture d'aujourd'hui* 8, no. 4 (April 1937): 3. Essays by Laprade and Moreux concerned historic garden styles, while

additional material featured public parks and promenades, playgrounds, botanical and zoological gardens, garden cities, private gardens (including projects by Le Corbusier and Richard Neutra), workers' gardens, and roof terraces. During the Vichy period, in response to the moral, physical, and economic destruction wrought by the war with Germany, Vera endorsed overcoming strict disciplinary distinctions among urbanists, architects, and landscape designers in favor of a broader, nationalistic approach to design. André Vera, "Manifeste pour le renouveau de l'art français," *Urbanisme* 10, no. 72 (1941): 53–59.

25. "Architecture . . . garden . . . landscape. There must be no antagonism between architecture and its natural setting. The architecture of the house embraces the garden. House and garden coalesce, a single unit in the landscape. The modern architect's aim is not to create a 'style' but to pursue a realistic unity of form and purpose, a concept whose implications are eligible not only for this or that type of building, this or that climate, but for all building problems wheresoever. Modern architecture is universal, infinitely adaptable." *New Architecture: An Exhibition of the Elements of Modern Architecture Organized by the MARS (Modern Architectural Research) Group* (London: New Burlington Galleries, 1938), 20.

26. "Members Work—Television and Garden Planning," *Landscape and Garden* 5 (Summer 1938): 118, cited by Dorothée Imbert, "The AIAJM: A Manifesto for Landscape Modernity," *Landscape Journal* 26, no. 2 (February 2007): 227.

27. G. N. Brandt, "The Garden of the Future," trans. Claire Jordan, *Oase* 56 (Summer 2001): 31; originally published as "Der kommende Garten," *Wasmuths Monatshefte für Baukunst und Städtbau* 14, no. 4 (April 1930): 161–76.

28. Fletcher Steele, "Landscape Design of the Future," *Landscape Architecture* 22, no. 4 (July 1932): 299.

29. Garrett Eckbo, review of *On Building: Mystery and Realities of the Site*, by Richard Neutra, *Landscape Architecture* 42, no. 1 (October 1951): 41.

30. Eero Saarinen lecture, Dickinson College, 1959, in *Eero Saarinen on His Work,* ed. Aline B. Saarinen (New Haven, Conn.: Yale University Press, 1962), 6, cited by Gregg Bleam, "The Work of Dan Kiley," in *Modern Landscape Architecture: A Critical Review,* ed. Marc Treib (Cambridge: MIT Press, 1992), 227.

31. Martha Schwartz, "Landscape and Common Culture since Modernism," in Treib, *Modern Landscape Architecture,* 261.

32. Horace Walpole, *Anecdotes of Painting in England . . . to which is added The History of the Modern Taste in Gardening* (London: Strawberry Hill Press, 1771), 4:137–38.

33. Vera, "Une Phase nouvelle," 3 (my translation). In his *Du principe de l'art* (1865), Pierre-Joseph Proudhon vowed that "we must transform France into a vast garden . . . where every landscape contributes to the overall harmony." Pierre-Joseph Proudhon, *Du principe de l'art et de sa destination sociale* (Paris: Garnier

Frères, 1865), 374 (my translation). Italian architectural historian Bruno Zevi reiterated Vera's complaint in a lecture to the International Federation of Landscape Architects in 1962: "The transition from city-design to town-planning took place a long time ago: the same cannot be stated of the transition from the architecture of gardens to the architecture of landscapes." Bruno Zevi, "The Modern Dimension of Landscape Architecture," in *Shaping Tomorrow's Landscape,* ed. Sylvia Crowe and Zvi Miller (Amsterdam: Djambatan, 1964), 18.

34. Joseph Hudnut, "Can the Modern House Have a Garden?" (lecture, Horticultural Society of New York, 15 December 1937), manuscript, Frances Loeb Library, Graduate School of Design, Harvard University, 13.

35. Rose, "Integration," 759.

36. Elizabeth Meyer, "Landscape Architecture as Modern Other and Postmodern Ground," in *The Culture of Landscape Architecture,* ed. Harriet Hedquist and Vanessa Bird (Melbourne: RMIT, 1994), 30–31.

37. Garrett Eckbo, *Landscape for Living* (New York: F. W. Dodge, 1950), 131.

38. Spartakus an Grün [pseudonym of Leberecht Migge], "Das grüne Manifest," *Die Tat,* no. 12 (1918–19): 912–19; see David Haney, "Leberecht Migge's 'Green Manifesto': Envisioning a Revolution of Gardens," *Landscape Journal* 26, no. 2 (2007): 201–18.

39. André Vera, "Manifeste pour le renouveau de l'art Français," *Urbanisme* 10, no. 72 (1941): 55, 56 (my translation).

40. Flouquet, "L'Association Internationale." Tunnard associated the demise of the AIAJM with the inability of landscape architects to adapt to the "needs of a changing society," as well as their focus on theoretical issues of style and reliance on private patronage. Christopher Tunnard, "Landscape Architecture in America," *Architects' Yearbook* 1 (London 1945): 30, 34–35. The AIAJM was supplanted in 1948 by the International Federation of Landscape Architects, founded in Oxford, England, following a conference in London titled "The Work of the Landscape Architect in Relation to Society" and its accompanying exhibition *Landscape of Work and Leisure.* See Imbert, "The AIAJM," 219–35.

41. Fletcher Steele, "Private Delight and the Communal Ideal," *Landscape Architecture* 31, no. 2 (January 1941): 69–71.

42. Achille Duchêne, *Premier Congrès Internationale des Architectes de Jardins* (Paris: Société Française des Architectes de Jardins, 1937), manuscript, Frances Loeb Library, Harvard University, 3 (my translation).

43. Efforts to provide housing for the working classes in these countries were part of a larger set of social reforms instituted during the interwar period and beyond to improve their quality of life; these included the institution of the eight-hour workday, the right to unionize, national health and unemployment insurance, universal suffrage, and expanded programs in education and public health.

44. See Gerry Andela, "The Public Park in the Netherlands," *Journal of Garden History* 1, no. 4 (October–December 1981): 367–92; Jan Woudstra, "Jacopus P. Thijsse's Influence on Dutch Landscape Architecture," in *Nature and Ideology: Natural Garden Design in the Twentieth Century,* ed. Joachim Wolschke-Bulmahn (Washington, D.C.: Dumbarton Oaks, 1997), 155–85; Anita Berrizbeitia, "The Amsterdam Bos: The Modern Public Park and the Construction of Collective Experience," in Corner, *Recovering Landscape,* 186–203; George Hargreaves, "Large Parks: A Designer's Perspective," in *Large Parks,* ed. Julia Czerniak and George Hargreaves (New York: Princeton Architectural Press, 2007), 146–55.

45. See Marco De Michelis, "The Red and the Green: Park and City in Weimar Germany," *Lotus International* 30 (1981/I): 109.

46. This distinction between aesthetic and "functional" landscapes echoes coeval distinctions in the United States between national parks, intended for aesthetic enjoyment, and national forests, originally slated to be managed purely for economic purposes; between the National Park Service, housed in the Department of the Interior, and the Forest Service in the Department of Agriculture; and between the professional specializations of landscape architecture and forestry. Such conflicting values have enormous political implications; despite attempts to bridge this ethical divide by private associations such as the Wilderness Society (founded 1935), the writings of Aldo Leopold (e.g., *A Sand County Almanac,* 1949), and the landscape practices and writings of Jens Jensen, Elsa Rehmann, or Garrett Eckbo, for example, they persist to this day. See Melanie Simo, *Forest and Garden: Traces of Wildness in a Modernizing Land, 1897–1949* (Charlottesville: University of Virginia Press, 2003), 139–56. The professional subdivision between landscape planning and landscape design that began in the United States during the 1930s reflects a corresponding tension between scientific and aesthetic values in the discipline of landscape architecture. Nina-Marie Lister makes a similar distinction between current approaches to ecological design: *"designer ecology* . . . that is vital . . . for educational, aesthetic, spiritual, and other reasons" and *"adaptive ecological design,"* which she associates with facilitating "the emergence and evolution of self-organizing, resilient ecological systems—a basic requirement for long-term sustainability." Instead, she advocates a combined approach. Nina-Marie Lister, "Sustainable Large Parks: Ecological Design or Designer Ecology?" in Czerniak and Hargreaves, *Large Parks,* 35. For a critique of analogous distinctions between practical and symbolic values in modern architecture, see Robert Levit, "Contemporary Ornament: The Return of the Symbolic Repressed," *Harvard Design Magazine* 28 (Spring/Summer 2008).

47. "We need not concern ourselves with the beauty of the garden. It is not invented, it grows: garden art arises solely from garden growth." Leberecht Migge, "Gardening and Garden Art," trans. Nijmegen Bookmakers, *Oase* 56 (Summer 2001): 79; originally published in *Gartenschönheit* (March 1927).

48. See Joachim Wolschke-Bulmahn, "From the War-Garden to the Victory Garden: Political Aspects of Garden Culture in the United States during World War I," *Landscape Journal* 11, no. 1 (Spring 1992): 51–57; Garrett Eckbo, "Site Planning," *Architectural Forum* 76, no. 5 (May 1942): 263–67.

49. Duchêne, "Premier Congrès," 16 (my translation). Duchêne initially set out this argument in his book *Les Jardins de l'avenir,* profusely illustrated with his own designs for various new programmatic garden types. Although best known for his restoration efforts at châteaux landscapes such as Vaux-le-Vicomte, Duchêne also worked on post–World War I reconstruction efforts in Albert (Somme), which he documented in *Pour la reconstruction des cités industrielles (étude économique et sociale)* (Paris: Bibliothèque de la Renaissance des Cités, 1919).

50. Duchêne, "Premier Congrès," 18.

51. Leberecht Migge, "Der kommende Garten," *Gartenschönheit* 8 (1927): 64, cited by Gert Groening and Joachim Wolschke-Bulmahn, "Changes in the Philosophy of Garden Architecture in the 20th Century and Their Impact upon the Social and Spatial Environment," *Journal of Garden History* 9, no. 2 (1989): 59.

52. Leberecht Migge, "Ernährungs-Siedlung," *Die Tat,* no. 5 (August 1920): 321; "Bodenproduktiv Siedlung," *Schlesisches Heim,* no. 6 (June 1922): 141–42; "Die Gartenstadt als Stadt der Gärten," *Gardenstadt,* no. 1 (1914): 2–5. Cited by De Michelis, "The Red and the Green," 115.

53. Fletcher Steele, "Modern Landscape Architecture," in *Contemporary Landscape Architecture and Its Sources* (San Francisco: San Francisco Museum of Art, 1937), 25.

54. Peter Walker, "The Practice of Landscape Architecture in the Postwar United States," in Treib, *Modern Landscape Architecture,* 250–51.

55. Galen Cranz traces a shift in American parks during the early twentieth century from pleasurable urban retreats, a phenomenon widely advanced in the nineteenth century by Olmsted and his followers, to active agents of reform—as playgrounds and sites for organized recreational activities that were more socially inclusive. Related to the rise in legislated leisure time for workers, this imperative led to a new focus on functional accommodation that she argues was often at odds with the aesthetic values of the City Beautiful movement. Yet Cranz overlooks the distinction between Olmsted's aesthetic approach to social reform and the more programmatic approaches of the early twentieth century. By 1930 such recreational facilities were ubiquitous in the American landscape and, in Cranz's account, their social motivations diminished. Galen Cranz, *The Politics of Park Design: A History of Urban Parks in America* (Cambridge: MIT Press, 1982).

56. Jean-Charles Moreux, cited by Marc Treib, "Sources of Significance," in *Denatured Visions: Landscape and Culture in the Twentieth Century,* ed. Stuart Wrede and William Howard Adams (New York: Museum of Modern Art, 1991), 107 and n4, from *Gardens and Gardening,* ed. F. A. Mercer (London: Studio, 1939), 17.

57. Walter Freiherr von Engelhardt, *Kultur und Natur in der Gartenkunst* (Stuttgart: Strecker & Schroder, 1910), cited by Barry Bergdoll, "The Nature of Mies's Space," in *Mies in Berlin,* ed. Terence Riley and Barry Bergdoll (New York: Museum of Modern Art, 2001), 73.

58. See Jules Buyssens, "Le Jardin moderne," *Bâtir,* no. 1 (15 December 1932): 20–21; "Jardins démocratiques," *Bâtir,* no. 11 (15 October 1933): 420–21.

59. Tunnard, "Modern Gardens for Modern Houses," 60; Kassler, *Modern Gardens and the Landscape,* 11; Alexander Pope, "An Epistle to Lord Burlington" (1731), in *The Genius of the Place: The English Landscape Garden, 1620–1820,* ed. John Dixon Hunt and Peter Willis (Cambridge: MIT Press, 1988), 212–13.

60. Kassler, *Modern Gardens and the Landscape,* 15.

61. Marc-Antoine Laugier, *An Essay on Architecture* (1753), trans. Wolfgang Hermann and Anni Hermann (Los Angeles: Hennessey + Ingalls, 1977), 128.

62. Gottfried Semper, "The Four Elements of Architecture" (1851), in *The Four Elements of Architecture, and Other Writings,* trans. Harry Francis Mallgrave and Wolfgang Hermann (Cambridge: Cambridge University Press, 1989), 101–21.

63. Vittorio Gregotti, "Lecture at the New York Architectural League," February/March 1983, quoted by Kenneth Frampton, "Rappel à l'Ordre: The Case for the Tectonic" (1990), in *Labour, Work, and Architecture: Collected Essays on Architecture and Design* (New York: Phaidon, 2002), 99.

64. Gio Ponti, *In Praise of Architecture,* trans. Giuseppina Salvadori and Mario Salvadori (New York: F. W. Dodge, 1960), 97.

65. Frank Lloyd Wright, *The Living City* (New York: Horizon Press, 1958), 112, 113.

66. Frank Lloyd Wright, "Broadacre City: A New Community Plan," *Architectural Record* 77 (April 1935): 246. Wright elaborates: "In an organic architecture the ground itself predetermines all features; the climate modifies them; available means limit them; function shapes them" (ibid., 247).

67. See Anne Whiston Spirn, "Frank Lloyd Wright: Architect of Landscape," in *Frank Lloyd Wright: Designs for an American Landscape, 1922–1932,* ed. David G. De Long (New York: Harry N. Abrams, 1996), 135–69.

68. Alvar Aalto, "Architecture in the Landscape of Central Finland" (1925), in *Alvar Aalto in His Own Words,* ed. Göran Schildt (New York: Rizzoli, 1998), 22.

69. Alvar Aalto, "Art and Technology" (1955), cited by Juhani Pallasmaa, "Alvar Aalto: Toward a Synthetic Functionalism," in *Alvar Aalto: Between Humanism and Materialism,* ed. Peter Reed (New York: Museum of Modern Art, 1998), 21.

70. Alvar Aalto, "Instead of an Article," *Arkkitehti,* nos. 1–2 (1958), cited by Marja-Riita Norri, "Appreciation," in Reed, *Alvar Aalto,* 11. The entire essay is published as "In Lieu of an Article" in Schildt, *Alvar Aalto in His Own Words,* 263–64.

71. Sigfried Giedion, *Space, Time, and Architecture* (Cambridge, Mass.: Harvard University Press, 1941), 552; this book is based on a series of lectures delivered at Harvard University, 1938–39.

72. Sigfried Giedion, *Space, Time, and Architecture,* rev. ed. (Cambridge, Mass.: Harvard University Press, 1954), 757.

73. Marc Treib, "A Setting for Solitude: The Landscapes of Luis Barragán," in *Luis Barragán: The Quiet Revolution,* ed. Federica Zanco (Weil am Rhein, Germany: Vitra Design Museum, 2001), 121; see Keith Eggener, *Luis Barragán's Gardens of El Pedregal* (New York: Princeton Architectural Press, 2001).

74. Richard Neutra, *On Building: Mystery and Realities of the Site* (Scarsdale, N.Y.: Morgan & Morgan, 1951), 14.

75. See David Leatherbarrow, *Topographical Stories: Studies in Landscape and Architecture* (Philadelphia: University of Pennsylvania Press, 2004), 72–77.

76. David Harvey, *Justice, Nature, and the Geography of Difference* (Malden, Mass.: Blackwell, 1996), 309, 306.

77. Sidney K. Robinson, "Picturesque Anticipations of the Avant-Garde and the Landscape," *Landscape Journal* 10, no. 1 (Spring 1991): 12.

78. Marc Treib, "Must Landscapes Mean? Approaches to Significance in Recent Landscape Architecture," *Landscape Journal* 14, no. 1 (Spring 1995): 50.

79. This idea is not new, as Thomas Whately argued in his *Observations on Modern Gardening* (London: T. Payne, 1770), 1: "The business of a gardener is to select and apply whatever is great, elegant or characteristic in [a park, a farm, or a riding]; to discover and to shew [sic] all the advantages of the place upon which he is employed; to supply its defects, to correct its faults, and to improve its beauties." Whereas Whatley is concerned primarily with the visual aspects of a site, designers today are compelled to take the site's broader cultural attributes and ecological qualities into account.

80. Julia Czerniak, "Introduction: Appearance, Performance; Landscape at Downsview," in *CASE: Downsview Park Toronto,* ed. Julia Czerniak (Munich: Prestel, 2001), 17.

81. Homi Bhabha, "DissemiNation: Time, Narrative, and the Margins of the Modern Nation," in *Nation and Narration,* ed. Homi Bhabha (London: Routledge, 1990), 314.

82. See, for example, David Ley and Marwyn Samuels, eds., *Humanist Geography: Prospects and Problems* (Chicago: Maroufa Press, 1978); Relph, *Rational Landscapes*; Paul C. Adams, Steven Hoelscher, and Karen E. Till, eds., *Textures of Place: Exploring Humanist Geographies* (Minneapolis: University of Minnesota Press, 2001).

83. Homi Bhabha, *The Location of Culture* (London: Routledge, 1994), 2.

84. Robert Morris, *Lectures on Architecture* (London: J. Brindley, 1759), 86; facsimile edition (Westmead, England: Gregg International, 1971). For discussion

of the significance of Morris's argument for architectural theory, see Leatherbarrow, *Topographical Stories,* 169–99.

85. John Beardsley, "A Word for Landscape Architecture," in *Nature, Landscape, and Building for Sustainability,* ed. William S. Saunders (Minneapolis: University of Minnesota Press, 2008), 185; originally published in *Harvard Design Magazine* 12 (Fall 2000).

86. Charles Eliot to Harvard University Board of Overseers member and university treasurer Charles Francis Adams, 12 December 1896, in Charles William Eliot, *Charles Eliot Landscape Architect* (Cambridge, Mass.: Harvard University Press, 1902), 630. In contrast, see the dire predictions for the discipline of landscape architecture by planner Denise Scott Brown, who included "the trivialization of landscape architecture" among current design trends, and landscape designer Diana Balmori, who argued more recently, "The profession of landscape architecture appears to be finished." Denise Scott Brown, "Another Battlefield of the Styles in Architecture" (response to editorial question "Looking from the Future into the Immediate Past"), *Architecture* 76, no. 5 (May 1987): 117; Diana Balmori quoted by Beardsley, "A Word for Landscape Architecture," 187; also see Heidi Hohmann and Joern Langhorst, "Landscape Architecture: An Apocalyptic Manifesto," accessed 29 July 2011, http://www.iastate.edu/~isitdead, with refutations published in "Landscape Architecture: A Terminal Case?" *Landscape Architecture* 95, no. 4 (April 2005): 26–45.

1. Social Idealism and Urban Landscape

1. Henry-Russell Hitchcock Jr. and Philip Johnson, *The International Style: Architecture since 1922* (New York: W. W. Norton, 1932), 77.

2. Henry-Russell Hitchcock Jr., "Gardens in Relation to Modern Architecture," in *Contemporary Landscape Architecture and Its Sources,* ed. G. L. McCann Morley (San Francisco: San Francisco Museum of Art, 1937), 15. This exhibition included works by several architects whom Hitchcock and Johnson associated with the international style: Le Corbusier, Ludwig Mies van der Rohe, R. M. Schindler, Richard Neutra, and André Lurçat.

3. Henry-Russell Hitchcock Jr., *Modern Architecture, Romanticism, and Reintegration* (New York: Payson & Clarke, 1929), 11.

4. For earlier use of this concept, see Walter Gropius, *Internationale Architektur,* Bauhausbücher 1 (Munich: Albert Langen Verlag, 1925).

5. Although Henry Wright studied architecture at the University of Pennsylvania, he is usually cited as a city planner and landscape architect. After graduating from Penn in 1901 he worked for landscape architect George Kessler and opened a branch office for Kessler's firm in St. Louis (to 1909). He served as town planner

for the Housing Division of the U.S. Emergency Fleet Corporation (1918) and was consultant to the New York State Commission on Housing during the 1920s and later, to the Public Works Administration. His numerous publications focus on housing issues, especially site strategies relative to land-use studies. The author of *Rehousing Urban America* (New York: Columbia University Press, 1935), during the 1930s he headed the architecture program at Columbia University, where he taught studios in town planning. Cautley received her degree in "landscape art" from Cornell University (1917) and worked for architect Julia Morgan on YWCA war housing projects in Illinois before establishing her independent landscape practice in New Jersey in 1921. She taught site planning and landscape design at the Massachusetts Institute of Technology (1934–37) and Columbia University (1935–37); in the 1940s she received a master's degree in city planning from the University of Pennsylvania. Her writings, infused with practical knowledge about soil preparation and plant materials suited to low-maintenance landscapes, contain an implicit social agenda.

6. There are numerous possible sources for this idea. Stein credits British planner Raymond Unwin with advocating the economic viability of providing common recreational spaces in the centers of urban blocks. Clarence S. Stein, *Toward New Towns for America* (1951; repr., New York: Reinhold, 1957), 22. See Raymond Unwin, *Nothing Gained by Overcrowding: How the Garden City Type of Development May Benefit Both Owner and Occupier* (London: Garden Cities and Town Planning Association, 1912). Henry Wright attributed the idea to his experience of visiting a town in southern Ireland in 1902; there he saw a villa fronting on gardens in the interior of an urban block: "I learned then that the comforts and privacy of family life are not to be found in the detached dwelling, but rather in a house that judiciously relates living space to open space, the open space in turn being capable of enjoyment by the many as well as by few." Henry Wright, "The Autobiography of Another Idea," *Western Architect* 39, no. 9 (September 1930): 139. In collaboration with architect Thomas C. Rogers, Cautley worked on a related site strategy at Oak Croft (1921), a demonstration housing complex in which six houses are grouped around a common lawn. See Marjorie Sewall Cautley, "A Group of Houses Planned and Planted as a Unit," *House Beautiful* 65, no. 1 (January 1929): 68–69. A further influence may have been the Backyard Playgrounds Association, established in New York City in the 1910s; Galen Cranz argues that it was "instrumental in tearing down fences, cleaning up rubbish and installing a common garden and interior court for centers of large, densely built city blocks." Galen Cranz, *The Politics of Park Design: A History of Urban Parks in America* (Cambridge: MIT Press, 1982), 84.

7. Henry-Russell Hitchcock Jr. and Philip Johnson, *Modern Architecture— International Exhibition* (New York: Museum of Modern Art, 1932). As Terence

Riley notes, there was little correspondence between the images Johnson featured in the exhibition and those in its catalog. Terence Riley, *The International Style: Exhibition 15 and the Museum of Modern Art* (New York: Rizzoli and Columbia Books on Architecture, 1992), 9.

8. Hitchcock and Johnson, *The International Style,* 90.

9. Ibid., 93, 92.

10. Lewis Mumford [and Catherine Bauer], "Housing," in Hitchcock and Johnson, *Modern Architecture—International Exhibition,* 189. Mumford wrote this essay in collaboration with Catherine Bauer; it avoided the aesthetic issues that were the focus of Hitchcock and Johnson's efforts in favor of the social attributes of the new communities. In a coeval essay, Mumford countered Hitchcock and Johnson's aesthetic biases, as well as their stylistic terminology: "I prefer Mr. Wright's term 'organic,' to the more current adjectives, 'modern' and 'international'; and this organic architecture is not merely a matter of using new materials and techniques or of conceiving new forms for their effective employment; it is a matter of relating air, sunlight, space, gardens, outlook, social intercourse, economic activity, in such a fashion as to form a concrete whole." Lewis Mumford, "The Sky Line: Organic Architecture," *New Yorker* 8 (27 February 1932): 46.

11. Mumford, "Housing," 183.

12. Ibid., 180, 182–83.

13. Ibid., 183, 186. In his *Gemeinschaft und Gesellschaft* (Community and civil society) of 1887, German social theorist Ferdinand Tönnies introduced the notion of society as consisting of communities, a concept that had a profound impact on architects of the *Neue Bauen* in Germany.

14. Mumford, "Housing," 184.

15. Clarence Stein, "Sunnyside as a Community," 30–31 August 1947, Clarence Stein archives, #3600, 1–9, Cornell University. Although Wright first visited Germany only in 1932, Stein visited housing developments based on garden city principles in Holland and Germany in July 1922. In 1924, as they were beginning plans for Sunnyside, Stein and Wright visited the English garden cities of Welwyn and Letchworth and met with Ebenezer Howard and Raymond Unwin, who, along with Ernst May, attended the first meeting of the International Garden City and Town Planning Federation in New York the following year. On that occasion the group spent a weekend at Hudson Guild Farm with members of the Regional Planning Association of America (RPAA), an organization that Stein initiated and led; it included Henry Wright, Lewis Mumford, Benton McKaye, Alexander Bing (developer of Sunnyside), Stuart Chase (an economist), and architect Frederick Ackerman. The RPAA was a group of like-minded individuals who sought to build garden cities in the United States by limiting the profit motive and maintaining communal control or ownership of land.

16. Architects who designed buildings for Römerstadt included Gustav Schaupp, C. H. Rudloff, Albert Winter, Karl Blattner, and Franz Schuster, while Austrian architect Grete Schütte-Lihotzky designed the Frankfurt kitchen and garden sheds for the allotment gardens. Landscape architects at Römerstadt included Max Bromme, who headed the Frankfurt Landscape Office (from 1912) and devised the system of flood control for the Nidda River valley (1928–30), and Leberecht Migge, his collaborator and ally from 1924.

17. Unwin advocated the merits of cooperative residential development; the integration of architecture and landscape; a hierarchical network of streets, alleys, and urban thoroughfares; and the elimination of roads to effect a more economical use of land. See his *Town Planning in Practice* (London: T. F. Uni, 1909) and *Nothing Gained by Overcrowding.* May served his apprenticeship working for Unwin in England, while Stein and Wright consulted with Unwin during a 1924 trip to England, sponsored by Sunnyside developer Alexander Bing, to examine the garden city developments there.

18. Both developments included two-family units as income-producing assets, while Sunnyside also had three-family units; in addition, both featured smaller apartments for individuals. Römerstadt also included a new school and some shops, whereas Sunnyside relied on existing neighborhood shopping facilities.

19. In both cases, rental and/or unit costs were above the means of the lowest income groups, restricting occupancy to the middle range of wage earners.

20. City Housing Corporation, *Your Share in Better Housing* (New York: City Housing Corporation, 1924), n.p.

21. Stein, *Toward New Towns for America,* 22. The development included one of the first cooperative apartment buildings in New York City.

22. City Housing Corporation, *Your Share in Better Housing,* n.p.

23. Clarence Stein, "Organization of the Community," 3 September 1947, Clarence Stein archives, #3600, 1–9, Cornell University.

24. Albert Gut, *Der Wohnungsbau in Deutschland nach dem Weltkriege* (Munich: F. Bruckmann Verlag, 1928), cited by John R. Mullin, "German City Planning in the 1920's: A North American Perspective of the Frankfurt Experience" (Occasional Paper no. 16, Faculty of Environmental Studies, University of Waterloo, 1975), 1.

25. Barbara Miller Lane compares May's powers with those of Albert Speer, principal architect to Adolf Hitler. Barbara Miller Lane, "Architects in Power: Politics and Ideology in the Work of Ernst May and Albert Speer," in *Art and History: Images and Their Meaning,* ed. Robert I. Rotberg and Theodore K. Rabb (Cambridge: Cambridge University Press, 1988), 283–310. In contrast, during May's lifetime he was described in National Socialist literature as the "Lenin of German Architecture." "Plattenpleite," *Die Deutsche Bauhütte* (1931): 23, cited by Christian

Borngräber, "The Social Impact of the New Architecture in Germany and the Building of the New Frankfurt," *Architectural Association Quarterly* 11, no. 1 (1979): 41.

26. May was sole editor of *Das neue Frankfurt* until 1927, when he began to share editorial duties with others.

27. See Jeremy Aynsley, "Graphic Change, Design Change: Magazines for the Domestic Interior, 1890–1930," *Journal of Design History* 18, no. 1 (2005): 56.

28. See *Die Wohnung für das Existenzminimum* (Frankfurt: Englert & Schlosser, 1930). Owing to the interest generated by this CIAM meeting, the city of Frankfurt set up an instructional program to teach architects and planners how to implement such a process. Catherine Bauer was the first American to attend this program, an experience she documented in her prizewinning essay "Art in Industry," *Fortune* 3 (1931): 96. An authority on modern housing, Bauer was active in the Regional Planning Association of America from 1932, serving as its executive-secretary and helping to write the organization's manifestos.

29. The Sunnyside Gardens site originally comprised wetlands and a hillside farm, Sunnyside Hill. In 1902, the Pennsylvania and Long Island railroads leveled the hill to fill in the wetlands and razed the existing farm buildings to make way for the rail yards, all to considerable opposition. Development in the vicinity began in earnest after the subway line was installed in 1915. See Franklin J. Havelick and Michael Kwartler, "Sunnyside Gardens: Whose Land Is It Anyway?" *New York Affairs* 7, no. 2 (1982): 67.

30. Cautley's planting strategy at Sunnyside echoed the approach she described for Radburn: "These low-cost homes . . . were planned and planted as garden groups, with tall-growing shrubs for privacy between porches and windows, with hedges staggered along property lines so that each owner might enjoy his share of blossoms, with trees that will give shade when mature, and with vines for shady and sunny locations. . . . To obtain interest and variety, a different foliage scheme was planned for each garden group and for each motor street." Marjorie Sewell Cautley, "Planting at Radburn," *Landscape Architecture* 21, no. 1 (October 1930): 26.

31. Marjorie Sewell Cautley, "Landscaping in the Housing Project," *Architecture* 72, no. 4 (October 1935): 184. Cautley based this article on her experiences at Sunnyside and Radburn. Consistent with the architects' emphasis on affordability, Cautley focused primarily on practical issues and means to develop low-maintenance landscapes. She lamented the low priority given to funding landscaping in such communal housing projects: "If the development of sixty percent of the land is considered as a permanent installation of definite sales' value, why should it receive an allotment which is equal only to such incidentals as radio outlets and awnings?" Marjorie Sewell Cautley, "Potted Plants? Or Adequate Landscaping for Community Projects?" *American City* 50, no. 8 (August 1935): 52.

32. The Weimar constitution (1918) guaranteed every citizen a home and plot of ground; the Allotments and Smallholdings Act was passed in 1919.

33. Leberecht Migge, *Die wachsende Siedlung nach biologischen Gesetzen* (Stuttgart: Frankische Verlagshandlung, 1932), 34, quoted by David Haney, "'No House Building without Garden Building!' ('Klein Hausbau ohne Landbau!'): The Modern Landscapes of Leberecht Migge," *Journal of Architectural Education* 54, no. 3 (February 2001): 154.

34. See Susan R. Henderson, "A Setting for Mass Culture: Life and Leisure in the Nidda Valley," *Planning Perspectives* 10, no. 2 (April 1995): 199–222.

35. Cautley adopted a similar staged approach to the planting at Radburn, which encompassed her notion of a community that would grow and change over time; see Cautley, "Planting at Radburn," 23–29.

36. Stein, *Toward New Towns for America*, 24.

37. In addition to separate playgrounds for small and larger children, Sunnyside Park included facilities for tennis, baseball, basketball, handball, volleyball, horseshoes, and croquet.

38. Owing to a combination of physical neglect and changing social mores, however, the ideological intentions and functional attributes of these landscapes are now considerably muted.

39. Lewis Mumford, "Introduction," in Stein, *Toward New Towns for America*, 17. Mumford lived in Sunnyside Gardens from 1925 to 1936.

40. See Charles S. Ascher, "The Enforcement of Deed Restrictions," *City Planning* 8, no. 4 (October 1932): 193–202.

41. For an account of preservation efforts at Sunnyside, see Havelick and Kwartler, "Sunnyside Gardens," 65–80.

42. Wright opposed both Sunnyside and Radburn for stylistic reasons, as he wrote to Lewis Mumford in 1933: "I am not too fond of what we did at Sunnyside or Radburn; but whatever it was, the important accomplishments were social rather than technical." Lewis Mumford, "A Modest Man's Enduring Contributions to Urban and Regional Planning," *Journal of the American Institute of Architects* (December 1976): 22.

43. Stein, *Toward New Towns for America*, 219.

44. Ibid., 218. Stein was consulting architect for Baldwin Hills Village, designed in a more modern idiom by Reginald D. Johnson with Wilson, Merrill and Alexander, Associated Architects.

45. Just as the suburban models that Stein and Wright ultimately promoted furthered their objective of urban decentralization, so May came to endorse a novel urban form based on *Zeilenbau* principles, in which issues of solar and wind orientation superseded communitarian planning aspirations. The standardization of units, buildings, and building orientation (north–south) in the *Zeilenbau* was

seen to reflect egalitarian, economic, and scientific benevolence, in which inflexibility was regarded as a virtue, yet these principles also ignored cultural, psychological, and topographic realities, resulting in a new version of the city that was detached from the old.

46. Stein, *Toward New Towns for America,* 19.

47. Clarence Stein, "City Patterns . . . Past and Future," *New Pencil Points* 23, no. 6 (June 1942): 52.

48. Stein, *Toward New Towns for America,* 220.

49. Richard Guy Wilson, *The A.I.A. Gold Medal* (New York: McGraw-Hill, 1984), 182.

50. Clarence Stein, "Communities for the Good Life," *Journal of the American Institute of Architects* 26, no. 1 (July 1956): 15.

51. Raymond Unwin, *Town Planning in Practice* (1909; repr., New York: Princeton Architectural Press, 1994), 381–82, 375–76.

52. Henry Wright, "Housing—Why, When, and How? Part Two: The Case for Group Housing," *Architecture* 68, no. 2 (August 1933): 83.

53. Fletcher Steele, "Comment" (on Christopher Tunnard's essay "Modern Gardens for Modern Houses"), *Landscape Architecture* 32, no. 2 (January 1942): 64.

54. Lewis Mumford, in City Housing Corporation pamphlet *Expert Opinion* (New York: City Housing Corporation, 1928), Clarence Stein archives #3600, 1–10, Cornell University.

55. Manfredo Tafuri, "L'Architecture dans le boudoir," *Oppositions* 3 (May 1974): 56.

56. Lewis Mumford, "Monumentalism, Symbolism, and Style," *Architectural Review* 105, no. 628 (April 1949): 180, 176, 177. In this essay Mumford associated monumentalism with social intention, rather than building morphology. In 1932 Mumford asserted: "I prefer Mr. Wright's term 'organic,' to the more current adjectives, 'modern' and 'international'; and this organic architecture is not merely a matter of using new materials and techniques or of conceiving new forms for their effective employment; it is a matter of relating air, sunlight, space, gardens, outlook, social intercourse, economic activity, in such a fashion as to form a concrete whole." Mumford, "The Sky Line," 46. By 1951, Hitchcock proposed that the term *international style* be dropped, arguing, "The living architecture of the twentieth century may well be called merely 'modern.'" Henry-Russell Hitchcock Jr., "The International Style Twenty Years After," *Architectural Record* 110 (August 1951): 97. By 1955 even Sigfried Giedion renounced the notion of the "international style," arguing: "Contemporary architecture has become a universal language, a language capable of being adapted to meet the needs of different conditions and different idioms in the varied regions of the world. This is something quite different from an 'international style'—a misnomer to be carefully avoided." Sigfried

Giedion, "History and the Architect," in *Architecture You and Me: The Diary of a Development* (Cambridge, Mass.: Harvard University Press, 1958), 107.

57. Mumford, "Monumentalism, Symbolism, and Style," 180.

58. Henry Wright, "Shall We Community Plan?" *Journal of the American Institute of Architects* 9, no. 10 (October 1921): 323.

2. The Barcelona Pavilion as Landscape Garden

I am indebted to the late Robin Evans for stimulating conversations about the Barcelona Pavilion and to Rafael Moneo and the late Alvin Boyarsky for their encouragement of this research. Mirka Beneš provided valuable feedback on an earlier draft.

1. See Wolf Tegethoff, *Mies van der Rohe: The Villas and Country Houses* (New York: Museum of Modern Art, 1985), 70–89; K. Michael Hays, "Critical Architecture: Between Form and Culture," *Perspecta* 21 (1984): 14–29; José Quetlas, "Fear of Glass: The Barcelona Pavilion," in *Revisions,* ed. Beatriz Colomina (Princeton, N.J.: Princeton Architectural Press, 1988), 123–51; Robin Evans, "Mies van der Rohe's Paradoxical Symmetries," *AA Files* 19 (Spring 1990): 56–68.

2. "We refuse to recognize problems of form, but only problems of building. Form is not the aim of our work, but only the result." From *G* no. 2 (1923), trans. in Philip Johnson, *Mies van der Rohe* (New York: Museum of Modern Art, 1947), 184. "Ours is not an age of pathos; we do not respect flights of the spirit as much as we value reason and realism." From *Der Querschnitt* (1924), in ibid., 186.

3. "Museum: Mies van der Rohe, Architect, Chicago, Ill.," *Architectural Forum* 78 (May 1943): 84.

4. Horace Walpole, *Anecdotes of Painting,* vol. 4 (1771), cited in Isabel Chase, *Horace Walpole: Gardenist* (Princeton, N.J.: Princeton University Press, 1943), 25.

5. From *G,* no. 2 (1923), in Johnson, *Mies van der Rohe,* 184.

6. Hays, "Critical Architecture," 24. Hays terms Mies's work "critical architecture," which he defines "in its difference from other cultural manifestations and from a priori categories or methods."

7. Eighteenth-century discussions of the picturesque vary from focusing on the qualities of the architectural object to examining the garden's psychological effects on the moving spectator. Such discrepancies were the basis of the "Picturesque Controversy" carried on by Richard Payne Knight and Uvedale Price during the 1790s. Yve-Alain Bois remarks on the mutually exclusive moments of the picturesque in "A Picturesque Stroll around Clara-Clara," trans. John Shepley, *October* 29 (Summer 1984): 36.

8. Pope never applied the term *picturesque* to landscape, although in later contexts he generally used it to refer to a setting appropriate to themes depicted

in poetry or painting. See John Dixon Hunt, "Ut Pictura Poesis, Ut Pictura Hortus, and the Picturesque," *Word and Image* 1, no. 1 (January–March 1985): 88–90.

9. Hays, "Critical Architecture," 24. Mies claimed that when the German government first approached him about the commission, he replied: "What is a pavilion? I have not the slightest idea. . . . I must say that it was the most difficult work which ever confronted me, because I was my own client; I could do what I liked. But I did not know what a pavilion should be." Quoted by H. T. Cadbury Brown, "Ludwig Mies van der Rohe," *Architectural Association Journal* (July/August 1959): 27–28.

10. Ludwig Glaeser deemed the onyx wall equivalent to the altarpiece of a Romanesque church. See Ludwig Glaeser, *Mies van der Rohe: The Barcelona Pavilion 50th Anniversary* (New York: Friends of the Mies van der Rohe Archive, Museum of Modern Art, 1979), n.p., cited by Tegethoff, *Mies van der Rohe,* 81. Tegethoff also draws analogies between the inner court and the cella of a Greek temple; neither can be occupied except by a cult figure—in the Barcelona Pavilion, Georg Kolbe's statue *Morning* (ibid., 80).

11. On Piet Mondrian's influence, Mies stated: "I think that was a mistake that the Museum of Modern Art made. . . . I never make a painting when I want to build a house. We like to draw our plans carefully and that is why they were taken as a kind of painting." Quoted by Peter Carter, *Mies van der Rohe at Work* (New York: Praeger, 1974), 180.

12. Tegethoff, *Mies van der Rohe,* 75.

13. As Robin Evans has observed, the columns, owing to their extremely thin proportions, appear insufficient to support the roof; indeed, the steel frame concealed within the marble walls contributes equally to the pavilion's structural integrity. Robin Evans, lecture, Harvard University Graduate School of Design, 20 October 1988.

14. Quoted in "6 Students Talk with Mies" (interview, 13 February 1952), *Master Builder* 2, no. 3 (student publication of the School of Design, North Carolina State College, Spring 1952), 28, cited by Tegethoff, *Mies van der Rohe,* 77. Credit for discovering the free plan must go to Le Corbusier, who published his "Five Points of a New Architecture" in conjunction with the housing project he carried out with Pierre Jeanneret for the Wiessenhofsiedlung in Stuttgart, which Mies directed. See Alfred Roth, *Zwei Wohnhäuser von Le Corbusier und Pierre Jeanneret* (Stuttgart: F. Wedekind, 1928), 8–9.

15. In this separation Mies acknowledged the influence of Schinkel's Altes Museum: "He separated the elements, the columns and the walls and the ceiling, and I think that is still visible in my later buildings." Quoted by Carter, *Mies van der Rohe at Work,* 182.

16. Sidney K. Robinson, "The Picturesque: Sinister Dishevelment," *Threshold* 4 (Spring 1988): 80.

17. See Kenneth Frampton, "Modernism and Tradition in the Work of Mies van der Rohe, 1920–1968," in *Mies Reconsidered: His Career, Legacy, and Disciples,* ed. John Zukowsky (Chicago: Art Institute of Chicago, 1986), 41–43; for discussion of Mies's neoclassicism, see Colin Rowe, "Neoclassicism and Modern Architecture," *Oppositions* 1 (1973): 1–26.

18. Quetlas, "Fear of Glass," 136.

19. On the silence of Mies's architecture, see Manfredo Tafuri and Francesco Dal Co, *Modern Architecture* (New York: Electa/Rizzoli, 1986), 1:134; and Hays, "Critical Architecture," 22.

20. Quoted by Goerd Peschken, *Karl Friedrich Schinkel Lebenswerk,* vol. 14, *Das Architektonische Lehrbuch* (Munich, 1979), cited by Barry Bergdoll, "Karl Friedrich Schinkel," *Macmillan Encyclopedia of Architects* (New York: Free Press, 1982), 3:682.

21. Ludwig Mies van der Rohe, "Prospectus of the Union of German Flate Glass Manufacturers" (1933), quoted by Tegethoff, *Mies van der Rohe,* 67.

22. Ibid.; Tafuri and Dal Co, *Modern Architecture,* 1:132.

23. Mies van der Rohe, "Hochhausprojekt für Bahnhof Friedrichstrasse in Berlin," in Johnson, *Mies van der Rohe,* 182; originally published in *Frühlicht* 1 (1922): 122–24.

24. Tafuri and Dal Co, *Modern Architecture,* 1:131.

25. Mies van der Rohe, inaugural address as director of architecture at the Armour Institute of Technology (1938), in Johnson, *Mies van der Rohe,* 194.

26. Interview with Mies van der Rohe (1959), in Carter, *Mies van der Rohe at Work,* 180.

27. See Tegethoff, *Mies van der Rohe,* 76–78.

28. Oswald Spengler, *Der Untergang des Abendlandes* (Munich, 1918), cited by Franz Schulze, *Mies van der Rohe: A Critical Biography* (Chicago: University of Chicago Press, 1985), 116. For an interpretation of the onyx wall as a reference to the horizon, see Evans, "Mies van der Rohe's Paradoxical Symmetries," 63.

29. Mies included a similar volume of light between the living and service spaces of his contemporaneous Tugendhat House in Brno (1928–30).

30. Grete Tugendhat, from *Die Form* 6, no. 11 (15 November 1931): 437ff., cited in Tegethoff, *Mies van der Rohe,* 97.

31. From an interview for the BBC, 1959, cited in Tegethoff, *Mies van der Rohe,* 13.

32. John Serle, *A Plan of Mr. Pope's Garden, as it was left upon his death, with a Plan and Perspective View of the Grotto* (London: R. Dodsley, 1745). The grotto survives, although the house was demolished in 1807.

33. Alexander Pope, *The Correspondence of Alexander Pope,* ed. George Sherburn (Oxford: Clarendon Press, 1956), 4:262.

34. Pope to Edward Blount, 2 June 1725, in ibid., 2:296–97.

35. "An Epistolary Description of the Late Mr. Pope's House and Gardens at Twickenham" (1747), in *The Genius of the Place: The English Landscape Garden, 1620–1820,* ed. John Dixon Hunt and Peter Willis (London: Elek, 1975), 249–50; originally published in *The General Magazine of Newcastle* (January 1748).

36. John Dixon Hunt, *Garden and Grove: The Italian Renaissance Garden in the English Imagination, 1600–1750* (Princeton, N.J.: Princeton University Press, 1986), 200.

37. I am grateful to Mirka Beneš for this observation.

38. Paul O. Kristeller, "The Modern System of the Arts," in *Renaissance Thought and the Arts: Collected Essays* (Princeton, N.J.: Princeton University Press, 1980), 226.

39. David Watkin, *The English Vision: The Picturesque in Architecture, Landscape, and Garden Design* (New York: Harper & Row, 1982), ix–x.

40. Quoted in Christian Norberg-Schulz, "Talks with Mies van der Rohe," *L'Architecture d'aujourd'hui* 29, no. 79 (September 1958): 100.

41. Michael Fried, "How Modernism Works: A Response to T. J. Clark," *Critical Inquiry* 9, no. 1 (September 1982): 225–27.

42. *G,* no. 1 (1923), in Johnson, *Mies van der Rohe,* 183.

43. *Die Form* (1928), in Johnson, *Mies van der Rohe,* 190.

44. Karl Friedrich Schinkel, quoted by Hermann G. Punte, *Schinkel's Berlin: A Study in Environmental Planning* (Cambridge: MIT Press, 1972), 195.

3. The Urban Landscapes of Erik Gunnar Asplund

I am grateful to Jöran Lindvall and the staff of the Swedish Museum of Architecture for their generous assistance in my research for this essay.

1. The term *functionalism* does not have the negative association in Sweden that it has in the United States; rather, it is considered an essential vehicle of the larger Social Democratic ambition to construct a new, more socially and economically egalitarian society.

2. The Bonde Palace (1662–73), by Nicodemus Tessin the Elder and Jean de la Vallée, served as the Stockholm City Hall between 1732 and 1915; in 1949 it was restored by Ivar Tengbom to house the Supreme Court.

3. Asplund adopted a similar site strategy for his temporary workers' housing in Stockholm (1917).

4. For discussion of Asplund's early site studies for the library, see Carl Bergsten, "Stockholms Stadsbiblioteks förläggning" [The location for the Stockholm Public Library], *Byggmästaren* (1923): 305–8; Gösta Drugge, "Arkitektur som mognadsprocess" [Architecture as a process of maturation], *Arkitekturmuseet Årsbok* (1983): 34–65.

5. Carl-Axel Acking, "Asplund as Teacher and Principal," in *Lectures and Briefings from the International Symposium on the Architecture of Erik Gunnar Asplund,* ed. Christina Engfors (Stockholm: Swedish Museum of Architecture and Royal Academy of Fine Arts, 1986), 65.

6. Gustav Adde, "Det nya förslaget till stadsbibliotek" [The new proposal for a public library], newspaper clipping, undated, Asplund archive, Swedish Museum of Architecture, Stockholm.

7. Asplund's scheme of February 1920 is similar to a plan dated 1922, published in Bergsten, "Stockholms Stadsbiblioteks förläggning," 307.

8. Milles's monument to Sten Sture resulted from a competition he won in 1902, bringing the sculptor international recognition; the monument was erected in Uppsala in 1925.

9. In a variation on this plan showing a carefully measured drawing of the plaza, Asplund extended the plaza's paving pattern into the streets to amplify the library's urban presence. This drawing includes construction lines for a perspective drawing (now lost?). Asplund archive 51A, Swedish Museum of Architecture, Stockholm.

10. See, for example, Stuart Wrede, *The Architecture of Erik Gunnar Asplund* (Cambridge: MIT Press, 1980), 112; Kristin Nielsson, "Stockholm Library," in *AJ Masters of Building: Erik Gunnar Asplund,* ed. Dan Cruikshank (London: Architectural Journal, 1988), 44–55; Elias Cornell, "The Sky as a Vault," in *Asplund,* ed. Claes Caldenby and Olof Hultin (New York: Rizzoli, 1986), 28–29.

11. Asplund's postcard collection includes images of the Villa Lante Fountain of Pegasus and the cascade at Tivoli. Asplund archive, Swedish Museum of Architecture, Stockholm.

12. "The detail planning of the site, including the entrance, the boundary walls, the roads and the burial grounds have been under the charge of architect Sigurd Lewerentz." E. G[unnar] Asplund, "Skogskapellet" [Woodland Chapel], *Arkitektur* (July 1921): 87 (my translation).

13. Construction of a subway line under the park during the 1940s made necessary the demolition of the reflecting pool and streambed, as well as the southeastern corner of the park toward Sveavägen, where the subway entrance is now located. Noted landscape architect Erik Glemme carried out a sensitive reconstruction of Asplund's park in 1950–51, although as a result it is difficult to ascertain Asplund's precise contribution to its present state.

14. Wrede, *The Architecture of Erik Gunnar Asplund,* 105.

15. Lars Olof Larsson, "The Stockholm Public Library," in Engfors, *Lectures and Briefings,* 37.

16. Asplund argued: "The Stockholm Exhibition hall constructions have had to be content with being the temporary frames around the exhibits, which it was

the intention to stress in place of the architecture of the buildings." Quoted in Gustav Holmdahl, Sven Ivar Lind, and Kjell Ödeen, eds., *Gunnar Asplund Architect* (Stockholm: AB Tidskriften Byggmästaren, 1950), 57. Reviewing the Stockholm Exhibition in the June/July 1930 issue of *Architect and Building News* (London), British architect Howard Robertson noted that the restrained exhibition design enhanced the beauty of the setting, but he also described this effect as "picturesque." Howard Robertson, "The Stockholm Exhibition, 1930," in *Gunnar Asplund, 1885–1940: The Dilemma of Classicism* (London: Architectural Association, 1988), 22–25.

17. Holmdahl, Lind, and Ödeen, *Gunnar Asplund Architect*, 59.

18. Thorbjörn Andersson speculates that the democratizing effects of Olmsted's public parks, which City Commissioner Yngve Larsson experienced during his study tour of the United States in 1936, may have inspired the Stockholm Parks Department to formulate its regional approach to public landscape design. Thorbjörn Andersson, "Erik Glemme and the Stockholm Park System," in *Modern Landscape Architecture: A Critical Review,* ed. Marc Treib (Cambridge: MIT Press, 1992), 133n16.

4. Toward a Spiritual Landscape

This essay is based on material from my book *The Woodland Cemetery: Toward a Spiritual Landscape* (Stockholm: Byggförlaget, 1994), for which research was carried out under the auspices of the Fulbright Commission of Sweden, the Peter and Birgitta Celsing Foundation, the Swedish Building Research Council, and the American–Scandinavian Foundation. I am indebted to Börje Olsson, manager of the Stockholm Cemetery Authority, and to Jöran Lindvall and the staff of the Swedish Architecture Museum, and particularly Karin Winter, who pointed me to many important facets of the Woodland Cemetery's development. Mirka Beneš, Robin Evans, Ed Robbins, and Charles Rose provided invaluable criticism of early book drafts, while Alison Constant and Julia Shivers provided thoughtful editorial assistance.

1. Asplund and Lewerentz collaborated on the Woodland Cemetery design from 1915 to 1935, when the Stockholm Cemetery Authority commissioned Asplund to design the main crematorium complex on his own, a decision that ended their professional relationship. After Asplund's death in 1940, Lewerentz continued to work on aspects of the cemetery complex until 1961.

2. See Stuart Wrede, *The Architecture of Erik Gunnar Asplund* (Cambridge: MIT Press, 1980); Janne Ahlin, *Sigurd Lewerentz, Architect, 1885–1975* (Cambridge: MIT Press, 1987).

3. Letter from Schlyter to Torsten Stubelius, 10 April 1913, in Gustav Schlyter, *Die Halle des Liebens* (Helsingborg: Hälsingborgs Litografiska Akitiebolag, 1937), 291 (my translation).

4. Leo Spitzer, *Classical and Christian Ideas of World Harmony: Prolegomena to an Interpretation of the Word "Stimmung"* (Baltimore: Johns Hopkins University Press, 1963), 5.

5. Ingrid Lilienberg, "Reflexioner med anledning af kyrkogårdstäflan," *Teknisk Tidskrift: Arkitektur* (1915): 79 (my translation).

6. "Program för pristävlan angående ordnande av ny begravningsplats i Malmö," 3, Lewerentz archive, Swedish Architecture Museum, Stockholm (my translation).

7. Undated jury report in *Sydsvenska Dagbladet Snällposten,* no. 259. 23 September 1916, Lewerentz archive, Swedish Architecture Museum, Stockholm (my translation).

8. Lilienberg, "Reflexioner med anledning," 79.

9. Hakon Ahlberg, *Modern Swedish Architecture* (London: Ernest Benn, 1925), 28.

10. Untitled and undated manuscript, Lewerentz archive, Swedish Museum of Architecture, Stockholm (my translation). Lewerentz submitted this manuscript to Lindfors Bokförlag of Stockholm in 1939, but publication was interrupted by World War II. When the second of two volumes was brought out by another publishing house in 1948, it lacked both Lewerentz's article and an accompanying piece by Dr. Sölve Gardell titled "History of the lying gravestone," also preserved in the Lewerentz archive. See *Trädgårdskonst: Den moderna trädgårdens och parkens form,* ed. Gregor Paulsson (Stockholm: Natur & Kultur, 1948). Lewerentz attempted to apply this principle at the Skövde Cemetery but lost the commission to Sven Ivar Lind in 1941 after he was unable to persuade the cemetery authority to pursue a policy of limiting grave markers to horizontal slabs.

11. Stockholm Cemetery Authority, Official Memorandum, 20 May 1958, cited in Cemetery Authority Minutes, 2 June 1958, para. 20 (my translation).

12. In his influential and widely disseminated book *On the Spiritual in Art* (1912), Wassily Kandinsky argued: "The spirit that will lead us into the realms of tomorrow can only be recognized as such through feeling (to which the talent of the artist is the path)." Wassily Kandinsky, *Kandinsky, Complete Writings on Art,* ed. and trans. Kenneth C. Lindsay and Peter Vergo (Boston: G. K. Hall, 1982), 141.

13. Gunnar Ekelöf, *Guide to the Underworld,* rendered from the Swedish by Rika Lesser (Amherst: University of Massachusetts Press, 1980), 81.

5. A Landscape "Fit for a Democracy"

Research for this essay was supported in part by grants from the Graham Foundation for Advanced Study in the Fine Arts and the College of Architecture, University of Florida; translation from the Czech was supported by the Division of Sponsored Research, University of Florida. I am indebted to Peter Krečič and Damjan Prelovšek, who assisted me with my research in Ljubljana, and to Zdeněk Lukeš, Jiří Hrůza, and Ivan Plicka, who arranged for my numerous visits to Prague Castle and the castle archives when the complex was still in communist hands. In addition to her able services as translator from the Czech, Katařina Finková offered valuable historic commentary on the primary source material, while Christopher Long, Andrew Herscher, and Paul Kariouk provided insightful feedback on earlier drafts.

1. As Marco Pozzetto argues, it is unlikely that Plečnik himself associated democracy with architectural form; rather, it was the enlightened patronage of Masaryk and his daughter Alice that prompted the "democratic" qualities of Plečnik's interventions in Prague Castle. See Marco Pozzetto, "Plečnik and Prague Castle: Architecture for the New Democracy," in *Josip Plečnik: An Architect of Prague Castle,* ed. Zdeněk Lukeš, Damjan Prelovšek, and Tomáš Valena (Prague: Prague Castle, 1996), 52. For discussion of various means for achieving a democratic architecture in the theoretical literature of the era, see Rostislav Švácha, "Czech Architecture in Plečnik's Time and the Ideal of Democracy," in Lukeš, Prelovšek, and Valena, *Josip Plečnik,* 27–37.

2. Records of Chancellor Sámal, cited in Věra Malá, "The Castle Architect and the Management of the Prague Castle Building Project," in Lukeš, Prelovšek, and Valena, *Josip Plečnik,* 127.

3. Masaryk letter to Plečnik, 10 April 1925, Plečnik archive, Museum of Architecture, Ljubljana, cited in *Josip Plečnik: Architecture for the New Democracy,* prospectus for an exhibition held in Prague Castle, 1996.

4. T. G. Masaryk, *Svetová revoluce* (Prague, 1925), 563, cited in Damjan Prelovšek, "Ideological Substratum in Plečnik's Work," in Lukeš, Prelovšek, and Valena, *Josip Plečnik,* 89.

5. Tomáš Masaryk, lecture, 7 March 1920, trans. in Damjan Prelovšek, *Jože Plečnik, 1872–1957: Architectura Perennis* (New Haven, Conn.: Yale University Press, 1997), 123. I am grateful to Professor Jiří Hrůza for calling my attention to this document.

6. During the Nazi occupation of Prague Castle, from 15 March 1939 to 8 March 1945, Deputy Reichsprotektor Reinhard Heydrich ordered the original flagstaffs destroyed, as their form made the German swastika appear to be hanging at half-staff. Reconstructed in 1962, the present flagstaffs are more economically built of slim wooden strips. See Malá, "The Castle Architect," 136–37.

7. Damjan Prelovšek cites the poles in the Piazza San Marco, Venice, as a source for Plečnik's flagstaffs, while Tomáš Valena argues for their roots in the pylons of Egyptian temple complexes. See Prelovšek, "Ideological Substratum,"

102; Tomáš Valena, "Courtyards and Gardens: Plečnik's Interventions in the Context of Prague Castle," in Lukeš, Prelovšek, and Valena, *Josip Plečnik,* 273.

8. In 1973–75 the communist regime aggrandized this processional route by enlarging Plečnik's entry door and inserting a monumental stair in the Columned Hall. The designers closed in the openings that linked the first and second courts, reducing the hall's function to that of a seldom-used ceremonial entry.

9. Objections from the Society for the Preservation of Old Prague (1929) prevented Plečnik's proposal for the Matthias Gate from being carried out.

10. Quoted by Anna Masaryková, "Masaryk a kontinuita Pražského Hradu" [Masaryk and the historical continuity of Prague Castle], in *Masarykuv sbornik,* vol. 7, *T. G. M. a naše současnost* [Masaryk memorial, vol. 7, T. G. M. and our time] (Prague: Academic Praha, 1992), 11 (trans. Katařina Finková).

11. While these modifications amplified the court's ceremonial value, they also remained controversial. Plečnik's unified ground plane countered the desire of the Society for the Completion of St. Vitus Cathedral to maintain the court's existing level in the vicinity of the cathedral, while the Mánes Society of Artists deplored the prospect of "a uniform and lifeless expanse of paving." Valena, "Courtyards and Gardens," 276. The Club for the Protection of Old Prague rejected the ruthless leveling of the third courtyard, declaring that Plečnik "didn't retain the historic character of the place and didn't respect its piety." J. R. Marek, 'Quo usque tandem . . . ?" *Národní listy* (5 December 1935): 131 (trans. Katařina Finková).

12. Věra Malá, "History of the Obelisk," in Lukeš, Prelovšek, and Valena, *Josip Plečnik,* 295n12. Masaryk originally wanted to place a Tomb of the Unknown Soldier in the obelisk's base. Plečnik's numerous proposals for completing the obelisk included a crystal pyramidion and a gilded one; a version of the latter idea was carried out in 1996.

13. A fragment of this tower is visible in the Royal Palace entry hall.

14. Bedřich Smetana's patriotic opera *Libuše* (1881) and Alois Jirásek's *Old Czech Legends,* first published in 1894, were popular nineteenth-century sources for these myths.

15. Prelovšek cites Plečnik's photograph of the gateway to a Slovak farm near Zvolen that is surmounted by a pair of oxen and a postcard depicting a bull atop a pillar. The latter is a funerary monument from Kerameikos Cemetery, near the Athenian acropolis, an image Plečnik sent to Otto Rothmayer in May 1927, which he inscribed: "Prague Castle—as an Acropolis." Prelovšek, "Ideological Substratum," 95–96.

16. Tomáš Valena, "Plečnik's Gardens at Hradčany: In Search of the Modern Architectonic Gardens of the 20th Century," *ab (arhitektov bilten/architect's bulletin)* 21, nos. 107/108 (May 1991): 41.

17. Although the Paradise Garden was intended as a private enclave for the president, his family, and guests, the entry gate that Plecnik created in 1924 adjoining the New Castle Steps diminished privacy within the garden, implying broader accessibility. During the 1930s Masaryk opened the garden to the public several times a year, and public access was increased to once a week under the communist regime. The gardens are now open daily.

18. Foundations for the obelisk can be seen in the vaulted "crypt" that Plečnik created under the monumental stair, where he intended to create a private chapel for Masaryk. This proposal was never completed, and the space is currently used for temporary exhibits.

19. Damjan Prelovšek maintains that Plečnik derived the idea of linking the obelisk and granite basin from Bernini's fountain in Rome's Piazza di Spagna and the form of the basin itself from the bowl in front of Schinkel's Altes Museum in Berlin. Yet unlike Schinkel, who provided steps so that visitors could look into his basin and view their reflections in its polished surface, Plečnik set his basin in a lawn, precluding any means of approach. Damjan Prelovšek, "Plečnik au château Hradčany," *L'Architecture d'aujourd'hui*, no. 305 (June 1996): 58.

20. Although the citizens of Prague gained the right to self-government in the revolution of 1848, the Germans prevailed in the elections of 1850 and maintained power until 1861, when the Czechs finally obtained a majority.

21. During the 1980s the communists replaced Plečnik's aviary with a semicircular transformer.

22. The communist government reconfigured this bastion, removing the winter garden and shifting the position of the stairs that descend to a lower level.

23. Zdena Pruchová, "Josef Plečnik a Praha," *Umění* 20, no. 4 (1972): 445 (trans. Katařina Finková).

24. As the son of a Slovak groom and coachman and a Moravian mother educated in German, Masaryk had a personal interest in the political union of Czechs and Slovaks. Plečnik felt special affinity with the Slovaks on account of their destiny as a "non-historical nation," a fate they shared with the Slovenes; see Prelovšek, "Ideological Substratum," 92. Alice Masaryk also encouraged her father's admiration for Slovak culture; through references to Slovakian folk art, which she viewed as "the Crete of Slav art," she anticipated that the renovation of Prague Castle might counteract Czech materialism. Prelovšek, *Jože Plečnik, 1872–1957*, 125.

25. Quoted by Vladimir Šlapeta, "Jože Plečnik and Prague," in *Jože Plečnik, Architect: 1872–1957*, ed. François Burkhardt, Claude Eveno, and Boris Podrecca, trans. Carol Volk (Cambridge: MIT Press, 1989), 92; Šlapeta's cited source for this quotation is incorrect.

26. Plečnik's proposals for restructuring the ascent to Prague Castle, dating from 1921, 1922, and 1928, were published in *Styl* 3, no. 7 (1921–22): 23; *Styl* 3,

no. 8 (1922–23): 43, 84; and *Uměni* 5 (1922): 445. For further elaboration of these proposals and the negative reactions they elicited, see Jörg Stabenow and Jindřich Vybíral, "Projects for Prague: Urban Projects for the Surroundings of Prague Castle by Josip Plečnik," in Lukeš, Prelovšek, and Valena, *Josip Plečnik,* 430–43; Andrew Herscher, "Prague and Ljubljana: Producing the Capital City," in Lukeš, Prelovšek, and Valena, *Josip Plečnik,* 445–54.

27. In his letter of resignation to President Edvard Beneš, who succeeded Masaryk in 1935, Plečnik argued: "I wish that someone else may succeed better, and I also wish for my loving, last but one work—the path from Powder Bridge, above the Stag Moat, along the Ball Game Hall to the Belvedere to be completed as soon as possible." Plečnik letter of 14 May 1936, Prague Castle archives, quoted by Prelovšek, "Ideological Substratum," 104. After 1945 the Royal Gardens and their historic buildings were restored in a conservative manner by Pavel Janák, who succeeded Plečnik as castle architect in 1936.

28. Architectural Museum correspondence 63, quoted by Richard Basset, "The Work of Josef Plečnik in Ljubljana," *AA Files* 1, no. 2 (July 1982): 43.

29. Pavel Janák, "Josef Plečnik v Praze," *Volné Směry* 26 (1928–29): 97, quoted by Šlapeta, "Jože Plečnik and Prague," 91. Janák succeeded Plečnik as both professor at Prague's School of Applied Arts (from 1921) and castle architect (from 1936).

30. For discussion of Plečnik's approach to historic preservation in relation to that of his Czech colleagues, see Karel Guth, *Lidové noviny* (24 December 1929), cited by Zdeněk Lukeš, "Plečnikův Hrad v dobových ohlasech," in *Pražský Hrad: Jiný pohled* [Prague Castle: Another view] (Prague: Prague Castle, 1995), 72. Guth was in charge of the archaeological survey of Prague Castle undertaken at Masaryk's request. Plečnik resigned from his post as castle architect in May 1936, although his last official visit to Prague was in November 1934. After Masaryk resigned because of ill health, the new Czech president, Edvard Beneš, sought to persuade Plečnik to continue in his position; when he declined, Beneš appointed Pavel Janák as his successor.

31. *Za starou Prahu, Vestnik pro ochranu památek* 19, nos. 3/4 (1935), quoted by Šlapeta, "Jože Plečnik and Prague," 92.

32. In 1994 Czech president Václav Havel appointed Professor Bořek Šípek, head of Prague's School of Decorative Arts, to serve as castle architect. While Šípek's work emulates Plečnik's stylistically, it lacks the ideological force of the work of his illustrious predecessor.

6. Collaborative Fruits

I am grateful to Dorothée Imbert, who provided valuable feedback on an earlier draft of this essay and whose groundbreaking work on Garrett Eckbo's communal landscapes inspired me to undertake this research; see Dorothée Imbert, "The Art of Social Landscape Design," in Marc Treib and Dorothée Imbert, *Garrett Eckbo: Modern Landscapes for Living* (Berkeley: University of California Press, 1997), 106–77.

1. Edwin Bergstrom, "Collaboration of the Professions," *Landscape Architecture* 31, no. 3 (April 1941): 141.

2. Henry Hubbard, "Editorial," *Landscape Architecture* 22, no. 3 (April 1932): 218.

3. A. D. Taylor, "Notes on Federal Activities Relating to Landscape Architecture," *Landscape Architecture* 25, no. 1 (October 1934): 41.

4. Phoebe Cutler, *The Public Landscape of the New Deal* (New Haven, Conn.: Yale University Press, 1985), 87, 88–89.

5. Alexis de Tocqueville, *Democracy in America,* trans. Arthur Goldhammer (1835; repr., New York: Library of America, 2004), 530.

6. See Richard Schermerhorn, "Landscape Architecture—Its Future," *Landscape Architecture* 22, no. 4 (July 1932): 281–87; and the series by A. D. Taylor, "Notes on Federal Activities Relating to Landscape Architecture," *Landscape Architecture* 24, no. 4 (July 1934): 215–17; vol. 25, no. 1 (October 1934): 41–45; vol. 25, no. 2 (January 1935): 104–6; vol. 25, no. 3 (April 1935): 164–71; vol. 25, no. 4 (July 1935): 211–14. See also Turpin Bannister, "An Architect Looks at Landscape Architecture and Sees a Larger Demand for It Than Ever Before," *Landscape Architecture* 39, no. 4 (July 1949): 164–66.

7. "Premier Congrès de l'Union internationale des architectes à Lausanne," *Das Werk* 35 (September 1948): 127 (my translation). For the persistence of these disciplinary conflicts in the United States, see Peter Walker and Melanie Simo, *Invisible Gardens: The Search for Modernism in the American Landscape* (Cambridge: MIT Press, 1996), 287–92.

8. Garrett Eckbo, "Architecture and Landscape, Landscape and Architecture," *Places* 4, no. 4 (1987): 49.

9. Garrett Eckbo, *Landscape for Living* (New York: F. W. Dodge, 1950), 238.

10. Garrett Eckbo, "Landscape Design in the USA as Applied to the Private Garden in California," *Architectural Review* 105, no. 625 (January 1949): 31.

11. Denise Scott Brown, "Another Battlefield of the Styles in Architecture" (response to editorial question "Looking from the Future into the Immediate Past"), *Architecture* 76, no. 5 (May 1987): 117, cited by Eckbo, "Architecture and Landscape," 51.

12. Garrett Eckbo, "Small Gardens in the City," *Pencil Points* 18, no. 9 (September 1937): 573–86.

13. Marc Treib, "The Social Art of Landscape Design," in Marc Treib and Dorothée Imbert, *Garrett Eckbo: Modern Landscapes for Living* (Berkeley: University of California Press, 1997), 38n59.

14. Eckbo, *Landscape for Living*, 178.

15. As a student at Harvard Eckbo participated in a design studio led by Walter Gropius in which he collaborated with four architecture students on the design of a park. See Garrett Eckbo, *Landscape Architecture: The Profession in California, 1935–1940, and Telesis,* interviews conducted by Suzanne B. Riess in 1991 (Berkeley: Regional Oral History Office, Bancroft Library, University of California, 1993), 16.

16. Reflecting this rejection of Beaux-Arts design principles is the series of three articles published in *Architectural Record* in 1939–40 in which Eckbo and his fellow Harvard landscape students Daniel Kiley and James Rose shifted the discussion of contemporary landscape architecture away from the private garden and toward issues of recreational landscapes in the public realm.

17. Garrett Eckbo, "Farm Security Administration Projects," *Arts and Architecture* 1, no. 4 (1982): 41. For further discussion of Eckbo's work with the FSA and its underpinnings in New Deal programs established by Franklin Roosevelt, see Dorothée Imbert, "The Art of Social Landscape Design," in Treib and Imbert, *Garrett Eckbo,* 115–47.

18. For Lange's FSA photographs in the Library of Congress, search the database at http://www.loc.gov/pictures/search.

19. Talbot Hamlin, "Farm Security Architecture: An Appraisal," *Pencil Points* 22, no. 11 (November 1941): 709.

20. See Vernon Armand DeMars, "A Life in Architecture: Indian Dancing, Migrant Housing, Telesis, Design for Urban Living, Theater, Teaching," an oral history conducted in 1988–89 by Suzanne B. Riess (Berkeley: Regional Oral History Office, Bancroft Library, University of California, 1992), 118–19. Thanks to DeMars's efforts, these projects were published in diverse venues. See Alfred Roth, "Co-operative Farm Community," *La Nouvelle Architecture présentée en 20 exemples, Die Neue Architektur, The New Architecture* (Zurich: Girsberger, 1940), 61–70; Elizabeth Mock, *Built in the USA: A Survey of American Architecture since 1932* (New York: Museum of Modern Art, 1945), 60–63.

21. Garrett Eckbo, "Site Planning: What Is It? What's It For?" *Architectural Forum* 76, no. 5 (May 1942): 265, 267.

22. William Wurster, "Architecture Broadens Its Base," *AIA Journal* 10, no. 7 (July 1948): 31.

23. Hamlin, "Farm Security Architecture," 709.

24. Ibid., 716, 711. It is unclear whether Hamlin visited these projects, or whether his comments merely reflect points gleaned from the design drawings and photographs or stressed by FSA team members. In either case, the time required for Eckbo's landscape elements to mature would have precluded the possibility of experiencing the spatial attributes of his camp landscapes—a problem evident in

contemporaneous site photographs, which provide limited evidence of new planting alongside the full-grown vegetation that preexisted the FSA's interventions.

25. Eckbo, "Farm Security Administration Projects," 42.

26. Eckbo, *Landscape Architecture*, 40.

27. Carey McWilliams, *Factories in the Field: The Story of Migratory Farm Labor in California* (Boston: Little, Brown, 1939), 7, 10. See Cletus E. Daniel, *Bitter Harvest: A History of California Farmworkers, 1870–1941* (Berkeley: University of California Press, 1982), 15–39. My argument relies heavily on McWilliams's account.

28. For discussion of failed state efforts to implement collective land colonization in California, see McWilliams, *Factories in the Field,* 200–10.

29. Dorothea Lange, interview by Richard Doud, New York City, 22 May 1964, Archives of American Art, Smithsonian Institution, http://www.aaa.si.edu/collections/oralhistories.

30. Such fears were not unfounded. In addition to the American Federation of Labor's long-standing efforts to unionize farm labor and related attempts associated with particular minority groups, the Communist Party of the United States became involved in organizing minority farmworkers in California's Imperial Valley beginning in 1930, leading to militant reprisals by growers. In reaction to the massive cotton strike of 1933 in Tulare County, farm owners forcibly evicted workers from grower-controlled housing, leading to the creation of a "strike camp" that in turn spawned laborers' further efforts at organization. Daniel, *Bitter Harvest,* 255. On efforts to unionize farm laborers, see McWilliams, *Factories in the Field,* especially 168–72, 212–29.

31. The National Labor Relations Act of 1935 explicitly excluded farmworkers from guarantees of the right to organize and bargain collectively, which the National Industrial Recovery Act of 1933 had granted to laborers in other industries. In a further concession to growers, workers employed at relatively high wages under the Works Progress Administration (established 1935) were required to return to harvesting on the farms at lower rates of pay whenever needed, leading Daniel to characterize such policies as "the Roosevelt administration's studied neglect of agricultural labor." Daniel, *Bitter Harvest,* 282.

32. U.S. Congress, Senate Subcommittee of the Committee of Education and Labor, *Violations of Free Speech and Rights of Labor,* Report no. 1150, 77th Congress, 2nd session (Washington, D.C.: Government Printing Office, 1942), pt. 1, 37; cited in ibid., 283.

33. For elaboration of programmatic and architectural developments in the migrant labor camps, see Vernon DeMars, "Social Planning for Western Agriculture," *Task,* no. 2 (1941): 4–9; Greg Hise, "From Roadside Camps to Garden Homes: Housing and Community Planning for California's Migrant Work Force, 1935–1941," in *Gender, Class, and Shelter,* ed. Elizabeth Collins Cromley and Carter L. Hudgins (Knoxville: University of Tennessee Press, 1995), 243–58.

34. Vernon DeMars anticipated that such a future of economic autonomy might await the FSA encampments: "Perhaps the decentralization of industry will really come, and a balance may be achieved between work in the factory and work in the field. Perhaps, with cheap electric power available, raw materials could be processed at their source into finished products." DeMars, "Social Planning for Western Agriculture," 9.

35. Walter Stein, "A New Deal Experiment with Guided Democracy: The FSA Migrant Camps in California," *Historical Papers* (1970): 133.

36. Ibid., 140–41, 133.

37. Ibid., 138–39. For an account of prejudice against minority agricultural workers in California, see McWilliams, *Factories in the Field,* especially 103–51.

38. Stein, "A New Deal Experiment," 145.

39. McWilliams, *Factories in the Field,* 4.

40. Ibid., 303, 324.

41. Daniel, *Bitter Harvest,* 270.

42. Paul Conkin, *Tomorrow a New World: The New Deal Community Program* (Ithaca, N.Y.: Cornell University Press for the American Historical Association, 1959), 222–23.

43. Eric Mumford, "National Defense Migration and the Transformations of American Urbanism," *Journal of Architectural Education* 61, no. 3 (January 2008): 30.

44. Marilynn S. Johnson, "Urban Arsenals: War Housing and Social Change in Richmond and Oakland, California, 1941–1945," *Pacific Historical Review* 60, no. 3 (August 1991): 285.

45. For discussion of Eckbo's "anger at the round up of Japanese-American people," see Robert N. Royston, "Garrett Eckbo, the Formative Years," in Eckbo, *Landscape Architecture,* 1. Eckbo's work at temporary assembly centers for Japanese American evacuees in Marysville and Tulare and the permanent relocation camp in Manzanar is examined in Imbert, "The Art of Social Landscape Design," 143. The FSA camp at Tulare accommodated close to five thousand Japanese American evacuees between 20 April and 4 September 1942, while Marysville housed roughly half that number from 8 May to 29 June. At Manzanar Eckbo developed landscape designs for staff housing, which facilitated that facility's transformation from a temporary assembly center to a more permanent internment camp. For information on relocation efforts and details of life inside the temporary centers, see *Personal Justice Denied: Report of the Commission on Wartime Relocation and Internment of Civilians,* chap. 5, at http://www.nps.gov/history/history/online_books/personal_justice_denied/chap5.htm.

46. The hexagonal layout of temporary housing units was typical of these migrant labor camps; see Eckbo, "Farm Security Administration Projects," 42.

Vernon DeMars describes the logic behind this layout in practical terms: in accordance with sanitation requirements for short-term migrant camps with no sewage disposal, a central water tower was ringed by privies seventy-five feet distant, and these were surrounded in turn by cabins another seventy-five feet away. See DeMars, "A Life in Architecture," 93.

47. Garrett Eckbo, "Space and People," *Architectural Record* 107, no. 1 (January 1950): 75.

48. Hamlin, "Farm Security Architecture," 720.

49. Ann Copperman, "The Changing West—Its Post-war Hope Is National Planning," *Task,* no. 6 (Winter 1944–45): 1. See Stephen Daniels, "Marxism, Culture, and the Duplicity of Landscape," in *New Models in Geography,* ed. Richard Peet and Nigel Thrift (London: Unwin Hyman, 1989), 2:196–220.

50. Garrett Eckbo, "Telesis," *Task,* no. 4 (1943): 42. Due to injuries sustained in an automobile accident in which FSA director Burton Cairns lost his life, Eckbo was active in Telesis only during its first six months, yet he served as the group's representative for two issues of *Task* (nos. 4 and 6), an annual publication started by faculty and students in and around Cambridge, Massachusetts, in 1941, and he guest edited its West Coast issue (no. 6, Winter 1944–45).

51. Notes of Francis Violich, cited in Eckbo, *Landscape Architecture,* 68.

52. Ibid., 52.

53. Serge Chermayeff, "Telesis: The Birth of a Group," *New Pencil Points* 23 (July 1942): 46; "Things Telesis Has Found Important," in ibid., 48. Telesis not only provided the groundwork for establishing the Department of City and Regional Planning at the University of California, Berkeley (1948), and helped pave the way for creation of the College of Environmental Design (comprising the Departments of Architecture, Landscape Architecture, Visual Studies, and City and Regional Planning) ten years later, but also inspired formation of the San Francisco Planning and Urban Research Association (SPUR), a public policy think tank established in 1959 to promote good government and effective planning.

54. Chermayeff, "Telesis," 48.

55. "Things Telesis Has Found Important," in ibid.

56. Edited proceedings of CIAM 4 were published as "Contestations" in the journal of the Technical Chamber of Greece, *Technika chronika—Les Annales techniques* (November 1933); see Le Corbusier, *La Charte d'Athènes* (Paris: Plon, 1943). CIAM included transport among the four functions of urban life.

57. Eckbo, "Telesis," 42, 43.

58. Garrett Eckbo, "North vs. South," *Arts and Architecture* 1, no. 4 (1982): 40.

59. Eckbo, "Site Planning," 263.

60. See John Dewey, *The Public and Its Problems* (New York: Henry Holt, 1927).

61. In 1942 Eckbo left the FSA to focus on the independent practice he had established with his brother-in-law Edward Williams in 1940, and in 1945 Robert Royston joined the practice as a third partner. In 1946, when Eckbo moved to Los Angeles, Royston and Williams remained in San Francisco to direct the firm's work there.

62. Transcribed notes of David Gebhard and Harriette Von Breton interview with Gregory Ain, 19 June 1973, David Gebhard papers, Architecture & Design Collection, University Art Museum, University of California, Santa Barbara, 3, cited by Anthony S. Denzer, "Gregory Ain and the Social Politics of Housing Design" (doctoral dissertation, University of California, Los Angeles, 2005), 205. Joseph Johnson and Alfred Day previously worked in William Wurster's San Francisco office; their professional affiliation as Ain, Johnson and Day, which grew out of Ain's commission to design Community Homes, extended from 1945 to 1952. Joseph Johnson's father, Reginald, a member of the team responsible for Baldwin Hills Village, offered to help Ain with securing Federal Housing Administration approval for Community Homes—a quest that was ultimately unsuccessful. Esther McCoy, *The Second Generation* (Salt Lake City, Utah: Peregrine Smith Books, 1984), 118–19. Both Ain and Johnson, as members of the Engineers, Architects and Chemists Federation, were implicated in Senator Joseph McCarthy's list of subversives that grew out of the fears of communism prompted by hearings of the House Committee on Un-American Activities (1938–44). Ibid., 119n5. The House Committee focused on investigating the possibility that the American Communist Party had infiltrated the Works Progress Administration; it also investigated security at the camps set up for wartime internment of Japanese Americans living on the West Coast.

63. For details of Ain's upbringing, ties to Communist Party members, and professional contributions, see Denzer, "Gregory Ain"; Anthony Denzer, "Community Homes: Race, Politics, and Architecture in Postwar Los Angeles," *Southern California Quarterly* 87, no. 3 (Fall 2005): 270–71. For discussion of Llano del Rio, see Dolores Hayden, "Feminism and Eclecticism: An Alternative to Los Angeles," in *Seven American Utopias: The Architecture of Communitarian Socialism, 1790–1975* (Cambridge: MIT Press, 1976), 288–317.

64. Gregory Ain, "In Search of Theory VI," *Arts and Architecture* 83 (January 1966): 15.

65. See ibid., 14–15; Gregory Ain, "Form Follows Faction," *Architectural Record* 137 (May 1965): 108–9.

66. Ain, "In Search of Theory VI," 14–15.

67. At Park Planned Homes, twenty-eight of sixty units were completed, and at Mar Vista, fifty-two of one hundred units. Prior to moving to Los Angeles, Eckbo collaborated on another cooperative housing project, Ladera Housing

Co-operative, with his partner Robert Royston, San Francisco architects Joseph Allen Stein and John Funk, and Nicholas Ciriano, an engineer with the FSA. Royston took primary responsibility for the design after Eckbo obtained the commission and carried out preliminary site analysis. See Reuben M. Rainey and J. C. Miller, *Modern Public Gardens: Robert Royston and the Suburban Park* (San Francisco: William Stout, 2006), 82. Ladera Housing met an end similar to that of Community Homes; of four hundred single-family houses originally planned for a hilly site in Palo Alto, only thirty-five were built using individual financing before the cooperative was dissolved owing to the Federal Housing Administration's refusal to finance the project on grounds that its principle of racial integration would limit the development's property values. The project was partially completed a decade later by developer Joseph Eichler, the first large-scale developer to openly encourage interracial occupancy in his housing projects. See Lizabeth Cohen, *A Consumers' Republic* (New York: Vintage, 2003), 218.

68. Garrett Eckbo, *The Art of Home Landscaping* (New York: McGraw-Hill, 1956), 261.

69. For elaboration of the communitarian point of view, see Arthur Eugene Bestor Jr., "The Communitarian Point of View," in *Backwards Utopias: The Sectarian Origins and the Owenite Phase of Communitarian Socialism in America, 1663–1829* (Philadelphia: University of Pennsylvania Press, 1950), 1–19.

70. Tocqueville, *Democracy in America,* 608.

71. Letter from Ruth Jaffee, executive secretary, Community Homes, to California representative Helen Gahagan Douglas, 11 July 1947, Helen Gahagan Douglas Collection, Carl Albert Congressional Research and Studies Center, University of Oklahoma, Norman. Jaffee studied landscape design at the University of California, Berkeley, graduating in 1943, and spent several years as apprentice in the office of Thomas Church.

72. Eckbo, "Architecture and Landscape," 49.

73. Eckbo, "Site Planning," 266. Eckbo credited his development of the ideas in this essay in large measure to his collaborative experience at the FSA (ibid., 267).

74. The first Los Angeles office of Eckbo, Day and Williams was in the Baldwin Village Golf Club. Clarence Stein, who consulted on the Baldwin Hills Village site layout, derived this concept of traffic separation from Frederick Law Olmsted's layout of Central Park, as well as from the writings of Raymond Unwin. See Stein, *Toward New Towns for America,* 218.

75. Eunice Grier and George Grier, *Privately Developed Interracial Housing: An Analysis of Experience* (Berkeley: University of California Press, 1960), 145. Although the Griers do not identify the project by name, their account is consistent with the circumstances surrounding Community Homes. On 4 April 1947 the

FHA rejected the original site plan in toto and recommended changes the board found unacceptable (ibid., 147).

76. Jürgen Habermas, *The Structural Transformation of the Public Sphere: An Inquiry into a Category of Bourgeois Society,* trans. Thomas Burger (Cambridge: MIT Press, 1991), 158.

77. Quoted by Denzer, "Gregory Ain," 222.

78. Garrett Eckbo, "Cooperatives," *Art and Architecture* 1, no. 4 (1982): 42.

79. Garrett Eckbo, "Outdoors and In: Gardens as Living Space," *Magazine of Art* 34, no. 8 (October 1941): 425, 422–23.

80. Eckbo, *The Art of Home Landscaping,* 266.

81. The Griers describe the existing condition: "The site was flat, surrounded on three sides by vacant land and on the fourth by scattered single-family homes costing $8,000 to $15,000. About half the land was subject to restrictive covenants against minorities. The price for the whole was approximately $230,000." Grier and Grier, *Privately Developed Interracial Housing,* 144–45.

82. Garrett Eckbo, syllabus for "Architecture 190ab, Landscape Design," University of Southern California (c. 1948), cited by Walker and Simo, *Invisible Gardens,* 120.

83. Articles of Incorporation, Community Homes, Inc. (11 March 1946), 2, 1, Helen Gahagan Douglas Collection, Carl Albert Congressional Research and Studies Center, University of Oklahoma, Norman.

84. Eckbo, *The Art of Home Landscaping,* 270, quotation adapted from Oscar Stonorov and Louis Kahn, *You and Your Neighborhood* (New York: Revere Copper and Brass, 1944), n.p.

85. American Public Health Association Committee on the Hygiene of Housing, *Planning the Neighborhood* (Chicago: Public Administration Service, 1948); Rainey and Miller, *Modern Public Gardens,* 45–46.

86. See, for example, publications of the Government Printing Office, Washington, D.C.: Federal Housing Administration, *Planning Neighborhoods for Small Houses* (Technical Bulletin 5, 1936); Federal Housing Administration, *The Structure and Growth of Residential Neighborhoods* (1939); National Housing Agency, *Mutual Housing: A Veterans' Guide* (1947); National Housing Agency, *Nonprofit Housing Projects in the United States* (1947). For a historic overview of restrictive covenants in housing developments in the United States, see Robert M. Fogelson, *Bourgeois Nightmares: Suburbia, 1870–1930* (New Haven, Conn.: Yale University Press, 2005).

87. Eckbo, "Site Planning," 266. Eckbo illustrated this essay with an aerial view of the FSA farmworkers' community in Granger, Washington. (I have attempted to correct typographic errors in this essay.)

88. American Public Health Association Committee on the Hygiene of Housing, *Planning the Neighborhood,* 22.

89. *Mutual Housing: A Veteran's Guide—Organizing, Financing, Constructing, and Operating Several Selected Types of Cooperative Housing Associations, with Special Reference to Available Federal Aids* (Washington, D.C.: National Housing Agency, 1947), 16.

90. Eckbo, "Site Planning," 263.

91. Catherine Bauer, "Who Cares about Architecture?" *New Republic,* 6 May 1931, 326.

92. Catherine Bauer, "Good Neighborhoods," *Annals of the American Academy of Political and Social Sciences* 242 (November 1945): 104.

93. Paul Conkin, *Tomorrow a New World: The New Deal Community Program* (Ithaca, N.Y.: Cornell University Press for the American Historical Association, 1959), 186. Although Conkin primarily addresses resettlement colonies established by the Resettlement Administration, this point applies equally to the FSA's migrant labor camps.

94. "By Laws of Community Homes, Inc.," art. IX, sec. 8 (undated document), Helen Gahagan Douglas Collection, Carl Albert Congressional Research and Studies Center, University of Oklahoma, Norman.

95. Ibid., art. XIV, sec. 1.

96. "A design must be reasonably good of its kind in order to be approved by or on behalf of the Board of Directors of the Corporation. A poorly designed example of any sort of architecture, regardless of its nominal 'style,' or of its cost, shall be disapproved." "Community Homes, Inc., Declaration of Establishment of Restrictions," 17 September 1946, art. I, sec. 5b, Helen Gahagan Douglas Collection, Carl Albert Congressional Research and Studies Center, University of Oklahoma, Norman.

97. Arnold R. Hirsch, "Containment on the Home Front: Race and Federal Housing Policy from the New Deal to the Cold War," *Journal of Urban History* 24 (January 2000): 160.

98. Quoted by Grier and Grier, *Privately Developed Interracial Housing,* 21. Among the deed restrictions encouraged by the FHA *Underwriting Manual* of 1936 is the following: "Prohibition of the occupancy of properties except by the race for which they were intended." Federal Housing Administration, *Underwriting Manual,* with revisions of 1 April 1936 (Washington, D.C.: Federal Housing Administration, 1936), pt. 2, sec. 284g.

99. Hirsch, "Containment on the Home Front," 163.

100. The Supreme Court decided *Shelley v. Kramer,* 334 U.S. 1, on 3 May 1948; see ibid., 158–89. A memorandum to President Truman from Thurgood Marshall, director of NAACP's Legal Defense and Education Fund, renewing allegations of racial discrimination by the FHA cited this decision relative to the examples of Community Homes and a similar cooperative development in Illinois, as well as restrictive covenants sanctioned by the FHA in the Levittown, New York,

development, where residents were required to limit use of the premises to members of the Caucasian race. Thurgood Marshall, "Memorandum to the President of the United States Concerning Racial Discrimination by the Federal Housing Administration," 1 February 1949.

101. Roughly half of the project acreage was subject to restrictive covenants against minority ownership at the time the cooperative purchased the property. Grier and Grier, *Privately Developed Interracial Housing,* 144–45. For details of the extensive negotiations with the FHA and other potential financing sources for Community Homes, see ibid., 143–55.

102. In August 1948 the Community Homes site plan was adjusted to subject the finger parks to private ownership in the manner of Sunnyside Gardens.

103. Ann Copperman, "The How and Why of Segregation," in "Ghettoes, U.S.A.," *Task,* no. 6 (Winter 1944–45): 4–6. In addition to Copperman's essay, the issue included an anonymous piece on Marin City, a racially integrated federal housing project for war workers ("Take San Francisco"), and one urging citizen participation in postwar planning efforts, prepared from material assembled by Ross Miller and former FSA landscape architect and planner Francis Violich ("What Californians Can Do").

104. Eckbo, "Site Planning," 264.

105. Quoted by Grier and Grier, *Privately Developed Interracial Housing,* 132; Denzer, "Gregory Ain," 226. Also see Lewis S. Feuer, "American Travelers to the Soviet Union, 1917–32: The Formation of a Component of New Deal Ideology," *American Quarterly* 14, no. 2 (Summer 1962): 119–49.

106. George Rand, "Evaluation: Three California Pioneers," *Architecture* 74 (July 1985): 88.

107. Larry Ceplair and Steven Englund, *The Inquisition in Hollywood: Politics in the Film Community* (Berkeley: University of California Press, 1979), 78.

108. The Molotov-Ribbentrop nonaggression pact, signed in August 1949, remained in effect until Germany invaded the Soviet Union in June 1941.

109. See Vernon DeMars, "Cooperative Housing" and "Build Your Own Neighborhood," *House and Garden* 99, no. 2 (February 1951): 44–55, 102–5 (includes Avenel Homes and Usonia in Pleasantville, New York, laid out by Frank Lloyd Wright); National Housing Agency, *Nonprofit Housing Projects in the United States* (Washington, D.C.: National Housing Agency, 1947), indicating growing interest in cooperative projects; National Housing Agency, *Mutual Housing: A Veteran's Guide* (Washington, D.C.: National Housing Agency, 1947), showing veterans how to organize a cooperative; Elsie Danenberg, *Get Your Own Home the Co-operative Way* (New York: Greenberg, 1949), with numerous examples in the United States based on principles developed by mill workers in Rochdale, England (1844), including a chapter titled "Mutual Housing Association, California," 56–61.

110. Joseph Hudnut, "Housing and the Democratic Process," *Architectural Record* 93 (June 1943): 43. Hudnut's essay addresses urban public housing projects, yet his comment applies equally to Community Homes and the FSA migrant labor camps.

111. Eckbo, *Landscape Architecture,* 70.

112. "It seems possible to hope that with co-operation, there may be introduced into our town suburbs and villages that sense of being the outward expression of an orderly community of people." Raymond Unwin, *Town Planning in Practice* (1909; repr., London: Ernest Benn, 1932), 381–82.

113. Eckbo, "Site Planning," 267.

114. Nancy Fraser, "Rethinking the Public Sphere: A Contribution to the Critique of Actually Existing Democracy," in *The Phantom Public Sphere,* ed. Bruce Robbins (Minneapolis: University of Minnesota Press, 1993), 25.

115. "Mutual Housing Association: A Project for Five Hundred Families in Crestwood Hills," *Arts and Architecture* 65 (September 1948): 32.

116. Grier and Grier, *Privately Developed Interracial Housing,* 155. Eckbo's landscape strategy for Crestwood Hills was never implemented. The site's hilly terrain, consisting of alternating ridges and valleys, precluded the type of communal articulation available in the flat locale of Community Homes. Although preservation of the site's natural character was deemed desirable, this goal was hindered by local regulations concerning street layout. The cooperative ultimately deemed Eckbo's master landscape plan too exotic, and the Crestwood Hills landscape was developed in a piecemeal fashion. Eckbo subsequently joined a third cooperative of sixty-seven households to create Wonderland Park in Laurel Canyon, where he designed roughly half of the private gardens as well as the master plan for the valley's trees. The site was previously subdivided and terraced to form individual lots along a curving hillside road, limiting the potential for communal expression. Josef Van der Kar, an associate of Gregory Ain, designed Eckbo's house.

117. Letter from Jaffee to Douglas, 11 July 1947.

118. Vernon DeMars, "Cooperative Housing—An Appraisal," *Progressive Architecture* 32 (February 1951): 64, 77. DeMars cites two projects with which Eckbo had been associated, Avenel Housing and Ladera.

119. Chantal Mouffe, "Democratic Citizenship and the Political Community," in *Dimensions of Radical Democracy: Pluralism, Citizenship, Democracy,* ed. Chantal Mouffe (London: Verso, 1992), 226; Mouffe refers to the argument made in Michael Sandel, *Liberalism and the Limits of Justice* (Cambridge: Cambridge University Press, 1982).

120. "The Valuator should investigate areas surrounding the location to determine whether or not incompatible racial and social groups are present, to the end that an intelligent prediction may be made regarding the possibility or probability

of the location being invaded by such groups. If a neighborhood is to retain stability it is necessary that properties shall continue to be occupied by the same racial and social classes." FHA, *Underwriting Manual* (April 1936), pt. 2, sec. 233.

121. DeMars, "Cooperative Housing—An Appraisal," 77.

122. "Mutual Housing Association," 61.

123. Eckbo, "Space and People," 75. Here Eckbo challenged the elitism inherent to a statement made in "Maze or Maize," *Landscape Architecture* 27, no. 4 (July 1937): 203.

124. Garrett Eckbo, "Study of the Profession of Landscape Architecture: Answers to Questions for Consultants," in Albert Fein, *A Study of the Profession of Landscape Architecture: Technical Report* (McLean, Va.: ASLA, 1972), sec. 6, 2–3.

125. Calvert Vaux to Frederick Law Olmsted, 22 May 1865, in *Frederick Law Olmsted Papers 5: The California Frontier, 1863–1865*, ed. Victoria Post Ranney (Baltimore: Johns Hopkins University Press, 1990), 376.

126. "Report by the Special Committee on Education AIA," *AIA Journal* 39 (April 1963): 129, 130. In focusing on a proposal to fuse architecture and engineering, the AIA report treats landscape architecture as a subsidiary aspect of this new professional outlook, broadly conceived of as environmental design.

127. "A Report on the Profession of Landscape Architecture," *Landscape Architecture* 54, no. 1 (October 1963): 35, 34. The following year the ASLA rejected the AIA conclusions even more emphatically, finding the AIA's "central concepts and specific proposals . . . unnecessary, unreasonable, unfeasible, untenable, and not in the interests of society or of the professions engaged in environmental design." "Reports: ASLA Responds to 'Centennial Challenges,'" *Landscape Architecture* 55, no. 1 (October 1964): 17.

128. Fein, *A Study of the Profession of Landscape Architecture*, sec. 1, 52. Although Eckbo served on the executive committee responsible for the study, he disagreed with this particular aspect of the report, submitting a separate assessment in which he espoused "an amalgamation of all of these fields [i.e., architecture, planning, and engineering], and others, in a new profession of Environmental Planning and Design" (ibid., sec. 6, 10).

129. Garrett Eckbo, "An Eckbo-Porterfield Exchange," *Landscape Architecture* 60 (April 1970): 201.

7. From the Virgilian Dream to Chandigarh

I am grateful to Peter Buchanan, former editor of the *Architectural Review,* who offered substantive feedback on an early draft of this essay.

1. For peripheral but illuminating discussions of the landscape in Le Corbusier's urban theories, see Mary McLeod, "Le Corbusier and Algiers," *Oppositions*

19/20 (Winter/Spring 1980): 54–85; James Dunnett, "The Architecture of Silence," *Architectural Review* 1064 (October 1985): 69–75; Manfredo Tafuri, "Machine et Mémoire: The City in the Work of Le Corbusier," in *Le Corbusier Archive,* vol. 10, *Urbanisme, Algiers, and Other Buildings and Projects, 1930–1933,* trans. Stephen Sartarelli (New York: Garland, 1983), xxxi–xlvi.

2. Elizabeth Meyer, "Landscape Architecture as Modern Other and Postmodern Ground," in *The Culture of Landscape Architecture,* ed. Harriet Hedquist and Vanessa Bird (Melbourne: RMIT, 1994), 30–31.

3. In 1912, as architect of the Ateliers d'art réunis in La Chaux-de-Fonds, Le Corbusier included *"architecture de jardins"* among the services on his letterhead; see Mary Patricia May Sekler, "Le Corbusier, Ruskin, the Tree, and the Open Hand," in *The Open Hand: Essays on Le Corbusier,* ed. Russell Walden (Cambridge: MIT Press, 1982), 5.

4. Le Corbusier, *Towards a New Architecture* [*Vers une architecture,* 1923], trans. Frederick Etchells (New York: Payson & Clarke, 1927), 212. Sekler discusses the roots of Le Corbusier's attitude toward nature in "Le Corbusier, Ruskin," 42–95; Christopher Green elaborates Le Corbusier's responses to nature through painting and sculpture in "The Architect as Artist," in *Le Corbusier, Architect of the Century* (London: Arts Council of Great Britain, 1987), 110–18.

5. Le Corbusier, *The Radiant City* [*La Ville radieuse,* 1935], trans. Derek Coltman (New York: Orion Press, 1967), 83.

6. Le Corbusier, *Towards a New Architecture,* 70.

7. See Dunnett, "The Architecture of Silence."

8. Le Corbusier's plan for the Ville Contemporaine (1922), for example, is organized in a Beaux-Arts manner, with cultural facilities isolated in a *"jardin anglaise."* The entire ground plane is public, an idea influenced by Tony Garnier's *Cité Industrielle,* and the *maisons à redents* (setback housing), borrowed from Eugène Hénard, are fragments of traditional courtyard blocks, open to a communal landscape of classical French *parterres,* inspired by the Palais Royal and the Tuileries in Paris.

9. Le Corbusier and Pierre Jeanneret, *Oeuvre complète, 1910–29* (Zurich: Girsberger, 1964), 17–21.

10. Le Corbusier, *Towards a New Architecture,* 189, 204.

11. Le Corbusier, *Last Works,* ed. Willy Boesiger, trans. Henry Frey (New York: Praeger, 1970), 177.

12. In his "Five Points of a New Architecture," initially published in 1927 in conjunction with the Stuttgart Weissenhofsiedlung, Le Corbusier also proposed the horizontal strip window to express the independence of the facade from the structural grid of the free plan; where the traditional vertical window is related anthropomorphically to the human body, the strip window is analogous to the

landscape. See Bruno Reichlin, "'Une petite maison' on Lake Leman: The Perret-Le Corbusier Controversy," *Lotus International* 60 (1988): 59–84. By denying the role of the window as frame, Reichlin argues, the strip window eliminates the real depth of the landscape to bestow a new objectivity on the image of nature it reveals. For the "Five Points," see Le Corbusier and Pierre Jeanneret, "Fünf Punkte zu einer neuen Architektur," in Alfred Roth, *Zwei Wohnhäuser von Le Corbusier und Pierre Jeanneret* (Stuttgart: F. Wedekind, 1927), 7–9.

13. For discussion of the Beistegui penthouse, see Tafuri, "Machine et Mémoire," xxxi–xxxii.

14. Le Corbusier compared the Marseille Block to an Ionic temple: "The modulor here smiles in the Greek, the Ionic fashion—smiling grace of mathematics, grace of proportion to the human scale." Le Corbusier, *Modulor* II [1955], trans. Peter de Francia and Anna Bostock (Cambridge, Mass.: Harvard University Press, 1980), 306/320.

15. Mary McLeod relates this shift to Le Corbusier's plan for Algiers of the 1930s and his growing involvement with syndicalism. See McLeod, "Le Corbusier and Algiers."

16. The Maison Monol derives from Gottfried Semper's little-noted second version of the primitive hut, based on the hearth and the wall.

17. "The spiral from the museum roof must become a track of gardens and dense rockeries set in the landscape and constituting landscape." Le Corbusier, *Le Corbusier Sketchbooks 4, 1957–1964* (New York: Architectural History Foundation, 1982), P59:447.

18. Le Corbusier intended the skylight of the Firminy Church to direct the sun's rays to illuminate the altar on Easter morning, recalling the effect of his skylight at the Assembly in Chandigarh.

19. Anthony Eardley, "Grandeur Is in the Intention," in *Le Corbusier's Firminy Church* (New York: Institute for Architecture and Urban Studies, 1981), 6.

20. Beatriz Colomina notes, for example, that in amending photographs of the Villa Schwob for publication "Le Corbusier discarded everything that was picturesque and contextual in the house, concentrating on the formal qualities of the object itself." Beatriz Colomina, "Le Corbusier and Photography," *Assemblage* 4 (October 1987): 12. In contrast, Stanislaus von Moos, in an otherwise cogent analysis of Le Corbusier's work, argues: "He even considers the relationship of the project to the site to be of secondary importance. . . . In fact, most of his projects were not bound to any particular location." Stanislaus von Moos, *Le Corbusier: Elements of a Synthesis* (Cambridge: MIT Press, 1982), 299. For analysis of the formative influence of site on Le Corbusier's work, see Alan Colquhoun, "The Strategies of the Grands Travaux," *Assemblage* 4 (October 1987): 66–81. For the spatial implications of Le Corbusier's photographic images, see Thomas Schumacher, "Deep Space, Shallow Space," *Architectural Review* 1079 (January 1987): 37–42.

21. Le Corbusier, *Le Corbusier Talks with Students,* trans. Pierre Chase (New York: Orion Press, 1961), 40–41.

22. Le Corbusier and Jeanneret, *Oeuvre complète, 1910–29,* 74.

23. The Villa Shodan (1951–56), originally commissioned by Surottam Hutheesin, was built without modification on a new site in Ahmedabad, where it is an isolated, freestanding object. In Firminy, owing to conflicting municipal authorities, Le Corbusier was required to shift his Maison des Jeunes to the opposite side of the sports stadium, which he also did without altering his original design. In 1965, when realization of the Firminy Church was in doubt, he negotiated to build the project in Bologna, subject to selection of an appropriate site, although none was ever agreed upon. See Martin Purdy, "Le Corbusier and the Theological Program," in Walden, *The Open Hand,* 313–17. Construction of the Firminy Church began after Le Corbusier's death and was completed by his protégé José Oubrerie in 2006.

24. Le Corbusier letter to Louis Secretan, July 1961, archives of the Bibliothèque de La Chaux-de-Fonds, quoted by Purdy, "Le Corbusier and the Theological Program," 291.

25. Le Corbusier, *Oeuvre complète, 1946–52* (Zurich: Girsberger, 1953), 72.

26. Le Corbusier, *Modulor* II, 148.

27. Describing his pilgrimage chapel at Ronchamp, Le Corbusier explained, "The requirements of religion have had little effect on the design, the form was an answer to a psycho-physiology of the feelings." Le Corbusier, *Oeuvre complète, 1946–52,* 72.

28. For analysis of Le Corbusier's buildings in Chandigarh, see Peter Serenyi, "Timeless but of Its Time: Le Corbusier's Architecture in India," *Perspecta* 20 (1983): 91–118; William Curtis, "Authenticity, Abstraction, and the Ancient Sense: Le Corbusier's and Louis Kahn's Ideas of Parliament," *Perspecta* 20 (1983): 181–94.

29. Le Corbusier, *Le Corbusier Sketchbooks 3, 1954–57* (New York: Architectural History Foundation, 1982), H34:190. See Tafuri, "Machine et Mémoire," for a different interpretation of the phenomenon of isolation in Le Corbusier's work.

30. Le Corbusier, *Le Corbusier Sketchbooks 2, 1950–54* (New York: Architectural History Foundation, 1982), F26:866.

31. Le Corbusier, *Sketchbooks 4,* P60:534.

32. Le Corbusier, *Sketchbooks 2,* G28:951: "June 14, 1953/ it is absolutely necessary to close off the whole horizon of the Capital by *horizontal hills/* But on the side of the Himalayas it's admirable to let the [farmlands] and the flocks run right up to a parapet. But watch out the goats will come gobble up everything."

33. See Le Corbusier, *Modulor* II, 214. Although he never resolved the materiality of the obelisks, Le Corbusier made repeated references to them in his

sketchbooks, attesting to their significance for the project. At different times he considered building them in reflective metal, brick, and concrete. Le Corbusier, *Sketchbooks 2,* H30:1042: "Think of the obelisks view upon arrival crossing the river, before Chandigarh/ a brilliant metal/ + color/ stainless steel." *Sketchbooks 3,* J38:430: "The Capital obelisks could be brick cones (matching the remaining walls) = recalling Muslim milestones in dark brick at Km. 61 on road from Delhi." He ultimately differentiated between them in size and material, according to the spaces they demarcate. See *Sketchbooks 3,* K41:587: "attention! the four obelisks ABCD/ large + the 4: 1.2.3.4./ small"; *Sketchbooks 4,* P60:538: "rounded square hole/ like in the pylons of the Assembly portico/ the obelisks 400 metres."

34. The dimension of 800 meters is the distance from the Louvre to the Place de la Concorde and from the Place de la Concorde to the Place Clemenceau, according to Le Corbusier's plan drawing in his *Oeuvre complète, 1946–52,* 117.

35. Le Corbusier, *Modulor* II, 211. The residential sectors of Chandigarh measure 800 by 1,200 meters.

36. Since the Club House on Lake Sukhna (1958–64) violated this principle, Le Corbusier depressed the building three meters below grade to maintain an unimpeded view of the mountains from the capital complex; see Le Corbusier, *Last Works,* 78.

37. Le Corbusier and François de Pierrefeu, *The Home of Man,* trans. Clive Entwistle (London: Architectural Press, 1948), 125. Fortuitously the site for Chandigarh was selected by airplane reconnaissance; see Norma Evenson, *Chandigarh* (Berkeley: University of California Press, 1966), 7.

38. Le Corbusier, *Sketchbooks 4,* M51:13; see *Modulor* II, 214–15; Le Corbusier, *Aircraft* (New York: The Studio, 1935), text adjoining fig. 122. His sketchbooks are replete with notes on perceptual site considerations; see, for example, *Sketchbooks 2,* E23:638, 675, 677; F26:866; G28:951; H30:1042.

39. See Le Corbusier, *Sketchbooks 3,* J38:140: "IMPORTANT Capital esplanade make a serious pattern with compartmentalization in cement (Beirut airport)/ slab 3.66 x 7.7/ Simla Stone, flowers and bushes used flush with the paving or projecting: 43, 86, 113." *Sketchbooks 4,* N56:360 (26 April 1959, from Rome airport): "Chandigarh esplanade courage of simplicity is needed"; K43:675: "L-C go to Orly to see for Chandigarh the various poured or prefabricated cement of the runways."

40. "*The 24 hours of the solar cycle* constitute the measuring rod of all human activities; they are what gives our lives their scale and their perspective." Le Corbusier, *The Radiant City,* 77. Le Corbusier credited Jane Drew with the suggestion that he include these symbols of his philosophy in the open plaza at Chandigarh; see Le Corbusier, *Oeuvre complète, 1946–52,* 157. In his sketchbook he noted "The *signs*! when the mind can conclude by a *sign* which henceforth will have something

like an algebraic value, then thought takes a leap forward; it has liberated a space, an expanse from then on qualified (signified) by a *term* or mark instantly understandable by anyone." *Sketchbooks 2,* F27:895. He noted that *radieuse* (the name he gave his utopian urban proposal of 1935), a term with no suitable parallel in English, has "the attribute of consciousness." *Le Corbusier Talks with Students,* 27. As hieroglyphs, Le Corbusier's personal signs are rendered at once primitive (hence comprehensible) and sacred.

41. "The Open Hand will turn on ball bearings like a weather-cock, not to show the incertitude of ideas, but to indicate symbolically the direction of the wind (the state of affairs). A movement of the spirit in 1948 has taken in 1951 an eminent part in the composition of a capital in India." Le Corbusier, *Oeuvre complète, 1946–52,* 155. For discussion of the symbolism of the Open Hand, see Sekler, "Le Corbusier, Ruskin," 69–83; von Moos, *Le Corbusier,* 291–93.

42. Le Corbusier, *Oeuvre complète, 1952–57* (New York: G. Wittenborn, 1957), 94.

43. Le Corbusier, *Modulor* II, 215. By "texturique" he means "connection, arrangement of parts" (ibid., 210).

44. Le Corbusier, *Sketchbooks 2,* G28:948 (1953); *Sketchbooks 4,* M1:39 (1957).

45. The name Chandigarh was borrowed from that of the nearest village, where there is a temple, erected centuries ago, in honor of the war goddess Chandi. Le Corbusier, *Last Works,* 52.

46. See Le Corbusier, *Aircraft,* ill. 14–18.

47. See Le Corbusier, *The City of Tomorrow and Its Planning* [*Urbanisme,* 1925], trans. Frederick Etchells (New York: Payson & Clarke, 1929), 168. Le Corbusier visited Egypt in April 1952 on his return from Chandigarh.

48. These paths were occasionally elevated to the heights of fruit trees; see Susan Jellicoe, "The Development of the Mughal Garden," in *The Islamic Garden,* ed. Elizabeth MacDougall and Richard Ettinghausen (Washington, D.C.: Dumbarton Oaks, 1976), 111.

49. See Alexander Gorlin, "An Analysis of the Governor's Palace of Chandigarh," *Oppositions* 19/20 (Winter/Spring 1980): 174. Gorlin's interpretation is flawed in its persistent references to Buddhism; Chandigarh was developed as a Hindu settlement.

50. Le Corbusier, *Sketchbooks 2,* E20:431. Le Corbusier repeated this form at different scales on each of the capital buildings: in the entry portico of the Assembly, over the door of the Secretariat, and in the topmost section of the High Court.

51. Norma Evenson, *Le Corbusier: The Machine and the Grand Design* (New York: George Braziller, 1969), 13–14.

52. Le Corbusier, *Last Works,* 174; *Sketchbooks 2,* E20:448 (1951).

53. Robert Slutzky, "Aqueous Humor," *Oppositions* 19/20 (Winter/Spring 1980): 30.

54. Le Corbusier, *Last Works*, 188.

8. Hilberseimer and Caldwell

I am grateful to Charles Waldheim, who provided valuable feedback on an earlier version of this essay.

1. Ludwig Hilberseimer, *Entfaltung einer Planungsidee* (Berlin: Verlag Ullstein, 1963), 22, quoted by Richard Pommer, "'More a Necropolis than a Metropolis': Ludwig Hilberseimer's Highrise City and Modern City Planning," in *In the Shadow of Mies: Ludwig Hilberseimer, Architect, Educator, and Urban Planner,* ed. Richard Pommer, David Spaeth, and Kevin Harrington (Chicago: Art Institute of Chicago, 1988), 17.

2. Detlef Mertins, "Living in a Jungle: Mies, Organic Architecture, and the Art of City Building," in *Mies in America,* ed. Phyllis Lambert (Montreal: Canadian Centre for Architecture, 2001), 623n117. See also M. Machler, "Das Siedlungensproblem," *Sozialistische Monatshefte* 27, no. 4 (1921): 182–87; "Wie ist das Sieldungproblem zu lösen?" *Sozialistische Monatshefte* 27, no. 5–6 (1921): 222–27, cited by Marco de Michelis, "The Green Revolution: Leberecht Migge and the Reform of the Garden in Modernist Germany," in *The Architecture of Western Gardens,* ed. Monique Mosser and Georges Teyssot (Cambridge: MIT Press, 1991), 419n18. Hilberseimer contributed articles on Paul Scheerbart, Dadaism, and American skyscrapers to this periodical in 1919, 1920, and 1922, respectively.

3. The *Zeilenbau* system, derived from hospitals and barracks buildings intended to reduce infection, originated in the housing designs of Theodor Fischer in Munich and Heinrich de Fries in Berlin just after World War I. See Richard Pommer, "The Architecture of Urban Housing in the United States during the Early 1930s," *Journal of the Society of Architectural Historians* 37, no. 4 (December 1978): 260–61.

4. Ludwig Hilberseimer, *The New Regional Pattern: Industries and Gardens, Workshops and Farms* (Chicago: Paul Theobald, 1949), 39.

5. Ludwig Hilberseimer, "Amerikanische Architektur," *G*, no. 4 (March 1926): 4–8, summarized in David Spaeth, *Ludwig Karl Hilberseimer: An Annotated Bibliography and Chronology* (New York: Garland, 1981), 5.

6. Hilberseimer's highly romanticized view of the Middle Ages parallels that which Sigfried Kracauer put forward in the *Frankfurter Zeitung* during the early 1920s, based on Ferdinand Tönnies's distinction of 1887 between organic community *(Gemeinschaft)* and technological-functional society *(Gesellschaft)*; see Thomas Y. Levin, "Introduction," in Sigfried Kracauer, *The Mass Ornament:*

Weimar Essays, ed. Thomas Y. Levin (Cambridge, Mass.: Harvard University Press, 1995), 13.

7. Hilberseimer wrote these drafts with lawyer and legal scholar Udo Rukser; see Pommer, "'More a Necropolis than a Metropolis,'" 27.

8. Daniel H. Burnham and Edward H. Bennett, *Plan of Chicago,* ed. Charles Moore (1909; repr., New York: Princeton Architectural Press, 1993), 43. Hilberseimer cited this motto in *The New Regional Pattern,* 149. Caldwell believed slum reclamation could achieve the spirit of Chicago's motto; Alfred Caldwell, "Order and Beauty," unpublished manuscript, n.d., Chicago Department of City Planning, 6, cited in *Alfred Caldwell: The Life and Work of a Prairie School Landscape Architect,* ed. Dennis Domer (Baltimore: Johns Hopkins University Press, 1997), 54.

9. Alfred Caldwell to Ludwig Hilberseimer, 13 September 1941, quoted in Domer, *Alfred Caldwell,* 266–67.

10. Wilhelm Miller, "The Prairie Spirit in Landscape Gardening," in *Illinois Agricultural Experiment Station Circular* no. 184, November 1915 (Urbana: University of Illinois College of Agriculture, 1915), 19.

11. Jens Jensen, *Siftings* (1939; repr., Baltimore: Johns Hopkins University Press, 2000), 19–20.

12. Ibid., 28.

13. "Oral History of Alfred Caldwell," interview by Betty J. Blum (1987), Art Institute of Chicago, 2001, 38. In 1932 Caldwell spent three weeks with Wright after the architect invited him to live at Taliesin East and restore the gardens that had fallen into disrepair after the fire that devastated the complex.

14. Alfred Caldwell, "The City in the Landscape," *Parks and Recreation* 28, no. 2 (March/April 1945): 59–64.

15. Alfred Caldwell, "The City in a Garden, Eagle Point Park, 1934," in *Architecture and Nature: The Work of Alfred Caldwell,* ed. Werner Blaser (Basel, Switzerland: Birkhäuser, 1984), 30.

16. Ludwig Hilberseimer, *The New City: Principles of Planning* (Chicago: Paul Theobald, 1944), 51. Both Hilberseimer and Caldwell owned copies of Kropotkin's *Fields, Factories, and Workshops,* and Hilberseimer cited Henry Ford frequently in his writings on urban planning.

17. Ibid., 69.

18. Hilberseimer, *The New Regional Pattern,* 121ff.

19. Ibid., 120.

20. Hilberseimer, *The New City,* 191.

21. Frank Lloyd Wright, *An Organic Architecture: Architecture of Democracy* (London: Lund Humphries, 1939), 1, 3.

22. Hilberseimer, *The New Regional Pattern,* xv.

23. Ludwig Hilberseimer, "Entwicklungstendenzen des Städtebaus," *Form: Zeitschrift für gestaltende Arbeit* 4 (1929): 209–11, cited in Spaeth, *Ludwig Karl Hilberseimer*, 9.

24. Ludwig Hilberseimer, *The Nature of Cities: Origin, Growth, and Decline; Pattern and Form; Planning Problems* (Chicago: Paul Theobold, 1955), 133.

25. Lewis Mumford, "The Garden City Idea and Modern Planning," in Ebenezer Howard, *Garden Cities of Tomorrow* (London: Faber & Faber, 1947), 47.

26. Hilberseimer, *The Nature of Cities*, 240–47.

27. Hilberseimer, *The New City*, 54.

28. Caldwell, describing his canyon houses project of 1951 in *Architecture and Nature*, 108.

29. Hilberseimer, *The Nature of Cities*, 140.

30. Hilberseimer, *The New Regional Pattern*, 136.

31. Hilberseimer, *The New City*, 190.

32. "America was settled to have a piece of land." "Oral History," 95.

33. Caldwell, *Architecture and Nature*, 56.

34. Ibid., 48. The forty-acre tract, deemed sufficient for the average family, became the official modular unit for settlement of the American Midwest in 1332.

35. Alfred Caldwell letter to Werner Blaser (1974), cited in *Architecture and Nature*, 12.

36. Hilberseimer, *The Nature of Cities*, 257.

37. Hilberseimer, *The New Regional Pattern*, 194. Caldwell undertook related studies of farm typologies from 1954 to 1965.

38. Ibid., 130.

39. Ludwig Hilberseimer, "Die Architektur der Grossstadt" (1914ff.), handwritten manuscript in Hilberseimer archive, Art Institute of Chicago 8/3 1/1, trans. and quoted by Pommer, "'More a Necropolis Than a Metropolis,'" 26.

40. Hilberseimer, *The New City*, 56.

41. In the late 1930s, when it was first marked for clearance, the sector of Detroit between the river and Gratiot Avenue constituted the poorest section of housing in the city, with more than two-thirds of its housing stock classified as substandard. "The Gratiot Redevelopment site . . . was the centerpiece of the 'Detroit Plan,' [1947] a comprehensive proposal for partnership between the city and private developers to clear the Lower East Side slum and rebuild the area as a private housing project." Thomas Sugrue, *The Origins of the Urban Crisis: Race and Inequality in Postwar Detroit* (Princeton, N.J.: Princeton University Press, 1996), 36–37, 49.

42. Pommer, "The Architecture of Urban Housing," 236.

43. The U.S. Housing Act of 1949 made federal funds available for site improvement and construction of streets; it encouraged private enterprise by calling

for plans that specified "proposed land uses and building requirements to control private development." Roger Montgomery, "Improving the Design Process in Urban Renewal," in *Urban Renewal: The Record and the Controversy,* ed. James Q. Wilson (Cambridge: MIT Press, 1966), 457. Montgomery argues: "The heavy criticism renewal has received for building luxury apartments on the ruins of slums seems pointless as long as ideological considerations place renewal at the mercy of the private market" (ibid., 466).

44. In contrast, the "Detroit Plan" of 1947 for the Gratiot Redevelopment area preserved the scale and alignment of the previous block structure, but not its street layout; culs-de-sac were positioned in the middle of the former blocks, with row housing at their edges.

45. "The broad view is the one that suggests infinity and power, and is the more inspiring for occasional visits; the long view is more human and intimate, and often more satisfactory to live with." Miller, "The Prairie Spirit," 17–18.

46. Describing an illustration that he made for Hilberseimer's study of the Chicago region, Caldwell argued: "The landscape is a productive landscape, comprising the farms and forests of the region. Thus the parks would be productive parks, containing, besides recreational facilities of every kind, vegetable gardens and small farms." *Architecture and Nature,* 48.

47. Alfred Caldwell, "Jens Jensen, the Prairie Spirit," *Landscape Architecture* 51, no. 2 (January 1961): 104–5.

48. Robert Fishman, *Bourgeois Utopias: The Rise and Fall of Suburbia* (New York: Basic Books, 1987), 6.

49. Hilberseimer, *The New City,* 49.

50. Patrik Schumacher and Christian Rogner, "After Ford," in *Stalking Detroit,* ed. Georgia Daskalakis, Charles Waldheim, and Jason Young (Barcelona: ACTAR, 2001), 48.

51. Hilberseimer, *The New Regional Pattern,* 69, figs. 40, 41.

52. Hilberseimer, *The New City,* 47–48.

53. See Mark Donchin, "Reflections on the Politics of a Non-political Planner," *Society for American City and Regional Planning History* (1988): 8, 10–11.

54. Kim Halik, "Modernity, Urban Planning, and the Metropolis: An Introduction to a Forgotten Treatise by Ludwig Karl Hilberseimer, *Groszstadtarchitektur* (1927)," *Australian Planner* 35, no. 3 (1998): 147–50.

55. David Spaeth, "Ludwig Hilberseimer's Settlement Unit," in Pommer, Spaeth, and Harrington, *In the Shadow of Mies,* 64; Albert Pope, *Ladders* (Houston: Rice School of Architecture, 1996), 85.

56. Paul Thomas, "Foreword," in Spaeth, *Ludwig Karl Hilberseimer,* xi.

57. Pope, *Ladders,* 91.

9. The Once and Future Park

I am grateful to my colleagues at the University of Michigan Institute for the Humanities for their feedback on a preliminary version of this essay, to Britt Eversole for always challenging my thinking in new directions, to Mireille Roddier for her ongoing support for this project, and to Tsz Yan Ng for generously sharing her insights into the Exposition Universelle of 1867 and its associated Parc des Buttes Chaumont. Britt Eversole and Keith Mitnick provided invaluable criticism of earlier drafts.

1. Paul Delouvrier, "Avant Propos," in *L'Invention du Parc: Parc de la Villette, Paris; Concours International, 1982–83*, ed. Marianne Barzilay, Catherine Hayward, and Lucette Lombard Valentino (Paris: Graphite Editions, 1984), 6.

2. For a comparison of the Parc des Buttes Chaumont and Bernard Tschumi's Parc de la Villette, see Elizabeth Meyer, "The Public Park as Avant-Garde (Landscape) Architecture: A Comparative Interpretation of Two Parisian Parks, Parc de la Villette (1983–1990) and Parc des Buttes-Chaumont (1864–1867)," *Landscape Journal* 10, no. 1 (Spring 1991): 16–26.

3. Quoted in "International Conference on Landscape Architecture," *Journal of the Town Planning Institute* (London) 34, no. 6 (September/October 1948): 192.

4. Nicos Poulantzas, *State, Power, Socialism* (London: Verso, 1978), 105.

5. Kenneth Robert Olwig, "Sexual Cosmology: Nation and Landscape at the Conceptual Interstices of Nature and Culture; Or, What Does Landscape Really Mean?" in *Landscape Politics and Perspectives*, ed. Barbara Bender (Providence, R.I.: Berg, 1993), 307.

6. Carl Bybee points out that "an official, widely used 1928 United States Army *Training Manual* stated that democracy led to 'mobocracy,' the rule of mobs, and that the democratic attitude toward property was 'communistic.' Democracy, the manual concluded, led to 'demogogism *[sic]*, license, agitation, discontent, anarchy.'" Carl Bybee, "Can Democracy Survive in the Post-factual Age? A Return to the Lippmann-Dewey Debate about the Politics of the News," *Journalism and Communication Monographs* 1, no. 1 (Spring 1999): 31–32.

7. Robert B. Westbrook, *John Dewey and American Democracy* (Ithaca, N.Y.: Cornell University Press, 1991), xv.

8. Stephen Daniels, "Marxism, Culture, and the Duplicity of Landscape," in *New Models in Geography*, ed. Richard Peet and Nigel Thrift (London: Unwin Hyman, 1989), 2:196. The invisible essence of politics and power relations in landscape is developed in several essays in Dianne Harris and D. Fairchild Ruggles, eds., *Sites Unseen: Landscape and Vision* (Pittsburgh: University of Pittsburgh Press, 2007).

9. Adrian Forty, "'Dead or Alive': Describing the Social," in *Words and Buildings: A Vocabulary of Modern Architecture* (New York: Thames & Hudson, 2000), 105.

10. Roger Connah, "An Unlikely Degree Zero?" *Perspecta* 38 (2006): 20. Manfredo Tafuri also interpreted the Modern Movement as "a program for modeling the 'bourgeois man' as an absolute type." Manfredo Tafuri, "Toward a Critique of Architectural Ideology" (1969), in *Architecture Theory since 1968,* ed. K. Michael Hays, trans. Stephen Sartorelli (Cambridge: MIT Press, 1998), 18.

11. Anita Berrizbeitia, "The Amsterdam Bos: The Modern Public Park and the Construction of Collective Experience," in *Recovering Landscape: Essays in Contemporary Landscape Architecture,* ed. James Corner (New York: Princeton Architectural Press, 199), 192.

12. Daniels, "Marxism, Culture," 206. See also Martin Jay, "Culture as Manipulation; Culture as Redemption," in *Adorno* (Cambridge, Mass.: Harvard University Press, 1984), especially 111–12.

13. Daniels, "Marxism, Culture," 217–18.

14. Rem Koolhaas, *Delirious New York: A Retroactive Manifesto for Manhattan* (New York: Oxford University Press, 1978), 7.

15. Ibid., 17–18.

16. Frederick Law Olmsted, "Public Parks and the Enlargement of Towns," in *The Public Face of Architecture: Civic Culture and Public Spaces,* ed. Nathan Glazer and Mark Lilla (New York: Free Press, 1987), 246.

17. See Frederick Law Olmsted, "Rules and Conditions of Service of the Central Park Keepers" (12 March 1859), image published in Elizabeth Barlow, *Frederick Law Olmsted's New York* (New York: Praeger, 1972), 110. The display of rules for appropriate garden use and behavior dates to the *lex hortorum* of Roman antiquity, revived in Renaissance Italy; see David R. Coffin, "The *Lex hortorum* and Access to Gardens of Latium during the Renaissance," *Journal of Garden History* 2 (1982): 201–32.

18. Olmsted, "Public Parks," 258, 241.

19. Roger Starr, "The Motive behind Olmsted's Park," in Glazer and Lilla, *The Public Face of Architecture,* 272.

20. Stephen A. Germic, *American Green: Class, Crisis, and the Deployment of Nature in Central Park, Yosemite, and Yellowstone* (Lanham, Md.: Lexington Books, 2001), 12, 7, 36–37. Construction of Central Park displaced roughly 1,600 poor residents, including a shantytown of Irish pig farmers and German gardeners, as well as Seneca Village, one of the city's most stable African American settlements.

21. Tafuri, "Toward a Critique of Architectural Ideology," 6.

22. Alain Orlandini, "Interview with Jacques Gourvénic," in *La Villette, 1971–1995: A History in Projects* (Paris: Somogy/Éditions d'art, 2004), 212. Koolhaas

voiced a similar sentiment when he argued that "architects' fanaticism [is] . . . a response to the horror of architecture's opposite, an instinctive recoil from the void, a fear of *nothingness*." Rem Koolhaas, "Imagining Nothingness," in Rem Koolhaas and Bruce Mau, *Small, Medium, Large, Extra-Large [S, M, L, XL],* ed. Jennifer Sigler (New York: Monacelli Press, 1995), 200.

23. Alphand also had the Parc de Vincennes, lying outside the eastern bounds of the city, modified from its former status as an elite hunting ground to serve its immediate working-class district, but this transformation was accomplished more modestly than were those of the other public landscapes he administered. Although Alphand took credit for the various landscaping projects carried out as part of Haussmann's extensive urban interventions, landscape gardener Jean-Pierre Barillet-Deschamps was responsible for the layout and planting of the Parc des Buttes Chaumont, and the work was supervised by his assistant Edouard André.

24. Cited by Ulf Strohmayer, "Urban Design and Civic Spaces: Nature at the Parc des Buttes-Chaumont in Paris," *Cultural Geographies* 13 (2006): 561, 558; also see Luisa Limido, *L'Art des jardins sous le Second Empire: Jean-Pierre Barillet-Deschamps (1824–1873)* (Seyssel: Champ Vallon, 2002), 126.

25. Georges-Eugène Haussmann, *Mémoires du Baron Haussmann,* vol. 3 (Paris: Victor-Havard, 1893), 234.

26. Haussmann quoted by Antoine Grumbach, "The Promenades of Paris," *Oppositions* 8 (Spring 1977): 51. When Napoleon III visited the site of Buttes Chaumont in 1865, he witnessed some thousand workers involved in the effort.

27. [Jean Charles] Adolphe Alphand, *Les Promenades de Paris* (1867–73; repr., New York: Princeton Architectural Press, 1984), lix.

28. D. A. [Dezallier d'Argenville], *Voyage Pittoresque de Paris,* 4th ed. (Paris: De Bure, 1765), iii–iv. D'Argenville's father wrote a popular treatise on landscape gardening, *La Théorie et la pratique du jardinage* (published anonymously, 1709).

29. Maria Luisa Marceca, "Reservoir, Circulation, Residue: J. C. A. Alphand, Technological Beauty, and the Green City," *Lotus International* 30 (1981): 63.

30. Barillet-Deschamps replicated certain of these constructional details in the temporary park surrounding the main exposition building and its horticultural "*Jardin réservé*" in the Champ de Mars, as well as the other public parks created under Haussmann; when spread over the expanse of the Bois de Boulogne or the Bois de Vincennes, such details have a diluted effect.

31. Frédéric Le Play, *Rapport sur l'Exposition Universelle de 1870 à Paris. Précis des operations* . . . (Paris: Imprimerie Impériale, 1869), 197, cited by Pieter van Wesemael, *Architecture of Instruction and Delight: A Socio-historical Analysis of World Exhibitions as a Didactic Phenomenon (1791–1851–1970),* trans. George Hall (Rotterdam: 010 Publishers, 2001), 757n578.

32. Nicholas Green, *The Spectacle of Nature: Landscape and Bourgeois Culture in Nineteenth-Century France* (Manchester: Manchester University Press, 1990), 83.

33. Koolhaas, *Delirious New York*, 7.

34. For parallels between the Parisian building programs of Haussmann and Mitterrand, see Annette Fierro, *The Glass State: The Technology of the Spectacle; Paris, 1981–1998* (Cambridge: MIT Press, 2003), 2–3, 10–38; Jean-Louis Cohen and Bruno Fortier, eds., *Paris: La Ville et ses Projects, a City in the Making* (Paris: Editions Babylone, Pavillon de l'Arsenal, 1988–89).

35. For details of the site's twentieth-century developments, see Alain Orlandini, "Chronology: From the Agony of the Abattoir to the Inauguration of the Cité de la Musique," in *La Villette*, 16–40. Orlandini reveals a fundamental misunderstanding of French landscape history, particularly the symbolic and ritual value of historic French landscapes, when he argues about Fainsilber's associated park proposal, "Like Le Nôtre's gardens, it was intended solely as a foil for the architectural object" (ibid., 40).

36. Delouvrier, "Avant Propos," 6.

37. François Barré, "Aux Portes du Parc," in Barzilay, Hayward, and Valentino, *L'Invention du Parc*, 16. Barré, who devised the competition brief, subsequently served as president of the Centre Pompidou (1993–96) and as president of the Grande Halle de la Villette exhibition center (from 1993).

38. Competition brief cited by Orlandini, *La Villette*, 41.

39. "Données sur l'Existant," cited by Lodewijk Baljon, *Designing Parks: An Examination of Contemporary Approaches to Landscape Design Based on a Comparative Design Analysis for the Concours International: Parc de la Villette, 1982–83* (Amsterdam: Architectura & Natura Press, 1995), 37–38.

40. Rem Koolhaas, "New York/La Villette," in *OMA/Rem Koolhaas: Architecture, 1970–1990*, ed. Jacques Lucan (New York: Princeton Architectural Press, 1991), 161.

41. Rem Koolhaas, "Parc de la Villette, Paris, 1982–1983," in Lucan, *OMA/Rem Koolhaas*, 86.

42. Georg Simmel, "The Metropolis and Mental Life" (1903), in *On Individuality and Social Forms*, ed. Donald Levine (Chicago: University of Chicago Press, 1971), 324.

43. Charles Baudelaire, "The Painter of Modern Life" (1863), in *The Painter of Modern Life, and Other Essays*, ed. and trans. Jonathan Mayne (New York: Da Capo Press, 1986), 13–14, cited in the dictionary compiled by Jennifer Sigler in Koolhaas and Mau, *S, M, L, XL*, 928.

44. Walter Benjamin, "Central Park," in *The Writer of Modern Life: Essays on Charles Baudelaire*, ed. Michael W. Jennings (Cambridge, Mass.: Harvard University Press, 2006), 139.

45. Rem Koolhaas, "Elegy for a Vacant Lot," in Koolhaas and Mau, *S, M, L, XL*, 937.

46. *Rem Koolhaas–Hans Ulrich Obrist: The Conversation Series* 4 (Köln: Verlag der Buchhandlung Walter König, 2004), 85.

47. Koolhaas, "Parc de la Villette," 86. Koolhaas's use of the term "Social Condenser" is a reference to Russian Constructivism, a topic he researched during a trip to Moscow and Siberia during his period of architectural studies at the Architectural Association in London (1968–72). See Rem Koolhaas and Gerrit Oorthuys, "Ivan Leonidov's Dom Narkomdtjazjprom, Moscow," *Oppositions* 2 (January 1974): 95–103; Rem Koolhaas, "A Foundation of Amnesia," *Design Quarterly* 125 (1984): 4–11. In *Delirious New York* Koolhaas argues, "In the Downtown Athletic Club the Skyscraper is used as a Constructivist Social Condenser: a machine to generate and intensify desirable forms of human intercourse" (128; cited in Koolhaas and Mau, *S, M, L, XL*, 210). He subsequently interpreted his Parc de la Villette proposal as a skyscraper turned on its side: "The bands across the site were like the floors of the tower, each program different and autonomous, but modified and 'polluted' by the proximity of the others." Koolhaas, "New York/La Villette," 161; also see "Universal Modernization Patent: 'Social Condenser'" (1982), in *Content*, ed. Rem Koolhaas (London: Taschen, 2004), 73.

48. Koolhaas, *Delirious New York*, 13.

49. Koolhaas, "Congestion without Matter," in Koolhaas and Mau, *S, M, L, XL*, 934.

50. Ibid., 931.

51. Koolhaas, "New York/La Villette," 161.

52. "Office for Metropolitan Architecture," in Barzilay, Hayward, and Valentino, *L'Invention du Parc*, 43.

53. Le Corbusier cited by Tafuri, "Toward a Critique of Architectural Ideology," 25; *Rem Koolhaas–Hans Ulrich Obrist*, 11.

54. *Rem Koolhaas–Hans Ulrich Obrist*, 52. In a related vein Koolhaas described Atlanta as "the wrong turn taken by a profession which can only talk about order and control." Rem Koolhaas, "Atlanta," in *The Idea of the City: Architectural Associations*, ed. Robin Middleton (London: Architectural Association, 1996), 91.

55. Koolhaas, "New York/La Villette," 160.

56. Robin Evans, "Towards Anarchitecture," *Architectural Association Quarterly* 2, no. 1 (January 1970): 58, 68. This essay precedes Gordon Matta-Clark's use of that term (a combination of *anarchy* and *architecture*) for the collaborative exhibition he orchestrated at 112 Greene Street, New York, in 1974.

57. See Yona Friedman, "Manifeste de l'architecture mobile," lecture delivered at CIAM 10 (1956); "A Trend in Architecture: Analysis and Prognosis," *Architectural Design* 35, no. 1 (January 1965): 52; *Architecture Mobile* (Paris: Casterman, 1970);

Vers une architecture scientifique (Paris: Pierre Belfond, 1974); *Towards a Scientific Architecture,* trans. Cynthia Lang (Cambridge: MIT Press, 1975); Reyner Banham, Paul Barker, Peter Hall, and Cedric Price, "Non-plan: An Experiment in Freedom," *New Society* 13, no. 338 (20 March 1969): 435–43. The Japanese Metabolists provided a related Eastern source of inspiration; see Rem Koolhaas, "Singapore: Portrait of a Potemkin Metropolis; Songlines: Thirty Years of Tabula Rasa," in Koolhaas and Mau, *S, M, L, XL,* 1043–51.

58. Le Corbusier's commentary on the CIAM 4 proceedings does not reflect the full range of ideas presented at the conference, devoted to "The Functional City" and held in 1933 aboard the Greek ship *Patris II.* An edited version of the proceedings of CIAM 4 was initially published as "Contestations" in the journal of the Technical Chamber of Greece, *Technika chronika—Les Annales techniques* (November 1933); see Congrès Internationaux d'Architecture Moderne, *La Charte d'Athènes* (Paris: Plon, 1943); Le Corbusier, *The Athens Charter,* trans. Anthony Eardley (New York: Grossman, 1973); Martin Steinmann, ed., *CIAM: Dokumente, 1928–1939* (Basel, Switzerland: Birkhäuser, 1979); Eric Mumford, *The CIAM Discourse on Urbanism, 1928–1960* (Cambridge: MIT Press, 2000).

Postwar CIAM meetings reflect reactions against the reductive programmatic aspects of the group's earlier urban analyses, focusing on more humanist goals propounded by the eighth congress ("The Heart of the City," held in Hoddesdon, England, 1951), a direction subsequently expanded upon by the members of Team 10. See Catherine Bain, "Team 10: The French Context" (paper delivered at the conference "Team 10—Between Modernity and the Everyday," Delft University of Technology, June 2003; http://www.team10online.org). Although Koolhaas embraced Team 10's emphasis on temporality and urban dynamism, as well as the group's prolific use of diagrammatic ideograms, he rejected its humanist approach to alleviating the alienation of the modern subject.

59. For a cogent comparison of Constant's New Babylon and the work of Archigram, see Simon Sadler, "New Babylon versus Plug-In City," in *Exit Utopia: Architectural Provocations, 1956–76,* ed. Martin van Schaik and Otakar Máčel (Munich: Prestel, 2005), 57–67.

60. For elaboration of French contributions to these issues, see Larry Busbea, *Topologies: The Urban Utopia in France, 1960–1970* (Cambridge: MIT Press, 2007).

61. Joan Littlewood, *Joan Littlewood's Peculiar History as She Tells It* (London: Methuen, 1994), 702, cited by Mary Louise Lobsinger, "Cybernetic Theory and the Architecture of Performance: Cedric Price's Fun Palace," in *Anxious Modernisms: Experimentation in Postwar Architectural Culture,* ed. Sarah Williams Goldhagen and Réjean Legault (Montreal: Canadian Centre for Architecture, 2000), 121.

62. Reyner Banham, "A Clip-On Architecture," *Design Quarterly* 63 (1965): 13.

63. Cedric Price, memorandum of 1964, quoted by Stanley Matthews, *From Agit-Prop to Free Space: The Architecture of Cedric Price* (London: Black Dog, 2007), 73.

64. Ibid., 67, 73, 75.

65. Ibid., 72. As both gardens levied admissions charges, the participating public would have been narrower than Price and Littlewood imagined.

66. Joan Littlewood, "A Laboratory of Fun," *New Scientist,* no. 391 (14 May 1964): 432; the issue is devoted to "leisure and the arts in 1984."

67. Cedric Price, "Objectives: Glengall Wharf, Isle of Dogs" (c. 1963), cited by Matthews, *From Agit-Prop to Free Space,* 68. Littlewood's interactive theatrical concept draws upon the work of Bertolt Brecht, who combined theory and practice in his epic theater, synthesizing and extending the experiments of Erwin Piscator and Vsevolod Meyerhold to explore the theater as a forum for political ideas.

68. Cedric Price, "Expediency," *Architectural Design* 35, no. 9 (1969): 493.

69. Gordon Pask, "The Architectural Relevance of Cybernetics," *Architectural Design* 35, no. 9 (1969): 494–95.

70. Alain Orlandini, "Interview with Rem Koolhaas," in *La Villette,* 180.

71. Koolhaas, *Delirious New York,* 240.

72. Ibid., 27, 28, 35.

73. Ibid., 23.

74. Rem Koolhaas, "Why I Wrote *Delirious New York* and Other Textual Strategies," (interview with Cynthia Davidson), *ANY,* no. 1 (1993): 42.

75. "With lapidary epigrams, skeletal drawings and a polemical zeal for mobilising the real against the pretensions of a still surprisingly megalomaniac profession, he changed the terrain of architecture." Rem Koolhaas, "Introduction," in Cedric Price, *RE-CP,* ed. Hans Ulrich Obrist (Basel, Switzerland: Birkhäuser, 2003), 6.

76. "Rem Koolhaas in Conversation with George Baird," *GSD News* (Summer 1996): 49.

77. Rem Koolhaas and Sarah Whiting, "Spot Check: A Conversation between Rem Koolhaas and Sarah Whiting," *Assemblage* 40 (December 1999): 50.

78. "The changing of landscapes from one hour to the next will result in total disorientation." Gilles Ivain [Ivan Chtcheglov], "Formulary for a New Urbanism" (1953), *Internationale Situationiste* 1 (Paris) (June 1958).

79. Rosalyn Deutsche, "The Question of 'Public Space'" (lecture delivered at the National Graduate Seminar, American Photography Institute, 1 June 1998; http://www.thephotographyinstitute.org/journals/1998/rosalyn_deutsche.html).

80. *Rem Koolhaas–Hans Ulrich Obrist,* 86, 87.

81. Anne Whiston Spirn, "The Poetics of City and Nature: Towards a New Aesthetic for Urban Design," *Landscape Journal* 7, no. 2 (Fall 1998): 108.

82. Rem Koolhaas, "What Ever Happened to Urbanism?" in Koolhaas and Mau, *S, M, L, XL,* 969.

83. Urban sociologist Robert Park and his student Louis Wirth developed the notion of human ecology at the University of Chicago during the 1920s. Contemporary research in social ecology goes beyond the biological and economic foundations posited by Park and Wirth to engage cross-disciplinary perspectives on the physical, political, legal, psychological, cultural, and societal forces that have impacts on human-environmental relations.

84. Koolhaas, "Congestion without Matter," 930. The opportunity to contribute to a collection of essays titled *Ecological Urbanism* has since elevated Koolhaas's ecological awareness. There he argues: "I still think architectural dialectics are between this building and this building—and are therefore not deep enough. We have all of these images of buildings that do not perform correctly, but our answers are not necessarily very deep. I don't exclude myself from any of these comments." Rem Koolhaas, "Advancement versus Apocalypse," in *Ecological Urbanism,* ed. Mohsen Mostafavi and Gareth Doherty (Cambridge, Mass.: Harvard University Graduate School of Design, 2010), 69.

85. John Beardsley, "Conflict and Erosion: The Contemporary Public Life of Large Parks," in *Large Parks,* ed. Julia Czerniak and George Hargreaves (New York: Princeton Architectural Press, 2007), 212.

86. Victor Papanek, *Design for the Real World: Human Ecology and Social Change* (Toronto: Bantam Books, 1973), 66–67.

87. Rem Koolhaas, "Imagining Nothingness," in Lucan, *OMA/Rem Koolhaas,* 156.

88. Richard Sennett, *The Conscience of the Eye: The Design and Social Life of Cities* (New York: Alfred A. Knopf, 1990), xi. For discussion of historic attempts to create architectural form suited to democratic principles in France, see Jean-Philippe Meurtin, "The Circle of Dissension and the Semicircle of Criticism," in *Making Things Public: Atmospheres of Democracy,* ed. Bruno Latour and Peter Weibel (Cambridge: MIT Press, 2005), 754–69; on the relationship between architectural form and democratic form, see Ludger Schwarte, "Parliamentary Public," also in Latour and Weibel, *Making Things Public,* 786–94.

89. Edward Soja, "The Socio-spatial Dialectic," *Annals of the Association of American Geographers* 70 (June 1989): 210, cited by Edward Dimendberg, "Henri Lefebvre on Abstract Space," in *Philosophy and Geography II: The Production of Public Space,* ed. Andrew Light and Jonathan M. Smith (Lanham, Md.: Rowman & Littlefield, 1998), 20.

90. "To form itself, the public has to break existing political forms." John Dewey, *The Public and Its Problems* (New York: Henry Holt, 1927), 31. In Dewey's analysis the American model of democracy is a process-driven rather than a

product-driven concept, inherently open to "experimentation and invention," leading historian James MacGregor Burns to refer to the United States as the "Workshop of Democracy." John Dewey, "Philosophy and Democracy" (1919), in *The Middle Works, 1899–1924,* vol. 11, ed. Jo Anne Boydston (Carbondale: Southern Illinois University Press, 1976–83), 50; James MacGregor Burns, *The Workshop of Democracy* (New York: Alfred A. Knopf, 1985).

91. Chantal Mouffe, *The Democratic Paradox* (London: Verso, 2000), 80–107. Mouffe posits an "agonistic model of democracy" based on a principle of deliberation "between free and equal citizens." Agonism "involves a relation not between enemies but between 'adversaries' [who] share a common symbolic space" but want to organize it in a different way (ibid., 13). Mouffe's model gives positive status to difference, addressing the need to construct a collective identity that would articulate the demands found in the different struggles against subordination.

92. Rosalyn Deutsche, *Evictions: Art and Spatial Politics* (Cambridge: MIT Press, 1996), 259, xiii.

93. Deutsche, "The Question of 'Public Space,'" 9.

94. Françoise Choay, "Critique," *Princeton Journal: Thematic Studies in Architecture* 2 "Landscape" (1985): 214.

95. The members of OMA launched their practice with this project. Elia Zenghelis describes "Exodus," influenced by Superstudio, as "primarily a critique of Megastructure, . . . [which] caricatured the humanist legacy of Team X and opposed Venturi's modesty as false masochism." Elia Zenghelis, "Text and Architecture: Architecture as Text," in van Schaik and Máčel, *Exit Utopia,* 260–61.

96. Koolhaas and Zenghelis elaborate that the "indoctrination" of the Voluntary Prisoners "is only accomplished by overwhelming previously undernourished senses." Rem Koolhaas and Elia Zenghelis, with Madelon Vriesendorp and Zoe Zenghelis, "Metropolis," in van Schaik and Máčel, *Exit Utopia,* 243. This is a complete version of the original text, initially published in *Casabella* 378 (June 1973): 42–45 (where it was awarded first prize *ex aequo* in the competition "The City as Meaningful Environment") and subsequently elaborated in Koolhaas and Mau, *S, M, L, XL,* 5–21.

97. Barré, "Aux Portes du Parc," 17.

98. Koolhaas, "Parc de la Villette," 86; republished as "Congestion without Matter," in *S, M, L, XL,* 894–935.

99. Henri Lefebvre, *Writing on Cities* [*Le Droit de la ville,* 1968], ed. and trans. Eleonore Kofman and Elizabeth Lebas (Cambridge, Mass.: Blackwell, 1996), 63–181; *Rem Koolhaas–Hans Ulrich Obrist,* 28.

100. Jürgen Habermas, "Modernity: An Incomplete Project," in *The Antiaesthetic: Essays on Postmodern Culture,* ed. Hal Foster, trans. Seyla Ben-Habib (Port Townsend, Wash.: Bay Press, 1983), 3–15.

101. Roland Castro, cited by Françoise Fromonot, "The Beaux-Arts: Model, Monster . . . Phoenix?" trans. Julie Rose, *Log* 13/14 (2008): 52. Castro was a candidate for the French presidency in 2007. Sarkozy's initiative to rethink the future of Greater Paris ("Le Grand Pari[s]") prioritized architectural over ecological concerns. The ten teams invited to participate in the study were all headed by architects or architect/urbanists; only the group headed by MVRDV took ecological concerns seriously. As a result, the opportunity to view the metropolitan region as part of a broader complex of ecological systems was lost.

102. Rem Koolhaas, "Generic City," in Koolhaas and Mau, *S, M, L, XL*, 1248.

103. Anthony Vidler, "Promenades for Leisure," *Oppositions* 8 (Spring 1977): 49.

104. "Rem Koolhaas in Conversation with George Baird," 49.

Afterword

1. See, for example, Mohsen Mostafavi and Gareth Doherty, eds., *Ecological Urbanism* (Cambridge, Mass.: Harvard University Graduate School of Design, 2010).

2. See Anita Berrizbeitia and Karen M'Closkey, "Criticality, Science, and the Rise of Landscape Architecture," in *Modernism and Landscape Architecture, 1890–1940*, ed. Therese O'Malley and Joachim Wolschke-Bulmahn (Washington, D.C.: Center for Advanced Studies in the Visual Arts, National Gallery of Art, forthcoming).

3. The outcome of the competition for Downsview Park in suburban Toronto (2000) is a case in point. Koolhaas's La Villette proposal had a significant impact on the Downsview competition requirements, which called for a structured transformation of the site that would remain open to change, engage the complexity of ecological thinking, and challenge disciplinary scopes and boundaries. Although the collaborative team of Bruce Mau, OMA, and Inside/Outside prevailed in the competition, they abandoned the social ramifications that underlay OMA's Parc de la Villette in favor of analogically modeling certain ecological principles—"Grow Culture; Grow the Park; Manufacture Nature." Yet their proposal, which is primarily graphic rather than tactical, also fails to take the complexity of ecological systems into account. The result offers little challenge to the traditional notion of the urban park as a counterpoint to the contemporary metropolis. See Julia Czerniak, ed., *CASE: Downsview Park Toronto* (Cambridge, Mass.: Prestel and Harvard Graduate School of Design, 2001); Julia Czerniak and George Hargreaves, eds., *Large Parks* (New York: Princeton Architectural Press, 2007).

4. See James Corner, "Ecology and Landscape as Agents of Creativity," in *Ecological Design and Planning*, ed. George Thompson and Frederick Steiner (New

York: John Wiley, 1997), 80–108; Chris Reed, "The Agency of Ecology," in Mostafavi and Doherty, *Ecological Urbanism,* 324–29.

5. Throughout the twentieth century, architects frequently collaborated with landscape architects, yet such initiatives were rarely undertaken with parity between the disciplines. The architectural practices of Alvar Aalto, Luis Barragán, Walter Burley Griffin and Marion Mahony Griffin, Louis Kahn, Richard Neutra, Rudolph Schindler, and Frank Lloyd Wright, or programs such as the Case Study Houses in California (to cite several examples not covered in this collection) are evidence of the inclinations of modern architects to address issues of humankind's relationship to the natural world, yet the contribution of landscape architects to such initiatives has drawn little scrutiny. Moreover, while the collaborative nature of certain architectural practices is occasionally acknowledged in the literature, the intricacies and nuances of such efforts remain relatively unexplored, suggesting fertile ground for future research.

PUBLICATION HISTORY

Chapter 2 was originally published in *AA Files* 20 (Fall 1990): 46–54.

Chapter 3 has been revised from "The Stockholm Public Library: Architecture between Nature and the City," *Arquitectura* 70, no. 280 (September/October 1989): 54–67.

Chapter 4 was published as "Verso un paesaggio spirituale: Il cimitero Woodland e la riforma cimiteriale svedese," *Parametro* 264/265 (July/October 2006): 82–89. A longer version was published as "Vers une paysage spirituel," *Pages Paysages* 6 (September 1996): 56–66.

Chapter 5 has been revised from an original version published in *Relating Architecture to Landscape,* ed. Jan Birksted (London: E & FN SPON, 1999), 120–46.

Chapter 7 is based on an essay originally published in *Denatured Visions: Landscape and Culture in the Twentieth Century,* ed. Stuart Wrede and William Howard Adams (New York: Museum of Modern Art, 1991), 79–93, which was revised from an earlier version published in *The Architectural Review* 181, no. 1079 (January 1987): 66–72.

Chapter 8 was originally published in *CASE: Lafayette Park,* ed. Charles Waldheim (Cambridge, Mass.: Harvard University and New York: Prestel Graduate School of Design, 2004), 95–111.

INDEX

Aalto, Alvar: and genius loci, 19
AIA (American Institute of Architects), 115; seeking expanded role for architects, 147–48
AIAJM (Association Internationale des Architectes de Jardins Modernistes), 6, 11, 231n22, 233n40. *See also* Canneel-Claes, Jean; Tunnard, Christopher
Ain, Gregory: collaboration with Eckbo, x, 117, 128, 130; communist sympathies of, 129, 261n62; influence on Eckbo, 133; social reform through architecture, 129, 130. *See also* Community Homes, Reseda, California
Almqvist, Osvald: director of Stockholm Parks department, 75
Alphand, Adolphe: bourgeois interests of capitalism in parks, 223; Parc des Buttes Chaumont, 199–202; Parc de Vincennes, 279n23; social betterment in parks, 215

Archigram: influence on OMA/Koolhaas Parc de la Villette, 213; social programming, 215
ASLA (American Society of Landscape Architects): response to AIA, 147–48, 267n127; work in public domain, 115–16
Asplund, Erik Gunnar: attitude to landscape, 61–64, 75–76, 77–78; European Secondary School, Karlshamn, 61–62; Stockholm Royal Chancellery competition entry, 62–63, 74. *See also* Stockholm Exhibition, 1930; Stockholm Public Library and park; Woodland Cemetery, Stockholm

Baldwin Hills Village, Los Angeles, 39, 132, 142, 262n74
Baltic Exhibition, Malmö, 79
Barcelona Pavilion (German Pavilion, Barcelona International Exposition, 1930), ix, 45–60; experiential

qualities of, 46, 49, 55; inspiration of Schinkel, 45, 46, 51, 56, 60, 246n15; materiality of, 50–55, 56–57; organic order in, 52; picturesque qualities of, 46–48, 57–58, 60; siting of, 49, 56; use by Eckbo, 118, visual rather than mathematical order in, 50. *See also* Mies van der Rohe, Ludwig; picturesque landscape garden; Pope, Alexander: house at Twickenham; Reich, Lilly; *Wunderkammer*

Barragàn, Luis: genius loci at El Pedregal, 20–21

Barrell, John: decline of landscape, 2, 228n6

Baudelaire, Charles: on modernity, 206

Bauer, Catherine, 139, 230n17, 240n10, 242n28

Benjamin, Walter: on modernity in Baudelaire, 206

Bijhouwer, J. T. P., 13

Bing, Alexander: developer of Sunnyside, 32; member Regional Planning Association of America, 240n15

Blom, Holgar: director of Stockholm Parks department, 75

Bospark, Amsterdam, 13, 16

Brandt, Gudmund Nyeland, 7

Bromme, Max: Nidda River landscape reclamation, 36, 241n16

Brown, Denise Scott, 117

burial reform: in Germany, 78–79; in Sweden, 78, 79. *See also* Baltic Exhibition, Malmö; Waldfriedhof, Munich; Woodland Cemetery, Stockholm

Burlington, Lord (Richard Boyle, 3rd Earl of Burlington), 58

Buyssens, Jules, 16–17

Cairns, Burton, 119, 127

Caldwell, Alfred, 276n46; Columbus Park, Chicago, 186; Eagle Point Park, Dubuque, 175; influence of Frank Lloyd Wright, 175; organic design principles, 170, 177; Prairie School of landscape gardening, 174–75, 185. *See also* Jensen, Jens; Lafayette Park, Detroit

Canneel-Claes, Jean: cofounder of AIAJM, 6; landscape manifesto, 11

Cautley, Marjorie Sewell: planting strategy, 242n30, 242n31; professional training, 239n5; Sunnyside Gardens landscape design, 26, 27, 35, 36, 42–43. *See also* Baldwin Hills Village, Los Angeles; Radburn, New Jersey

Central Park, New York, 196–98; collaboration of Olmsted and Vaux, 147; compared to Parc de la Villette, 192, 196; compared to Parc des Buttes Chaumont, 198–200, 203; emblem of metropolitan condition, 196; isolation of pedestrian from vehicular movement, 39, 175; landscape of, 200; social displacement caused by construction, 278n20; vehicle of social reform, 196–98, 199, 203, 205. *See also* Olmsted, Frederick Law

Chandigarh, ix, 20, 149, 157–68; boundaries of capital complex, 159–61, 270–71n33; capital complex, 159–61; cosmic references, 162–63; Governor's Palace and garden, 164–67, 168; history of commission, 158; influence of aviation, 161–62; influence of Mughal paradise garden, 149–50, 157–58, 165–68; urban plan, 158; vision

altered in execution, 164. *See also* Le Corbusier; Mayer, Albert
Chermayeff, Serge: Telesis, 127–28
CIAM (Congrés Internationaux d'Architecture Moderne): Athens Charter, 213; correlation between physical form and social form, 212; Functional City, 128, 282n58; meeting in Frankfurt, 33–34, 242n28; model for AIAJM, 6, 11; premise of tabula rasa, 10
City Housing Corporation, 32, 33–34, 37–38. *See also* Sunnyside Gardens, Queens
collaboration between architects and landscape architects, 226; advocated by Bergston, 115; advocated by Eckbo, ix–x, 116, 117, 129, 139, 146; at FSA, 116, 121; lack of acknowledgment in literature, 287n5; in Telesis objectives, 127; in Weimar Republic, 7
communist sympathies: of Ain, 129, 261n63; of Community Homes members, 143; in FSA, 125, 143; in Los Angeles cooperative housing projects, 142–43
Community Homes, Reseda, California, 129–48, 263n81, 264n100; civic aspirations, 137–38; communitarian ethos, 129, 130–31, 137–38; democratic aspirations, 145, 148; landscape design, 133–36; organizational structure, 140–41; project background, 131; restrictive covenants and, 141–42, 264–65n100, 265n101; site organization, 131–32; social potential of collective space, 132–33, 140. *See also* Ain, Gregory; Eckbo, Garrett; Eisner, Simon; FHA
Contemporary Landscape Architecture and Its Sources (San Francisco Museum of Art, 1937), 14, 25–26. *See also* Hitchcock, Henry-Russell, Jr.
Corner, James: ecology as scientific and aesthetic design vehicle, 226; landscape discipline, 5; *Recovering Landscape,* 2; stewardship, 3, 230n15
correlation between physical form and social form: for Bauer, 139; in CIAM urban planning precepts, 212; at Community Homes, 144; Eckbo's attempts to counteract, ix–x, 119–20, 125–26; at FSA migrant labor camps, 122–24, 140–41, 144; in Modern Movement, 215; at Sunnyside Gardens, 37; for Unwin, 144
Cosgrove, Denis: decline of landscape, 2, 228n4
Courajoud, Claire and Michel: collaboration with Koolhaas, 209–10
cremation rituals, 79–80
Cremation Society of Sweden, 79–80
Crestwood Hills, Los Angeles, 143, 145, 146, 266n116
Cutler, Phoebe, 116, 121

Daniel, Cletus, 121, 125
Daniels, Stephen, 194, 195
Delirious New York (Koolhaas): analysis of Central Park, 196, 203; analysis of Manhattan grid, 208; concept of Manhattanism, 216–17; Koolhaas's reason for writing, 217; process of retroaction, 203. *See also* Koolhaas, Rem; Parc de la Villette, Paris
DeMars, Vernon: head of FSA western division, 119; on housing cooperatives, 145–46; member of Telesis, 127. *See also* FSA
democracy: for Alfred Caldwell, 179, 180; in Czechoslovakia, ix, 93; for

Eckbo, 117, 138, 144; in FSA migrant labor camps, 124; for Hilberseimer, 179–80; for and space, 220; for Unwin, 144; in Weimar Republic, ix

democracy and landscape design, viii, 220; at Community Homes, 128, 135–36, 138, 139–40, 145–46; at Crestwood Hills, 145; at Parc de la Villette, 220–22, 223; at Parc des Buttes Chaumont, 201–2; at Prague Castle, 97, 106, 109, 114 252n1; in public parks, 193–94; at Sunnyside Gardens, 32, 43

democratic theory: of Bybee, 277n6; of Deutsch, 218, 220; of Dewey, 129, 220, 284–85n90; of Jefferson, 121–22, 180; of Mouffe, 220, 285n91; of Tocqueville, 131

Dewey, John, 129, 220, 284–85n90

Duchêne, Achille: landscape theory of, 3, 12, 14–15; professional work, 235n49

Eckbo, Garrett, 5, 6, 7, 10, 116–48; on architecture as discipline, 147; on architecture as source of inspiration, 133, 148; attempts to counteract strict correlation between physical and social forms, ix–x, 119–20, 125–26, 144–45; challenge to conventional disciplinary hierarchies, 132; on collaboration with architects, ix–x, 116, 117, 129, 139, 146; on landscape architecture as discipline, 147; on landscape as medium, 133–34; opposition to racial segregation, 142; process of collaboration equated with democratic processes, 144. *See also* Community Homes, Reseda, California; Crestwood Hills, Los Angeles; FSA; Mar Vista, Los Angeles; Telesis

ecology: in architectural practice (as metaphor), 219, 226; for Hilberseimer, 176; human ecology, 284n83; for Koolhaas, 218–19, 284n84, 286n3; in landscape architecture practice, 218–19, 226; in urbanism, 225–26, 286n101

Eisner, Simon: planning of Community Homes, 131–35, 137

Eliot, Charles (landscape architect), 23, 229n10

Eliot, Charles W. (Harvard University president), 3, 229n10

Evans, Robin: "anarchitecture," 212–13

FHA (Federal Housing Administration): fostering cooperative ownership, 143; restrictive covenants, 141–42, 145, 146; stipulations for Community Homes, 141–42

First International Congress of Garden Architects, 6, 14–15. *See also* Duchêne, Achille

Fourier, Charles, 123–24

FSA (Farm Security Administration), western division, 14, 116; communist sympathies in, 125; defense housing, 125; historians' negative assessments, 121–22, 124–25; Japanese internment camps, 125–26, 259n45; migrant labor camps, 119–27, 131, 132, 142, 259–60n46; racial segregation in housing, 124, 125. *See also* DeMars, Vernon; Lange, Dorothea

Fun Palace (Price and Littlewood), 213–15

garden city principles, 169, 174, 240n15; at Lafayette Park, 170; at Sunnyside Gardens, 32, 39; in

Weimar Republic, 172. *See also* Howard, Ebenezer
genius loci: for architecture, 17–22; for landscape architecture, 17. *See also* Aalto, Alvar; Barragàn, Luis; Giedion, Sigfried; Le Corbusier; Neutra, Richard; Viollet-le-Duc, Eugène-Emmanuel; Wright, Frank Lloyd
Giedion, Sigfried: and genius loci, 19–20; internationalist aims, 18; renunciation of "international style," 244n56
Grässel, Hans, 79
Greenwald, Herbert: developer of Lafayette Park, 182, 184, 188
Gregotti, Vittorio, 17–18
Gropius, Walter, 18, 119, 229n13

Habermas, Jürgen, 222
Hamlin, Talbot: on FSA migrant labor camps, 119, 120, 126
Haussmann, Baron George-Eugène: hygienic urban operations in Paris, 199; meat markets and slaughterhouses, 204; Parisian boulevards, 208; public parks, 192, 201, 222; spatialization of class distinctions, 203
Helsingborg Crematorium, 80–81, 88
Hilberseimer, Ludwig: assessments of urban theories, 189–90; collaboration with Caldwell, 174–77; ecological perspective, 176; Fish Spine scheme, 172; Highrise City, 1924, 171; isolation of pedestrian from vehicular movement, 171–72; and Leberecht Migge, 172; mixed-height housing development, 1930, 171; organic design principles, 170, 177–78; settlement unit, 170–71, 172–73, 188; urban principles, 170–74, 180–81, 187. *See also* Lafayette Park, Detroit
Hitchcock, Henry-Russell, Jr.: art of gardening, vii, xi, 2; *Contemporary Landscape Architecture and Its Sources*, 14, 25–26; rejection of "international style," 244n56. *See also* Johnson, Philip; *Modern Architecture—International Exhibition*
Howard, Ebenezer, ix, 172, 178; meeting Stein and Wright, 240n15. *See also* garden city principles
Hudnut, Joseph, 2, 9; Dean of Graduate School of Design, Harvard University, 5–6, 118, 119; housing as act of segregation, 143–44
Hunt, John Dixon, 58

Jackson, J. B., 1
Janák, Pavel, 112–13
Jefferson, Thomas, 121–22, 180, 189
Jensen, Jens, 173, 174, 186
Johnson, Philip, 18; bias against landscape design, 28, 31; critique of *Siedlungen*, 27–28; "international style" approach to landscape, 25–26, 42; *Modern Architecture—International Exhibition*, 7, 26–27, 29, 42. *See also* Hitchcock, Henry-Russell, Jr.
Johnsson, Ivar, 60, 73

Kassler, Elizabeth, 4–5, 17, 23, 230n17
Kent, William, 9, 46, 47, 58
Kolbe, Georg, 52, 54, 55
Koolhaas, Rem: challenges to architecture discipline, 211–12, 218, 223; Downsview Park, Toronto, 286n3; and ecology, 218–19, 284n84, 286n3; "new urbanism," 218–19.

See also Delirious New York; Parc de la Villette, Paris
Kviberg Cemetery competition, 90

Ladera Housing Cooperative, 261–62n67
Lafayette Park, Detroit, ix, 22, 169–70, 181–89; collaboration in, 174–75; garden city principles in, 172; Hilberseimer's settlement unit in, 171, 188; landscape design, 184–87; and Prairie School of landscape gardening, 174; project background, 181–83; and *Zeilenbau,* 172–73. *See also* Caldwell, Alfred; Hilberseimer, Ludwig; Mies van der Rohe, Ludwig
landscape, as cultural medium, 1; decline, 2, 58–59, 117, 228n4–6, 231n19, 238n86; neglect by architectural historians, 31; resurgence, 2, 3, 228–29n7
landscape architecture: emergence as professional discipline, vii, 1; in twentieth century, 8–9, 12–17
landscape architecture vs. architecture, x, 26; attempts at mutual understanding, 6; differing theoretical bases, 10–12, 149; disciplinary boundaries, 5–6, 8, 9, 46; disciplinary differences, 3–6, 7–8, 23, 25–26, 191; disciplinary hierarchy, 26, 115, 116, 117–18, 131–32, 138–39, 147–48; disciplinary reevaluations, x, 225
landscape design: duplicity in, 126–27, 194, 195; as expression of democratic values, 16, 32, 220–22, 139, 148, 193–94, 220–23; as expression of intended social form, 37, 122–24, 139, 140, 144, 194, 212, 215; as expression of regional or national identity, ix, 10, 11, 75, 76, 94;

figuration vs. abstraction, ix, 93–94, 114; as force for social and political action, 192, 220–22; formal versus informal, 15–17, 59, 129, 195; in public realm, viii, x, 6, 8, 9, 12, 133; in Social Democratic countries, ix, 12–13, 61; socially contingent, 207
landscape design, as vehicle of social reform, 2–3, 9, 12, 14–15, 16, 64, 201–2; for Bauer, 139; for Caldwell, 175–76, 185; at Central Park, 196–98, 199, 203, 205; for Eckbo, 139–40; at FSA migrant labor camps, 119–20, 123, 124, 140; for Hilberseimer, 178–79, 185, 188–89; at Lafayette Park, 187–88; for Mumford, 29; for Olmsted, 3, 185, 196–97, 215; in Parc de la Villette, 205; at Parc des Buttes Chaumont, 201–2; rejection by Koolhaas, 206–7; at Römerstadt, 30–31, 33, 35–36; at Sunnyside, 30–31, 34–35; in Telesis, 127; in twentieth-century landscape design, 193–95; in Weimar Republic, 32, 1 40, 172
Landschaft: in allotment gardens, 10, 13; and *Landskap,* viii, 2, 195; at Parc de la Villette (OMA/Koolhaas), x, 195, 222
Lange, Dorothea: FSA photographer, 119, 121, 122
Laugier, Marc-Antoine, 17
Le Corbusier, 39, 49–50, 211, 216; architect as organizer, 211; attitude to landscape, 20, 149–50; attitude to nature, 150–51; attitude to site, 156–58, 269n20, 270n23; Beistegui penthouse, Paris, 153–54; Carpenter Center for the Visual Arts, Cambridge, 155; Church of Saint-Pierre, Firminy, 155–56; and genius loci, 20; Maison de Weekend, La

Celle St.-Cloud, 155; Mother's house, Vevey, 156–57; Obus A (project), Algiers, 20; Radiant City, 39; Ronchamp, 152, 157, 163; Unité d'Habitation, Marseille, 154; urbanism, 19, 20, 151. *See also* Chandigarh

Lewerentz, Sigurd: expertise in cemetery design, 61, 80, 89; unpublished manuscript on cemetery design, 90, 251n10; Woodland Cemetery Memorial Ground, 90–91. *See also* Helsingborg Crematorium; Kviberg Cemetery competition; Malmö Eastern Cemetery; Stockholm Exhibition, 1930; Woodland Cemetery, Stockholm

Lilienberg, Ingrid: commentary on Stockholm South Cemetery competition, 87

Littlewood, Joan: Fun Palace, 213–14, 216, 283n67. *See also* Price, Cedric

Malmö Eastern Cemetery, ix, 87–89. *See also* Lewerentz, Sigurd

Mar Vista, Los Angeles, 130, 142

Masaryk, Tomáš Garrigue: aims for Prague Castle and environs, 93, 94, 95–96, 99, 101, 106; death, 99; political philosophy, 107–8, 109, 254n24; presidential bastion, 111

May, Ernst: advocate of *Zeilenbau* principles, 243–44n45; apprenticeship under Unwin, 241n17; and CIAM, 34; cited by Tafuri, 42; *Das neue Frankfurt,* 33; Frankfurt planning, 32–33, 39–40; International Garden City and Town Planning Federation, 240n15; powers of, 241–42n25; Römerstadt, 27, 31. *See also* Römerstadt, Frankfurt

Mayer, Albert: plan for Chandigarh, 158–59

McWilliams, Carey, 122, 124–25

Mies van der Rohe, Ludwig: Brick Country House, 48; collaboration with Lilly Reich, 56; Farnsworth House, 59; Friedrichstrasse Skyscraper, 52; Glass Room, Stuttgart Werkbund Exhibition, 51, 54; Lafayette Park, Detroit, 169, 174, 177, 178, 179, 182, 183–84, 187, 188; Museum for a Small City, 45; Nolde House, 59; Project for a Glass Skyscraper, 51; Resor House, 59; Tugendhat House, 59; working methods, 49. *See also* Barcelona Pavilion

Migge, Leberecht, 13; garden of the future, 15; "The Green Manifesto," 10; "growing settlement," 10, 18; land reform, 172; practical basis of garden design, 36

Miller, Wilhelm, 174, 185, 276n45

Milles, Carl, 66, 87

Mitterrand, François: *Grands Projets,* 192, 203, 207

Modern Architecture—International Exhibition (Museum of Modern Art, New York): aesthetic biases in, 26; inclusion of Sunnyside Gardens, 27, 29; untouched landscape as background for modern architecture, 7, 42. *See also* Hitchcock, Henry-Russell, Jr.; Johnson, Philip

Modern Movement: correlation between physical form and social form, 215; and genius loci, 18; issue of meaning, 91; lack of theoretical concern with landscape, 149; social and political ideology vis-à-vis landscape, viii, 194

Moreux, Jean-Charles, 6, 16

Mouffe, Chantal: agonistic model of democracy, 220, 285n91

Mughal garden: inspiration for capital complex, Chandigarh, ix, 150, 162; inspiration for Governor's Palace precinct, Chandigarh, 165–68

Mumford, Lewis: advocacy of Sunnyside Gardens, 38, 41–42; critique of "international style," 42; curator of Modern Housing section, *Modern Architecture—International Exhibition,* 28–29, 42, 240n10; Regional Planning Association of America, 240n15

Mutual Housing Association. *See* Crestwood Hills, Los Angeles

Neutra, Richard: and genius loci, 21; significance of site, 7

New Babylon (Nieuwenhuys), 213, 216

New Deal, 16; antiunion bias versus paternalism, 122; collective ideology, 116, 124; housing as vehicle for social reform, 140, 141; neglect of minority voices, 145; racism in housing policies, 139

Non-plan, 213

Olmsted, Frederick Law: parkways and urban infrastructure, 9; partner of Calvert Vaux, 147; public park as antithesis of city, 186, 187; public park as vehicle of social reform, 3, 185, 196–97, 215; public parks, 14, 76; regional planning powers, 39; separation of pedestrian and vehicular routes, 175; use of term "landscape architect," 2. *See also* Central Park, New York

Owen, Robert, 123–24

Pacassi, Niccolo: eighteenth-century modifications to Prague Castle, 96, 98, 100, 106

Papanek, Victor, 219

Parc de la Villette, Paris (OMA/Koolhaas competition proposal), x, 191–92, 203–23; competition brief, 204–5; as democratic landscape, 220–23; formal and programmatic malleability in, 206–7, 211–12; Koolhaas's tactics, 205–11; landscape in, 208–10; site for, 203–4; as social instrument, 206, 212, 217–18, 220–23. *See also Delirious New York;* Koolhaas, Rem

Parc des Buttes Chaumont, Paris, 198–203; "democratic" motivation, 201–2; and Exposition Universelle, 200, 201–2; and Haussmann's hygienic urban operations, 192, 199–200; history of site, 199–201, 204; integration with metropolitan setting, 200; precursor to Parc de la Villette, 198–99, 203; spatialization of class distinctions, 203, 205

Park Planned Homes, Altadena, California, 130, 261n67

Parlér, Petr of Gmünd, 97, 100

Pešan, Damian, 102, 108

picturesque landscape garden: and Barcelona Pavilion, 45, 48, 50, 55, 60; detachment from realities of world in, 194; evolution of concept, 46–47, 245n7; invisibility of social forces in, 198; "new picturesque," 16; and Parc des Buttes Chaumont, 201; and Stockholm Library park, 76. *See also* Pope, Alexander: house at Twickenham

Plečnik, Jože: architectural philosophy, 93–94, 97, 111; Church of the Holy Spirit, Vienna, 94; interest in Slavic art, 94–95; Zacherlhaus, Vienna, 94. *See also* Prague Castle

Ponti, Gio, 18
Pope, Alexander, 17, 46; house at Twickenham, 46, 57–58
Prague Castle, ix, 21, 93, 95–114; figuration versus abstraction, ix, 93–94, 114; historic milieu, 96–97, 99–100, 102, 106; issues of interpretation, 113–14; Masaryk's aims for castle and environs, 93, 94, 95–96, 99, 101, 106; Plečnik interventions, 98–111; Plečnik response to manifestations of Habsburg rule, 97, 111–12; resistance to Plečnik interventions, 93, 112–14, 253n11. *See also* Masaryk, Tomáš Garrigue; Plečnik, Jože
Prairie School of landscape gardening, 174–75, 185
Price, Cedric: challenge to architectural discipline, 217; Fun Palace, 213–15, 216

racial segregation: challenges to, 142; in federal housing policy, 141; in FSA defense housing, 125; in FSA migrant labor camps, 124
Radburn, New Jersey, 27, 39, 118, 132, 172
Reich, Lilly, 56–57
reintegration of art and life, ix, 2, 74, 147, 213
restrictive covenants: at Community Homes, 141–42, 264–65n100, 265n101; at Crestwood Hills, 145; in federal government publications, 138; in FHA guidelines, 141–42, 155; at Sunnyside, 26–27, 35
Römerstadt, Frankfurt, ix, x, 22; correspondence between social aims and landscape, 32, 34, 36; *Das neue Frankfurt*, 33–34; landscape of, 35–36; in *Modern Architecture— International Exhibition*, 27, 28, 42; parallels with Sunnyside Gardens, 30–31
Rose, James C., 5–6, 9
Rothmayer, Otto, 106
Ryberg, Ture: collaboration with Asplund, 62–63

Schinkel, Karl Friedrich: as inspiration for Mies van der Rohe, 45, 46, 51, 56, 60, 246n15
Schlyter, Gustav, 79–80, 81
Semper, Gottfried, 17
Sennett, Richard, 220
SI (Situationist International), 213, 216, 217
Simmel, Georg: on metropolitan condition, 206
Soja, Edward, 220
Spengler, Oswald, 53, 56
Spirn, Anne Whiston: ecological approach to urban design, 218–19
Steele, Fletcher, 7, 12, 15–16, 41
Stein, Clarence: attitude to city planning, 40, 240n15, 262n74; rejection of Sunnyside planning, 39. *See also* Baldwin Hills Village, Los Angeles; Radburn, New Jersey; Sunnyside Gardens, Queens
Stockholm Exhibition, 1930, 61, 74–75, 249–50n16
Stockholm North Cemetery, 78
Stockholm Public Library and park, ix, 61, 63–76, 249n13; assessments of park landscape, 73–74; landscape development, 65–66, 67–68, 69–73; library design, 64–67, 68–69. *See also* Asplund, Erik Gunnar
Stubelius, Torsten. *See* Helsingborg Crematorium
Sunnyside Gardens, Queens, ix, 22, 26–43, 132; adaptation of European

housing principles to American cultural conditions, 29–30; cited by Tafuri, 42; compared to Römerstadt, 30–31; correlation between social and physical organization, 37; garden city principles at, 32, 39; landscape of, 26–27, 34–35, 36, 42–43; restrictive covenants, 26–27, 38–39; site, 31, 34, 242n29. *See also* Bing, Alexander; Cautley, Marjorie Sewell; City Housing Corporation; Howard, Ebenezer; Mumford, Lewis; Stein, Clarence; Unwin, Raymond; Wright, Henry

Tafuri, Manfredo, 42, 52; "Critique of Architectural Ideology," 212, 278n10; critique of bourgeois art, 198
Telesis, 127–28, 142, 260n50, 260n53
Tengbom, Ivar, 68, 70, 73
Tocqueville, Alexis de, 116, 131
Tschumi, Bernard: Parc de la Villette, 191, 192, 225
Tunnard, Christopher: cofounder of AIAJM, 6, 11, 233n40; lamenting disciplinary focus on private garden, 3; teaching at Harvard, 229n13

Unwin, Raymond: garden cities advocate, 30; isolating pedestrian from vehicular circulation, 39; meeting with Stein and Wright, 240n15; *Town Planning in Practice*, 40–41, 144, 241n17

Vaux, Calvert. *See* Central Park, New York; Olmsted, Frederick Law
Vera, André, 6; advocating nationalistic approach to design, 231–32n24; humility of designer, 23; "Manifesto for the Revival of French Art," 11; scale of landscape concerns, 9
Violich, Francis: planner for FSA, 119, 127
Viollet-le-Duc, Eugène-Emmanuel: genius loci in building design, 17, 18

Wagner, Martin: economic benefits of urban parks, 3
Waldfriedhof, Munich, 79
Walker, Peter, 16
Walpole, Horace, 9; Chiswick House, 47; on the ha-ha, 46
Woodland Cemetery, Stockholm: and burial reform, ix, 77–80; collaboration of Asplund and Lewerentz, 61, 250n1; competition design, 80–82; influence on Stockholm Library park, 70, 72; landscape design, 81–86; Lewerentz's Memorial Ground, 90–91; precedents, 78–80; ritual and spiritual significance, 91–92. *See also* Helsingborg Crematorium; Waldfriedhof, Munich
Wright, Frank Lloyd: architecture as landscape, 18–19, 21; Broadacre City, 176; and genius loci, 18; organic architecture, 177; Prairie Style houses, 175; technology and urbanism, 187
Wright, Henry: approach to landscape, 42; consultant to Housing division of Public Works Administration, 182; professional training, 238–39n5; Regional Planning Association of America, 240n15. *See also* Baldwin Hills Village, Los Angeles; Radburn, New Jersey; Sunnyside Gardens, Queens
Wunderkammer, 58
Wurster, William, 120

Caroline Constant is professor of architecture and Emil Lorch Collegiate Professor of Architecture and Urban Planning at the Taubman College of Architecture and Urban Planning, University of Michigan. She is author of *The Palladio Guide, The Woodland Cemetery: Toward a Spiritual Landscape,* and *Eileen Gray,* and coeditor, with Wilfried Wang, of *Eileen Gray: An Architecture for All Senses.*